Doing Collaborative Research in
PSYCHOLOGY

To our children–
Rory, Roan, and Coriander

Doing Collaborative Research in
PSYCHOLOGY
A Team–Based Guide

Jerusha B. Detweiler–Bedell

Brian Detweiler–Bedell

Lewis & Clark College

Foreword by Philip Zimbardo

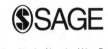

Los Angeles | London | New Delhi
Singapore | Washington DC

Los Angeles | London | New Delhi
Singapore | Washington DC

FOR INFORMATION:

SAGE Publications, Inc.
2455 Teller Road
Thousand Oaks, California 91320
E-mail: order@sagepub.com

SAGE Publications Ltd.
1 Oliver's Yard
55 City Road
London, EC1Y 1SP
United Kingdom

SAGE Publications India Pvt. Ltd.
B 1/I 1 Mohan Cooperative Industrial Area
Mathura Road, New Delhi 110 044
India

SAGE Publications Asia-Pacific Pte. Ltd.
3 Church Street
#10-04 Samsung Hub
Singapore 049483

Acquisitions Editor: Reid Hester
Editorial Assistant: Sarita Sarak
Production Editor: Astrid Virding
Copy Editor: Judy Selhorst
Typesetter: Hurix Systems Pvt. Ltd.
Proofreader: Dennis Webb
Indexer: Molly Hall
Cover Designer: Anupama Krishnan
Marketing Manager: Lisa Sheldon Brown
Permissions Editor: Karen Ehrmann

Copyright © 2013 by SAGE Publications, Inc.

Printed in the United States of America

Library of Congress Cataloging-in-Publication Data

Detweiler-Bedell, Jerusha Beth.
Doing collaborative research in psychology : a team-based guide / foreword by Philip Zimbardo ; Jerusha B. Detweiler-Bedell, Brian Detweiler-Bedell.

p. cm.

Includes bibliographical references and index.

ISBN 978-1-4129-8817-9 (pbk.)

1. Psychology—Research. I. Detweiler-Bedell, Brian Thomas. II. Title.

BF76.5.D43 2013

150.72—dc23   2012008888

This book is printed on acid-free paper.

SUSTAINABLE FORESTRY INITIATIVE
Certified Chain of Custody
Promoting Sustainable Forestry
www.sfiprogram.org
SFI-01268
SFI label applies to text stock

12 13 14 15 16 10 9 8 7 6 5 4 3 2 1

Contents

9 Presentations

10 Research Write-Ups   183

Foreword

Engaging Students' Curiosity as Research Creators

Philip Zimbardo

In education there is a striking difference between the *consumers* and the *creators* of knowledge. Most students are cast in the role of consumers. They consume the facts, ideas, theories, and values handed down to them by their expert elders, and they ask, "What does it all mean?" By contrast, individuals who create knowledge reshuffle existing information in order to explore the unknown. They ask, "What if this idea or theory were changed?"

A similar distinction all too often separates liberal arts colleges from research universities. University professors are the creators. They focus on designing research paradigms that will generate new knowledge, and they avoid teaching undergraduates because teaching takes time away from their research. Meanwhile, liberal arts professors are accomplished teachers who work closely with undergraduates. They pass on to students the knowledge and evidence created by their colleagues at research universities.

These traditional distinctions have always been flawed, and they need to be abandoned. Each of us should consume as much knowledge as possible and aspire to be effective teachers, *and* we should be endlessly curious about exploring new realms of ideas and creating new knowledge. This applies as much to undergraduates as to anyone else. Indeed, what is wonderful about psychology, and the social sciences in general, is the endless variety of unanswered questions that can be investigated by students even at the very start of their academic journeys. But recasting undergraduates in the role of knowledge creators requires a new tradition of teaching and learning. The key, as Jerusha and Brian Detweiler-Bedell advocate in this new guide to team-based research, is for professors to organize bright, motivated students into effective research groups.

I have valued such learning–doing collaborations ever since I was an undergraduate researcher, whose first original study emerged from an urban sociology course at Brooklyn College. Growing up in New York's South Bronx ghetto, I was aware of the confrontations between incoming Puerto Ricans and the African Americans who had lived in the neighborhood for many years. So I organized a small research team of fellow students to do extensive interviews of members of these groups, and I published our findings while I was still an undergraduate in the sociology journal *Alpha Kappa Delta*.

Later, as a graduate student instructor at Yale, I insisted that each of the 25 students in my introductory psychology course do an original study. Most of them ended up doing studies at their daddies' corporations, but one team helped me do a fascinating study of *shoeness*. Shoe was the quality of everything cool at Yale, especially the style of clothing considered "in" among the all-male Yalies at the time. We had seniors rate items of clothing according to how *shoe* they were, then my team raided the dorms and gave a summary *shoe* rating to each student's wardrobe. We found that prep school freshmen were much more *shoe* than their public school classmates, but this divergence shrank until, by senior year, everyone was *Yale Shoe True Blue*—perfectly cool, perfectly acculturated.

Then came my forty-plus years at Stanford, where the students were blazing with smarts and boundless energy that only needed to be focused on the excitement of doing research. I admit, I get excited about too much, but each "much" ends up as a research program, typically in collaboration with a team of undergraduate honors students and graduate students. These teams worked with me in developing research programs on time perspective, shyness, the cognitive and social bases of madness, and that oldie but goodie, the Stanford Prison Experiment. Through it all, my undergraduates were not simply research assistants. They were my collaborators, and I took their ideas seriously. The prison experiment grew out of a class project conceived by undergraduate student David Jaffe, who played a central role as the warden of our Stanford County Prison and coauthored the original articles reporting the study. Similarly, Bob Norwood's in-class question stimulated my pioneering research on shyness in adults. Bob, a shy student himself, helped me develop this line of research and coauthored the project's *Psychology Today* article.

The bottom line for me, and my message to my colleagues everywhere, is to inspire inquiry and curiosity in undergraduate students, while also empowering them to be active creators of knowledge and understanding. Some of these students will go on to an academic career in psychology, but many others will translate the lessons of psychology and their experience as *creators* into inspired accomplishments in a host of other fields and in their personal lives as well.

Among the hundreds of students in my research teams and the thousands I taught in many different classes, two stood out as special. Jerusha Detweiler was the smartest kid in the class, smashing the uppermost grade barriers, and she was one of the most sensitive neophyte researchers I had encountered. Brian Bedell was a "*do it right*" and "*do it all now*" kind of guy who could organize any number of his peers into an effective research ensemble. So imagine what these two could do in collaboration! I did imagine it, and so I did everything I could to make this vision into a reality, into a permanent unity of the Detweiler-Bedells.

And so here we have this guide to team-based research, one of the best labors of love that I have ever seen. It is written in an accessible, even charming style, filled with interesting material, exciting adventures for students and mentors, and a detailed exposition of how to get from a *clueless here* to *clue-filled there*. You will find that it covers all the essential steps in the research endeavor. Where do good ideas come from? How do you translate the curiosity of "*What if?*" into a testable hypothesis? How do you design a logically convincing study and then execute it in a way that stands up to the messy realities of implementing any research design? And how do you analyze the data generated by your research so that your findings provide meaningful evidence in support of equally meaningful conclusions? These steps culminate in the take-home message of your research, which you must preach to the world—not just to your choir. This means becoming a polished speaker and presenter. It also means writing up your research as a technical report, thesis, or poster for a conference, and ideally as an article for submission to a professional journal. This book will walk you through the process of making your oral presentations and write-ups accurate, meaningful, and interesting. In this way, your hard work can achieve the highest goal—of being memorable.

What is so unique and special about this guidebook is that it spells out the how and why of organizing undergraduates into effective research teams, enabling students to share their energy, naive excitement, and dedication to the goal of creating new knowledge in ensembles of like-minded peers. Undergraduates are continually expanding their own intellectual boundaries, and working together in teams they have the ability to expand the available knowledge in our field, perhaps in unexpected ways. That is the lesson of this book. What more could a student, teacher, or reader of this extraordinary book want? Not much more—from my view as a former student, ancient teacher, and current reader of this very timely team-based guide.

Preface

When colleagues or friends ask what we enjoy most about our jobs as professors, the answer comes quickly and easily. *The students*. When we were undergraduates two decades ago at Stanford University, we had the great fortune of being mentored by professors who were passionate about the *process* of learning, not just about the *content* of their courses. They taught us that learning should be immersive and fun, and, above all else, they taught us that learning should be a collaborative endeavor. Within psychology, this type of learning happens when professors and students work together *doing* science. This means conducting research in the classroom and in the lab. Our professors at Stanford instilled in us the belief that undergraduates have amazing potential and can grow rapidly into promising researchers. Now that we are professors ourselves, we think of our students as our youngest, most vibrant colleagues, and these colleagues are the best part of our jobs.

This spirit of collaboration is essential because psychological research is a team effort. As undergraduates, we worked closely with graduate students and their faculty advisers. Our regular team meetings ushered research projects from start to finish. During these meetings, each team member, including the undergraduates, had the ability to make key contributions to a project's success. Later, as doctoral students, we collaborated with one another. (Our marriage and children have been long-term side effects of what began as a purely academic relationship.) As we worked together, we reached up to faculty mentors and down to undergraduate assistants to help us pursue our lines of research. This team-based approach to research is the norm at larger universities, where professors, graduate students, postdoctoral students, and undergraduates all work together to conduct research. In such an environment, teams form naturally as people with different skills and different levels of experience and expertise interact.

After we earned our doctorates, we found ourselves on a long drive from Connecticut to Oregon. We were about to begin our jobs as faculty members at Lewis & Clark College, a small, primarily undergraduate liberal arts institution. As we drove, our minds kept returning to our best experiences in learning and conducting research. In every case, these experiences were collaborative. The line between teaching and learning was often blurred, and the line between learning and research seemed artificial. Doing science was doing science, period. These musings led us to a clear vision of how we would involve undergraduates in collaborative research. We planned to do so *systematically*, engaging ourselves and our students in collaborative research both in the classroom and in our research lab. Together with our students, we wanted to *own* the ideas and questions of psychology.

We have been pursuing this goal for more than 10 years. In classes ranging from Community Psychology to Advanced Statistics, we ask our students to work in teams in order to tackle challenging, real-world research questions. Similarly, in our lab, we have developed a laddered, team-based method of collaborating with our students. As we developed and refined this approach to teaching and learning, it became clear to us that our focus on teamwork and many of the skills we were teaching our students were not emphasized in standard research methods texts. Students should know what goes on behind the scenes of research. They should learn to work effectively with their peers and their professors, and they should develop a clear understanding of how to move a project from a vague set of ideas to a polished presentation of data. These skills require a concrete understanding of collaborative research. In other words, students master research only through doing it.

This type of hands-on learning calls for careful guidance. Our goal in this book is to offer guidance to undergraduates who are actively involved in research, whether in their courses or in collaboration with faculty or graduate student mentors. The book is designed to lead students on an engaging journey through the process of conducting collaborative research. We emphasize an approach that promotes effective teamwork and reflects the collaborative nature of experimental psychology. Students will learn to work as a team to generate creative research ideas, design studies, recruit participants, collect and analyze data, write up results in APA style, and prepare and give formal research presentations. We conclude the book with something most undergraduates crave: a practical discussion of how they can market their research skills when they apply to jobs or graduate schools.

ORGANIZATION OF THE TEXT

The book's first chapter introduces students to the virtues of team-based learning and teaching, and we emphasize three principles of effective collaboration that we revisit throughout the book: vision, togetherness, and ownership. After reading this first chapter, students can read Chapters 2 through 12 either sequentially or separately. Instructors and research mentors have the flexibility of assigning particular chapters that are most relevant to the current state of a research project or the content of a course. Regardless of the order in which the chapters are read, each chapter builds on the theme of how research is enhanced by effective teamwork, and we use examples from classic and contemporary research studies to bring research concepts to life.

Chapter 2 focuses on creative idea generation, including step-by-step guidance on how to brainstorm effectively. Chapter 3 teaches students how to develop testable predictions by first grounding their ideas in relevant theories and research. This chapter includes many details about the nuts and bolts of successful literature searches using databases such as PsycINFO. In Chapter 4, we focus on ethical issues, paying particular attention to the use of human participants in research, and we provide detailed guidance on preparing an institutional review board application.

Chapter 5 transitions to the concrete aspects of research design. This chapter focuses on translating predictions into elegant research methodologies and selecting or designing effective outcome measures. Chapter 6 offers a primer on statistics and data, highlighting how the best experimenters pay attention to what their data will look like during the design phase of a study, well before data collection ever begins. We then devote the entirety of

Chapter 7 to something that is often overlooked in traditional research methods texts: piloting an experiment. Chapter 8 focuses on conducting a study and includes detailed discussions of recruiting and running participants.

Chapter 9 transitions to advice on how to present research findings. In this chapter, we discuss research talks and poster presentations. We then devote Chapter 10 to the process of writing an APA-style paper, focusing on the importance of peer editing in addition to the mechanics of good writing. The book's two final chapters discuss how students can extend and make the most of their research experiences. In Chapter 11, we describe how a student can link his or her research interests with those of a faculty or graduate student mentor in order to develop and carry out a student-initiated project. Finally, in Chapter 12, we reflect on the many benefits of undergraduate research. We emphasize how much a student learns from and is shaped by a team-based research experience, and we describe how the benefits of such an experience generalize outside the research lab and well beyond college. We conclude the book by discussing how students can assess their experiences and market their skills to potential employers and graduate programs.

USE OF THE TEXT IN THE CLASSROOM AND RESEARCH LABORATORY

We designed this text as a hands-on, explanatory guide to conducting research, with a focus on the skills needed to collaborate effectively. We cover many of the traditional topics of research methodology, but we also provide detailed advice, backed by numerous research findings, concerning the nuts and bolts of the research process. Moreover, we introduce students to the practical issues of day-to-day, team-based research. This emphasis on team-based research is unique, as is the assumption that students will be *doing* research while they are reading the book. In other words, we intend this guide to accompany students' engagement in collaborative research, not precede it.

This text is aimed at undergraduates taking basic and advanced courses in research methodology, as well as students enrolled in courses requiring independent or collaborative research theses. An equally ideal audience is the undergraduate research assistant or student collaborator who is working with a professor or a graduate student research mentor in a laboratory setting. It is a high-level text for first-year or second-year undergraduates, and it is particularly well suited to juniors and seniors. Although the text is written with the undergraduate psychology student in mind, it may be equally appealing to master's-level psychology students as well as students working toward degrees in health sciences, education, behavioral economics, experimental philosophy, or public health.

In beginning and advanced psychology methodology courses for undergraduates, this text would be a supplement to a traditional research methods text. Likewise, it would be a supplementary text in lab courses in any of the subdisciplines of psychology (i.e., neuroscience, cognition, developmental, social, clinical). As a supplement, the text would play a central role as students design and conduct original experiments as part of their course work.

In more advanced research courses such as independent research or honors research, instructors can rely on our book as a primary text. Alternatively, instructors can use it as a stand-alone text in career-oriented courses such as those focused on professional issues or careers in psychology. Faculty or graduate students who run research labs with undergraduate assistants will also find it useful as a stand-alone text because it quickly immerses students in the day-to-day practice of collaborative research.

Throughout the book, we emphasize the skills needed to succeed as part of a research team, but it is important to note that "team" can be construed broadly as any type of research collaboration extending beyond a single individual. Indeed, the book is designed to help students and research mentors alike develop more effective collaborations with one another. In this vein, it also can be used in graduate-level teaching development courses, such as those concerning pedagogical issues in psychology, to give graduate students a template for mentoring undergraduates to be more effective research assistants.

PEDAGOGICAL FEATURES OF THE TEXT

Unlike some traditional research methods texts, this book is purposely engaging and conversational in tone. Our goal is to treat the reader as if she or he were sitting in the classroom or laboratory with us. To enhance this experience and to make the text as useful as possible to students, we include the following pedagogical features:

1. *Vivid, extended research examples drawn from classic and contemporary studies.* Each chapter immerses students in compelling experiments that bring to life the key concepts and lessons of the book. We use these studies as thought-provoking points of entry for our undergraduate audience, and they help "lift the curtain" on the methodological issues we discuss. In selecting these research studies, we have drawn from a wide range of topics spanning the subdisciplines of psychology, and the studies discussed have unique features or challenges that underscore the advantages of team-based research.

2. *Quick, key-lesson summaries at the beginning of each chapter.* The feature "Seven Lessons (Plus or Minus Two)" prefaces each chapter, introducing the chapter's most important lessons in five to nine succinct, reader-friendly bullet points. This is intended to jump-start discussion among members of a research team so that they can set goals related to their research project. It also serves as a learning check for the student reader, as well as a discussion guide for the instructor or research mentor when the chapter's lessons are covered in class or in the lab.

3. *Concrete tips, sample materials, and key sources indexed at the end of the text.* We expect students to utilize many of the resources that we feature in the text, including websites, reference books, and hands-on materials (e.g., samples of an informed consent form, a peer editing sheet, a poster template, a job application cover letter). To facilitate easy access to these resources, we have indexed these resources in a feature called the "Researcher's Toolbox," which appears as an appendix to the volume. Students can jump-start their collaborative research with the aid of this wide array of references and ready-to-use tools.

Acknowledgments

Writing this book has been a labor of love in many ways. Our shared love of teaching motivated and sustained us throughout the writing process. Likewise, our love of research and of seeing the research process through the eyes of our students made it a joy to develop the book's content and select the classic and contemporary research examples used throughout the text. And of course, our love and understanding of one another made this project possible in the first place and enabled us to take the idea for our book and shape it slowly over time into a reality. But just as with any endeavor worth pursuing, this book would not have been possible without the inspiration, support, ideas, and guidance we received from many individuals.

First, we thank Sarita Sarak and our editors at SAGE for their invaluable advice. We also thank the reviewers who provided extensive feedback on the first draft of our manuscript: Steven A. Branstetter, Pennsylvania State University; Kristin Lane, Bard College; Stuart Marcovitch, University of North Carolina at Greensboro; Simon Moon, La Salle University; Melanie O'Neill, Vancouver Island University; Jean Pretz, Elizabethtown College; Eshkol Rafaeli, Barnard College, Columbia University; and Andrew Ward, Swarthmore College. We took your suggestions to heart and appreciated your encouragement. We also thank the National Science Foundation for generous support of our work under Grant No. 0737399, but we remind the reader that any opinions, findings, and conclusions or recommendations expressed in this book are our own and do not necessarily reflect the views of the National Science Foundation.

This book would not have been conceived, nor would we be the teachers we are today, without the mentoring we received from our own beloved professors. In particular, we thank David Rosenhan, Mark Lepper, Susan Nolen-Hoeksema, Lee Ross, Al Bandura, Peter Salovey, Sheila Woody, Duane Wegener, and Mike Barnes. Special thanks go to our Introduction to Psychology professor, research mentor, and lifelong cheerleader, Phil Zimbardo. Even when he was half a world away hobnobbing with every *who's who* in the field, Phil provided continued support to this project, once e-mailing us after giving a talk to thousands of people to say he would "rather be with students at the local café." This is precisely the spirit he instilled in us when we were his students. At heart, we still are those students and always will be.

Next, we thank our own students, past and present, at Lewis & Clark College. Particular thanks go to Abigail Hazlett, who helped us compile the material for the original BHS lab manual; to Nicolia Eldred-Skemp, who worked with us when the idea of transforming our little lab manual into something more took shape; to Kelsey Domann-Scholz, who helped us with the many logistical hurdles we needed to clear to get the book's first draft completed; and to Emily Umansky, who provided us with the structure we needed to launch the writing process, enthusiastically jumped into the project again when we sought her help, and always seemed able to read our minds. We also thank the 2010–2011 Behavioral Health and Social Psychology research lab members, who devoted so much time to discussing what this book should include: Richie LeDonne, Corinne Innes, Dmitri Alvarado, Kelsey Domann-Scholz, Eli Klemperer, Emilie Sanchez, Amanda Hamilton, Stephanie Schwartz, Claire Beatus, Rachel Ludovise, Azalea Lewis, and Ashley Beck.

To our other BHS labbies from 2001–2011, this project grew out of your hard work and the time you shared with us: Julia Boehm, Chris Murray, Alexa Reynolds Delbosc, Anisa Goforth, April Lapotré Hein, Lisa Williams, Casia Freitas, Devon D'Ewart, Kim Sackmann, Tom Armstrong, Talia Ullmann, Zoey Cronin, Liesl Beecher-Flad, Elena Welsh, Miya Barnett, Linnaea Schuttner, Shannon Brady, Jessica Johnson, Kerry Balaam, Mihana Diaz, Nicole Garrison, Caitlin Standish, Chelsea Heveran, Melia Tichenor, Laura Gadzik, Tess Gilbert, Amy Baugher, Brooks Fuentes, Katrina Liukko, Lauren Tracy, Maura Walsh, Pat MacDonald, Lauren Haisley, Natalie Chernus, Julie Robertson, Melanie Cohen, Clare Montgomery-Butler, Laurel Anderson, Alex Steahly-Jenkins, Clara Laurence, Hilary Gray, Peaches Baula, Danielle Fagre, Emily Wilson, Hannah Tierney, Allison Sweeney, Kelsey Chapple, and Peter Fisher.

There are many others who inspired us throughout the writing process. We thank the graduate students who first mentored us when we were undergraduates: Andrew Ward, Tracy Mann, and Ronaldo Mendoza. We thank the undergraduates whom we first mentored when we were graduate students: Mike Shin and Brian Lizotte. We thank our peer mentors: the Null Set and many others who shared the classrooms of Kirkland and offices of SSS at Yale between 1995 and 2001. We thank our colleagues at Lewis & Clark, especially Kelly DelFatti, Jennifer LaBounty, Erik Nilsen, and the biologists across the hall. For sustaining us amidst our work, we thank Homa Bambechi, Sharon and our gym, caffeine, and the "penultimate hotel" where we completed the first draft of this book. And for giving us a life outside of work, we thank the usual suspects (Mark, Brooke, Rachel, Paul, Becko, Greg, Ana, and Peter), the coffeehouses and brewpubs of Portland, and the Oregon coast.

Finally, we express our deepest gratitude to our family for being the ultimate source of meaning in our lives. Thanks to Mom and Dad Bedell for your unwavering support and unconditional love, along with Harry, Darren, Karen, Derrick, Alexandra, Anthony, Heidi, and Natalie. Thanks to Mom and Dad Detweiler for your support and love as well as your guidance and expertise as a fellow book writer (Mom) and psychology professor (Dad). Thanks to Natasha (who was always there not only for us but also for our kids), and to Carrick, Courtney, and Nola. And most of all, we thank our three precious children, Rory James, Roan Walker, and Coriander Carolyn, for the collective energy and joy you bring to our lives. We are so proud of and amazed by each of you. We can imagine no better product of our collaboration.

About the Authors

Jerusha B. Detweiler-Bedell is Associate Professor of Psychology at Lewis & Clark College in Portland, Oregon. She received her B.A. and M.A. in psychology from Stanford University and her Ph.D. in clinical psychology from Yale University. Her program of research brings together investigations of human decision making, health psychology, and clinical psychology, with the goal of promoting health behaviors by understanding why people fail to do "what's best" for their physical and mental well-being. She codirects the Behavioral Health and Social Psychology laboratory, where she conducts research with undergraduate student collaborators. The Detweiler-Bedells were awarded a National Science Foundation Course, Curriculum, & Laboratory Improvement (CCLI) grant in 2008 to further develop and disseminate their methods of mentoring undergraduates in research. Jerusha has coauthored a number of journal articles and the book *Treatment Planning in Psychotherapy: Taking the Guesswork Out of Clinical Care*. In 2008 she was named the United States Professor of the Year for Baccalaureate Colleges by the Council for Advancement and Support of Education (CASE) and the Carnegie Foundation for the Advancement of Teaching.

Brian Detweiler-Bedell is Associate Professor and Chair of Psychology at Lewis & Clark College in Portland, Oregon. He received his B.A. and M.A. in psychology from Stanford University and his Ph.D. in social psychology from Yale University. His research examines the influence of emotion on social judgment and decision making. Together with Jerusha, Brian codirects the Behavioral Health and Social Psychology laboratory, which provides an immersive research experience to more than a dozen undergraduate student collaborators each year. In 2008 the Detweiler-Bedells were awarded a grant from the National Science Foundation for their project, *Using Laddered Teams to Promote a Research Supportive Curriculum*. Brian has authored a number of journal articles on emotion and decision making, and he recently served as director of Lewis & Clark College's Howard Hughes Medical Institute–funded undergraduate science education program, *Collaborative Approaches to Undergraduate Science Education (CAUSE)*.

CHAPTER 1

Teams

Seven Lessons (Plus or Minus Two)

My problem is that I have been persecuted by an integer. For seven years this number has followed me around, has intruded in my most private data, and has assaulted me from the pages of our most public journals. This number assumes a variety of disguises, being sometimes a little larger and sometimes a little smaller than usual, but never changing so much as to be unrecognizable.

—George A. Miller (1955, p. 343)

Seven was the recurring number that inspired famed psychologist George Miller. His paper "The Magical Number Seven, Plus or Minus Two," is among the most widely cited articles in all of psychology (Kintsch & Cacioppo, 1994), and led many to believe that seven items of information, plus or minus two, is the definitive capacity of short-term memory. This conclusion is misleading, and Miller himself withheld judgment about the number seven. Nevertheless, each of our chapters naturally gravitated toward this number of key concepts, so we decided to recognize this with a nod to Miller by beginning each chapter with five to nine succinct "lessons." These summaries are intended to jump-start discussion among members of your research team so that you can set goals related to your research project. They can also serve as a learning check for you and a discussion guide for your instructor or research mentor when the chapter is covered in class or in the lab.

1. Engage in undergraduate research! It will impart lifelong personal and academic skills.

2. Scaffold your experiences by relying on both your professors and your peers to learn something new about the research process.

3. Although research experiences take place in diverse settings (e.g., small colleges, large universities) and contexts (e.g., classrooms, laboratories), the underlying

(Continued)

> goals for the researcher remain the same: to acquire new knowledge, to share findings, and to become a better researcher in the process.
>
> 4. Successful team-based research is characterized by the development of a strong personal connection with the goals of the group (*vision*), the other people in the group (*togetherness*), and the contributions that you and others are making to the group's success (*ownership*).
>
> 5. An immersive and well-structured research experience encourages collaboration, produces high-quality research, and enables you to apply your newly acquired skills to your life within and beyond the halls of academia.

Bringing together a diverse set of research skills by forming a team of scientists . . . can make your empirical contributions far more profound and influential than they would otherwise be.

—Shelley E. Taylor (2008, p. 51)

Congratulations! You are reading this book because you are about to engage in team-based, collaborative research. This should be a rewarding and productive endeavor, and it could be life changing. Doing science rather than simply reading about it can be transformative, and numerous studies have shown that undergraduates who engage in research develop a number of personal and academic skills that continue to benefit them long after graduation (Hunter, Laursen, & Seymour, 2007; Landrum & Nelsen, 2002). Time and time again, our own students report that their collaborative research experiences have been both gratifying and extremely practical, helping them to shape and succeed in their future pursuits. These students have gone on to careers as research practitioners, medical and public health professionals, statisticians, lawyers, and educators. Many of them have completed or are now pursuing advanced degrees in psychology at top graduate schools, and a few are now professors collaborating with their own undergraduates. So whatever path you take after completing your undergraduate degree, your research experiences and skills will serve you well.

Many students have the option or are required to complete an independent research project. However, the notion of independent research is misleading, and at the core of this book is a steadfast dedication to the benefits of team-based collaborations. Yes, there is an important role for individual efforts throughout the research process, but the very best work ultimately comes from collaborative endeavors. If you are new to psychological research, you will have to trust us when we say that team-based efforts add a level of depth and intensity to your experience that you cannot achieve on your own. If you are an experienced research assistant already, you may be seeing glimpses of the benefits of collaboration in your own work. Perhaps you have even considered enlisting your own collaborators (i.e., younger research assistants) to help you complete an "independent" project, or what we prefer to call a *student-initiated* project or thesis. If you have not considered building your own team, you should. Researchers, especially in psychology and other lab-based sciences, rarely work alone. They seek out collaborators whose efforts and abilities will contribute to their projects' success. The benefits of working as a team go well beyond additional person-power. Effective teams are truly synergistic, bringing an unmatched level of energy, intellect, creativity, and commitment to any project. Because of this, teams of scientists typically produce the most compelling research. As an added bonus, working side by side with other researchers is great fun.

Our goal, then, is to help you develop into a collaborator that your peers and mentors will find indispensable: one who brings vigor, insight, and considerable talent to every project. Whether you are a student new to research methods, a seasoned research assistant, or an individual who is preparing to complete a research-based thesis, this book's collaborative approach will encourage you to progress to the next level of inquiry and intellectual challenge. At the same time, a well-structured research experience can be extraordinarily rewarding. Your research team will be pursuing a common intellectual goal, and this shared pursuit will create a vibrant atmosphere of collaboration among you, your fellow undergraduates, and your research mentor or professor. Many undergraduate researchers find that team-based collaborations foster a strong sense of community, a supportive "academic home," and a base of activity that uniquely prepares them for their future pursuits.

We look forward to guiding you through the process of conducting collaborative research, helping you develop the perspective and skills that will make the most of your research experiences. The chapters of this book are organized around the crucial tasks that span a research project: generating creative research ideas, searching for relevant literature, designing a study, considering ethical issues, writing a research proposal, piloting methods and materials, recruiting participants, collecting and analyzing data, writing up the results, and giving formal presentations of your team's research findings. Each chapter is explicitly designed so that novice and more advanced students alike will have something important to learn. If you are new to research methodology or want a systematic review of the process, you can follow the order of the book. Alternatively, you may find it just as informative to read the chapters out of order once you have finished this introductory chapter. Research on effective teaching suggests that people learn best while engaged in an activity. So if you are starting from scratch, begin with the chapter about ideas. If you are about to run participants, start instead with our chapter on piloting or the one on conducting a study. If your project is in the data analysis phase, read the statistics chapter first. Applying what you are reading about in these pages will be essential if the work you are doing is to take shape and thrive.

THE UNDERGRADUATE RESEARCH EXPERIENCE

The day-in, day-out experience of "doing" research as an undergraduate varies depending on the setting, but it often includes many hours running participants through experimental procedures. It seems fitting that in this introductory chapter we introduce you to the first laboratory-based research experience that one of us had as an undergraduate student. To frame this experience, imagine that you are a participant in the study. At the appointed time, you take an elevator to the third floor of the psychology department, where you are greeted by a research assistant. She walks you to a small laboratory, where you encounter an array of tasty junk food spread out on the table in front of you. It is midafternoon, you feel hungry, and the heaping plates of Doritos, M&Ms, and chocolate-chip cookies look, quite simply, irresistible.

The experimenter asks you to take a seat in front of the food, and then she explains that this is a study of the effect of emotion on memory. She tells you that other researchers use stimuli such as pleasant music to induce moods, but for this study the researchers are using delicious snacks. She says that you should feel free to eat as little or as much of the snacks as you would like, although you should eat at least some. Your main "job" during the study is to watch and memorize a series of slides of famous paintings. Later, you will be tested on your memory of the slides. Finally, as a measure of your attention to the memorization task, you will hear a beeping noise every 30 seconds or so. As soon as you hear the noise, you should quickly press a button on the floor with your foot. With these instructions in mind, you hunker down, grab some food, and begin the process of juggling snacks, slides, and beeps for the next 10 minutes.

When the slide show is over, the experimenter sits down and explains that the project is not exploring mood and memory at all, so there will be no test on the slides. Instead, the research question involves the effects of cognitive load (i.e., how much attention you were paying to a distracting task) on eating behavior. You were in the "high" cognitive load condition, requiring you to respond to a series of beeps as you tried to memorize the art slides. Moreover, in your Psychology 101 class a few months earlier, you and your peers filled out a questionnaire about eating habits, enabling the researchers to identify the extent to which you generally restrain your eating (i.e., stick to a diet). The researchers hypothesize that nondieters will eat *less* when their attentional resources are being taxed. That is, they will be too busy to eat. In contrast, people who typically restrict their diets will eat *more* under the same conditions. That is, they will be too busy to *control* their eating. Before you leave the study, you are reassured that all participants tend to eat a wide range and amount of snacks during the study and that the study's data will be analyzed as a group, thus assuring the anonymity of your individual behavior.

That is the study in a nutshell from the point of view of the participant (for additional details, see Ward & Mann, 2000). But what was happening behind the scenes? Much of the allure of conducting research is the process of becoming a partner in the drama that unfolds during the collection of data. Whether you are administering a survey, conducting an interview, or carrying out an experimental manipulation in the research lab (as in this example), you are becoming a partner in staging a smooth and efficient "performance." For this study, research participants completed a survey assessing their level of dietary restraint even before they came into the lab. Through random assignment, half of the restrained eaters (i.e., dieters) were assigned to the high cognitive load condition, and half were assigned to the low cognitive load condition. Similarly, the nonrestrained eaters were randomly assigned to one of these two experimental conditions. However, the research assistant running the study was *blind* to the participant's level of dietary restraint, meaning that she did not know whether the participant in a given session was a dieter or not.

The nitty-gritty of setting up this study is worth mentioning as well because the logistics were not trivial. First, the research assistant had to set up the computer that would deliver the beeps and the slide projector that would display the artwork. Then she counted the number of cookies she put on the plate and used a scale to measure the weight of the bowl of M&Ms and plate of Doritos. All of this information was carefully recorded. After each participant completed the study, this same process of counting, weighing, and recording had to be repeated, and this had to be done with precision because the amount of food consumed by the participant was the study's primary outcome measure, or *dependent variable*. Weighing snacks meticulously over and over again was a tedious chore. The research assistant also was responsible for discarding the leftover cookies and chips at the end of each day. At least initially, this meant devouring the delicious leftovers and was a nice benefit, but after a few weeks of running the study she found the mere thought of these snacks thoroughly unappealing.

One of the most challenging aspects of running this study was the debriefing. Telling a (potential) dieter that the researchers were scrutinizing how much she had just eaten felt like an unfair violation of trust. What if she felt devastated because she broke her diet and ate a large amount of snacks during this experiment? What if she went home after the study and tried to make herself vomit? What if she never trusted the motives of psychology researchers again? The importance of being sensitive while explaining a study to participants, especially when deception has taken place, is covered in detail later in the book. For now, rest assured that with time and practice, the research assistants for this experiment learned to explain the study in a caring manner and in a way that emphasized the study's important scientific questions.

TEAM-BASED LEARNING AND TEACHING

From the experiment we just described, you might get the impression that being a research assistant is a relatively solitary experience. Yes, you interact regularly with participants, but the act of conducting a study often falls on just one research assistant during any experimental session. Many undergraduate research assistants spend much of their time alone, gathering journal articles, setting up experiments, and collecting and entering data. But this is a limited picture of psychological science. When we were undergraduates, we were part of a much more immersive, team-based research environment. We each started out working under the supervision of a graduate student mentor, who in turn worked in collaboration with other graduate students and a faculty adviser. Later, we collaborated more directly with a faculty adviser and worked on projects in parallel with graduate students.

Throughout all of this, our strongest connections were always with other undergraduates. Some were older than us and helped show us the ropes, some were younger than us and learned the ropes as our own research assistants, and some had roughly the same amount of research experience as we did. This cohort of students learned a great deal from one another, shared ideas, and socialized. These were the people we talked to in the hallways between running participants, on the roof of the psychology department while studying for statistics exams, and in the campus coffeehouse as we contemplated graduate school. (This pretty much covers how the two of us got to know each other, by the way.) Between our interactions with our research mentors and these peers, we were part of a rather ideal community of researchers. We were not alone at all.

Within that community, what solidified our appreciation for collaborative research was the experience of sitting in the offices of our professors, side by side with other students, learning about the history and future of psychology and engaging in expansive conversations about intriguing hypotheses and compelling experimental designs. We were trained not only in the procedures of a research project but also in the process of playing with ideas. Our professors lit the spark of our imaginations, and our peers' contagious enthusiasm kept the ideas flowing long after we left those meetings. Even as we worked in the relative isolation of the lab or library, we were able to connect our moment-to-moment tasks back to those big-picture conversations. As a result, the conversations were always ongoing. This shaped our passion for psychological research and gave us a sense of the immense benefits of collaborative research.

We learned only later that having this kind of open-door relationship with professors is the exception rather than the rule at most universities. Time is precious, some universities have tens of thousands of undergraduates, and professors can be extraordinarily busy. Still, research opportunities exist for undergraduates at almost every institution. These opportunities vary a great deal from school to school, however, and no specific model for undergraduate research will fit every situation. Fortunately, the field of psychology is full of outstanding models for involving students in research, whether in the classroom or in a mentor's lab, at a small college or large university, during the summer or throughout the academic year (for numerous examples, see Miller et al., 2008).

The good news, of course, is that you are reading this book because your instructor or research mentor has a commitment to involving you in research. The structure of your research experience might differ substantially from how we involve our own students in research, and your school might seem massive compared to the small liberal arts college where we teach. Nevertheless, your instructor or mentor shares with us a common goal. Simply assigning this book reflects a desire to have you function less as a mere laborer (e.g., someone who mindlessly enters data into a computer) and more as a collaborator. You will come across the word *collaborator* often in our writing, but we do not use this term lightly. Being a good collaborator is an extremely valuable skill. Moreover, it is a skill that can be taught. We are confident that, in reading and applying what we teach in these pages, you can become a successful collaborator and develop a strong sense of contributing to your research team.

THE EVOLUTION OF EXPERTISE

Collaborating with others and becoming a better researcher are two sides of the same coin. This is because expertise truly *evolves* in the company of others. The subject matter of any research project and the process of conducting research together involve a substantial amount of uncertainty and complexity. Because of this, it takes multiple trial-and-error exposures to the ideas and methods of a research project for learning to sink in and for mastery to emerge. This learning process will require you to challenge yourself on a regular basis. You will need to take ownership of your learning, and you will need to take on things that are slightly beyond your current level of comfort and competence. Rather than sticking to familiar tasks, it is crucial to ask, "What more can I do?" and "What more might I learn?"

Although you could attempt to do this entirely on your own and in relative isolation, how would you gauge your successes? How would you track your progress? What would you do when you felt completely stuck? Who would help you to break set and think of novel ideas and new directions? Psychological science is too rich and open-ended for anyone to go it alone. All of us need to scaffold or ladder our experiences in the presence of others. We need to challenge ourselves and gather corrective feedback from our collaborators. We need to seek out information and ideas from those whose strengths differ from our own, and we need to refine our own strengths by teaching and learning from others. Laddering your experiences in this way will benefit you personally, and it will benefit your research team and project as a whole.

As an undergraduate, you can expect the evolution of your research skills to take some time, so be patient. As you will see, even a seemingly straightforward research question is rarely "answered" quickly. Because most studies need to be repeated and extended before they are publishable, a research psychologist may spend a few years or more on a particular line of research. If you are reading this book in the context of a research methods class, the experiment you complete by the term's end is likely to raise many unanswered questions. If you end up enjoying the research process, you can then transform these unanswered questions into directions for future research. You can fulfill a desire for continuing your research on your own (see Chapter 11, on student-initiated projects), or you might join a research mentor's lab group. Classroom-based experiences often provide an "in" to a professor's research lab because they allow you to draw on what you have learned and demonstrate that you would be a valuable addition to a research team. And once you become part of a professor's or graduate student's research lab (or if you are currently in this position), you will steadily learn new skills and techniques as you progress through various stages of one or more research projects. This is a path that you can follow as far as you want, through graduation, into graduate school, and even on to a career in research and mentoring.

RESEARCH IN THE LAB OR THE CLASSROOM?

Most psychology professors earned their doctorates in programs that rely on the natural hierarchies that come from coordinating the efforts and expertise of faculty, postdoctoral students, advanced graduate students, and a cadre of younger graduate students and undergraduate research assistants. Together, these groups help further the research agenda of the project's lead investigator (typically the professor). Researchers who have advanced through this hierarchical system on the path toward their master's or doctoral degrees think of it matter-of-factly. It suits both the research and its setting, and it happens to be an effective training model as well. In contrast, the goal of most undergraduate research is primarily educational. Most undergraduates conduct research for the first time in the context of course projects, and only a small number go on to assist faculty advisers or graduate students with research outside the classroom. In an undergraduate setting, faculty and other research mentors tend to work one-on-one or in the classroom with students by supervising independent study projects, theses, or small-group projects.

Although research takes place in many contexts, it is important that you not allow the particular setting to obscure the overall purpose of conducting research. The goals underlying all research in psychology are to learn something about a phenomenon that interests you, to convey what you have learned to others, and to become a better researcher in the process. When you work as part of a research team, learning and teaching happens not just through the results of your research project but also through your day-to-day interactions with your collaborators. This is the real value of team-based research efforts. Within collaborative projects, each person (from the most inexperienced to the most expert) should make a point to learn from and teach something to all members of the research team.

Laboratory-Based Research

Our professors in graduate school were experts in their fields, but the very best among them had a passion for learning from the experiences of their graduate and undergraduate students. This was also true of our professors when we were undergraduates. (If you have read Philip Zimbardo's foreword to this book, you know that his prison study and subsequent work on shyness grew out of ideas and questions from his undergraduate students.) Likewise, our very best undergraduate research assistants have always found something to teach us. Younger researchers tend to see phenomena with a fresh eye, and they are more willing to build bridges between different disciplines and draw ideas from disparate sources. Younger students also may have more experience with new technologies that can benefit the research process. Finally, everyone (including your professors) has his or her own strengths and weaknesses, so research mentors and more advanced students must recognize and harness the comparative strengths of their younger counterparts. We have known first-year undergraduates whose organizational skills were so refined that they were able to keep their mentors on task and manage the logistics of experiments better than anyone else in the lab. Some of our students have had an uncanny eye for detecting mistakes in experimental materials, while others have had a special knack for devising new ways to recruit study participants. Some of them have been superb writers. These strengths need to be utilized by a research team. Team members, regardless of their levels of expertise, must be prepared to teach *and* learn from one another.

Effective teamwork gives rise to an efficient teaching–learning approach to doing collaborative research. At our school, we have adapted this general model to an undergraduate liberal arts environment. We recruit teams of undergraduates, and each team works on a separate project. Three-student teams are the norm, with a senior or advanced psychology major (the team leader) supervising a younger major and a student new to psychology (the team associate and assistant, respectively). This model ladders student experiences and lends a sense of continuity to projects over an extended period of time. Ideally, team members advance from novices to accomplished team leaders, and as they do so there is an explicit progression of responsibilities (see Detweiler-Bedell & Detweiler-Bedell,

2004; Detweiler-Bedell & Detweiler-Bedell, 2007; Detweiler-Bedell, Detweiler-Bedell, & Eldred-Skemp, 2010).

Team leaders have the highest level of responsibility (i.e., organizing and overseeing daily team operations and weekly team meetings, attending team leadership training, delegating tasks to team members and subsequently integrating the members' efforts, analyzing study results, and writing literature reviews and drafts of manuscripts). Team associates take a lead role in preparing research materials, running studies, and collecting literature for review. Team assistants are charged with learning as much as possible about the various aspects of the research by assisting with the team's many tasks, and they are required to help other project teams when needed (again to learn as much as possible about the research process). But, importantly, the teaching of new skills is not just "top-down." Younger team members often find themselves in the position of explaining concepts to more senior team members. As suggested by the quotation from UCLA professor Shelley Taylor that we used to open this chapter, members of a research team bring different strengths to the table, and this is true regardless of seniority.

We are by no means alone in recognizing the benefits of having students mentor one another and ladder their experiences in a team-based undergraduate research setting. At Baldwin-Wallace College, for example, Andrew Mickley and his colleagues have developed an undergraduate research model similar to ours (Mickley, Kenmuir, & Remmers-Roeber, 2003). Like us, they started their lab at a primarily undergraduate institution and had the goal of engaging students in research beyond the classroom by pairing each student with a faculty member and other peers. Being able to view both your peers and your professors as sources of knowledge, guidance, and inspiration is central to such models.

Of course, the value of the teaching–learning model of collaborative research is not limited to a liberal arts setting. Anyone involved in research can seek out mentors, assistants, and peers with a variety of skills and abilities. For instance, if you are being asked to conceive and complete an independent research project, our team-based approach might seem incompatible with your assignment, but quite the opposite is true. You should reach out to a mentor, typically a professor or graduate student, to help you formulate your research question and methods. At the same time, you should ask your mentor if you are permitted to recruit research assistants to help you refine and conduct your research. We hope your mentor will answer with a resounding yes, because teamwork epitomizes the research process and your assistants will benefit immensely from the experience. You can assure your mentor that you will be the project's team leader, or *principal investigator,* as researchers more generally refer to this position. In addition, a few ground rules might be helpful. For instance, you should be in charge of the project's design and statistical analyses, and you should write up the research on your own, allowing for feedback from your assistants. In the end, the effect of this arrangement is to put into place a vibrant team that can benefit from the teaching–learning model of collaborative research.

Classroom-Based Research

What about carrying out team-based research in the context of a classroom rather than a laboratory? In the classroom, students who work together on a research project are likely to have a similar base of knowledge and experience. This levels the playing field. Although there are certain benefits to this, one of the weaknesses of the typical classroom-based model of group work is the lack of a clear leader. This can result in misunderstandings, inefficiencies, and the feeling that someone has to "step up" whether or not he or she is prepared to do so.

The best way to avoid many of the common misunderstandings and inefficiencies associated with group projects is to assign transparent but flexible roles and responsibilities to each team member. Before doing this, it is helpful for the group to identify the component tasks of a typical research project. These include the following:

- Coordinating the team (e.g., establishing a meeting schedule, defining the group's structure)
- Generating ideas and hypotheses
- Designing the study
- Considering ethical issues
- Creating materials
- Scheduling participants and experimenters
- Piloting the study
- Running the study
- Overseeing participant compensation
- Handling data
- Synthesizing results
- Presenting the findings
- Writing up the findings
- Identifying future directions for research

These tasks, in turn, can be grouped fairly naturally into the following three roles:

1. Organization and logistics
2. Design and analytics
3. Storytelling and writing

The organization and logistics role focuses on coordination of the research team, ranging from scheduling team meetings and setting deadlines for individual tasks to scheduling participants. The design and analytics role focuses on operationalizing variables (i.e., selecting experimental manipulations and outcome measures), weighing ethical issues, and working with the project's data. Finally, the storytelling and writing role focuses on creating a coherent whole out of the research process, beginning with the generation of hypotheses and following through to the presentation of the project's results.

Although it is useful to keep these three roles in mind, we are *not* suggesting that each member of the team take on just one role for the entire duration of a project. Instead, we encourage you to evaluate your strengths and weaknesses honestly by asking, "Do I naturally gravitate more toward one role than another?" And, if so, "Why?" Your most important first tasks as a member of a nonhierarchical team are to recognize your own strengths and weaknesses, to identify which unique skills you bring to the group, and to make a commitment to develop the skills you currently lack.

In order to assess your skills, we encourage you to complete the questionnaire included in Table 1.1, which is adapted from an activity developed by Dr. Michael Bednarski. After you have completed this exercise, return to your research team to discuss the skills you currently possess and the skills you would like to develop. As you review your skill set individually and with your team, be aware that a person's strengths and weaknesses may be related to the topic of your research (e.g., familiarity with the literature) or specific technology (e.g., comfort with statistical software) or with an approach to group work (e.g., interpersonal style).

Ideally, your group's members will find that they have a mixture of interests, talents, and personality characteristics. Such diversity will serve your team well. If it happens that one member of your team is especially detail oriented, another is a whiz at statistics, and yet another is a talented writer, then each of you can play to your strengths by taking the lead role in organization, analytics, and storytelling, respectively. However, do not fret if your team lacks such a perfect balance of these skills. Much more often, team members' strengths will overlap substantially, and some tasks (such as conducting statistical analyses) might be outside everyone's initial comfort zone. This reality is a good thing. The point of undergraduate research is to learn *new* skills, and your team should never completely divide responsibility for any task. Groups work best together when individuals take lead roles on different tasks but the team as a whole shares responsibility for accomplishing each task. With this in mind, the best approach is to acknowledge the strengths each person brings to the group and to support each person as he or she strives to develop additional skills.

PRINCIPLES OF EFFECTIVE COLLABORATION

Identifying the different types of expertise within your team is a crucial first step in the research process, but developing and sustaining an effective collaboration requires even more attention to *melding* your team's efforts. What are the core principles underlying successful team-based efforts? To answer this question, think back on a time when you felt deeply fulfilled as a member of a group. Perhaps you were part of an athletic team, a choir, or a theater group. Perhaps you were involved with a student newspaper, a religious organization, or a grassroots political campaign. Your sense of fulfillment in such a group likely came from a strong personal connection with the *goals* of the group, a connection with the other *people* in the group, and a connection with the *contributions* that you and

TABLE 1.1   Research Skills Exercise

Below is a list of skills. Please place a checkmark (✓) by the five skills you feel confident about having mastered through past work, classes, or other experiences. Next, circle (O) five other skills that you would like to learn or develop. Finally, star (✱) the five skills that you most enjoy doing, regardless of your level of mastery.

1. ___ **Present before groups:** Deliver a message or point of view to an audience with the intent of informing or motivating
2. ___ **Evaluate and assess:** Determine the needs of a situation in order to identify a particular course of action
3. ___ **Implement and follow through:** Initiate and follow the steps that need to be taken to start and complete a project
4. ___ **Write:** Construct written reports and recommendations requiring skills in using vocabulary, grammar, and punctuation
5. ___ **Invent:** Develop a new service or process through creative thinking and experimentation
6. ___ **Analyze:** Examine data, concepts, and ideas to determine how they all fit together
7. ___ **Plan:** Develop and organize a series of steps and timelines to meet goals and objectives
8. ___ **Inspire:** Motivate groups or individuals to take action for producing optimal results
9. ___ **Memorize:** Bring together facts, faces, and knowledge from the past
10. ___ **Supervise:** Work directly with others to monitor work projects and ensure that performance goals are met
11. ___ **Synthesize:** Pull together separate pieces of data or information to form a new way of thinking or conceptualizing
12. ___ **Build consensus:** Communicate knowledge in a way that engages the interest and action of others
13. ___ **Edit:** Improve or revise written material for final use
14. ___ **Coordinate:** Organize separate facts, ideas, or concepts into a working model, theory, or product
15. ___ **Design:** Think through and form a plan that can be carried out as an outline, service, or invention
16. ___ **Categorize:** Organize information, ideas, or objects into groups or classifications
17. ___ **Display:** Present ideas and products in a manner that is designed to get others' attention
18. ___ **Investigate:** Systematically explore different sources of information to determine their relation to each other for the goal of supporting ideas or drawing conclusions
19. ___ **Direct:** Create order and direction from different types of events, activities, and information
20. ___ **Conceptualize:** Develop new ideas, theories, or processes, or redesign old ones
21. ___ **Monitor:** Observe and manage work assignments, projects, or processes
22. ___ **Calculate:** Use math and statistical operations to answer questions or explain data
23. ___ **Delegate:** Achieve desired goals through enlisting the use of other people's skills
24. ___ **Facilitate group action:** Motivate teams for the purpose of creating agreement on and attaining common goals
25. ___ **Brainstorm:** Freely generate ideas without restriction or judgment
26. ___ **Keep records:** Organize and save important information through databases, written material, and classification systems
27. ___ **Make decisions:** Comfortably use information to make and communicate choices and options among alternatives
28. ___ **Plan events:** Coordinate information, people, timelines, and logistics to actualize projects or events
29. ___ **Solve problems:** Pull apart different and sometimes conflicting elements of a situation to identify possible solutions
30. ___ **Explain:** Express information, beliefs, and so on in a clear manner so that others will understand

(Continued)

TABLE 1.1 (Continued)

List the 5 skills you have checked off above as **Skills I Already Have.** To the right, list the 5 skills you have circled as **Skills I Want to Develop.** Next, list the 5 skills you have starred as most **Enjoyable.** Finally, from your **Skills I Already Have** and **Enjoyable Skills** columns, select the 5 skills you think would be most helpful to **Utilize** in your team-based research. List these 5 skills in order of importance (1 = most important, 2 = next most important, and so on) under the column **Skills to Utilize.**

Skills I Already Have

1. _____
2. _____
3. _____
4. _____
5. _____

Skills I Want to Develop

1. _____
2. _____
3. _____
4. _____
5. _____

Enjoyable Skills

1. _____
2. _____
3. _____
4. _____
5. _____

Skills to Utilize (in order of importance)

1. _____
2. _____
3. _____
4. _____
5. _____

Source: Adapted with permission from Michael Bednarski (2012).

others were making to the group's success. These three types of connection highlight the core principles underlying effective collaboration: *vision, togetherness,* and *ownership* (see Table 1.2).

Vision

Having a sense of connection with the goals of a group typically motivates a person to join the group in the first place. If you don't believe that human activity is a cause of global warming, then it is highly unlikely that you will join a grassroots campaign in favor of a "green" tax on gas-guzzling cars. On the other hand, if you love writing about and discussing current events, joining the staff of a newspaper makes good sense. But what happens when you find yourself joining a group that has less certain goals? This is one

TABLE 1.2 Three Principles of Effective Collaboration	
Vision	Develop a shared vision by discussing with your team the purpose of the research project and routinely reminding one another of the overarching goals of your work.
Togetherness	Develop a feeling of togetherness by building relationships with and respect for the members of your team and by relying on one another to give support, advice, and critical feedback.
Ownership	Develop a sense of ownership by recognizing individual and group contributions to the success of the project and by creating a shared sense of responsibility for and pride in the group's work.

of the challenges of research. In the earliest phases of a research project, the only thing that is certain is that you will have to conduct an experiment and report the results. If you are being asked to conduct research as a class requirement, you might have to develop a project from scratch. The specific purpose of your research and what your results might look like will be entirely up in the air. Alternatively, if you are working in a lab as a beginning research assistant, you might be assigned small tasks at first that reveal very little about your mentor's research goals. So to have a successful team-based research project, the first challenge is to develop a shared *vision*. Developing a shared vision is necessary for the success of any project because, just as in any other positive group experience you have had, knowing *why* you are doing something and believing in the rationale for doing it serve as potent motivators.

Especially if you are creating a project from scratch, the process of developing a vision will take time, and it will require both individual and group effort. One of the key ingredients of vision is being able to step back from the concrete or day-to-day details of the task in order to take in the bigger picture. Perhaps the bigger picture for your group is to learn more about why stereotyping occurs or how to help people who suffer from major depressive disorder. No single study will get close to answering either of these big questions, but single studies are needed to crack the surface of these problems. When you find yourself feeling dissatisfied with the small day-to-day details of research or a bit despondent because any particular study can get at only a narrow range of questions, remind yourself of the importance of the bigger picture, and make sure that you and your teammates see the connections between your research and this bigger picture. This is the vision that will connect your specific efforts to your broader goals.

Togetherness

Vision is great, but having a connection with the people in your group is what will keep you coming back to the group even on days when you feel too tired or busy to do any work. Having a solid connection with and respect for the people who surround you is important in any group setting. Imagine a skilled soccer player who doesn't respect the other members of her team. The trust she needs to pass the ball won't always be there, and the team's cohesiveness will suffer. Imagine a deeply spiritual individual who nevertheless feels detached and uncomfortable around the other members of his religious congregation. Such a feeling of alienation, especially if it spreads, will quickly undermine the strong sense of community that characterizes most religious groups and enables these groups to flourish.

A positive interdependence between you and the other members of your team is *togetherness*. It results from members of the group relying on one another for support, advice, critical feedback, and motivation to persevere in the face of challenges. Team members must trust that they can delegate tasks to one another, and each person must be confident that the group will respect his or her contributions. As with the principle of vision, developing a sense of togetherness takes time and effort. Developing trust in others does not come quickly for everyone, so it is possible that you might find yourself slower or faster than others in forming these connections. Interestingly, and contrary to popular belief, togetherness is not always guaranteed or even enhanced when a team forms among friends. Friendship groups have added layers of complexity that often undermine a more professional sense of togetherness. But whether or not the members of your team knew each other before the team was formed, the goal is to be *intentional* in your efforts to work collaboratively. Togetherness requires thoughtfulness; it is not simply a function of getting along.

Ownership

Feeling a strong sense of connection with your particular role and contributions to your group, not just with the group's purpose and other members, is the final principle of successful teamwork. This is *ownership*. In Western culture, the idea of ownership is very individualized. We tend to view what can be "owned" as finite, so ownership is often associated with competition. This connotation might make it difficult to appreciate how ownership can be both personal and shared within a group, as well as how this merged sense of ownership is crucial to a team's functioning. We urge you to let go of the negative connotations of ownership. Instead, focus on the quality of your team's efforts and how everyone benefits from the team's success.

Looked at this way, ownership develops when you come to recognize that your contributions directly support the success of your group. Because you are engaging in a collaborative effort, your sense of ownership is further enhanced when your teammates make contributions that usher the project along. One person's accomplishments become the team's accomplishments, thus deepening each person's sense of responsibility for and pride in the project. Moreover, team-based research tends to be an iterative process. The group sets goals, individuals do some initial work on their own, the group comes back together for an exchange of ideas and reassigns or trades individual tasks, and so on. As a research project moves forward through this process, each goal that is checked off of the team's "to do" list represents a shared accomplishment. Instead of being a matter of competition, this type of ownership deepens the group's shared vision and sense of togetherness over time.

Conclusion

The total effect of an immersive, well-structured research experience is to create a vibrant atmosphere of collaboration among undergraduates and their research mentors. This teaching–learning approach is an efficient mechanism for producing high-quality research, and it is a system that will enable you to make the very most of your undergraduate education. By the time you finish this book, you will have learned how to generate creative research ideas, design studies, write research proposals, pilot methods and materials, recruit participants, collect and analyze data, write up research in APA style, and give formal presentations of research findings. By engaging in well-structured team-based research, you will be involved in a caliber of work usually reserved for graduate students and faculty members. Based on this experience, you might be inspired to continue doing research, perhaps working with a professor over the summer or during the academic year. Later, you might find yourself on an airplane to Washington, D.C., or Cancún, along with your fellow students and research mentor, on your way to present your research at a national conference. You might find yourself applying to graduate school so you can continue to build on your excitement for research. Or you might find yourself talking to a future employer about your team-based research experiences. In other words, doing collaborative research could easily shape your future pursuits, and whatever path you take after completing your undergraduate degree, your research experiences and skills will serve you well.

References

Bednarski, M. (2012, February 22). *Research skills exercise.* Personal communication.

Detweiler-Bedell, B., & Detweiler-Bedell, J. (2004). Using laddered teams to organize efficient undergraduate research. *Council on Undergraduate Research Quarterly, 24,* 166.

Detweiler-Bedell, J., & Detweiler-Bedell, B. (2007). Transforming undergraduates into skilled researchers using laddered teams. In K. K. Karukstis & T. Elgren (Eds.), *How to design, implement, and sustain a research-supportive undergraduate curriculum* (pp. 402–405). Washington, DC: Council on Undergraduate Research.

Detweiler-Bedell, J. B., Detweiler-Bedell, B., & Eldred-Skemp, N. (2010). Establishing the flow of collaborative research. *Eye on Psi Chi, 14,* 18–22.

Hunter, A. B., Laursen, S. L., & Seymour, E. (2007). Becoming a scientist: The role of undergraduate research in students' cognitive, personal, and professional development. *Science Education, 91,* 36–74.

Kintsch, W., & Cacioppo, J. T. (1994). Introduction to the 100th anniversary issue of the *Psychological Review. Psychological Review, 101,* 195–199.

Landrum, R. E., & Nelsen, L. R. (2002). The undergraduate research assistantship: An analysis of the benefits. *Teaching of Psychology, 29,* 15–19.

Mickley, G. A., Kenmuir, C., & Remmers-Roeber, D. (2003). Mentoring undergraduate students in neuroscience research: A model system at Baldwin-Wallace College. *Journal of Undergraduate Neuroscience Education, 1,* A28–A35.

Miller, G. A. (1955). The magical number seven, plus or minus two: Some limits on our capacity for processing information. *Psychological Review, 101,* 343–352.

Miller, R. L., Rycek, R. F., Balcetis, E., Barney, S. T., Beins, B. C., Burns, S. R., Smith, R., & Ware, M. E. (Eds.). (2008). *Developing, promoting, and sustaining the undergraduate research experience in psychology.* Retrieved from http://teachpsych.org/resources/e-books/ur2008/ur2008.php

Taylor, S. E. (2008). From social psychology to neuroscience and back. In R. V. Levine, A. Rodrigues, & L. Zelezny (Eds.), *Journeys in social psychology: Looking back to inspire the future* (pp. 39–54). New York: Psychology Press.

Ward, A., & Mann, T. (2000). Don't mind if I do: Disinhibited eating under cognitive load. *Journal of Personality and Social Psychology, 78,* 753–763.

CHAPTER 2

The Idea

> ## Seven Lessons (Plus or Minus Two)
>
> 1. Go beyond your typical course work by seeking ownership of the ideas that make a research project exciting.
>
> 2. Idea generation is not without constraints. Creative ideas must also be relevant, theoretically sound, and feasible.
>
> 3. Fuel idea generation by paying attention to day-to-day experiences, questioning your assumptions, exploring cause-and-effect relationships, and referencing past research in areas that interest you.
>
> 4. To invent and refine compelling ideas, utilize the quasselstrippe, lively and rigorous back-and-forth conversations with your collaborators.
>
> 5. Encourage productive brainstorming by approaching it as an iterative process, alternating between individual and group idea generation. In team meetings, take turns playing the roles of scribe, process monitor, and assumption chaser.
>
> 6. Be patient and postpone feelings of ownership during this early idea-generation phase. You will use the literature to ground your ideas and shape them into a good hypothesis.

The sound of one hand clapping . . . and the wrong hand.

—William J. McGuire (1973, p. 450)

The best educations are those that we outgrow. Do you remember your grade school grammar lessons? Proper grammar provides an essential foundation for *good* writing, but *great* writing often breaks these rules and invents new forms of expression. In other words, great writers must go *beyond* grammar. Likewise, there is no substitute for high school and college training in critical reasoning. An unruly mind is the mind of a sucker, willing to believe just about anything that can be made to sound reasonable. But critical reasoning only ensures decent thinking. Great thinkers invent new ideas, and they place enough belief in these untested ideas in order to give them a fair hearing. In other words, great thinkers go *beyond* being critical. On occasion, this means that a new idea must be tolerated even though it seems unreasonable. An idea that seems eccentric, far-fetched, or flat-out wrong must be championed despite the likelihood of its failing. This chapter is about outgrowing your critical reasoning skills so that you can invent and champion new ideas. This is how research goes beyond course work, and it is what makes psychological science so exciting.

IDEA GENERATION

The hunch. The vision of something new and exciting. The idea. How do researchers come up with that idea, that cool insight that changes how we think about ourselves and the world around us? Does it come as a flash of brilliance, perhaps in a dream? Or is the idea a faraway destination reached after tireless hours of searching, pondering, and questioning? The quest for an idea gives rise to images of a long and exhausting journey. A journey fraught with false starts, wrong turns, and great difficulty. A solitary journey ending in a sudden, serendipitous discovery. These are romantic images, but they are of little use. Trekking alone through a dark cave, hoping for a flash of light to illuminate hidden treasure—this is no way to go about research. It is far too chancy, and, besides, it is too scary. So for now, set aside your preconceptions of how researchers come up with their ideas.

Instead, imagine transporting yourself to your local coffeehouse or neighborhood pub. Surround yourself with the sounds of boisterous conversation, and envision being encircled by other scholars who love puzzling through the realities of day-to-day life in order to identify compelling questions that are worth answering. This is the true spirit of idea generation in psychology, and undergraduate researchers can and should participate in the lively "coffeehouse" conversations that give rise to exciting research ideas. Although most psychological research appears to build on what has been done before, every idea should be vetted from the ground up through a rigorous series of conversations among collaborators.

The Need for Creativity

This chapter describes the first step in designing a high-quality experiment: coming up with an idea worth pursuing. Unfortunately, most college students never have the opportunity to participate in the lively invention and testing of new ideas. Imagine having to capture and keep the attention of a lecture hall full of students on a daily basis. Your professors, at least the good ones, can do this. They pass along some information. They model critical thinking. They motivate and inspire. But going beyond this to harness and direct each student's imagination is something else entirely. This can be done in smaller classes and labs, but the ability of professors and undergraduates to collaborate with one another evaporates quickly as class size increases beyond a dozen or so students. Inquiry-based learning loses out to mere instruction, as good as that can be. But you, as a student, need to wring the most out of your education. Certainly, you need to engage yourself as much as possible in large lectures, medium-size classes, and smaller sections and labs. But that is not enough. You need to outgrow and go *beyond* your typical course work. Research is a perfect vehicle for doing this.

Outgrowing your typical course work does not mean setting out entirely on your own. The backdrop for your thinking will be the lessons and theories of psychology, and you should look to your instructor or research mentor for extensive guidance. These are truisms. If you are intent on understanding your eccentric aunt, or if you want to pursue a self-styled theory of cyberpunk novels and their ability to nurture extrasensory perception, you are coming at psychological research from the wrong direction. Successful undergraduate research requires close collaboration between student and mentor, and, more often than not, student projects should piggyback on a professor's or graduate student's existing interests or lines of research. This will ensure that your efforts are sufficiently grounded in relevant theory and will be meaningful to other researchers in the field. In addition, your instructor or research mentor will help you develop a realistic project that you can complete in a set amount of time and with available resources. These considerations are essential. The most exciting, creative idea for a research project will go absolutely nowhere unless it is relevant, theoretically sound, and feasible.

In light of these constraints, many research mentors argue that undergraduates should "think small" as they conceive and design any research project. This sentiment is understandable from a practical standpoint. Yes, you will have to attend carefully to psychology's prevailing theories and current research literature. Yes, you will have to focus your thinking at some point in order to develop a set of good, workable hypotheses. And, yes, even the most independent student research must be doable and should reflect a partnership between the student and a research mentor or instructor. But you will have plenty of time to address these concerns. (You will read more about the research literature and theory-driven predictions in the next chapter, and you can skip at any time to our discussion of student-initiated research, in Chapter 11, if you are developing an independent thesis.) Moreover, emphasizing the many constraints on the research process often has the undesirable effect of crippling researchers' thinking. Students, especially, need to enter into research with a sense of their important role in contributing to psychological science. So whether you are in a methodology course, are participating in a thesis seminar, or are serving as a research assistant in a professor's lab, you should make a point of *owning* the ideas that make a research project exciting.

How do you own an idea? If you are anything like our students, you will struggle. We often assign papers requiring undergraduates to generate their own novel ideas for studies. Our students respond with blank stares, and they overflow our office hours seeking these elusive ideas. In a classic paper published decades ago, William McGuire (1973) recognized this challenge and called for a drastic change in the teaching of psychology research methods. To his dismay, McGuire noted that undergraduate and graduate training in psychology was focused almost exclusively on critical hypothesis testing. What about *creative idea generation*? After all, a bad idea is not worth testing. Adapting a traditional Zen Buddhist

TABLE 2.1	"Needed Innovations and Correctives" for Psychologists in the Form of Seven Koans
Koan 1:	The sound of one hand clapping . . . and the wrong hand.
Koan 2:	In this nettle chaos, we discern this pattern, truth.
Koan 3:	Observe. But observe people, not data.
Koan 4:	To see the future in the present, find the present in the past.
Koan 5:	The new methodology where correlation can indicate causation.
Koan 6:	The riches of poverty.
Koan 7:	The opposite of a great truth is also true.

Source: McGuire (1973, pp. 446–456).

koan (that is, a thought-provoking puzzle), McGuire described this state of affairs as "the sound of one hand clapping . . . and the wrong hand" (p. 450; see Table 2.1 for a complete list of McGuire's koans). The entire framework of hypothesis testing is boring and mute on its own. On the other hand, the process of idea generation can be profound and, as we have suggested, quite boisterous.

As McGuire noted, "The neglect of the creative phase in our methodology courses probably comes neither from a failure to recognize its importance nor a belief that it is trivially simple. Rather, the neglect is probably due to the suspicion that so complex a creative process as hypothesis formation is something that cannot be taught" (pp. 450–451). Because of this, the problem persists unchanged today, and most course work pays scant attention to the creative phase of psychological research. Even so, all hope is not lost. In his 1973 paper, McGuire boasted of knowing a "dozen or so" effective ways to promote creative idea generation. Alas, he described only nine of them. Humbled by readers clamoring to hear more of his suggestions, McGuire (1997) set to work and eventually came up with a list of 49 ways to generate creative ideas!

Building from McGuire's sage advice, we suggest the following tips to kick-start your idea generation (see Table 2.2). First, look around you. What do you observe in the course of your day-to-day life that captures your attention or curiosity? The ordinary and extraordinary are fair game here, and your goal is to take note of these occurrences and ask yourself *when, how,* and *with whom* these natural events occur. Second, question the things you take for granted. Do you find yourself making assumptions about cause-effect relationships without any "proof" that your assumptions are accurate? If so, what alternative patterns of cause and effect might exist, and how might you test them? (The goal here is to play with ideas. For example, are heated arguments the sign of a troubled romantic relationship? Perhaps not. Maybe what really matters in a healthy relationship is that romantic partners share the same inclination to argue.) Third, ask *why*. Even if a presumed cause-effect relationship holds up to closer scrutiny, there might be an unexpected *mechanism* (that is, an explanation for what links A to B) lurking in the background. What might this explanation be? (Okay, perhaps frequent arguments are a bad sign for relationships, but

TABLE 2.2	Four Approaches to Developing Research Ideas, Inspired by McGuire's "Creative Hypothesis Generating in Psychology" (1997)

Look around you. What do you observe in the course of your day-to-day life that captures your attention or curiosity?

Question the things you take for granted. What assumptions do you make about cause-effect relationships? What alternative patterns of cause and effect might exist, and how might you test them?

Ask why. If a cause-effect relationship holds up under scrutiny, what explains the relationship between the cause and effect?

Look at past research. Are there simpler explanations for complex conclusions? Ways of linking disparate ideas together? Questions left unanswered by a particular study? Qualitative data that suggest new questions?

this might be true because couples who argue more never argue about arguing. Ironically, heated discussions *about* arguing might be needed to resolve relationship issues, decrease the frequency of future arguments, and bolster the health of a romantic relationship.) Finally, look at past research. Are there simpler explanations for complex conclusions? Ways of linking disparate ideas together? Questions left unanswered by a particular study? Qualitative data (e.g., interviews) that capture your attention and suggest new questions? If so, pursue these possibilities.

Metaphor as a Powerful Tool: An Example

With these suggestions in mind, let us illustrate an instance of effective idea generation. Brainwashing became a hot topic following the Korean War, when a number of Americans who had been prisoners of war appeared to have been "broken" by their Chinese and North Korean captors. These once-loyal soldiers denounced the United States and appeared to embrace communism. Motivated by these troubling reports, a handful of social psychologists, including McGuire, felt a compelling need to change the focus of their research. Rather than continuing to study various means of persuading individuals, they switched their attention to ways that individuals might be able to *resist* persuasion. In other words, what could be done to prevent brainwashing?

McGuire's extraordinary idea was that persuasion can be considered metaphorically as the transmission of a disease. The process of persuasion communicates new attitudes and beliefs, which are like an illness. If attitude change works like the transmission of a disease, how can we protect ourselves and others from "falling ill"? Based on this analogy, McGuire and his colleagues reasoned that "we can develop belief resistance in people as we develop disease resistance in a biologically overprotected man or animal: by exposing the person to a weak dose of the attacking material, strong enough to stimulate his defenses but not strong enough to overwhelm him" (McGuire, 1970, p. 37). In other words, we should be able to develop a vaccine that inoculates our attitudes against persuasive attacks.

This is an intriguing idea, and, as McGuire (1970) remarked, "the notion is such a beautiful one that it really deserves to work" (p. 37). That, in a nutshell, is the essence and spirit of creative idea generation. Indeed, McGuire and his colleagues went on to demonstrate that attitude inoculation is a particularly effective means of developing resistance to persuasion. Exposure to a weak form of an argument prompts individuals to counterargue and build their defenses against a persuasive attack. Later, when the individuals are confronted with much stronger persuasive attacks, these bolstered defenses enable them to resist being persuaded (e.g., Papageorgis & McGuire, 1961).

So how did McGuire get his idea for attitude inoculation? We were not there, so we cannot be sure. Still, when we were graduate students, we interacted with McGuire a number of times. Our discussions with him had that characteristic frenzied intellectual quality of all coffeehouse conversations, and we are confident that the idea of attitude inoculation arose and was vetted through these types of interactions between McGuire and his colleagues and students back in the 1950s. In other words, idea generation is inherently social.

The Quasselstrippe

How can we formalize the coffeehouse conversations that lead to great ideas? To formalize something that is inherently informal might seem contradictory, but it would be a mistake to characterize the fun and play of these conversations as frivolous and merely entertaining. The goal is to be productive, and this goal must be taken seriously. Idea generation is comparable to the serious, disciplined focus of professional athletes who nevertheless lose themselves in their sport when they play a game or match. Likewise, researchers can immerse themselves in the flow of creative idea generation through the *quasselstrippe*, an informal environment for generating research ideas. The quasselstrippe is a process of lively and determined "yapping" that follows the winding thread of an idea from its first principles to a workable, theoretically driven research hypothesis. Kurt Lewin, one of the fathers of modern psychology, famously championed this method. The beauty of the quasselstrippe is that it can take place just as effectively in the classroom or lab as in the coffeehouse.

The quasselstrippe is inherently collaborative. It relies on the contributions of each group member, and the process fuels a sense of passion and excitement among the group as a whole. In regular, free-ranging meetings, members of a research team step back and play with ideas in the characteristically Lewinian fashion of "searching and seeking—working a problem this way, working it that way, turning it upside down, inside out, left to right, right to left" (Marrow, 1977, p. 234). The process should be fun rather than discouraging. Any observation could be the seed of an idea, but, importantly, no single observation should dominate any part of the conversation. Although there will come a time for constraining the group's ideas, the initial process of quasselstripping should be freewheeling and open-ended. Only after the group generates and fully explores a broad collection of ideas should the members focus their discussion and commit to a particular question.

This process of idea generation may appear to be an exercise in tolerating chaos, but it will be much less chaotic and more productive if one key prerequisite is met: Each individual must engage in his or her own brainstorming session *before* the group's quasselstrippe. This is comparable to an athlete practicing before the big game, and it will provide a solid foundation for your group's conversation. Then, after each group session, it is the individual's job to revisit the ideas, sort them, push them further, and assign a value to each one. The results of this independent work are brought back to the group's subsequent discussions.

Of course, researchers have generated countless ideas, and it would be naive to assume that the only effective means of creative idea generation is to iterate between individual brainstorming sessions and the quasselstrippe. Still, we think this process is a crucial means of melding a team's efforts, enabling all team members to take collective ownership of a research project. This point is essential. Individuals, on their own and before the quasselstrippe, must develop their own thinking, processing their own experiences and reflections alongside whatever relevant and thought-provoking theories, research, and ideas have been proposed by others. Then, when the group sits down to the quasselstrippe, it will be "pre-armed" with the varied perspectives of the participants. Each person comes to the conversation already invested in the issue, and the participants agree to let their ideas mingle and clash. Done in the spirit of collaboration (even if the conversation gets heated now and then), this process transforms the substance of individual ideas into a much more compelling vision that is owned collectively by the team.

PUTTING EFFECTIVE BRAINSTORMING INTO PRACTICE

This book is devoted to the idea that the group can be much more effective than the individual in conducting psychological research. But as we have noted, effective brainstorming requires time for the individual to consider ideas away from the group. Research suggests that group brainstorming in and of itself can have a serious downside, stifling creativity and the group's ultimate productivity because it preempts individual thinking (Mullen, Johnson, & Salas, 1991). So you must think of effective brainstorming as an iterative process (see Brown & Paulus, 2002; Girotra, Terwiesch, & Ulrich, 2010). Individual team members should first ponder ideas they find interesting, and then they should bring these ideas to the group for a freewheeling discussion. The highlights of the group's conversation are taken up again by the individual for further thought and consideration. And so the circle of brainstorming continues. To help you prepare for this process, we have developed a number of concrete recommendations for putting effective brainstorming into practice.

Keep a Written Record

In addition to a mug of strong coffee, soothing tea, or hoppy beer, there is a prerequisite of any brainstorming session that should not be overlooked: paper and pencil, or your favorite electronic equivalent. In practice, it works best to have one team member take notes at every meeting. But because note taking is likely to pull this person's attention away from his or her own thoughts, the position of *scribe* should rotate among team members from one meeting to the next. Similarly, when each individual engages in his or her own brainstorming sessions, taking notes is crucial. Ideas are fleeting, ephemeral creatures. Unless they are captured immediately, on paper or electronically, they tend to disappear and be forgotten. Ideally, each team member should keep an individual lab notebook and record ideas in it as they occur across the entire span of the project. Many of these ideas will be irrelevant to the current project, but they should all be recorded. Good ideas will wait patiently for your future self to dig them up and make use of them. This is yet another reason a written record is essential.

Identify an Area of Interest

How does the brainstorming process begin? Sometimes researchers begin the process of idea generation with certain predetermined parameters in place, such as a specific question or topic of study. This will be true more often than not for undergraduates collaborating with faculty or graduate student mentors within a research lab. It also will be true in classes if the professor proposes a general topic or theme to guide everyone's projects. Other times, the field of inquiry is wide open. Having an open field is both a blessing and a curse. Freedom of choice maximizes the chance that the group will come up with a project that interests all the members, but, as Swarthmore College professor Barry Schwartz (2000) argues, too much choice can be paralyzing and rarely leads to happiness. So if a research mentor or professor focuses your attention on a particular area of study, be glad and work contentedly within this constraint.

If your team does have to develop its own idea entirely from scratch, first be sure to acknowledge that this is a difficult (though certainly not insurmountable) challenge. The interests and suggestions of group members may be so far-ranging that it may seem impossible to reconcile the disparate ideas. To sidestep this difficulty and organize a more effective planning meeting, your team needs to set as its first goal the identification of a broad theme that is of common interest to the group. If you are not sure where to start, flip through your Introduction to Psychology textbook. Is there a particular chapter *subtopic* (e.g., children's development of gender identity) that captures your attention? Do the other members of your group share this area of interest? If so, you have created the appropriate boundary conditions to begin brainstorming.

Brainstorm Individually

After identifying the theme of your group's research, it is time for your group to part ways for a while and do some individual brainstorming. Some people prefer to brainstorm in a quiet location. Others find the din of conversation and background music of a coffee shop to be the ideal setting for coming up with ideas. The objective of individual brainstorming is to record as many ideas as possible. To do this, it is important that you refrain from dismissing, critiquing, or fixating on any particular idea. There is an approach to meditation that urges practitioners to allow their thoughts to flow by unobstructed. The person "watches" these thoughts in much the same way he or she would watch clouds pass by in the sky. Clouds cannot be judged; they are neither good nor bad. Clouds cannot be held on to; they will pass by at a pace all their own. Apply this perspective to your ideas. Do not judge the character of your thoughts. Do not hold on to any particular thought. Unlike in meditation, however, you will be recording your thoughts as they occur. Simply list your ideas; you will return to this list later.

For most individuals, successful brainstorming requires more than one session. Breaks are incredibly helpful for allowing ideas to stew and develop. Some of your best ideas may come to you after a nap or a distracting activity. Take a brisk walk, go chat with friends for a while, or treat yourself to an indulgent bowl of ice cream. Your mind will continue important work on your project even when you let it slip outside your conscious awareness (Wallas, 1926). Taken as a whole, individual brainstorming cannot be forced or done quickly at the last minute. When done well, the process is time-consuming. But it is worth it in the end.

Monitor the Group's Dynamics

When your team gets together to quasselstrippe, your initial objective is to keep the conversation playful. Your group's thoughts must be allowed to flow at this early stage; developing specificity and focus will come later. Insisting on structure or working too quickly toward a full-blown research design will interfere with the development of *the idea*. Each individual should be asked to share his or her ideas, but not necessarily as one long list. A balance must be struck between giving each individual the time and opportunity to share ideas and giving the group time to build on, discuss, and develop any ideas of mutual interest. For this reason, we recommend that one person in the group be assigned the explicit role of monitoring the group brainstorming process.

The *process monitor* should be as engaged in brainstorming as the other members, but he or she should assess periodically whether the focus of the conversation should slow down or, alternatively, shift. The group's string of thoughts must be allowed to wind back and forth. Generally, it is not appropriate to go around the circle rigidly, having each person take turns suggesting an idea. Instead, try having one person begin talking about his or her ideas with the understanding that other group members will jump in to elaborate and build on these ideas. Sometimes this will lead to a new idea or to other group members adding ideas from their own individual brainstorming sessions. It is up to the process monitor to elicit contributions from every team member (e.g., "Julia, you look like you have something to say about this"), put the conversation back on track by returning to an individual's original idea (e.g., "Alexa, say more about what you were thinking"), and redirect conversations that have become bogged down (e.g., "Let's back up and think about what else we can do with this idea"). In addition, the process monitor might notice that an individual has not spoken much at all, and in this case it is appropriate to prompt the person by saying, "What's on your list that we have not discussed, Chris?" Alternatively, someone might be dominating the conversation. It helps for everyone to know that this is commonplace, and a handy expectation to cultivate is that the process monitor will occasionally ask more talkative participants to "go completely silent" for a few minutes.

As the string of ideas grows longer, it is likely that the group will be able to identify a common area of interest or excitement. Perhaps the topic represents an area of maximal overlap of all the members' interests, or perhaps the questions emerging from the team's discussion fill each group member with a feeling of anxious anticipation because the prospect of searching for an answer is so compelling. Feelings such as these are clear indicators that the idea is close.

Avoid Groupthink

Although it is thrilling to imagine arriving at an idea for your research project, we should pause for a moment to discuss a potential pitfall of group brainstorming. Brainstorming in a group can quickly go awry because of a phenomenon known as *groupthink,* first described in detail by Irving Janis in the 1970s. Janis observed that groups have a strong tendency to latch onto a single, narrow vision, essentially putting up psychological barriers to the further exploration of good ideas. This can happen in many different settings. For instance, Janis (1972) attributed the Kennedy administration's ill-fated decision to orchestrate an invasion of Cuba in 1961 to groupthink. The Bay of Pigs invasion failed miserably and helped precipitate the Cuban missile crisis, which brought the United States and the Soviet Union to the edge of nuclear war. Although the stakes are not nearly as high in your brainstorming sessions as they were for President Kennedy and his advisers, the lesson is the same: Do not settle on any particular idea too quickly.

To avoid groupthink, be particularly aware of the *illusion of unanimity* (Janis, 1972). Sometimes it will appear as if everyone else in the group, except you, is in complete agreement about a particular idea. However, actual unanimity in groups is quite rare, and the only way the illusion of unanimity will be dismantled is if someone speaks up. Unfortunately, the illusion of unanimity can be especially powerful in small, self-managed teams (see Moorhead, Neck, & West, 1998), and individuals may feel too intimidated to offer a perspective that contradicts the group's vision or train of thought. Our first bit of advice is simple: Just say it! Your team needs to establish a norm of good-natured nonconformity in these brainstorming sessions. As this norm takes hold, you will find that other individuals or perhaps the whole group will share your questions and concerns. Even if you are alone in your perspective, your insight might be correct or otherwise invaluable to the group's full consideration of an idea. So try to avoid fearing that others will judge you or your ideas harshly. It is much better to contribute often during this early stage of work than it is to wait until later to express concerns.

Ironically, a cohesive team mentality can be dangerous in the initial stages of brainstorming. Because of this, we highly recommend that another group member adopt the role of *assumption chaser* (see Cress, Collier, & Reitenauer, 2005). The assumption chaser is responsible for recognizing and calling attention to groupthink and to illusions of unanimity. It is also the assumption chaser's job to play devil's advocate by explicitly bringing the group's attention to important concepts that have been overlooked or dismissed too quickly. The assumption chaser must help the group avoid stifling some ideas altogether and criticizing other ideas too harshly. The goal of the assumption chaser (and, indeed, the group as a whole) is to keep the conversation open, flowing, and wide-ranging. The narrowing of ideas will come, but only later.

Take Time to Pause and Reflect

Groups, just like individuals, must take breaks from the brainstorming process. Although it would be nice to assume that only one brainstorming session will be necessary before your group decides on a topic, we urge you not to make that assumption. Time pressure is yet another contributor to groupthink. With this in mind, it can be especially helpful for each individual to take the group's ideas home and return a few days later to continue the conversation. Having time to pause and reflect not only enhances the overall quality of the final idea but also allows group members to recognize any constraints put on the team's initial brainstorming by groupthink.

Conclusion

In the first chapter of this book, we discussed how to engineer a series of relationships among you, your group, and the project that will maximize the likelihood of successful collaborative research. The overarching goal is to create an experience that builds a collective sense of vision, ownership, and togetherness. At the idea-generation stage of a research project, these characteristics of the group are in their infancy. Rather than seeing this initial lack of vision, ownership, and togetherness as a problem, you should see their absence as advantageous. Each group member needs to bring a different perspective and disparate ideas to the table.

Getting to know the other members of your team is a process, just like the development and execution of your research idea is a process. In some cases, you may be part of a brand-new team. In other cases, some team members may have preexisting relationships. Although many students look forward to working with friends, the truth is that friendships can make the process of working together more challenging. In large part this is because friends' interpersonal comfort with one another may be interpreted mistakenly as shared vision. This is not ideal at this early stage of the process. Rather, this is a rare time when it is advantageous for each individual in the group to bring a strikingly different perspective to the discussion. As you work at brainstorming, facing the pitfalls head on, you will begin to feel the first hints of interpersonal connection that we think of as professional togetherness. But be patient at this early stage; only after you and your teammates have collaborated for a longer period of time will a sense of shared experience be cemented.

Likewise, as you engage in the process of developing *the idea* for your team's research project, your group must be patient. When you are immersed in idea generation, you are at the starting gate. Individual ideas must be treated with care at this point, for they are the delicate beginnings of what will eventually become the common threads of a unified vision. Giving each individual idea a role in these initial conversations is vital. At the same time, too much courtesy can lead to the acceptance of an idea before the time is right. When, you might ask, is the time right? Our answer? Not now! Your project is still in its earliest phase of development, and becoming too attached to any particular idea (as an individual or group) could lead to disappointment as the project progresses. Experienced researchers know that the path from first ideas to a final project is neither straight nor narrow. You should avoid any sense of ownership for now, and prepare yourself to use the research literature to link your team's ideas to relevant theories and to narrow your ideas into a compelling hypothesis.

References

Brown, V. R., & Paulus, P. B. (2002). Making group brainstorming more effective: Recommendations from an associative memory perspective. *Current Directions in Psychological Science, 11,* 208–212.

Cress, C. M., Collier, P. J., & Reitenauer, V. L. (2005). *Learning through serving: A student guidebook for service-learning across the disciplines.* Sterling, VA: Stylus.

Girotra, K., Terwiesch, C., & Ulrich, K. T. (2010). Idea generation and the quality of the best idea. *Management Science, 56,* 591–605.

Janis, I. (1972). *Victims of groupthink: A psychological study of foreign-policy decisions and fiascoes.* Boston: Houghton Mifflin.

Marrow, A. J. (1977). *The practical theorist: The life and work of Kurt Lewin.* New York: Teachers College Press.

McGuire, W. J. (1970, February). A vaccine for brainwashing. *Psychology Today,* pp. 36–39, 63–64.

McGuire, W. J. (1973). The yin and yang of progress in social psychology: Seven koan. *Journal of Personality and Social Psychology, 26,* 446–456.

McGuire, W. J. (1997). Creative hypothesis generating in psychology: Some useful heuristics. *Annual Review of Psychology, 48,* 1–30.

Moorhead, G., Neck, C. P., & West, M. S. (1998). The tendency toward defective decision making within self-managing teams: The relevance of groupthink for the 21st century. *Organizational Behavior and Human Decision Processes, 73,* 327–351.

Mullen, B., Johnson, C., & Salas, E. (1991). Productivity loss in brainstorming groups: A meta-analytic integration. *Basic and Applied Social Psychology, 12,* 3–23.

Papageorgis, D., & McGuire, W. J. (1961). The generality of immunity to persuasion produced by pre-exposure to weakened counterarguments. *Journal of Abnormal and Social Psychology, 62,* 475–481.

Schwartz, B. (2000). Self-determination: The tyranny of freedom. *American Psychologist, 55,* 79–88.

Wallas, G. (1926). *The art of thought.* New York: Franklin Watts.

CHAPTER 3

Theories, Predictions, and the Literature

Seven Lessons (Plus or Minus Two)

1. The best research ideas are firmly rooted in theory.

2. Avoid narrowing your team's idea too soon. Keep an eye on the big picture as you approach the literature.

3. Be aware of two common missteps that fall on opposite ends of the same continuum: becoming overwhelmed and stifled by the literature or failing to consult it.

4. Use PsycINFO whenever possible. It is a precision tool that will enhance your likelihood of finding relevant literature.

5. Start with broad search terms and focus on articles published in high-impact journals. Scour the reference sections of highly relevant articles to find additional sources.

6. To narrow your findings, limit your search to peer-reviewed journal articles, literature reviews, and meta-analyses.

7. Use established theories to shape your team's idea into a hypothesis that builds on or challenges the existing literature.

8. Increase the likelihood of your team's success by ensuring that your idea is testable, your predictions are compelling, and your data are informative no matter what the results turn out to be.

There is nothing more practical than a good theory.

—Kurt Lewin (1952, p. 169)

Scientists are storytellers. They scour the scientific literature for inspiring story lines, blend in their own observations, and arrive at rough ideas for new stories or, more likely, sequels to existing story lines. But the idea for a scientific story is only the beginning of the tale. Ideas are loosely formed and limited, a bit like a hazy vision of a key scene in a play. Suppose you have an idea for a research project. What comes next? Before you proceed, you need to insert your idea in the full, rich arc of a story. The arc of a story is the guiding motif, an organizing principle that lends a sense of coherence to the story and moves the plot along in a compelling way. In research, such an organizing principle is called a *theory*.

Welcome to the next phase of the research process: the search for a theory that helps to define and expand the ideas that are of interest to you and your research team. This chapter covers the process of identifying and using a psychological theory as a foundation for transforming an idea into concrete, testable predictions. We intend to help you answer the following three questions:

1. What makes for a good theory?

2. How are previous theories, research findings, and new ideas blended together to advance psychological research?

3. How do theories help make an idea testable? That is, how do researchers transition from idea to theory to prediction?

Answering these questions will enable you to place your team's research within a compelling theoretical framework—that is, a broad organizational structure that lends credibility to your team's ideas and helps you look beyond one simple study to see how your ideas fit within an entire line of research.

THEORIES ARE CLEAR AND CONCISE EXPLANATIONS

Some of the earliest research in psychology concerned a basic question about human performance: Does having an audience help or hinder a person's success at a task? Initial observations by Norman Triplett in 1898—yes, that long ago!—suggested that cyclists go faster when they are being observed by an audience, and, similarly, young children wind string onto a spool more quickly in the presence of other children compared to when they are alone. This phenomenon, referred to as social facilitation, was supported by the findings of scores of follow-up studies. People seem to work harder when they are being watched, and, for the most part, they are unaware of doing so. But wait, doesn't an audience sometimes make a person so nervous that he or she goofs up and performs worse? Sure enough, the gospel of social facilitation was later questioned by researchers who observed many instances in which human performance suffered in the presence of an audience.

Who was right, and why? Now we have a horse race! The key to this puzzle, as with most puzzles in science, is that both social facilitation and its opposite (i.e., the ability of an audience to interfere with performance) hold true under different circumstances. Rather than create a laundry list of these different circumstances, Robert Zajonc (1965) proposed a rather elegant theory that identified the key boundary condition separating these two seemingly contradictory findings. Zajonc proposed that the presence of others is the source of a general "drive" that aids performance in certain situations and hinders it in others. At the time, researchers had used rats and even goats to test the impact of social contact on performance. Zajonc chose cockroaches. He hypothesized and found that the presence of an audience (of roaches, in this case, watching another roach run a maze) enhances the performance of a dominant or familiar response but interferes with the performance of a more complex or unfamiliar response (Zajonc, Heingartner, & Herman, 1969). What implications might this have for human beings? The simple answer is that Zajonc's theory, which gained initial support with cockroaches, was later tested and held true with human participants.

The beauty of Zajonc's "dominant response" theory is that it clearly and concisely explains a boundary condition for observing social facilitation. Social facilitation does not happen all of the time, and we can explain why. Being in the presence of others causes a person (or even a cockroach) to become physiologically aroused, and as a rather straight-forward result of this basic biological arousal, the person is most likely to "lean on" his or her most practiced or automatic behavior (i.e., the dominant response). A professional basketball player has practiced making free throws for decades, so being in the presence of others will tend to bring out this highly routine, perfected behavior. But we cross over the boundary of social facilitation when an action is unpracticed for someone. We, your authors, have no basketball skills worth mentioning. In the presence of an audience, our most automatic response would be to throw the ball in some stereotypical, grossly mis-taken way (e.g., straight at the hoop, which makes it physically impossible for the ball to arc through the air and fall down and through the hoop), making it far less likely for us to make a shot.

This work highlights the fact that a good theory will specify the boundary conditions of a phenomenon. When does an effect occur? When does it disappear? When would you observe the opposite behavior? *And why?* As your team begins to search for a theoretical framework connected to *the idea,* you should clearly discuss and identify the *boundary conditions* that limit the predictions you made during your brainstorming sessions. This is the first step in the process of developing and explaining your team's predictions.

INITIALLY, KEEP YOUR IDEA ABSTRACT

When you and your group hit upon a compelling idea, your instinct probably will be to make the idea and your initial predictions far too specific. If you are currently taking a methods course (or have done so already), or if you are interested in a particular applied area, your tendency will be to narrow your idea almost immediately to a specific study that asks a specific question and uses a specific procedure or set of materials to answer the question. This way of proceeding is a mistake we all make. Giving in to the urge to operationalize an idea immediately is the surest way of losing a sense of the big picture and the meaning of a research project. Quickly and reflexively moving from a rough idea to a specific research question and design has another serious downside as well: Unrefined ideas tend to be wrong. So at this point in the process, we urge you to resist the temptation to narrow down your team's idea any further. As you explore your team's area of interest, perusing the psychological literature for related insights and explanations of these insights, your idea is likely to change shape somewhat. It should expand as its meaning deepens. At the same time, it should become more precise as you better understand which processes you are studying and as you distinguish these from other processes. This will have a direct impact on your team's final choice of what idea to test.

If you have done the idea-generation process justice, at this point you and your team-mates will feel consumed by uncertainty, asking yourselves: Where will the idea go next? This is an uncomfortable state, but these feelings indicate that you are perfectly positioned to begin the search for related theories. Evans (2005) has compared the process of narrow-ing down ideas to reading a gripping but unfinished novel (p. 16). When you discover that the next chapter does not yet exist, your mind will run wild with what could happen next. This state of curiosity and anticipation soon will be replaced by a much more certain state: transforming your team's rough idea into a compelling prediction based on past theories and your own thinking.

When you and your teammates begin to search out theories, you are positioning your-selves not as the consumers of an unfinished book but as the authors. However, you are not writing the book from scratch. The process of research in psychology looks a lot like the improvisational theater game called "Story-Story." In the most straightforward version of this game, the actors stand in a circle and one person begins to narrate a tale and then passes the story to another actor. This next person builds on the story and passes it to yet another actor, and so on. In the psychological research process, you are entering the story as one of a number of authors, whose work stretches over years, decades, or even centu-ries. But unlike the players of "Story-Story," *you* were not standing in the circle when the story began. So before you craft the next chapter of the story, you will need to review the story thus far. Your goal is to make the arc of the story a coherent one, and understanding the theories that have been proposed in the past will help you to continue the story into the future. Good theories are, in fact, the foundations for stories about human behavior. And by searching out these theories, you will be able to move your story along to its next, logical, compelling chapter.

In an abstract sense, the concept of searching out relevant theories should be quite motivating. Your research team has brainstormed various ideas and settled on a rough direction for moving forward, and now it's time to see if other researchers in the field of psychology share a fascination with your topic. Imagine how rewarding it would be to consult the literature and get a firm sense of the state-of-the-art science on this topic. Then, after doing so, you would take the existing theories and your group's rough idea to the next logical step, refining the idea into a well-explained, testable prediction that builds on and contributes to the scientific literature. Indeed, many of our colleagues in the natural sciences characterize the search for their next research questions this way. Given a topic and a firm sense of past and current theories and findings, a researcher can tell what has already been studied and what remains unknown. A biologist friend of ours who studies the tiny roundworm *C. elegans* can say with relative certainty that no one knows the relationship between particular aspects of the roundworm's genome and how these genes are expressed in the structure and function of the worm's nervous system and other organs. These relationships are important, and a rigorous approach to illuminating them should result in informative, publishable research. But there are countless questions to ask about the roundworm's genome and its expression, so our biologist friend must choose wisely among specific lines of research. To do so, he and his students carefully consider past theories and findings together with their own creative and experience-based insights. If the theoretical framework they develop leads to questions and answers with far-reaching implications, then they will produce great research. This great research about worms is done in the service of great theory, which ultimately goes beyond worms. Kurt Lewin's (1952) admonition that "there is nothing more practical than a good theory" (p. 169) suggests that a good theoretical framework leads to concrete applications. In other words, good theory directs meaningful action.

If only the theoretical underpinnings of psychological concepts could be this straightforward in practice! Psychological research is both blessed and cursed by a wealth of perspectives on even the simplest of questions. Indeed, much of human behavior is incredibly complex, and therefore multiple, competing hypotheses and theories pepper the research literature. Because of this, you and your teammates must initially keep your minds open to how others approach and discuss ideas similar to yours.

THE PITFALLS OF "THE LITERATURE"

As a result of this complexity, identifying appropriate theories requires a careful search of the literature. This process of searching is often a source of stress for students and faculty alike. Moving from an abstract idea to the nitty-gritty details of the literature search gives rise to a multitude of questions, especially among novice researchers: What keywords should I use? Who are the major players in this area of research? What journals are well respected? How do I know that I have "covered everything" in my search?

These and other questions are likely to dominate your thinking at this phase in the process, whether or not you have conducted literature searches in past classes. In our experience, students face two major pitfalls in their attempts to develop an idea. The pitfalls are related yet at opposite ends of a continuum. The first is to fixate on the literature. This pitfall can be paralyzing, because it will undermine your creativity, intuition, and initiative. The truth is you can *never* read enough to cover absolutely every angle. Just when you feel set on explaining your team's idea within a particular theoretical framework, you might stumble on another line of research that seems important yet incompatible with your current thinking. Knowing that this can happen fills many students with doubt, making it all but impossible for them to commit to an idea until they read "just a bit more." But, again, you can never read enough to overcome this concern completely. One result of being paralyzed by the literature is a temptation to play it safe and test smaller ideas that trivially extend past research. But this saps the life out of a project. Constrained excessively by the literature, researchers might end up testing an idea that is a pale reflection of the enthusiasm they originally experienced during the brainstorming phase of the project.

At the other extreme, we have seen students who fail to consult the literature, assuming instead that their ideas can "stand on their own" without relying on past work or theoretical foundations. Perhaps a quick check of the literature fails to turn up a journal article reporting a similar idea, so you assume that no one else has tackled your question. This is a big mistake. Yes, it is refreshing to brainstorm freely, without much if any consideration of past research. It is even rumored that Kurt Lewin forbade his graduate students to read the literature so that they would avoid the potentially boring or trivial ideas that can come from attempts to "extend" past work. But once your team has an idea and needs to refine it, you *must* scour the literature because every idea represents a conversation with the ideas of other scientists.

Your goal is to find the various lines of research that have something to say about your team's idea, and you need to learn how to express your team's idea in a way that relates to these lines of research. If it seems you cannot find related research, you are not approaching the literature correctly. You might not know the language that other researchers have used to discuss related ideas, or you might be looking for studies that are superficially similar to your team's idea without recognizing that what matters is the *theoretical* similarity between your idea and past research. Two ideas are theoretically similar if the underlying psychological mechanisms are closely related, even if the specific research is quite different. Would you, based on your idea, be interested in sitting down and talking with certain authors about the *deeper* ideas and implications of their work? If so, theirs are lines of research you need to consult.

THE NUTS AND BOLTS OF A SUCCESSFUL LITERATURE SEARCH

Our goal in this chapter is to help your team strike a balance between too much and too little, achieving the Goldilocks ideal of just the right amount of emphasis on the research literature. This balance allows past theoretical work to guide you in the process of creating the best possible test of your team's research ideas. To achieve this balance, you should capitalize on the strengths that come from being part of a team. We recommend that you begin by discussing potential search strategies with your teammates. Then, when it actually comes time to search the literature, you should split up and work alone. After putting in time individually, you and your teammates will come back together to compare and consolidate results. If important pieces of the literature are missing, or if your team has distinct questions that require additional follow-up, you can split up once again to tackle these issues. But as soon as your team has a relatively clear picture of the literature, you should wrap up the search process so that you can move forward.

Using Databases Such as PsycINFO

When we were undergraduates, a literature search took place in a library. We had to flip through a thesaurus of keywords and their synonyms in order to translate our ideas into the language of published research. We then rummaged through card catalogs to locate relevant journal articles and books. If you don't know what a card catalog is, don't worry. Just imagine a Google search in which a person at Google headquarters reads your search terms, runs to a somewhat organized vault of little cards describing each and every website in the world, and then rummages through the vault and collects the relevant cards. This Google assistant would then run between five or more storage buildings scattered miles apart, gathering printouts of the material on the identified sites. After skimming all the printouts, he or she would sort them roughly in order of usefulness before sending them to you for your perusal.

This is more or less how our mentors did literature searches when we were undergraduates, and we were their Stone Age Google assistants. This took forever! Tracking down a single article meant following a winding trail, locating each physical journal, and then paging through numerous articles in order to access a source that might or might not be useful. This occasionally led to the serendipitous discovery of a neighboring book or journal article that seemed relevant, but the process as a whole was daunting and had serious drawbacks. Chief among these was the very real possibility of overlooking important sources simply because the search process was terribly inefficient. Now, well into the 21st century, the practice of seeking out sources is quite different. The computer is your conduit to past knowledge, and the card catalog has been replaced by online databases.

When you are conducting research in psychology, the first step in the process is to search and read the *abstracts* (brief summaries) of relevant journal articles and book chapters. For 80 years, ending in 2006, the American Psychological Association produced *Psychological Abstracts,* a monthly print publication containing summaries of new articles, books, chapters, and reports in the field of psychology. This used to be how students found sources related to their research ideas. Now, the digital equivalent of *Psychological Abstracts* is a database called PsycINFO. This database allows you to access abstracts from more than 2.5 million sources related to psychology, and it is updated weekly. Depending on your library's electronic subscriptions to various journals, some of the articles you locate using PsycINFO will be available for you to download immediately. You will need to locate other sources in your library's stacks or request them through an interlibrary loan process.

PsycINFO is not the only database of psychology-related articles; others include (but are not limited to) PsycARTICLES, PsycCRITIQUES, and PUBMED. Subscriptions to these databases are quite expensive, so not all of them will be available at your college or university. Free databases, such as Google Scholar, can aid in your search of the literature, but you should think of them as blunt instruments, best utilized when you are interested in casting a wider net in order to see what might be related to your research terms. PsycINFO, in contrast, is a precision tool; it will more immediately and efficiently find relevant sources. Unless your professor asks you to do otherwise, make use of databases such as Google Scholar only after you have spent some time learning about and utilizing an official research database. For the purposes of this discussion, we will focus on advice related to PsycINFO because of this database's prominence and widespread availability (see Table 3.1 for a brief overview of PsycINFO search strategies). You can also visit the American Psychological Association's webpage for a collection of search guides (http://www.apa.org/pubs/databases/training/search-guides.aspx).

TABLE 3.1   PsycINFO Search Strategies
• *Know your search terms:* The more specific you are, the better. Use the Thesaurus of Psychological Index Terms, available online within the PsycINFO search engine, to locate additional terms. • *Narrow your search:* By age group (e.g., childhood, adolescence, adulthood), population (e.g., human, animal, female, male), publication type (e.g., article, book), publication year, methodology (e.g., field study, literature review, meta-analysis), and so on. • *Look for partial words:* You can search for words in different forms by using an asterisk (*). For example, searching for "adult*" would yield results for "adult," "adults," and "adulthood." • *Use quotation marks:* For exact phrases, place quotation marks (" ") around your search terms. • *Use "or," "and," or "not":* These modifiers will help you refine your search by adding or ruling out particular terms.

Source: American Psychological Association (2012).

Beginning the Search

The beginning of any literature search is likely to feel somewhat forced and awkward. Many students (and some faculty too) have an aversion to the entire process. This aversion becomes especially strong if you think of a literature search as something that has a "right" versus "wrong" answer associated with it. If you expect to find a perfect article about your group's idea, one that will support your hypotheses and make way for an obvious follow-up study, you are bound to be frustrated. Instead, you should think of searching the literature as a series of successive approximations. Certain search terms will get you close to your team's idea, but not close enough. Other search terms will lead to a windfall of topics related to your idea, but they will produce too much information for you to digest.

For a literature search to be rewarding, you must be patient, take your time, and remind yourself that you are not alone in this search. Your teammates are likely to find sources that you missed, and you are likely to stumble on things that they overlooked. The overarching goal of this process is to find the best research that is related to your team's idea, broadly construed. Do not worry about digesting every single article on the topic—this is an impossibility, and struggling to take in all that information will only cause stress. Instead, follow the tips we offer below to come up with a solid number of articles that you can use as a foundation to formalize your team's idea (see Table 3.2 for a summary of these tips).

Start by selecting a few broad search terms that you believe will be relevant to your idea. You should be able to determine quickly whether your search terms are too broad (providing hundreds of potential articles) or too narrow (providing only a handful). If your search is too broad, you can narrow it to certain types of publications or participant populations using preexisting settings in PsycINFO. At this stage, however, we encourage you to limit your search by revising your search terms or adding additional terms to increase the specificity of your search. If, on the other hand, your search is too narrow, first check to see if any of the articles that come up on the list are on-target. If you find that any of them are, click on those articles' titles to see lists of keywords and index terms, which are

TABLE 3.2 Tips for Conducting Literature Searches
<ul><li>Start your search with one to three broad keywords, and slowly get more specific.</li><li>To narrow your search: Select relevant subject population (e.g., children, adults) Sort articles by publication year and focus first on the most recent. Limit your search to literature reviews and meta-analyses. Look only at peer-reviewed journals.</li><li>To broaden your search after locating one or two "good" articles: Scan the abstracts of these articles and locate their keywords and index terms. Go through the reference sections of these articles to identify additional sources. Search for other publications by the same author(s). Look at the "Cited By" field in order to find others who reference these articles.</li><li>Retrieve the best articles in order to read them in their entirety. If your library does not have access to the articles, try searching in Google Scholar or requesting them through interlibrary loan.</li><li>Take a step back: Sometimes doing literature searches can be frustrating. If you are hitting a wall, be sure to give yourself a break and come back to your search later with a fresh perspective.</li></ul>

provided for most articles. These terms can guide you in making your search broader. Or start again, this time by choosing broader terms encompassing your idea.

Knowing When (and How) to Be Strategic

You will know you are on the right track when many of the articles produced by your search look interesting to you. When this happens, we encourage you to be strategic. Don't just read one abstract after another. What does it mean to be strategic? In our experience, it means that you should temporarily limit your search to *literature reviews* or *meta-analyses* in order to determine if any comprehensive reviews have been written on your topic. If they have, the authors of these papers have already done the hard work of reading and summarizing the literature. The typical literature review offers a coherent overview of a topic and systematically integrates a large number of relevant papers. A meta-analysis also provides an overview of a topic, but the purpose of this type of paper is to reanalyze the data from past studies in order to draw overarching conclusions about the statistical trends in the literature. You can learn a great deal about a topic from these types of articles. In particular, the reference section of a good literature review or meta-analysis is a potential gold mine that will help you identify the most important or influential articles in a given area of research.

As you scour the literature for relevant research and theories, you should assume an attitude of humble elitism. You want to learn who the experts are, who is most influential, and who first proposed the theories related to your team's idea. You also want to focus your attention on the "best" journals in psychology. One method of assessing the quality of a journal is to find out its *impact factor* (see Garfield, 1994), or how often other scholars in the field are citing articles from that journal. The more citations, the greater the "impact" and respectability of the journal. If your library has a subscription to *Journal Citation Reports,* produced by Thomson Reuters, you can access impact factors directly (available at http://wokinfo.com/products_tools/analytical/jcr/). In addition, your professor or research adviser can guide you in the process of evaluating the credibility and impact of particular journals. Some of the most influential journals in psychology are listed in Table 3.3.

By focusing on articles from top journals, you and your teammates can avoid the all-too-common problem of becoming attached to ideas that appear only in obscure journals or dissertations (i.e., the final projects written by students working toward their Ph.D.s). Although doctoral students work very hard on their dissertations (often taking many years to complete their projects), a dissertation is not the same as a published paper. The gold standard in published research is a process called *peer review,* and PsycINFO allows you to limit your search to peer-reviewed journals. A peer-reviewed publication has been scrutinized by other experts in the field, and, as a result, is more highly respected and more likely to be theoretically and methodologically sound than non-peer-reviewed work. Generally, we encourage you to focus on peer-reviewed articles, but there is also a place for non-peer-reviewed publications, specifically books and book chapters. Many books are not peer reviewed, but they are often the best sources for detailed descriptions of important theories. If you were to look only for peer-reviewed papers, then you might miss out on these important resources.

Utilizing the Team to Identify Themes

After you have identified a reasonable number of sources that seem related to your topic of interest, it is up to your team to sort them into groups and identify the main themes or stories they contain. Now is when you should look more carefully at the abstracts. Abstracts can tell you a great deal, but, contrary to what some students believe, reading abstracts is *not* the end point of your literature search. After you identify informative papers based on their abstracts, you *must* track down the articles themselves. As we mentioned earlier, some of the articles will be available instantly online through your library. You might be able to locate others by using a standard Internet search engine to find reprints, which many authors make available on their own websites. Alternatively, you may need to locate physical copies of some articles and most books on your library's shelves. If your library does not have a particular source, then you will have to request it through interlibrary loan. The process of securing materials through interlibrary loans can take some time, so be prepared and try to avoid leaving your requests for articles until the last minute.

As you begin to compile and read the articles related to your team's topic, you will be piecing together a sense of how past researchers have talked about the ideas relevant to your interests. Throughout this stage of the process, your team should meet regularly to share what each person has found and to identify what's missing, and then work individually to fill these gaps before meeting again. Our advice here is counterintuitive: Team members should duplicate one another's efforts. Separate searches of the literature are likely to yield different resources as well as some clear areas of overlap. Both are highly informative. Areas of difference will often highlight potential directions in which you can take your group's idea. Some of these competing directions will prove more useful than

TABLE 3.3 High-Impact Journals in Psychology by Subject Area

General

    American Psychologist
    Annual Review of Psychology
    Journal of Applied Psychology
    Journal of Experimental Psychology
    Psychological Bulletin
    Psychological Inquiry
    Psychological Methods
    Psychological Review
    Psychological Science

Social and Personality

    Advances in Experimental Social Psychology
    Journal of Experimental Social Psychology
    Journal of Personality and Social Psychology
    Personality and Social Psychology Bulletin
    Personality and Social Psychology Review

Developmental

    Child Development
    Developmental Psychology
    Developmental Science
    Journal of Child Psychology and Psychiatry
    Psychology and Aging

Clinical and Abnormal

    Clinical Psychology Review
    Development and Psychopathology
    Journal of Abnormal Psychology
    Journal of Clinical Psychiatry
    Journal of Consulting and Clinical Psychology

Cognition and Neuroscience

    Behavioral and Brain Science
    Biological Psychology
    Cognition
    Cognitive Psychology
    Journal of Cognitive Neuroscience
    Neurobiology of Learning and Memory
    Neuropsychologia
    Trends in Cognitive Science

Other

    Addiction
    Educational Psychologist
    Health Psychology
    Psychosomatic Medicine

others, and it is just as important to identify what your project is *not* as it is to identify what your project *is*. Shedding some articles will undoubtedly be necessary, so resist the temptation to become overly attached to the articles you have found. On the other hand, when you and your team members come across the same sources (when, for example, three of you arrive at a meeting with the exact same article in hand), you can be confident that you have begun to identify the key players in this area of research. Your search for good theory is on the right track, and your team's combined understanding of past research will begin to deepen. Finally, you will possess the tools necessary to transform your group's idea into testable predictions.

FROM THEORY TO PREDICTION

It is time to discuss the process of moving from theories (which help to shape your group's idea) to predictions (which help to shape your group's research design). By now, you probably sense that the "logical next step" in psychological research is not always clear. Findings are often conflicting, and there are many directions that a research question could go. This reflects the fact that psychologists work at the border between the sciences and the humanities: The methods of psychological experimentation are orderly, concrete, and clear, but the questions of interest are disparate, abstract, and complex. It also reflects the fact that the pace of psychological research is fast, and this makes it difficult for those working in the field of psychology to coordinate their efforts. Evans (2005) notes that psychological research is so "cutting edge" that it can be vague and, at times, completely subjective (p. 11). One scholar's interpretation of an experimental finding may be completely different from another scholar's, and many psychological theories are conflicting and selective in their scope. We urge you not to become discouraged by this. Instead, focus on the theories that your team finds most compelling in order to move forward with your project.

Searching through the literature is a humbling process, and it is likely that now that you know what's out there, you will question many of your team's initial predictions. Just remember that the aim of experimental prediction is to build on or challenge what already exists. There are always unanswered questions, novel methodologies, untested participant populations, and so forth that can help you shape a set of predictions. Your goal is to join in the existing "conversation" among researchers, as expressed through the theories and research you identified in your literature search. For instance, many students find success in bringing two seemingly disparate theories together in order to explain an otherwise well-researched phenomenon. Or perhaps your team believes that a theory from one area of research can help explain a seemingly unrelated phenomenon from another area of research. In any case, it is natural to feel overwhelmed as you try to think of a novel prediction, so don't despair. Just stick with it and continue working with your ideas.

Ultimately, your team will need to ask and answer the following two questions: What makes for a compelling story? And how will you translate this story into a clear vision moving forward? Answering these questions requires a clarity of purpose and method that you cannot get prepackaged or "off-the-shelf." Your team must develop a clear and compelling prediction, and this will take a great deal of effort and a willingness to consider a range of potential methodologies. Keep at it until you are convinced that you have a *testable* hypothesis. Theories rapidly lose their utility, and ideas are far less compelling, if they cannot be tested.

Testability of the Prediction

The notion of testability is its own beast and deserves special attention. Researchers must strike a balance between the desirability of a research question and how easily it can be translated into a clear, testable hypothesis. A testable hypothesis is one that specifies an unambiguous relationship between observable events. If you will be conducting an experiment, your hypothesis should clearly predict an outcome that will occur under certain conditions but not under other conditions, and you must have a good rationale for this expected pattern of findings. Some hypotheses are fascinating but extremely difficult, if not impossible, to test. For instance, ideas such as Freudian repression or that people regularly conceal distasteful opinions are extremely difficult to test because these phenomena are by definition "hidden" or unobservable. Hypotheses that merely predict null effects (i.e., that two experimental conditions will lead to the same outcome) also should be avoided. These predictions tend to be somewhat uninteresting, and they are difficult to test because observing little or no difference between two experimental conditions in a single study generally provides only weak evidence of there being no difference.

Another aspect of testability is more practical. Researchers must identify the limitations of their projects. Sometimes it is impractical to bring a fascinating idea into the research laboratory because of the complexity of the phenomenon being studied. Recall the cockroach experiment that we described at the opening of this chapter. The researchers considered conducting their initial studies with human participants, but they recognized that doing so would be of limited value and would provide only a weak test of their hypotheses:

> Had the present been experiments using human subjects one could easily raise questions about self-disclosure, evaluation apprehension, the approval motive, etc. But one finds it rather awkward to attribute this sort of motivation to the cockroach, even though we have no idea if these seemingly spiritless creatures aren't vulnerable to some of the very same passions and weaknesses which beset our sophomore population of subjects. (Zajonc et al., 1969, p. 91)

Zajonc and colleagues were determined to isolate the impact of social facilitation on behavior, and they wagered that cockroaches would be seen as a simpler and far less biased model of behavior than humans (especially college sophomores). Their bet paid off, and it laid the necessary groundwork for subsequent research using human participants. Would you have settled for cockroaches as your initial participants? Ensuring that your ideas are testable is difficult and requires keen insight.

Characteristics of Strong Hypotheses

Good researchers must be logicians of an unusual breed; they must be alternatingly clever and sensible. Transforming an idea that is informed by theory into a prediction that can be tested in the context of a research laboratory is a true challenge. To succeed at this, the researcher must balance a variety of competing needs: the originality of the idea, the constraints of time and available resources, the research setting, and the likelihood of finding the desired outcome. Generally, the "desired outcome" is your team's prediction: You want results that are consistent with your team's hypothesis. So how do you develop the best possible hypothesis? In our experience, we have found that some of the best hypotheses are those that set up a horse race between competing ideas. That is, the researcher pits two or more competing theoretical predictions against one another.

A classic example of a horse race like this is Zanna and Cooper's (1974) "dissonance and the pill" study, which pitted cognitive dissonance theory against self-perception theory. The theory of cognitive dissonance argues that people experience an uncomfortable and "dissonant" psychological state marked by a physically unpleasant sense of arousal when their behavior contradicts their beliefs. This physical tension persists until, most often, their beliefs change in order to align more comfortably with their actions. In contrast, self-perception theory dismisses the idea that any subjective, visceral experience of "dissonance" occurs in these situations. Instead, self-perception theory argues that people's beliefs are generally weak and ephemeral. When asked to report their beliefs, individuals dispassionately consider the most salient evidence available to them—that is, their own actions—and they report beliefs that are logically consistent with these actions. According to self-perception theory, people are *not* emotional cauldrons of conflicting thoughts and actions; they are rather simple and relatively calm observers of themselves.

In Zanna and Cooper's study, each college student participant was given a "pill" (actually a placebo) and was told (depending on the experimental condition) that it would cause feelings of tension, cause feelings of relaxation, or have no effect. Immediately after taking the pill, each participant was instructed to write an essay in favor of banning speakers from the college campus, a writing task that ran counter to the beliefs of these politically active college students of the 1970s. Participants who thought the pill would make them feel relaxed changed their attitudes dramatically toward the controversial position they had just advocated; they must have experienced an uncomfortable, visceral tension, made all the more alarming by the fact that they should have been feeling the "relaxing" effects of the pill. In contrast, participants who thought the pill would make them feel "tense" did not demonstrate a change in attitude toward the controversial position (which would otherwise be typical in this type of research), presumably because they were able to attribute the dissonance caused by writing the controversial essay to the pill. These findings support the idea that tension is a natural by-product of asserting something you do not believe in. But once you have an alternative explanation for your feelings (e.g., it was the "pill" that made me feel on edge), the need to allay the tension by changing your attitude disappears.

These findings clearly supported cognitive dissonance theory over self-perception theory. The subjective experience of "dissonance" does matter. This type of horse race between competing ideas is especially compelling, but it takes a great deal of effort and insight to design such a study. Zanna and Cooper's hypothesis stemmed from the researchers' careful examination of many previous studies on cognitive dissonance and self-perception theory. Only after understanding past work could they make a novel prediction using a clever experimental paradigm.

Utility of the Data

A final consideration to take into account when you are developing a compelling hypothesis is the broader utility of the data you collect. Even if your team's hypothesis is wrong, you want your results to be meaningful. As we discuss later, in Chapter 6, data have the ability to speak in a number of important ways. In this early phase of developing your predictions, it is crucial that you think ahead to the conclusions you will reach if your study's findings differ from your expectations. Setting up a horse race between competing ideas can help in this respect. If your hypothesis is wrong, at least you might learn that the competing idea is more accurate. But even if a study results in nonsignificant findings (that is, you observe little or no difference between the experimental conditions), this can convey important information, especially if your predictions acknowledge this possibility in advance.

The little-discussed reality is that researchers frequently do not see differences between their experimental conditions. A biologist looking to find a bacterial contaminant in a local stream might complete her investigation without finding any evidence of the contaminant's presence. This might suggest that her prediction or methods were flawed, or it might suggest that she consider, instead, that the stream is healthy and therefore has salubrious effects on its inhabitants. In this case, the lack of results should prompt additional research. No study stands alone, and a single study should never disqualify an idea. Instead, as in the case of investigating a stream's health, the researcher's goal should be to consider the data as potentially meaningful regardless of the outcome. Genius is the failed prediction that leads to a meaningful discovery.

Conclusion

We started our discussion of theories and predictions by talking about cockroaches and how these disgusting, ordinary creatures played a central role in Robert Zajonc's development of an important theory about social facilitation. This quirky example is fascinating, and not just because it illustrates the creative evolution of a theory. It also has implications for team-based research. Tasks that are unfamiliar and challenging are best tackled individually, especially at first. From the initial brainstorming to the literature search process to the development of a prediction, we have urged you to begin these tasks alone before bringing your individual efforts back to the group. This is because much of the process of coming up with a testable idea involves flexibility, creativity, and openness to new ideas. Unfortunately, as the limitations on social facilitation suggest, groups tend to stifle creativity. In the presence of others, individuals are inclined to fall back on more stereotypical ideas and ways of thinking.

On the other hand, some tasks lend themselves particularly well to being done in the presence of other team members. Groups make efficient work of labor-intensive activities, and they increase excitement for a project. Moreover, the shift in gears from individual work to group work represents an important change in perspective in the course of a project. The wild ideas of individuals might spark related ideas among other team members, or they might be reeled in or discarded as the dynamics of group work lend focus to a project. Both of these processes signal progress.

Up until this moment in time, your team might have experienced only a tenuous sense of togetherness. The initial coordination of group work is much like an awkward first date. It is natural to feel uncertain, overwhelmed, disconnected, and even frustrated. But as you and your teammates identify common interests, you will gain confidence in a shared vision. You will have "Aha!" moments that are amplified by their being felt together. And you will begin to appreciate how valuable your differences in abilities, experiences, and perspectives are to translating your team's idea into a compelling prediction. As your research team becomes more comfortable working together, your shared vision of the project will enable you to develop a joint understanding of how you can test *the idea*. And the more frequently your research team revisits its shared vision, the more invested you will be in the project itself. Perhaps not surprisingly, ownership begins to develop through this process. Mapping your ideas onto a theory is the first step, but ownership truly comes when you place your bets by making a prediction: "We think it works like this, but let's see!"

References

American Psychological Association. (2012). APA PsycNET Help Menu. Retrieved from http://helpdocs.apa.org/PsycNET-help.html

Evans, J. St. B. T. (2005). *How to do research: A psychologist's guide*. New York: Psychology Press.

Garfield, E. (1994, June 20). The Thomson Reuters impact factor. *Current Contents*. Retrieved from http://thomsonreuters.com/products_services/science/free/essays/impact_factor

Lewin, K. (1952). *Field theory in social science: Selected theoretical papers by Kurt Lewin*. London: Tavistock.

Triplett, N. (1898). The dynamogenic factors in pacemaking and competition. *American Journal of Psychology, 9,* 507–533.

Zajonc, R. B. (1965). Social facilitation. *Science, 149,* 269–274.

Zajonc, R. B., Heingartner, A., & Herman, E. M. (1969). Social enhancement and impairment of performance in the cockroach. *Journal of Personality and Social Psychology, 13,* 83–92.

Zanna, M. P., & Cooper, J. (1974). Dissonance and the pill: An attribution approach to studying the arousal properties of dissonance. *Journal of Personality and Social Psychology, 29,* 703–709.

CHAPTER 4

Ethics

Seven Lessons (Plus or Minus Two)

1. Avoid the slippery slope of fraud by treating research methods, data, and findings as sacred.

2. Respect for persons, beneficence, and justice are the ethical principles that guide the conduct of all research involving human participants.

3. Your goal as a scientist is to be honest, accurate, efficient, and objective throughout the research process.

4. Plan ahead if you are required to submit an application to the institutional review board on your campus. The lag time between submission and acceptance can be a month or more.

5. Your responsibilities as an ethical researcher include providing informed consent, communicating risks and benefits, allowing participants to withdraw without penalty, using deception judiciously if at all, and debriefing participants thoroughly.

6. Debriefing can serve as a vehicle for sharing vision, ownership, and togetherness with your participants, allowing them to feel like collaborators instead of mere data points.

7. When faced with ethical uncertainties, consult early and often with your instructor, your adviser, other professors, and your research team.

It is psychologically easy to ignore responsibility when one is only an intermediate link in a chain.

—Stanley Milgram (1974/2009, p. 11)

Imagine being a research assistant at the University of Pennsylvania in the late 1960s. Your adviser is conducting research funded by the National Science Foundation, the National Institute of Mental Health, and the National Institutes of Health. The experimental procedure is summarized in the *Annual Review of Medicine* as follows:

> When an experimentally naive dog receives escape-avoidance training in a shuttle box, the following behavior typically occurs: at the onset of the first painful electric shock, the dog runs frantically about, defecating, urinating, and howling, until it accidentally scrambles over the barrier and so escapes the shock. On the next trial, the dog, running and howling, crosses the barrier more quickly than on the preceding trial. This pattern continues until the dog learns to avoid shock altogether . . . . However, in dramatic contrast to a naive dog, a typical dog which has experienced uncontrollable shocks before avoidance training soon stops running and howling and sits or lies, quietly whining, until shock terminates. The dog does not cross the barrier and escape from shock. Rather, it seems to give up and passively accepts the shock. On succeeding trials, the dog continues to fail to make escape movements and takes as much shock as the experimenter chooses to give. (Seligman, 1972, p. 407)

Most students find this experimental procedure to be horrifying, and they assume that any reasonable professional code of ethics would forbid such research. Yet federal granting agencies funded this work on learned helplessness, which was conducted by Martin Seligman and his colleagues. Still, regardless of whether or not the federal government supported the work, the investigator conducting this research must have been some kind of sadist, right? Not necessarily, and in this case *not at all*. Seligman today is widely known as the "father" of positive psychology, the study of human resilience and thriving. But his earlier work troubles many of us, and it should. Most students today could not imagine assisting with an experimental procedure such as this, and the truth is, you most likely never will. Why? Because the code of ethics in psychology has changed over the years, and research that was considered acceptable a generation ago is no longer acceptable today.

THE GOALS AND ETHICS OF SCIENCE

Science pursues two closely related ends: raw knowledge and practical know-how. On one hand, *basic* science accumulates empirically verifiable facts about the world and its inhabitants. Here the goal is truth for truth's sake. Some discoveries are more profound and far-reaching than others, but no truth is too small. Each and every discovery is a clue contributing to the unraveling of life's many mysteries. *Applied* science, on the other hand, puts a premium on knowledge that is more immediately useful. The goal here is to make life better. To accomplish this, scientists must refine raw knowledge and put it to work "in the real world," and this is a messy, high-stakes business. For instance, translating basic research on psychoactive compounds into an effective psychotherapeutic drug often takes decades and runs up against unexpected setbacks, such as unacceptable side effects when the drug is tested in human trials. If the development of a particular drug fails, millions of dollars and decades of work are lost. When a drug succeeds, however, millions of lives can be saved or improved, and the drug maker earns billions of dollars. Of course, many new drugs are only somewhat successful and perhaps no more effective than older, cheaper generic drugs. Some patients may respond quite favorably to the new treatment, while others suffer serious side effects or benefit little or not at all. In its effort to advance society's practical know-how, applied science must wrangle with all of these trade-offs.

What do the goals of science have to do with research ethics? The answer turns out to be rather straightforward, and it grounds research ethics in just two simple ideas. First, *science values truth*. This is why honesty, objectivity, and accuracy are so important to scientists. Dishonesty, bias, and inaccuracy undermine the whole enterprise. Some sins against science, such as fabricating data, are unforgivable and can lead to the overnight evaporation of a career in academia. Retractions of research articles are on the rise as instances of scientific misconduct have been exposed. In a recent case at Tilburg University in the Netherlands, social psychologist and prolific researcher Diederik Stapel resigned in the face of overwhelming evidence of fraud and fabrication of data (Carey, 2011). In another case, an eminent psychologist at Harvard University was found guilty of numerous ethical lapses "involving data acquisition, data analysis, data retention, and the reporting of research methodologies and results" ("FAS Dean Smith Confirms," 2010).

As these cases suggest, many aspects of the research process are vulnerable to scientific misconduct. Instances of misconduct can range in seriousness from negligent mistakes to willful and egregious fabrications. The past president of the Society for Personality and Social Psychology, Jennifer Crocker, likens the process of committing fraud to the experience of Stanley Milgram's research participants, who were led to believe they were delivering true electric shocks to another person. Although the majority of participants ended up giving seemingly lethal shocks to the confederate, the escalation in strength of the shocks was *gradual* (Milgram, 1963). According to Crocker (2011), "To understand fraud, we should think about how it begins and escalates, not how it ends. By the time such fraud is exposed, bad choices that would usually lead to only minor transgressions have escalated into outright career-killing behavior" (p. 151). Thus, we urge you to be truthful at all times about every aspect of the research process. Fabricating or fudging data is always wrong. Theories, methods, and results must be treated as sacred, and your reports to others must be honest and accurate.

It is important to point out that many sins against the truth appear to be "honest" mistakes. For instance, adjusting or throwing out data from a subset of participants whose answers are unusual is occasionally warranted, but this must be done transparently and with extreme caution. Ideally, you should develop and follow *preestablished* rules for working with your data. If you look at your results and only then decide to delete cases or adjust extreme scores, you are likely to do so in a manner that favors your predictions. At the very least, you should *always* explain precisely why, how, and when you decided to manipulate your data. Then your audience can decide for themselves whether or not to trust your findings. Failing to disclose your data-handling procedures is an ethical violation whether or not you intended to act dishonestly. That is, you have an ethical responsibility to identify and report any aspect of your methods that might distort or bias your findings. This is a high standard to meet. As a student, you might overlook a potential source of bias that a more experienced researcher would identify, so enlisting the aid of your mentor or instructor is crucial. Even if such a mistake or omission results from ignorance, it still matters.

The second simple idea that grounds research ethics is this: *Science values quality of life.* The pain and suffering of others, whether human or not, is real. Needlessly inflicting misery on others in the course of the quest for knowledge ought to be troubling. Clearly, the intentional infliction of unmitigated harm on study participants directly violates this principle. But what if there is a small risk of harm coupled with the prospect of gaining significant knowledge? Modern research ethics grew out of this dilemma. Today's researchers must take care to inform potential participants about their studies' procedures so that a person's consent to participate is meaningful and given freely. In brief, your personal and professional standard of ethics should always begin and end with a careful analysis of the potential benefits versus the potential costs of your actions in relation to the goals of science.

THE FORMATION OF ETHICS COMMITTEES

The first American Psychological Association Committee on Ethical Standards for Psychologists was convened in 1947, with the express purpose of creating a set of professional standards that would help psychologists with the moral dilemmas they faced. The result of this committee's work was the first APA ethics code, published in 1953, which focused primarily on the ethical goals psychologists should *aspire* to achieve (Fisher, 2009). This code of ethics did not provide clear guidance for research such as Seligman's learned helplessness experiments. Indeed, the field of psychology of the 1960s and 1970s is filled with vivid images of controversial experiments: kittens forced to live in partial or complete blindness (Wiesel & Hubel, 1965); rhesus monkeys confined to a "pit of despair" for weeks or months at a time (Suomi & Harlow, 1972); innocent men confined to a mock prison and subjected to the cruelty of their peers (Haney, Banks & Zimbardo, 1973); and hundreds of human participants persuaded to deliver what they perceived to be dangerous if not deadly electric shocks to another human being (Milgram, 1963).

The potential and real harm that could be caused by experimental paradigms did not become a focus of national attention until the early 1970s, when the Tuskegee syphilis study became public. The U.S. Public Health Service admitted to having infected hundreds of African American men with syphilis since 1932, observing the progress of the disease and failing to provide these individuals with treatment even after antibiotics were shown to be an effective cure (Centers for Disease Control, 2009). This scandal brought to the forefront the importance of having more than just a single researcher's aspirational goals guide the design and conduct of a research study. An objective body was needed to oversee researchers' plans for using animal and human research subjects. The responsibility for this oversight landed in the halls of academia; every university and college in the United States became responsible for convening a committee that would review research proposals, make suggestions, and grant permission for researchers to conduct their work. The institution-based bodies that regulate research using human participants are known as institutional review boards (IRBs) or human subjects committees. Those that review research proposals involving animal participants are known as institutional animal care and use committees.

It is crucial to note that policies regarding the institutional review of research apply to all researchers, not just psychologists. Protection of research participants is mandated by the U.S. government and is required of all scientists who receive federal funds. In 1974, the National Commission for the Protection of Human Subjects of Biomedical and Behavioral Research was formed, and its first job was to identify the ethical principles that should guide the conduct of all human subjects research. The result of the commission's deliberations, the Belmont Report, was adopted on April 18, 1979 (the full report is available online at http://www.hhs.gov/ohrp/humansubjects/guidance/belmont.html). The core of the Belmont Report is the discussion of three *basic ethical principles:* respect for persons, beneficence, and justice (see Table 4.1 for an explanation of each principle). The commission proposed a way to apply each of these principles, respectively: (a) the requirement of full and informed consent, (b) a formal assessment of the risks and benefits of research participation, and (c) a system of distributive justice in the selection of research participants (which includes protections for particular groups, such as children, pregnant women, institutionalized individuals, and people who are mentally or physically ill).

More recently, in 1991, the U.S. Department of Health and Human Services published the Federal Policy for the Protection of Human Subjects, known as the "Common Rule," which includes the formal regulations associated with IRBs, informed consent, compliance

TABLE 4.1 The Three Basic Ethical Principles	
Ethical principle	*Explanation*
Respect for persons	• People are capable of forming their own opinions, making choices, and carrying out independent actions; therefore, investigators should treat every individual as an autonomous agent by providing the information necessary to make choices and allowing freedom of action. • Some people are less capable of autonomy because of age, illness (mental or physical), disability, or other circumstances (such as incarceration or institutionalization); therefore, investigators should offer additional protections to these individuals.
Beneficence	• Investigators are obliged to avoid harming individuals who participate in research. • In cases where the research involves some level of risk, it is the investigator's duty to minimize these risks and to maximize all possible benefits to the research participant.
Justice	• Investigators must take care to distribute the advantages and disadvantages of research participation in a balanced (i.e., just) manner, so that no particular group reaps greater benefits or suffers greater burdens.

Source: Based on the National Commission for the Protection of Human Subjects of Biomedical and Behavioral Research's Belmont Report (1979).

assurances, and protections for vulnerable populations (the full text of the Common Rule is available online at http://www.hhs.gov/ohrp/humansubjects/commonrule/index.html). These regulations, which have been unchanged for more than 20 years, are currently being revisited and are likely to be revised in light of numerous changes in the scope and context of modern research practices ("HHS Announces," 2011). A discussion of possible revisions to the Common Rule is beyond the scope of this chapter, but we encourage you to visit the Department of Health and Human Services website and to talk with your instructor about the most current regulations and practices. You may find that your institution provides or perhaps requires a training course in ethics, many of which are available online.

Although specific ethics requirements will change from time to time, the ethical values behind these requirements are likely to remain constant. In a report published by the Office of Research Integrity of the U.S. Department of Health and Human Services, Steneck (2006) describes four values that should be shared by all researchers, regardless of discipline: honesty, accuracy, efficiency, and objectivity (p. 3). In fulfilling the value of honesty, you should ask yourself, "Are these ideas my own? Am I satisfying the promises I made to my collaborators? Am I conducting the study in the manner that I said I would?" Accuracy speaks to the importance of minimizing and correcting errors and reporting findings clearly, as well as being scrupulous in how data are analyzed and presented. It is sometimes easy to overlook the value of efficiency, which recognizes that resources (e.g., money, time) are limited. As a result, you should avoid purchasing unnecessary equipment, misusing experimenter time, or subjecting participants to unnecessary procedures. Finally, being objective means trying your best to avoid bias and approaching each research question with a scientific attitude rather than the attitude of an activist.

You should apply the values of honesty, accuracy, efficiency, and objectivity throughout your daily life, inside and outside the classroom and research laboratory. Even as you describe your research to your family and friends, you should keep these values in mind. Table 4.2 provides a number of examples of how these values play out in real-life situations experienced by psychology students.

RESEARCH IS NOT REALITY TV . . . OR IS IT?

The era of intensely immersive, emotionally challenging research studies is over, at least within the psychologist's laboratory. Most researchers appreciate the importance of the current ethical restrictions and the oversight of committees such as IRBs for one central reason: These constraints help to protect participants. But here is a (not-so-secret) secret: Many researchers look wistfully back on the days when creativity was unfettered. Even though you can no longer design a study without careful outside scrutiny of your planned procedures, there is no reason to assume that today's research projects need to be bland or mundane. Indeed, it is possible to translate ethically impossible scenarios into acceptable experimental paradigms.

As an example, let's look to one place in the 21st century where ethical standards seem not to apply: so-called reality television. With titles like *Temptation Island, Fear Factor,* and *Wife Swap,* many reality television shows seem ethically questionable, and it is highly

TABLE 4.2	Examples of Ethically Questionable Behaviors

Read the following brief examples of ethically questionable behaviors and try to identify how the values of honesty, accuracy, efficiency, and/or objectivity (as described by Steneck, 2006) are being violated. Some of these behaviors are more serious ethical violations than others, but all of these behaviors should be avoided:

- You e-mail a sensitive data file to your adviser that includes participants' names, phone numbers, and addresses.
- You tell your classmate about the experience you had running a challenging experimental participant, providing a vivid description of the participant's annoying behaviors.
- You discuss confidential details of your mentor's current research project while you are sitting in the university cafeteria.
- You initially miss a typographical error in the experimental materials and have to reprint all 500 pages.
- You discover that the participant you are supposed to run is your roommate, but you have her complete the study (and receive compensation) anyway.
- You find yourself being more laid back when running participants in the control condition than you are when running those in the experimental condition.
- You enter the data from a lengthy survey after pulling two all-nighters and feeling as if you can barely keep your eyes open.
- You make a mistake during the experimental procedure and decide not to tell your adviser.
- You list your name as first author on a poster presentation, even though your collaborator did the majority of the work.

unlikely that any IRB would approve the activities depicted on these shows for scientific research. So it should be impossible for reality TV to inspire an ethical research study, right? And no ethical study is titillating enough to inspire a reality TV program, right? Think again. Take the reality television series *Room Raiders* as an example. This show, originally aired on MTV in 2004, gets very personal. One individual in each episode is featured as a contestant, and that person gets to "raid" the bedrooms of three potential romantic partners. The contestant does not meet or see photos of the potential partners. Instead, he or she chooses whom to date based on the content of their rooms, which includes everything from what's under the bed to what's written in cell phone text messages. As you can imagine, the show's producers are able to push this to its limit by revealing to a television audience a wide array of very private items.

Here is where serious science and popular culture collide. A researcher named Samuel Gosling and his colleagues published a paper in one of the premier psychology journals, the *Journal of Personality and Social Psychology,* titled "A Room With a Cue: Personality Judgments Based on Offices and Bedrooms." Much like the television program, the series of studies reported in this paper involved individuals going through other persons' belongings in their bedrooms or offices in order to find out something about their personalities. Unlike the television program, all participants granted informed consent, confidentiality was maintained, and dating preferences were ignored. But which came first, the show or the study? Gosling, Ko, Mannarelli, and Morris published their paper in 2002, two years before the first episode of *Room Raiders* aired. Although it is unclear whether their research directly inspired *Room Raiders,* the similarity of the premise is uncanny, and Gosling (2008) has since reported being contacted by a television producer interested in developing yet another, similar reality show. This is an example of how scientists can be creative in how they ask their research questions *while holding true to ethical standards.* And, for better or for worse, this is also an example of how a psychological study can inspire the mass media's salacious attempts to produce a hit show.

PROTECTING RESEARCH PARTICIPANTS

We opened this chapter with a very unsettling description of the dogs that were used as subjects in Seligman's research on learned helplessness. Because animals can never "consent" to participate in research, some people believe that experimentation on animals is simply unacceptable. Others recognize that human welfare can be directly affected by what scientists learn in working with animals, so they deem the trade-off worthwhile. Indeed, most lifesaving medications prescribed to humans were first tested on animals. That said, there is widespread recognition that animals, like humans, need research protections. The federal Animal Welfare Act, which regulates how animals are treated in the United States, was signed into law in 1966. Since that time, it has been amended more than half a dozen times (the text of the most current version is available online at http://www .gpo.gov/fdsys/pkg/USCODE-2009-title7/html/USCODE-2009-title7-chap54.htm).

Today's researchers seeking to use animal subjects are required to justify their choices of animal species and must demonstrate that they have considered nonanimal models for their research. In addition, they must provide appropriate housing for the animals, minimize the animals' pain and distress, sedate or anesthetize the animals whenever possible, and painlessly kill any animals whose distress cannot be relieved (a complete list of the requirements that researchers must meet is available online at http://grants1.nih.gov/grants/olaw/references/phspol.htm). The National Academy of Sciences' Institute of Laboratory Animal Resources has published the *Guide for the Care and Use of Laboratory Animals,* which can be accessed online (at http://www.nap.edu/catalog.php?record_id = 12910), and a detailed overview of the regulations can be found at the website of the Association for the Assessment and Accreditation of Laboratory Animal Care (http://www.aaalac.org).

Because most research in psychology relies on human participants, the remainder of this chapter focuses on the ethical considerations and requirements associated with this type of research, which often involves submission of a detailed application to an IRB. It is important to keep in mind that if you are reading this book as part of a research methods class, your instructor may not require you to write an IRB application. If your instructor does ask you to complete an IRB application, it is likely that he or she (rather than your institution's actual IRB) will be the one reviewing your work and approving your research. This is because, at most institutions, research that is conducted for the purpose of a class project is not subject to review by the IRB. The assumption here is that your professor acts as the "ethical checkpoint" for your project. In contrast, if you are completing a thesis or independent study, or if you are working in a research lab, it is likely that you (typically in collaboration with your adviser) will be preparing and formally submitting an actual IRB application.

There is no universal template for IRB applications. Some required elements are common across IRBs (see http://www.hhs.gov/ohrp/archive/irb/irb_introduction.htm), but the applications themselves vary in length, content, and structure from one institution to the next. Similarly, there is great variability in how "strict" IRBs tend to be, as well as the length of time it takes between the IRB's receipt of an application and when the researcher is notified of the board's decision. In our experience, most IRBs are perceived (by at least someone on campus) to be too slow and too harsh or picky. These are relative concepts, of course, so we encourage you to take lightly any rumors you have heard about your institution's IRB. That said, it is typical for the average IRB to take at least a month to return an application. It is also commonplace for an IRB to ask for revisions in a research plan. If you are working with any kind of special population, such as children or individuals with psychiatric disorders, there are additional steps you must take to gain IRB approval. Altogether, this means that the average researcher must wait a month or two from the time he or she submits an IRB application to the time when the IRB grants formal permission to conduct the study. This is something you need to keep in mind as you embark on a career in research; planning ahead is crucial!

Informed Consent

When you are conducting research with human participants, certain ethical issues should play a central role in your thinking, beginning early in the design stage. The first issue is informed consent. All potential participants must be told what they can expect to experience if they take part in the research study. This means giving them an overarching description of the study's procedures and questions, an idea of how much time they will be asked to commit to the study, and details about what compensation they should expect (if any). Table 4.3 lists the most common elements of informed consent forms, along with example phrasing, and Table 4.4 provides a complete sample of an informed consent form. Because there is some variability in style, level of detail, and required elements in such forms, you should always check with your research mentor and local IRB when you develop your consent procedure.

A careful reading of the sample informed consent form in Table 4.4 should draw your attention to two additional concepts associated with informed consent that are worth highlighting. These are the discussion of the risks and benefits of participation, and the inclusion of an explicit statement that participants can withdraw from the research at any time without penalty or loss of compensation.

Weighing Risks and Benefits

What is the risk-benefit ratio? All IRBs require an explicit discussion of the risks and benefits of participation in a research study. Any risk that comes from participation must be outweighed by the potential benefits of the research. For example, imagine that your team would like to conduct a research study that involves a negative mood induction. One of the

TABLE 4.3 Common Elements of Informed Consent Forms	
Element	*Example of appropriate phrasing*
Purpose of the research	"I hereby consent to participate in this study involving a word association task followed by a short questionnaire."
Expected duration of the procedures	"I understand that this study will take about fifteen (15) minutes to complete."
Voluntary nature of the experiment	"I understand that my participation in this study is completely voluntary."
Potential risks or discomfort the participant may experience	"I understand that aspects of this study may elicit feelings of discomfort, but these feelings should dissipate quickly."
Participant's right to terminate participation at any time without loss of compensation	"I understand that I have the ability to withdraw at any time without penalty or loss of compensation."
Extent to which the participant's individual data will remain confidential	"I understand that no individual data will be reported and that subject codes will be used to maintain confidentiality."
Incentives or benefits of participation	"I understand that I will be compensated with five dollars ($5) for my participation in this study."
How to contact the experimenter in case the participant has any questions relating to the study	"I understand that matters relating to this study may be directed to [experimenter's name and contact information]."
Acknowledgment of the participant's legal age and comprehension of the consent form	"I acknowledge that I am at least eighteen (18) years old and that I have read and understand the above explanations."

risks is that the experimentally induced mood may become severe or long-lasting, having a greater impact on the participant than expected. This is a potential risk, but it is a risk that can be mitigated in at least two ways. First, the risk can be mitigated if care is taken that the experimental induction of mood does not go beyond something that a person might come across in his or her own day-to-day life. This means that a negative mood could be induced by a sad song or a sad video clip; either is something a participant might encounter by listening to the radio, going to a movie, or watching television. It would be more risky for the researcher to create a video of high-impact images of death, devastation, or heartbreak. These would increase the risk of having the negative mood transcend the experimental procedure and influence the participant beyond the confines of the laboratory.

Second, the risk can be mitigated by what is done at the end of the study. That is, the experimenter can attempt to reverse any potential harmful effects of the experimental manipulation. To alleviate an induced sad mood, for example, your team could show

TABLE 4.4 Sample Informed Consent Form

Informed Consent Form

Please acknowledge that you have read and agree to each paragraph by checking each box.

☐ I hereby consent to participate in this study, which will ask me to (1) think about personal finances and (2) view and evaluate a number of short video clips. This study will take about twenty (20) minutes to complete. I further acknowledge that I have not already participated in this study.

☐ I will receive $6 compensation for my participation in this study. I understand that my participation in this study is completely voluntary and that I have the ability to withdraw at any time without penalty or loss of compensation.

☐ I understand that no individual data will be reported and that subject codes will be used to maintain confidentiality. I permit publication of the results of the experiment with the agreement that participant confidentiality is ensured.

☐ I understand that I may contact the experimenter in order to ask any questions that I might have after I have participated in the study. I understand that matters relating to this study may be directed to Joe Psychology, Ph.D., at joe@mycollege.edu, or the college Human Subjects Research Committee at irb@mycollege.edu. The investigators reserve the right to answer questions relating to the results of the study until after the experiment has been completed.

☐ Again, I understand that my participation in this study is completely voluntary. If I feel uncomfortable during the study, or for any other reason, I may terminate my participation at any time without penalty or loss of compensation.

☐ I acknowledge that I am at least eighteen (18) years old and that I have read and understand the above explanations.

_____   _____
Signature   Date

I certify that I have presented this information to the participant and have obtained his or her consent.

_____   _____
Experimenter's Signature   Date

a humorous film clip or play uplifting music at the end of the participant's session. In addition, you could suggest resources or strategies that the participant could utilize if he or she finds that the effects of the experimental manipulation linger. These are relatively straightforward approaches to dealing with the potential risks of a negative mood induction.

So far we have discussed the ways in which risks must be addressed. Equally important, however, is the need to weigh any risks against the potential benefits of the research. Yes, your procedure may lead the participant to feel sad, but are you inducing sadness for a good reason? Here is where your value judgments and personal ethics will enter into your answer. Different individuals have different opinions about the range of benefits that could come from a particular research study. Under what circumstances is it worthwhile to make a person feel sad in the laboratory? Is this acceptable if the purpose of the study is to determine whether a sad mood influences memory? Social interactions? Decision making? Political opinion? Pain tolerance? Sexual arousal? Smoking behavior? Self-esteem? Shoe preference? (No, that isn't a typo!)

A study that answers a question such as "Does a sad mood lead a person to perform better (or worse) on a memory task?" may have important implications for our understanding of the connection between human emotional and cognitive processes, which in turn could have implications in classrooms and in treatment approaches for chronic mood problems. In contrast, one might argue that the question of whether or not a sad mood has an impact on preference for *shoes* has fewer merits. Yet this exact question was explored by Walther and Grigoriadis, whose article "Why Sad People Like Shoes Better: The Influence of Mood on the Evaluative Conditioning of Consumer Attitudes" (2004) was published in the journal *Psychology and Marketing*. The savvy student might ask, at this point, about the researchers' methods. How was the mood manipulation achieved? The answer is that the researchers induced a happy mood by showing participants scenes from the movies *Shrek* and *The Little Bear*. They induced a sad mood by showing participants "two films, one about child abuse and the other about the last day of a doomed man" (p. 764).

Clearly the researchers were taking the mood induction seriously, and a reasonable reaction would be to scrutinize the potential impact of participating in this study. Could the research have been done without the laboratory-based mood induction? What are the broader implications of this research topic? If your team is uncertain about the potential benefits of a research topic, it is likely that an IRB evaluating the research will be uncertain as well. Beginning at the stage of study design, your team must be able to articulate the potential benefits of participating in your study. Such benefits are often linked to the idea of advancing the scientific understanding of an important principle or practice. Rather than speculating about what Walther and Grigoriadis felt were the potential benefits of their study, we quote from the conclusion of their paper:

> Taken together, the studies reported in this article provide support for the hypothesis that attitudes toward products can be formed through simple processes of evaluative conditioning. Interestingly, and counterintuitively, there is evidence that sad mood enhances the attitude-formation process, whereas happy mood decreases it. (p. 771)

If you were a member of the IRB reviewing these researchers' hypotheses and procedures, would you have given approval? Clearly their IRB did approve the study, but it is important to keep in mind that such judgments are always subject to a variety of perspectives and opinions.

The Ability to Withdraw Without Penalty

Another protection that is granted to participants, according to current ethical guidelines, is the ability to withdraw from a study at any time without penalty or loss of compensation.

Some of the more famous (and, one might argue, notorious) studies in psychology placed significant hurdles in the way of participants' withdrawing partway through the experimental procedure. In the Milgram (1963) study, the authority figure's mantra was, "The experiment requires that you continue." And indeed, the vast majority of subjects continued to participate, despite clear discomfort, subjective stress, and disagreement. In the Stanford Prison Experiment (Haney et al., 1973), the "release" of "prisoners" happened only in the face of very serious circumstances: Four participants were released from the study because of "extreme emotional depression, crying, rage, and acute anxiety," and another participant was released "after being treated for a psychosomatic rash which covered portions of his body" (p. 81).

In part because of participant experiences such as these, researchers today must take great care to inform potential participants that they need not continue in a study if they feel uncomfortable. This idea is explicitly addressed in the informed consent form. In addition, it is the experimenter's responsibility to monitor participants' reactions continually and to ensure that any ill effects of the procedure are quickly addressed. Most important, each participant must be allowed to make a true choice in deciding to participate in a study—not just once, but throughout the experimental procedure.

The Debriefing and the Use of Deception

At the end of the experiment, your team has another opportunity to interact with your participants in an ethical manner. Whether you are sitting face-to-face in the research lab or on the other side of the country administering an online survey, your job is to provide a *debriefing* that is sensitive, meaningful, and informative. The debriefing is your opportunity, first and foremost, to share the purpose of your team's research study (focusing in particular on the anticipated benefits that could come from this line of research). It is also your opportunity to involve each participant in the process of understanding what your team hypothesized and why. In conducting a debriefing, you should avoid the use of jargon. Instead, describe in a clear and concise manner the details of the study and its anticipated implications. For studies that elicit strong reactions from participants, or for studies that lead participants to behave in ways that they would not be comfortable admitting to in the "outside world," it is critical that researchers normalize the participants' experiences. That is, they must help participants understand that the experiment was intentionally designed to elicit certain behaviors and attitudes, and that other participants exposed to the same experimental paradigm are likely to respond in the same way.

The debriefing is also the point at which you describe to the participant, in detail, any deception that has taken place in the research project. One of the challenges you will face in describing the use of deception to participants is to make sure that they don't end up feeling like fools for "falling for it." Again, the key is to normalize the participants' experiences, this time by assuring them that they were not supposed to know what was really being studied and that the experiment depended on the success of the deception. In effect, you are thanking the participants for believing what they were supposed to believe and for contributing useful data to the study.

What if the experimental paradigm is disturbing to a participant, and what if it becomes clear that the experiment could trigger distressing memories or emotions for some individuals? This does happen, even in protocols that have been approved by IRBs. In studies where such outcomes can be anticipated, it is usually wise for the researchers to plan to give all participants referral information for local, affordable counseling services, health care providers, and/or hotlines. As a student researcher, you are required to report any negative participant responses to your adviser, who in turn has a responsibility to report these cases to the IRB.

Some forms of deception used in past research are considered egregious today. For example, many now argue that Milgram (1963) violated ethical standards through his elaborate, emotionally damaging deception. IRBs would consider his studies too risky and deceitful to approve today. On the other hand, Milgram did a fairly good job of conducting debriefings of his participants, which he describes in some detail in his discussion of the original results. Milgram orchestrated a "reunion" between each participant and the confederate (that is, the person the participant had thought he was shocking), allowed for extensive conversation between them, and made clear that the participant was not alone in "going all the way" in obeying the authority figure's advice.

Two Types of Harm

This highlights a subtle, yet important, point about experimental research. Consider two types of harm. One is the harm that occurs within the context of the experiment itself; receiving or giving a painful shock is just one example. The other, more subtle, type of harm is the harm that occurs when a participant leaves the experiment and realizes something upsetting (even terrible) about him- or herself as a result of participating in the study (Ross, 2011). Perhaps a participant learns that she is capable of behaviors that violate her sense of self: that she is capable of being gullible, prejudiced, or even cruel. The truth is that all of us are likely to be any one of these things under the wrong circumstances, but being led to recognize this as the result of an experimental procedure can be particularly damaging. This potential harm must be addressed head-on before the participant leaves the lab or closes the survey.

Lest you believe that these types of harm occurred only in the distant past, consider a study in which one of us participated as an undergraduate. (We know our undergraduate days weren't yesterday, but the early 1990s were firmly rooted in more "modern" ethical standards.) Imagine that you are invited into the research laboratory to participate in a study on attitudes and social perceptions. After filling out some initial questionnaires, you are told that your college is considering whether or not to increase funding to make the campus more accessible to disabled students. The committee charged with this decision has been collecting opinions on the matter and has found that it is helpful to examine arguments on both sides of the issue. Because the committee has received numerous letters in support of such funding, you are asked to help out by writing a powerful and persuasive essay in opposition to funding for disabled students. You agree, with some trepidation, because you want to be helpful. After you go through the fairly torturous process of writing the essay, the experimenter collects it from you, seals it in a manila envelope, gives you a follow-up survey, and debriefs you.

If you have taken classes in social psychology, you might recognize that this procedure is based on one used by Steele and Liu (1981) to demonstrate the effects of performing a counterattitudinal behavior on dissonance-based attitude change. Steele and Liu found that participants who wrote an essay opposing funding for disabled students were likely to change their attitudes about such funding so that their attitudes became more consistent with the counterattitudinal essay. Although we both participated in numerous experiments as undergraduates, this one remains the most vivid more than 20 years later. Why? In part because I (JDB) obeyed the experimenter in doing something I found to be very distasteful: writing an essay in opposition to something I believed in. Perhaps even more important, I remember worrying about the lingering aftereffects of the experiment. I was told in the debriefing that the follow-up questions I completed included an assessment of my attitude about government funding for chronically ill and disabled individuals, and if I were like most participants, I was likely to be *less* in favor of such funding after having written the essay. I knew this was true, and it shook me to the core. Was my attitude really that malleable? Why didn't I refuse to write the essay in the first place? How might I be similarly influenced in day-to-day life? I left the experiment feeling deeply troubled.

Was there a way to minimize my experience of "harm"? Maybe. If the debriefing had done a better job of "normalizing" my behavior, perhaps I wouldn't have felt so troubled by what I experienced. On the other hand, one could argue that I learned something important about myself, and that it is not the experimenter's job to dull responses such as mine. We focus on this example in depth in order to emphasize that researchers should always strive to keep the participant's perspective in mind. Even if your team uses a well-tested paradigm such as Steele and Liu's, it is possible that your study will have a lifelong impact on the participants. It is not always possible to avoid this impact, but it is crucial that you be as prepared as possible to help the participants handle it. Some ethical issues are very clear-cut; others are less so. It is the experimenters' responsibility to monitor participants as closely as they monitor themselves. Indeed, even when deception is minimal, challenging ethical situations may arise. (For example, consider what you would do in the situation presented in Table 4.5.)

THE NUTS AND BOLTS OF AN IRB APPLICATION

Now that you have read about the many issues associated with using human participants in research, we should cover some additional details of the IRB application process. First, let's take a bird's-eye view of the process. The IRB application will typically require your research team to provide all of the following information: a brief review of the background literature, a detailed description of what participants will experience (including how your team will recruit participants, how you will maintain participant confidentiality, and what specific procedures you will follow), a description of how you will secure voluntary and fully informed consent, and a discussion of any compensation to be provided to study participants. In addition, you will need to discuss the risk-to-benefit ratio of your research, and, if your experimental procedure involves deception, you will need to provide a highly convincing rationale for its use. Most IRBs are wary of the use of deception

TABLE 4.5   Ethical Debriefing Activity

This example highlights a situation where the deception is minimal, but the impact of the study may be far-reaching.

Imagine that you are conducting a research project to explore an online computer game's effects on attitudes toward the Israeli–Palestinian conflict. This game is available to the public and displays a simple, animated "choose-your-own-adventure" scenario that promotes human rights in the Middle East. Specifically, the game focuses on atrocities committed by one side of the conflict, the Israelis. The experiment utilizes this game and has a simple methodology: participants are randomly assigned to play the online game or to read the information presented in the game but without the game's animation. In this way you hold constant the information presented while manipulating the participants' level of interaction with the information. Your goal is to determine whether participants' interaction with the game's animated information has a greater effect on their attitudes toward the situation in the Middle East than the same written material.

Consider the following:
- The simulation is persuasive, and opinions may be swayed to concur with or react against the message being promoted.
- The information is factual but one-sided and controversial. It takes a strong stance as "the truth" on a highly charged humanitarian issue embedded in religious, cultural, and political issues.
- The ideas are powerful; presenting these concepts to undergraduate college students could have lasting effects on these individuals and the community.

This experiment does not involve any true deception, but participants are exposed to only one side of a controversial and complex situation. Moreover, you hypothesize that the game could lead participants to develop new (or more extreme) biases based on their experimental condition (see Klemperer, LeDonne, & Nilsen, 2012).

Discussion points:
- Is it ethical to change the attitudes and/or feelings of individuals?
- How should you account for (or correct) changes in opinion caused by a study?
- How should you conduct the debriefing in order to respond to the predicted changes in participants' attitudes?

Activity:
- When presenting this project to an IRB, how might you resolve the ethical issues presented above?
- Develop a debriefing that adequately addresses the potential concerns raised above.

Source: LeDonne and Klemperer (2010).

in research studies. If you intend to use deception, the IRB will likely ask, "Is there any way the research question could be answered without the use of deception? If not, is the research question compelling enough to warrant the use of deception?" You also will need to provide the IRB with a detailed description of your procedure for debriefing participants, including an accurate and easily understood explanation of the study and its hypotheses, your rationale for deceiving the participants (if applicable), and any relevant follow-up or referral information (e.g., for counseling services) you will provide to participants if the study touches on sensitive issues or elicits negative emotions.

To supplement the elements described above, some IRBs (including our own) ask for a "first-person scenario," which is a description of the experimental procedure from start to finish from the perspective of the participant. In our opinion, the first-person scenario is one of the most useful, though undervalued, components of an IRB application. If it is not required by your IRB, it should be! This section of an IRB application requires your team to write, in the first person, exactly what the participant experiences. Most first-person scenarios start with recruitment—for example, "I was in the dining hall and a researcher approached me to ask if I had time later this week to participate in a study on emotion and decision making." These descriptions then go on to detail the experimental procedure and conclude with the participant's perception of the debriefing. For a complete example of a first-person scenario, see Table 4.6.

One of the reasons the first-person scenario is so useful is that it requires the researchers to put themselves in a participant's shoes and imagine what it would be like to participate in their study. Whether or not you find yourself having to write a first-person scenario, we urge your team to at least simulate the experiment from the point of view of the participant. Expose yourselves to the paradigm, practice answering all of the questions, imagine being told the purpose of the study. Would the flow of the study make sense? Would you understand the study's questions? How would you feel? The extent to which you feel awkward, embarrassed, or confused is highly important. These emotions are indicative of potential problems with the procedure, problems that are much better fixed now than after the study is launched.

Equally important is to practice reading your debriefing out loud—to yourself, your teammates, friends, or family members. The debriefing, when done well, should incorporate and share the principles of vision, ownership, and togetherness with your participants. Participants develop a shared vision when they hear you articulate the purpose and hypotheses of your team's study. The more compelling the explanation you give, the more meaningful the participants' shared sense of vision will be. The participants should gain a sense of ownership not only because some of the data are theirs but also because they become invested in the importance of the research question. Ask your participants if they are interested in learning the results of the study when it has been completed, and be sure to follow up by providing a summary of your findings to those who say yes. Finally, a sense of togetherness is achieved through the tone of your debriefing: It should be supportive, honest, collegial, respectful, and gracious. The overarching goal is to help participants feel more like collaborators in the research process and less like simple data points.

ETHICS IN ACTION

In this chapter, we have touched on a number of ethical issues and considerations. It is important to note, however, that your research adviser might err on the side of caution, especially if your team is completing a classroom project. For example, your adviser might

TABLE 4.6 Example of a First-Person Scenario

While I was walking across campus after my lunch break, a fellow student approached me and asked if I had about twenty minutes to do a taste test study. The study was for psychological research. On our way to the lab, I was asked if I had taken any classes in social psychology or research methods. I had not, so we proceeded to where there were chairs lined up for waiting participants. I was thanked for agreeing to participate and handed a one-page questionnaire about my preferences for certain foods. I also was given a bottle of water and told that I should bring it with me when the taste test study began.

Once I completed the questionnaire, an experimenter greeted me and led me to a private room. I was told that while the experimenter prepared the first part of the taste test, I should fill out a questionnaire for a separate study they were developing. In this questionnaire, I thought about and wrote down on a sheet of paper three ways to achieve financial success. Once I finished that, the experimenter came in with a tray of chocolates. The chocolate tray had six types of chocolates with a wide range of cacao levels. I was asked which of the chocolates presented I would prefer to taste if given the choice. After I gave my answer, I was told I had been chosen to taste the sweetest and the most bitter chocolates. After trying each piece separately, and with a drink of water in between, I was asked to rate my enjoyment on a scale the experimenter provided. I also rated the two types of chocolates in comparison with each other.

The experimenter then told me that she needed to prepare the second part of the taste test study and that she had a separate questionnaire for me to fill out, similar to the one I did before, but this time I listed three ways for avoiding dissatisfaction in my personal relationships. When that was completed, the experimenter returned with the second part of the taste test. I was handed a paper with pictures of jelly beans and asked to choose whether I would prefer the sweet or sour version of each color. After indicating my preferences for the sweet and sour jelly beans, I handed the sheet back. The experimenter then had two sweet and two sour jelly beans for me to taste. After tasting the sweet and sour jelly beans separately, also with drinks of water in between, I was again asked to rate my enjoyment of them based on the scale the experimenter provided. I also was asked to compare the sweet and sour jelly beans and rate which of the two I preferred.

This was the end of the taste test study, and I was then given a final questionnaire to fill out regarding my experience and whether I noticed anything unusual about the study. After this, I was taken to another room and debriefed about the purpose of the study. I was told that the questionnaires about financial success and relationship satisfaction were not part of a separate study (as I was led to believe); instead, the researchers hypothesized that the wording of the questionnaires would temporarily change my taste preferences. Finally, before leaving, I was given a choice of candy bars as my compensation for participating in the study.

be much less comfortable with the use of deception in the context of a classroom project than he or she would be in the context of faculty-student collaborative research. An independent study or honors project is likely to fall somewhere in the middle of this "comfort" scale. Fortunately, most ideas can be tested along a continuum that varies in terms of the ethical complexity and intensity of the participant's experience.

To illustrate this idea, here is an example from our own research lab. One of our lines of research examines the extent to which information can be "framed" (that is, described in objectively equivalent terms that are subjectively quite different) in order to be most persuasive. For instance, we have studied the use of message framing to encourage people to provide social support to someone with depression. One version of this work, which could easily be carried out as a classroom project, involves exposing participants to one of two brochures: one that describes the benefits individuals experience when they provide social support to someone with depression (a "gain-framed" message), and one that describes the losses experienced by individuals who fail to provide such support (a "loss-framed" message). Immediately following exposure to the brochure, each participant is asked to imagine a series of hypothetical scenarios, including one in which he or she is asked to provide support to a depressed friend. The experimental question is whether the gain- or loss-framed message is more likely to increase participants' willingness to help the (hypothetical) depressed friend.

A research methods student who finds encouraging results in a study such as this might take the question a bit further as a student-initiated project. A more involved experimental design would include greater separation between the initial exposure to the framed message and subsequent assessment of the participant's intentions to help the hypothetical friend. In our lab, we created a fictional website that was purported to be under development for the Mount Hood Center for Depression Support (Detweiler-Bedell & Detweiler-Bedell, 2009; Detweiler-Bedell, Detweiler-Bedell, Hazlett, & Friedman, 2008). Participants were asked to read and evaluate the website, paying particular attention to the section of the website that described what volunteers could expect. Embedded in this part of the website was the experimental manipulation (either a gain-framed or a loss-framed message). One week later, participants were contacted again and asked to imagine the conditions under which they would provide social support to a (hypothetical) depressed friend.

As you can see, the two studies that we just described parallel each other exactly. However, the second study involves deception (the website was created by our research lab, not the depression support center), and, furthermore, the deception was not revealed until a week later, when the debriefing occurred. On one hand, this version of the experimental paradigm presented a higher level of "risk" to participants, but on the other hand, if the manipulation worked (which it did), this would suggest that a framed message can influence participants even a week after they were exposed to it.

We took the same paradigm one step further by bringing it into the research lab, this time under the close supervision of the faculty mentor. In order to stage a more "real-world" helping scenario, we used the same initial setup (exposure to the Mount Hood Center for Depression Support website) followed by an in-lab session one week later. Participants came to the research lab ostensibly to participate in a pilot program being run by the college's admissions department. Each participant was told that he or she would be interacting via instant messaging (IM) with a prospective undergraduate student. What the participant didn't know was that the "prospective student" was actually a member of our research team (sitting in a nearby room) and the experiment was not being run by the admissions department.

We scripted the IM conversation so that our confederate disclosed having depression midway through the interaction. Our interest was in the extent of social support the participant was willing to provide to the prospective student. The ethical issues involved in this study were far more significant than those raised by our earlier studies. This study was much more realistic and intense for participants, but it also included a great deal more deception and a need for a very careful debriefing procedure (see Table 4.7 for the text of the debriefing). We give this example to illustrate the ways in which ethical issues can increase in intensity depending on one's approach to exploring the research question. We also share this example to reassure you that, even if your team has to be cautious when designing a study for classroom use, you can take promising ideas into more and more immersive contexts with the appropriate support of a research mentor.

TABLE 4.7 Example of a Debriefing for a Study Involving Substantial Deception

I'm going to spend the next few minutes telling you more about the study you just completed. But before I do this, I'd like to thank you for taking time out of your busy schedule to participate in this research. The data that you provided will allow us to answer some very important questions. In a minute I'll describe how this study is aimed to address questions whose scope and importance are bigger than that of the college admissions process. In fact, our main purpose is to better understand how to provide social support to people who need it.

Before I explain the true nature of the study, I ask that you please do NOT discuss this information with other students. Doing so would compromise the study design by influencing other students' responses.

The study you participated in today was not really a joint project between our lab and our college's admissions office. We used the admissions cover story to create a believable, highly involving situation in which participants would interact with another person. The person you interacted with was not actually a prospective student, but was instead a member of our research team. However, the study was designed so that all participants would believe that the prospective student was real. We're sorry to have misled you, but the purpose of this deception was to create a highly realistic situation, and we used a member of our research team to keep one end of the online conversation constant. This was why we asked you to use a script when you asked the questions.

This study is about how the wording used in volunteer recruitment materials affects a person's willingness to provide social support to someone with depression. In previous studies, we've found that perceptions of reward are highly related to one's willingness to provide social support. In this study, we're investigating whether someone's perception of reward can be influenced by wording social support in terms of the gains of volunteering or the losses of not volunteering.

About one or two weeks ago, you participated in a study where you evaluated a website for the Mount Hood Center for Depression Support. This was actually the first phase of our two-part study. The Mount Hood Center for Depression Support was created by our research team. We used the center's simulated website to create a believable situation in which to present information about providing social support to someone with depression.

In this first phase of our study, one-half of the participants evaluated a website that emphasized the gains of providing social support (the upside of volunteering), and one-half evaluated a website that emphasized the losses of *not* providing social support (the downside of *not* volunteering). In phase 2, we invited you back for a seemingly "unrelated" study. In all cases, the prospective student in phase 2 (who was actually a member of our lab) divulged that she had been diagnosed with depression. We hypothesize that participants who initially evaluated the website emphasizing the upside of volunteering would be more likely to offer support to a depressed prospective student than would those who evaluated the website emphasizing the downside of not volunteering.

(Continued)

TABLE 4.7 (Continued)

It is important to note that, during the IM conversation, many participants chose to tell the prospective student personal information after she disclosed having depression. This is a positive response, and if you shared information, please be assured that it is completely confidential and will not be published.

We hope you understand the reason for the deception involved in this study. We believe that this study will help researchers and practitioners to better understand how to motivate people to volunteer to help depressed individuals. To date, no one has studied whether the words used to recruit volunteers actually make a difference in whether the person chooses to volunteer. This study is a good first step in discovering the most effective ways of describing volunteer opportunities. Please remember that your individual data will never be released or reported with your name attached. All data are anonymous and analyzed in groups. If you are interested in the results of this study, you may sign up to receive them once the study is completed.

Conclusion

Throughout this chapter we have emphasized that being ethical involves paying close attention to the experience of the participant. Your goal as a researcher is to ensure that the participant is informed of what will happen during the procedure, is told about the risks and benefits of participating in the study, and understands that participation is completely voluntary from start to finish. In addition, participants should receive a thorough debriefing, during which any ill effects of the procedure are ameliorated and the purpose of the study is clearly explained. Although today's researchers must always keep in mind what would be considered appropriate or inappropriate from the perspective of an IRB, you should remember that the research team—not the IRB—is ultimately responsible for the ethics of the research project. As a student, you should be aware that any unethical behavior by you or your teammates also becomes the responsibility of your mentor or professor. So err on the side of caution, and if you are uncertain about the ethics of a particular issue, talk with the members of your team and seek guidance from other researchers and your professors.

References

Carey, B. (2011, November 2). Fraud case seen as red flag for psychology research. *New York Times*. Retrieved from http://www.nytimes.com/2011/11/03/health/research/noted-dutch-psychologist-stapel-accused-of-research-fraud.html

Centers for Disease Control. (2009, February 12). U.S. Public Health Service Syphilis Study at Tuskegee. Retrieved from http://www.cdc.gov/tuskegee/index.html

Crocker, J. (2011). The road to fraud starts with a single step. *Nature, 479,* 151. doi:10.1038/479151a

Detweiler-Bedell, J., & Detweiler-Bedell, B. (2009, April). *Aiding depressed individuals using framed messages*. Paper presented at the meeting of the Western Psychological Association, Portland, OR.

Detweiler-Bedell, J. B., Detweiler-Bedell, B., Hazlett, A., & Friedman, M. A. (2008). The effect of diagnosis and perceived reward on perceptions of depressive symptoms and social support. *Journal of Social and Clinical Psychology, 27,* 1–35.

FAS Dean Smith confirms scientific misconduct by Marc Hauser. (2010, August 20). *Harvard Magazine.* Retrieved from http://harvardmagazine.com/2010/08/harvard-dean-details-hauser-scientific-misconduct

Fisher, C. B. (2009). *Decoding the ethics code.* Thousand Oaks, CA: Sage.

Gosling, S. D. (2008). *Snoop: What your stuff says about you.* New York: Basic Books.

Gosling, S. D., Ko, S. J., Mannarelli, T., & Morris, M. E. (2002). A room with a cue: Personality judgments based on offices and bedrooms. *Journal of Personality and Social Psychology, 82,* 379–398.

Haney, C., Banks, C., & Zimbardo, P. (1973). Interpersonal dynamics in a simulated prison. *International Journal of Criminology and Penology, 1,* 69–97.

HHS announces proposal to improve rules protecting human research subjects. (2011, July 22). Press release, U.S. Department of Health and Human Services. Retrieved from http://www.hhs.gov/news/press/2011pres/07/20110722a.html

Klemperer, E., LeDonne, R., & Nilsen, E. (2012). Promoting human rights while polarizing political perceptions with a serious game. *Proceedings of the Games, Learning, and Society Conference.*

LeDonne, R., & Klemperer, E. (2010, November 15). Ethical debriefing activity. Personal communication.

Milgram, S. (1963). Behavioral study of obedience. *Journal of Abnormal and Social Psychology, 63,* 371–378.

Milgram, S. (2009). *Obedience to authority: An experimental view.* New York: HarperCollins. (Original work published 1974)

National Commission for the Protection of Human Subjects of Biomedical and Behavioral Research. (1979, April 18). Belmont Report: Ethical principles and guidelines for the protection of human subjects of research. *Federal Register, 44,* 23192–23197.

Ross, L. (2011, July 7). Two types of harm. Personal communication.

Seligman, M. E. P. (1972). Learned helplessness. *Annual Review of Medicine, 23,* 407–412.

Seligman, M. E. P., & Maier, S. F. (1968). Alleviation of learned helplessness in the dog. *Journal of Abnormal Psychology, 73,* 256–262.

Steele, C. M., & Liu, T. J. (1981). Making the dissonant act unreflective of self: Dissonance avoidance and the expectancy of a value affirming response. *Personality and Social Psychology Bulletin, 7,* 393–397.

Steneck, N. H. (2006). *ORI introduction to the responsible conduct of research.* Rockville, MD: U.S. Department of Health and Human Services, Office of Research Integrity. Retrieved from http://ori.hhs.gov/images/ddblock/rcrintro.pdf

Suomi, S. J., & Harlow, H. F. (1972). Social rehabilitation of isolate-reared monkeys. *Developmental Psychology, 6,* 487–496.

Walther, E., & Grigoriadis, S. (2004). Why sad people like shoes better: The influence of mood on the evaluative conditioning of consumer attitudes. *Psychology and Marketing, 21,* 755–773.

Wiesel, T. N., & Hubel, D. H. (1965). Extent of recovery from the effects of visual deprivation in kittens. *Journal of Neurophysiology, 28,* 1060–1072.

CHAPTER 5

Experimental Design

Seven Lessons (Plus or Minus Two)

1. Avoid complex designs. You will be rewarded with happy participants (who provide better data), manageable analyses, and a focused test of your team's hypothesis.

2. Work as a team to design a strong experiment. Consider multiple perspectives, refrain from putting any single idea on a pedestal, and be willing to compromise.

3. Minimize unwanted effects by using random assignment and carefully attending to and controlling for extraneous variables that might interfere with your results.

4. Select your measures with care, because no matter how strong your independent variable may be, your team will not find an effect if the dependent variable is weak or inappropriate.

5. Evaluating whether a variable such as age or personality influences the strength of the relationship between your team's manipulation and the primary outcome is a search for *moderators*.

6. Think of any given experiment as the first in a series. Over time, multiple studies will come together to clarify the answer to a good research question.

> *I have so heavily emphasized the desirability of working with few variables and large sample sizes that some of my students have spread the rumor that my idea of the perfect study is one with 10,000 cases and no variables. They go too far.*
>
> —Jacob Cohen (1990, p. 1305)

Experimental design begins once your team has identified relevant theories and formulated predictions. Now it is time to transform your team's idea into something concrete. To launch our discussion of experimental design, let's begin with an example. We would like you to spend the next few minutes writing a brief description of what excites you most about the process of research. But here is the catch: You are not allowed to use the letter *a* or the letter *n* in any of the words you write. Begin now. (The best researchers have a knack for simulating and therefore experiencing the phenomena they study. This means you have to try things out. So, we're serious: Start writing!)

Immediately after completing this writing exercise, quickly assess your current feelings. How energetic do you feel? *If you resemble most people who try to write without these two letters, you'll feel tired out.* (It took us a full two minutes to write the preceding, italicized sentence according to the rules, so we share this feeling.) This type of writing task requires a great deal of mental self-control, and after you have completed the task, the energy that fuels your self-control has been depleted. You might feel some combination of being tired and a bit frustrated, but at the same time engaged and perhaps a little relieved that you are done. Overall, your mood will not be particularly positive or negative, but you will feel like you have done some strenuous mental exercise. Indeed, exercising self-control is like exercising your muscles. It's draining.

So what? Here is where the story of self-control gets fascinating. Imagine you are reading this chapter in a bustling public setting such as a coffeehouse, the library, or a lounge (perhaps this is actually the case). Nearby, on the floor, you see a $5 bill. Would you pick it up? Would you then ask the people around you if they dropped the money? Or would you pocket it? Based on recent theory and research concerning self-control, right now you are *much* more likely to pocket the money than to ask others if they dropped it. Don't worry; we do not think you are a dishonest person. Instead, that annoying writing task sapped your internal reserve of self-control, and now you have less energy "left over" to do something else that involves self-control. It is much easier to give in to temptation and keep the money than it is to go through the effort of finding its rightful owner. Mead, Baumeister, Gino, Schweitzer, and Ariely (2009) designed two studies much like this that were published in the *Journal of Experimental Social Psychology*. The title of their article says it all: "Too Tired to Tell the Truth: Self-Control Resource Depletion and Dishonesty."

Before describing these studies in greater detail, we would like to remind you that there are a number of different approaches to carrying out research in psychology, ranging from descriptive (e.g., case studies) to correlational (e.g., opinion polls) to experimental (e.g., laboratory-based studies). Self-control could be studied with any of these approaches. A researcher could do a descriptive study by observing children diagnosed with attention-deficit/hyperactivity disorder in their classrooms in order to determine the situations in which their impulse control is most likely to break down (e.g., before lunch, after recess). A researcher could do a correlational study by surveying a random sample of adults and asking them to answer a questionnaire about a time when they acted impulsively. Or a researcher could do an experiment by bringing participants into the lab and randomly assigning them to experience one of two events (i.e., one designed to deplete their self-control resources and the other designed to maintain those resources) and then looking at the impacts of these two events on a subsequent measure of impulsivity. Table 5.1 provides examples of the most common research designs in psychology. For additional information about various research methodologies, we encourage you to consult a traditional research methodology text or a reputable online resource such as the Research Methods Knowledge Base (http://www.socialresearchmethods.net/kb/index.php).

TABLE 5.1	Three Types of Research Design in Psychology, With Representative Examples
Design type	**Examples**
Descriptive	Naturalistic observation Case studies Focus-group interviews
Correlational	Surveys Psychological testing Research using archival data
Experimental	Between-subjects designs, where participants are randomly assigned to either an experimental or a control group Within-subjects designs, where the same participant experiences more than one experimental condition

In this book, we focus exclusively on experimental design because experimentation is the single best approach for determining causal relationships, and we believe that mastery of experimental methods is an important goal for all students of psychology. We begin our discussion of experimental design by taking a look at Mead and colleagues' (2009) first experiment. Participants came to the research lab and were randomly assigned to write a short essay without using the letters *a* and *n* (the self-control *depletion condition*) or, alternatively, without using the letters *x* and *z* (the *nondepletion condition*). After participants completed this exercise, they were told that the experiment was over. (Yes, there is some deception going on here because the experiment was not over, and this would need to be justified in the researchers' IRB application.) Then, as part of a "separate" experiment, participants were given a sheet with 20 matrices of numbers, and their goal for each matrix was to find the two numbers summing to 10.00 (e.g., 7.79 and 2.21). They were told they would earn 25 cents for each matrix they solved. This search task was tricky, and participants had only five minutes to work.

Then came the key part of the experiment. Half of the participants were randomly assigned to have the experimenter score their worksheets and compensate them appropriately. This provided a baseline for participants' typical performance, and the average participant earned about 50 cents whether they wrote the draining essay (without *a* or *n*) or the easier essay (without *x* or *z*). This is important. Being drained of self-control does not seem to undermine just any intellectual task. Instead, it should undermine tasks that require *self-control*. Self-control is the ability to override, for instance, undesirable impulses. To test this, the experimenters had the other half of the participants score their own worksheets and take the appropriate amount of money out of an envelope containing twenty quarters. These participants were told to score their worksheets, recycle them using the room's paper shredder, pay themselves from an envelope containing $5 in quarters, and then tell the experimenter they were done. *Nobody would know if they cheated and awarded themselves a couple extra quarters.*

What did the experimenters find in the self-scoring condition? Clearly, participants were tempted to be dishonest. Even participants in the nondepletion condition cheated a bit. On average, the nondepletion participants awarded themselves *one* extra quarter. But the real story is how participants who wrote the essay without the letters *a* and *n* responded to this tempting situation. By now you can anticipate the results. These participants had depleted their resources of self-control, and for them the impulse to take the easy money was much more difficult to override. Compared to their counterparts who earned only two quarters in the experimenter-scored condition, these participants awarded themselves *five* quarters on average. These participants didn't just fudge their scores a bit, they more than doubled their legitimate earnings. They were *stealing*.

Every good study has a moral—that is, a meaning that goes well beyond the specific research design. This is the hallmark of a well-conceived and well-designed experiment. In this study, the moral is that people generally resist the urge to be dishonest, but their success in doing so quickly deteriorates when they have access to fewer psychological resources enabling them to exercise self-control. If your self-control has been depleted in one domain, you are less likely to exert control in another domain. The implications of this relatively straightforward experiment should serve as a warning to all of us. Never go to an all-you-can eat restaurant that has wonderful desserts right after having a "delicate conversation" with your significant other. You won't eat healthfully. Never fill out a time sheet or prepare your tax return when you are trying to avoid thinking about missing the party that your neighbors are throwing next door. The temptation to tinker with your numbers is likely to be too great and could get you into serious trouble. And never leave a basket of candy out on Halloween expecting children to be honest and take just one piece each. The poor kids have already used up their self-control at previous houses as they put candy directly into their buckets, as told, rather than into their mouths.

DESIGNING YOUR STUDY

With the preceding examples in mind, you can begin the process of designing your team's study. At the outset, we should say that some people like this part of research because it focuses their efforts. Others feel like they are giving too much up when they narrow an otherwise big idea down to a specific experimental test. For just about everyone, crafting a new experimental design evokes a complex set of emotions. This is the moment when the ideas that inspire you, the theories that guide you, and the many practical considerations that constrain you (e.g., ethical requirements, limited time, the availability of participants) come together in one place. It is finally time to bring your team's research question to life.

Lesson 1: Avoid Complexity

We began this chapter with a tongue-in-cheek statement made by Jacob Cohen (1990), one of the most influential figures in statistics and experimental design in the behavioral sciences. The absurdity of his suggestion that "the perfect study is one with 10,000 cases and no variables" is meant to reinforce a key principle of designing studies: *Less is more.* Human behavior is breathtakingly complex, but experiments *must* be focused. So take it as a cardinal rule that you should manipulate and measure only a few select variables in your studies. This admonition may seem obvious. Simplicity is elegant. But researchers, and especially students, too often propose overly complex research designs. After all, if you are interested in understanding a rich theoretical concept, and if your participants will be taking time out to come to the research lab or complete your online survey, why not expose them to a variety of experimental manipulations? This should enable you to test a number of hypotheses at once, right? And why not ask your participants hundreds of questions and have them complete every measure under the sun? This should enable you to detect and precisely specify each and every effect of the experimental manipulation, right? The answers to these four questions are, respectively, *don't do it, no, don't do it,* and *no!*

Complex designs typically backfire. There are many reasons for this, including participant fatigue, overly complex and cumbersome data, and the likelihood of diluting and therefore weakening your ability to test any particular hypothesis. In marketing research, phone surveys are kept to 8–12 minutes for a reason. Survey participants grow tired after a short while, and at that point their attention to the details of new instructions or questions wanes. As a result, participants' responses become less and less reliable. Have you ever taken an online survey only to catch yourself daydreaming or speeding up your responses halfway through? This is a typical reaction, and it is one that your team would like to avoid in your own studies. To the extent that an experiment is more engaging than a question-after-question survey, you can get away with a somewhat lengthier study. Likewise, participant fatigue has less of an effect on some phenomena, including many simple cognitive tasks. Still, you should streamline your team's study as much as possible.

Even if you can keep a person's attention for an extended period of time, having a large number of experimental manipulations or outcome measures can lead to overwhelming complexity when you try to analyze your data. We once ran three related studies in our lab, each of which included more than 100 loosely organized questions spread over two experimental sessions. One of these studies required participants to answer nearly 200 questions over four distinct stages of the study, including an initial experimental session and three time points during a lengthy follow-up session one week later. The data from these studies paralyzed one of us (who had won an award for teaching graduate-level statistics at Yale) for almost two years. Simply put, there were too many somewhat related yet somewhat distinct questions to manage and neatly reduce into a smaller number of compelling variables. And because of this, it was nearly impossible to tell a consistent story across the three studies. There are other problems associated with having too many variables (e.g., the increased likelihood of type I errors), but our point here is that you do not want to put your team in this position when it comes time to tackle the data.

Finally, complex studies with too many experimental conditions rarely provide clean, direct tests of any particular hypotheses. Moreover, they spread researchers' most precious commodity, participants, too thinly across conditions. So even if the theory behind your idea is complex, the ideal approach is to isolate and test pieces of the theory systematically, *one step at a time.* For example, you might hypothesize that a person's making a healthy snack choice depends on that individual's mood and the social setting. Great, go ahead and test this! But don't design a study that puts each participant into one of four mood states (e.g., happy, sad, afraid, neutral) and then asks the participant to choose a snack in one of three social settings (e.g., alone, in the presence of a friend, in the presence of a stranger). This design results in *twelve* separate experimental conditions (i.e., four mood conditions further divided into three social settings), and the number of interrelationships among these conditions is potentially overwhelming. Your data will make a fool of you more often than not if you insist on running studies like this. Trust us, we've been there.

No matter how compelling your team's hypothesis, or how tempted you are to try out all possible variations of your question, you are better off conducting a series of much simpler studies that build from and inform one another. Your team might start off by comparing the influence of three mood states (e.g., happy, sad, neutral) in only one social setting, demonstrating that moods can, in fact, influence snack choice. You can then follow up with a study using the two mood states and two social settings that you think are most likely to interact. Does sadness result in unhealthy snacking when a person is alone but healthier snacking in the presence of a stranger, whereas a neutral mood leads to about the same level of somewhat healthy snacking regardless of the social setting? That would be a great finding. Then your team could build another study from there.

Lesson 2: Utilize the Design Team

How exactly does the research team come into play during the design phase? Unlike some parts of the research process, designing the study is not best accomplished through the divide-and-conquer strategy. Instead, the design process benefits tremendously from the absolute immersion of all team members. Entertaining multiple perspectives as you go about trying to develop your methods is an ideal place to start off. Imagine that your research team is interested in exploring the extent to which people mimic each other's facial expressions, posture, and movements without being consciously aware of doing so (a phenomenon known as the *chameleon effect*; Chartrand & Bargh, 1999). There are a number of ways to go about investigating this topic, ranging from observational studies (e.g., watching pairs interact at a coffeehouse) to experimental ones (e.g., seeing if participants can be led to mimic one another in the research laboratory). There are also individual differences that may be of interest to the research team, leading to other possible questions: Are women more likely than men to engage in mimicry? Are highly empathetic people more skilled at mimicry than less empathetic ones? Your team also might consider the effect of mimicry on the person being imitated. Under what conditions does the person become aware of being mimicked? Does being mimicked make an individual more or less fond of the person he or she is interacting with? Are therapists more effective when they mimic their clients?

As you and your teammates engage in the process of considering all possible designs, you will solidify a sense of togetherness and learn how to work best with one another. Everyone has something to contribute based on his or her unique perspective. This process is naturally chaotic at times, and it is sometimes frustrating. We liken the group process to a line dance, where you and your teammates are on one side of the dance floor and the design ideas you are considering are on the other. You should each take turns dancing with the ideas, joining together then moving apart, but always passing along each idea (no matter how attractive) to the person dancing next to you. Gradually the feelings of chaos will be replaced with confidence and control. And one of the secrets to gaining control is letting go. It is crucial to avoid putting any particular idea on a pedestal. Working together requires compromise, but compromise is not a painful process if you are willing to give up your own idea in order to entertain another.

Going back to the example of the chameleon effect, imagine that your team has decided to run an experimental study to investigate the extent to which a naive participant unconsciously imitates the behavior of a confederate in a laboratory-based personal interaction. At this point your team needs to *operationalize* the concepts that are of interest. By "operationalize," we are referring to the process of making the *independent variables* (i.e., what is manipulated in the experiment) concrete and the *dependent variables* (i.e., the outcomes) measurable. More specifically, what will the confederate do in this study? And what type of participant behavior will "count" as mimicry? The process of operationalizing your independent variables (IVs) and dependent variables (DVs) helps to clarify, crystallize, and sharpen the vision for your project. This is the moment when the team commits to a certain set of specialized materials in the hopes of finding a particular result.

It is through the process of putting together these materials that ownership is developed. In order to investigate the chameleon effect, you would consider questions such as the following: What aspects of mimicry interest us most (e.g., posture, facial expressions, body movements)? How closely scripted should the confederate's behavior and conversation be? What questions should we ask the participants before they meet the confederate? What should the *cover story* of our study be (that is, what should the participants think is happening in the study so that they won't guess the purpose of the research)? What questions should we ask the participants after their interactions with the confederate? And how in the world are we going to keep track of and quantify our primary dependent variable, imitation of the confederate? As you continue to conduct group brainstorming about the design, feel free to let the chaos enter and leave the conversation. Play around with ideas and engage in freewheeling discussion until you feel comfortable with the methodology. At a certain point the number of unanswered questions will seem overwhelming, but over time the answers will outnumber the questions, and ultimately you will have a neat package of methods and a tentative plan.

TRANSLATING YOUR PLAN INTO AN ELEGANT METHODOLOGY

Let us remind you again that simplicity of design is crucial. There clearly are a number of directions that one could take any given experimental question, and the reality is that most published research today describes more than just a single study. It is common, and in fact expected, for researchers to collect and report data on two or three studies before they are able to "package" a compelling set of studies for publication.

The most basic experimental designs set up a comparison between a treatment condition and a control condition (or conditions), in which participants are not exposed to the "active ingredient" of the treatment condition. In the study we described at the start of this chapter on the depletion of self-control, participants in the "experimenter-scored" conditions were considered to be controls because they were not given the opportunity to cheat on the task. Their data were useful in providing a baseline for the number of correct responses participants produced under conditions of depleted versus nondepleted self-control. But the primary hypothesis that depletion of self-control would lead to cheating was not tested directly among these control participants. The "treatment" or experimental condition in this study was the self-scored group. These participants also were randomly assigned to have their self-control resources either depleted or not, but unlike participants in the control condition, they were given the opportunity to cheat. Moreover, within this group, participants who did not have their self-control resources depleted by the more challenging writing task served as controls for the focal "treatment" group: participants whose self-control was depleted and were given the opportunity to cheat.

Experimental Control

To shape the remainder of our discussion of concepts that are crucial during the design stage, we will take Chartrand and Bargh's (1999) series of research studies on the chameleon effect as an example. Chartrand and Bargh conducted three studies, each building on the last, in order to create a more comprehensive picture of the natural human tendency toward imitation. Let's begin with Experiment 1. The hypothesis for this first study was that participants would unintentionally imitate the facial expressions and bodily movements of a confederate, who was a member of the research team but was presented to each true participant as another student taking part in the study. Each participant worked with the confederate on a task that was ostensibly part of a process of pretesting experimental measures. The participant and confederate took turns describing pictures that had been taken from magazines. After interacting with the first confederate, the participant "switched partners" and worked with another confederate. Depending on condition, the confederate in the first interaction smiled and rubbed his or her face or, alternatively, avoided smiling and shook his or her foot. The second confederate always exhibited the opposite set of behaviors from the first confederate (e.g., if confederate 1 smiled and rubbed her face, then confederate 2 avoided smiling and shook her foot). The confederates' behavior was the independent variable in this study. All participants were videotaped, and their behavior was later coded for smiles, face rubbing, and foot shaking. The participants' behavior as recorded by the coders was the dependent variable in this study.

In any research study, it is crucial to attend to *experimental control,* or the process of protecting the integrity of the experiment's conditions. Researchers accomplish this by minimizing and/or measuring any variables that might have an unintended influence on participants' responses to the experimental manipulations. In an investigation such as this one concerning the chameleon effect, the question to ask yourself is this: What variables other than the experimental manipulation might interfere with the observed results? One concern that Chartrand and Bargh had was that some people might be more smiley in general or they may be chronic foot shakers or face rubbers (no, these aren't the official scientific terms for such behaviors). What could you do to determine whether this is true? It would not be a good idea to ask participants, "How much do you smile?" in the prescreening questionnaire. Not only are people notoriously bad at giving objective responses to questions like that, but also such a question might give away the purpose of the study. Instead, Chartrand and Bargh videotaped participants for one minute prior to their interactions with the confederate in order to gather "baseline" observations of the frequency of their smiling, foot shaking, and face rubbing. These observations were coded and accounted for in the data analysis.

Another way in which experimental control was introduced into this paradigm was by having the participant interact with two different confederates. In this way, the participant served as his or her own control; the experimenters were able to see if they could produce one set of behaviors (e.g., face rubbing and smiling) during the first part of the study and another (e.g., foot shaking and not smiling) in the second part of the study. Being able to demonstrate one effect and then changing the nature of the effect within the same experimental session can be a very powerful application of experimental control. In addition, the researchers had the legitimate concern that participants might imitate one research assistant (i.e., confederate) more than another. If so, it would be problematic to have participants interact with just one confederate, because any observed imitation could be a product of the confederate in particular rather than the chameleon effect in general.

Randomization and Counterbalancing

When we first began to describe the methods of this experiment, you probably noted that we mentioned that participants were *randomly assigned* to experimental condition. This means that there was nothing systematic in how participants were dispersed across conditions of the experiment (i.e., they were assigned by chance). Remember, the second confederate always performed the behaviors that were *not* demonstrated by the first confederate, and all participants interacted with both of the confederates. The confederates demonstrated two of four behaviors (smiling or not; foot or face movement), and the likelihood that the participant was assigned to one particular set of behaviors in the first interaction also was determined by chance. The experimenters made sure to *counterbalance* the confederates' behaviors, so that confederate 1 performed each mannerism and facial expression as often as confederate 2. In counterbalancing, the researchers make sure that all possible orders in which participants are exposed to elements of the experiment are utilized. Counterbalancing is deemed important whenever there is a concern that the order in which a person experiences aspects of the experiment could matter, because of familiarity, practice, or fatigue. Attention to random assignment and counterbalancing is crucial because researchers need to rule out the possibility that something other than the experimental manipulation is responsible for the study's observed effects. For instance, what if all participants who completed the study during the month of March were exposed to one sequence of events, whereas all participants who completed the study in April were exposed to another sequence? There might be additional systematic differences between conditions (e.g., the weather during these months) that could account for the results. Similarly, what if the same confederate were always the nonsmiling foot shaker? It's possible that incidental characteristics of the confederates (e.g., differences in attractiveness) could account for the results. Random assignment and counterbalancing help to address these concerns.

SELECTING MEASURES

To maximize the likelihood of finding an effect, most researchers emphasize conducting studies with an adequate number of participants. Two other considerations are equally important, however. Ideally, your team should increase the strength of the manipulation as much as possible without making the hypothesis so obvious to participants that they simply try to confirm your predictions (i.e., fall prey to demand characteristics).

Moreover, your team should strive to increase the precision of your dependent variables (i.e., decrease the statistical noise or error in your measures). This, along with choosing appropriate measures for your experiment, is a crucial part of the design process.

Measures can be placed at different points within a study. Many studies include "pre-questionnaires" to assess variables that will be taken into consideration during data analysis. This is especially useful in evaluating *changes* that occur as a result of the experimental manipulation. Of course, the questions that you ask after the experimental manipulation are your *primary dependent variables*. However, many researchers place demographic questions that are not likely to be affected by the experimental paradigm (e.g., self-reports of age and sex) at the very end of the experiment, immediately prior to debriefing. This helps to prevent participants from becoming fatigued prior to the experimental manipulation and primary measures. In some cases, these demographic data might relate directly to your hypotheses (e.g., women might be more likely than men to demonstrate the chameleon effect). This is a question of moderation, which we discuss at the end of this chapter. In other cases, demographic data might enable you to identify and eliminate the influence of nuisance variables on your primary measures (e.g., younger people might be much more likely than older people to shake their feet).

Coding Participant Behavior

Chartrand and Bargh obtained the data for their experiment by "coding" videotapes of the participants. Participants were told as part of the informed consent procedure that their responses during the experiment would be videotaped. Then, after all of the participants had completed the study, two "judges" who had not been involved in the earlier part of the experiment viewed and rated the frequency of each participant's facial expressions and mannerisms. These judges were *blind to experimental condition,* which means they did not know what behaviors were being exhibited by the confederate. The researchers achieved this by positioning the camera so that only the participant was visible on the video recording. Three distinct time periods were coded: the one-minute baseline, the interactions with confederate 1, and the interactions with confederate 2. The coding resulted in ratings of the number of times each participant smiled, shook his or her foot, and rubbed his or her face.

Lest you get the impression that the coding of such videotapes is as straightforward as a simple behavioral count, let's take a moment to do a reality check. What were some of the stumbling blocks that these researchers faced when it came time to translate the video material into usable data? The overarching issue that challenges every study that involves coding of data is *interrater reliability,* or the extent to which different judges evaluate a particular phenomenon in the same way. Adequate interrater reliability is notoriously difficult to achieve, especially if there is any ambiguity in what should be coded, which causes judges to guess when they rate certain things. In the evaluation of the chameleon effect, interrater reliability was lower for face rubbing than it was for the foot shaking or smiling. There are a number of reasons participants might rub their faces (e.g., to move their hair away, to scratch an itch), and some of these instances might be irrelevant to "mimicking." The best that the researchers could do was to create a detailed coding sheet (which included a description of the specific nature of the participant's face rubbing) to increase the reliability of the ratings across judges.

Another question about measurement is also relevant here: Is the *number of times* the participant engaged in a behavior actually the best measure of mimicking? Or would it be more informative to rate the *length of time* the participant smiled, shook a foot, or rubbed his or her face? As it turns out, the experimenters coded both variables, but because the two sets of ratings were so similar (that is, they were highly correlated), only the *number of times* ratings were discussed in the results.

This study highlights just one example of the types of measures experimenters can use. Although using video recordings of participants is appealing for many reasons (e.g., the measure gets at "real" behavior), coding the material reliably can be quite challenging. Not only do you have to worry about interrater reliability, but also you have the challenges associated with obtaining the necessary physical space and equipment to conduct this type of study. Unless your team is working with a research adviser who has recording equipment in his or her lab, it is unlikely that you will be able to create the right environment in which to collect this type of data. Thus, your team must consider using other types of measures.

Utilizing Existing Measures

Potential dependent variables come in many forms. We have just described how researchers can utilize observations (e.g., behavioral coding) as a study's primary measures. However, self-report measures are the most common type of measure used in psychological research. Self-reports come in many forms, ranging from simple reflections by participants on their own thoughts or feelings (e.g., "liking of partner") to multi-item scales that have been developed and validated by other researchers (e.g., the Young Adult Alcohol Problems Screening Test developed by Hurlburt & Sher in 1992).

The selection of appropriate measures is crucial, because no matter how strong your experimental manipulation is, you will not be able to find an effect if your dependent variables are ambiguous, irrelevant, or otherwise flawed. We encourage you to rely on the strengths and expertise of your team members throughout the process of choosing measures. For example, perhaps your team will be bringing romantic partners to the lab in order to study the impact of relationship satisfaction on expressions of emotion during a problem-solving task. Your hypothesis is that greater relationship satisfaction will be associated with a balance between positive and negative emotional displays, whereas lower relationship satisfaction will be associated with predominantly negative *or* predominantly positive (that is, unbalanced) emotional displays. You decide to use the Dyadic Adjustment Scale (Spanier, 1976) as your measure of relationship satisfaction (the IV). But how will you measure "expressions of emotion" (the DV)?

Again, being part of a team is a great advantage here. We suggest having each team member search out ideas, keeping in mind that there are a number of types of measurement techniques (e.g., observational, self-report, psychophysiological) that you might use. One team member might return with a well-established and validated self-report mood questionnaire such as the Profile of Mood States (Cella et al., 1987), which is a brief measure of transient mood. Perhaps another team member is a research assistant with a professor who studies emotion. As a result, she has been trained in the Facial Action Coding System (Ekman & Friesen, 1978), a method of coding emotion-specific facial movements (a system popularized, at least loosely, in the 2009–2011 television drama series *Lie to Me*). She therefore proposes that the participant dyads' interactions should be videotaped so she can code their moods. All smiles are not the same, you learn, and she can distinguish an insincere and voluntary "Pan American smile" from a sincere and involuntary "Duchenne smile" (the key is the additional contraction of the inferior part of orbicularis oculi, in case you were curious). This team member argues that taking videos of participants and later coding participants' facial expressions would be worthwhile because self-reported emotions could be biased.

As for you? You worry less about the biases associated with self-reports and more about a questionnaire relying on participants' faulty memories of their emotions during the interaction. You would prefer a "real-time" (presumably more accurate) measure of mood. The Ekman coding system would address this concern, but you are wary of the time and effort involved in the painstaking process of coding participants' each and every facial expression. As an alternative, you propose having participants use "mood dials" throughout their problem-solving session. The mood dial is a relatively simple, handheld device that is connected to a computer via a USB port. The dial is 360 degrees and color coded from dark blue (very unhappy) to bright orange (very happy). Participants would be told to start their conversation with their dials set to the midpoint (neutral) and then turn them toward blue as their feelings become more negative and toward orange as their feelings become more positive. Not only does this method capture data on a person's mood as it happens, but in your study it would allow you to map each partner's data onto those of the other, so that mood-related questions (such as "To what extent does relationship satisfaction predict congruence in the mood of partners?") could be answered in real time. By sharing with one another the experiences and knowledge that you possess individually, you and your teammates can together shape the design of your experiment in a way that makes use of the best possible measures.

Creating Your Own Measures

In some cases it may be appropriate for your team to create your own measures. Perhaps, for example, you are researching how a college student's place of residence (IV) affects his or her perception of the college experience as a whole (DV). Although other researchers surely have created scales to assess students' perceptions of their college experiences, it may be important for you to tailor questions so that they include statements specific to your own campus. For example, you may want to assess the extent to which students see the college as (a) a community of scholars, (b) committed to diversity, and (c) cultivating civic engagement. It isn't likely that any preexisting, validated scales tap into these three constructs in a way that would be meaningful to your participants, so you will need to create a measure.

Creating a measure is not an easy or quick process, and the best measures are thoroughly pretested before they are used within a larger study. How does one go about doing this? First, some definitional issues. A *construct* is a specific psychological attitude or property that you, as the researcher, are attempting to measure. When you *operationalize* your dependent variables, you first will need to identify how many distinct constructs you plan to measure. (The student perceptions listed above might map neatly onto three constructs; alternatively, there might be more than one distinct aspect of, say, "cultivating civil engagement" that should be measured as separate constructs.) After your team has identified the constructs, it is time to come up with particular questions that tap into each of them. Our advice is to develop three to four reliable questions for each construct. The questions will be worded slightly differently and susceptible to somewhat different biases, but combined together they will help your team "triangulate" on the overarching construct.

As an example, take the idea of assessing the extent to which students on your campus feel as though they are immersed in a *community of scholars.* There are a number of possible statements you could ask your participants to endorse (using a scale from 1 = *strongly disagree* to 7 = *strongly agree)*: "I feel engaged intellectually both inside and outside of the classroom"; "I rarely have conversations with friends that draw on ideas that I learned in my classes"; "I am part of a campus culture that values lifelong learning." Each of these questions taps into the *community of scholars* construct. As you probably noticed, the second item is worded in the direction opposite that of the first and third, so that a high score (7) on that item reflects a belief that the campus does not cultivate a community of scholars. We encourage your team to include such *reverse-coded* items in your scales for one simple reason: Sometimes participants answer questions somewhat mindlessly, giving very similar, often positive ratings across all items. By having some items worded in the opposite direction from others, you will increase participants' attention to the questionnaire, and the combined measure will correct somewhat for any positive-response bias. Ultimately, the hope is to increase the overall *validity,* or accuracy, of participants' responses.

Earlier in this chapter we discussed interrater reliability, but when it comes to survey design, a different type of reliability matters: *internal consistency reliability.* This term refers to the idea that a set of items designed to measure a particular construct should be consistent with each other in a given survey. Reliability estimates range from 0 (no consistency whatsoever) to 1 (complete overlap). A number of measures are available for estimating internal consistency reliability, but the one you are likely to encounter most frequently (particularly when there are a large number of items to assess) is Cronbach's alpha or α (Cronbach, 1951). A discussion of how to calculate α is beyond the scope of this chapter, but you can find a comprehensive description of this and other measures of reliability online at the Research Methods Knowledge Base website (http://www.socialresearchmethods.net/kb/reltypes.php). In Table 5.2 we provide a list of these and other considerations that you should be mindful of when creating measures.

An Application of Measurement Concepts

The overarching principle in experimental design is to measure specific, predicted outcomes while minimizing all influences on the participant except for those that are deliberately introduced by the experimental paradigm. Going back to Chartrand and Bargh's line of research, how might the chameleon effect be measured using self-report questionnaires? Could you simply ask participants to chart how often they match their own physical movements to those of other people? Most likely not. It is doubtful that people have an unbiased view of the extent to which they mirror others; indeed, the definition of the

TABLE 5.2 Twenty Helpful Tips to Consider When Designing Measures

1. Give your team enough time for the initial brainstorming and revision process.
2. Identify the independent variables you intend to manipulate in your study.
3. Think about the broader, theoretical concepts motivating each measure.
4. Brainstorm questions—the more the better (at least initially).
5. Make sure your questions cover all aspects of your predictions.
6. Meet with your research mentor and teammates to compare ideas for measures.
7. Whenever possible, adapt constructs from previous research, especially if your team hopes to replicate past findings.
8. Select three to four items for each subscale (i.e., construct).
9. Pay attention to internal consistency reliability when measuring constructs.
10. When using established measures, locate an original article that reports reliability statistics and a factor analysis of the items, which can guide the selection of a subset of items for use in your team's experiment.
11. As a general rule, avoid yes/no questions because they reduce the statistical power of any test. Instead, use scaled items such as Likert-style 7-point scales or semantic differentials.
12. Reverse the direction of some questions in order to correct for response biases.
13. Ask participants demographic questions in order to test hypotheses related to potential moderators, or to identify and eliminate the influence of nuisance variables on your primary dependent variables.
14. Edit your questions for content, word choice, and tense.
15. When necessary, edit the phrasing of questions to fit the end points of the scale.
16. Rearrange the ordering of the questions to enhance the overall flow.
17. Confirm that the questions are phrased in a way that does not bias or distort participant responses.
18. Keep in mind Cohen's admonition to minimize the number of DVs and delete unnecessary items.
19. Have all team members and your research mentor scrutinize your measures before your team pilots the experiment.
20. Be prepared to do additional editing and rewriting of items based on feedback from pilot participants.

chameleon effect includes the idea that it is an automatic, passive, nonconscious process. So we remind you again of the importance of utilizing your whole team in designing your study. Some of the constraints that you and your teammates must impose on yourselves are practical ones. In this case, you should reach a point where you realistically assess the resources your team can access for the purpose of your study. If you are unable to investigate the participant's likelihood of *demonstrating* the chameleon effect, how about investigating the impact of the chameleon effect *on* the participant? Would the participant report greater comfort, liking, and connection with a person who mirrors his or her behavior? This might be a more testable hypothesis if you plan to use self-report measures.

Chartrand and Bargh asked this very question in their second experiment. In this study, the participant again interacted with another "participant" (actually a confederate), taking turns describing what they observed in a series of photographs. The experimental design was relatively straightforward. Half of the participants were randomly assigned to a confederate who was instructed to imitate the behavioral mannerisms of the participant; other participants were assigned to a confederate who was instructed to engage in neutral, unremarkable mannerisms. The primary dependent variables were participants' self-reports of how much they liked the confederate and how well they felt the interaction went. Here is the researchers' description of the measures, as stated in the methods section of their write-up of the experiment:

> The key items read, "How likable was the other participant?" and "How smoothly would you say your interaction went with the other participant?" To help camouflage the hypothesis of the study, we embedded these two items among eight other questions that asked about the task itself and the group format (e.g., how easy or difficult it was for them to generate responses to the photos, and whether they thought the various photographs went well together as a single "set"). All items were rated on 9-point scales (for the smoothness item, 1 = extremely awkward, 9 = extremely smooth; for the likability item, 1 = extremely dislikable, 9 = extremely likable). (Chartrand & Bargh, 1999, p. 902)

We would like to believe that Cohen (whom we quoted at the outset of this chapter) would have approved of Experiment 2. This study included one independent variable (mirroring or not mirroring the participant) and two primary dependent variables (liking and smoothness of interaction). This makes for a simple and elegant test of the impact of the chameleon effect on participants.

Before we transition to our next topic concerning experimental design, it only seems fair that we should report the results of Chartrand and Bargh's Experiments 1 and 2. What were the hypotheses? And were they supported? In the first study, the researchers hypothesized that the participants would imitate the facial expressions of the confederates and that this process of imitation would be a nonconscious experience. The results supported these hypotheses. Indeed, participants smiled more times per minute with a smiling confederate than they did with the nonsmiling confederate. In addition, the predicted relationship between confederate behavior (foot shaking, face rubbing) and participant behavior was observed. These results are depicted graphically in Figure 5.1. Finally, at the end of the experimental session, participants were asked if anything stood out to them about the confederate's behavior, including mannerisms or way of speaking. Out of 35 participants, only 2 stated that they noticed something unusual: One noted that the confederate made hand motions while speaking, and a second noted that the confederate slouched. In short, none of the participants noticed the expressions or mannerisms being studied.

In the second study, Chartrand and Bargh hypothesized that the chameleon effect serves to increase liking and feelings of comfort during interpersonal interactions. As predicted, participants in the experimental condition reported liking the confederate more and feeling that the interaction went more smoothly in comparison with those in the control condition. Further, just 1 of the 37 participants in this study reported noticing anything unusual about the confederate's behavior during the interaction, again suggesting that effects of mimicry come about through a nonconscious process. Taken together, the two experiments support the idea that people do engage in automatic, nonconscious mimicry of their interaction partners and that there are social benefits (e.g., increased liking) that accompany this phenomenon.

FIGURE 5.1   Results of Chartrand and Bargh's (1999) study showing a strong correspondence between confederate and participant behavior.

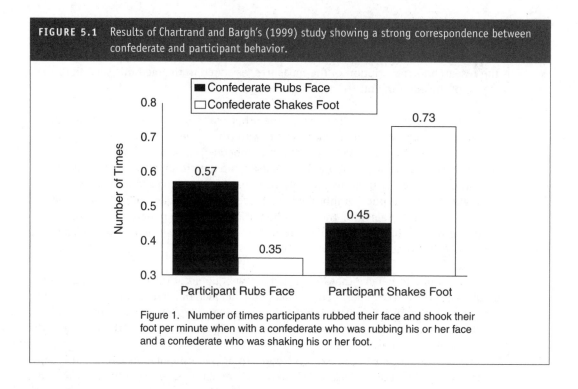

Figure 1.   Number of times participants rubbed their face and shook their foot per minute when with a confederate who was rubbing his or her face and a confederate who was shaking his or her foot.

INVESTIGATING MODERATORS

In this chapter we have focused quite a bit on the chameleon effect. What questions about this effect remain? The answer is likely to be "many," but we will highlight just one more: Is it possible that some people are "better" chameleons than others? If so, what distinguishes skilled imitators from less skilled ones? Chartrand and Bargh wondered if any personality variables might predict how likely a person is to engage in mimicry. When researchers are interested in determining the extent to which a third variable (e.g., personality) influences the strength of the relationship between the independent variable (e.g., the confederate's body movements) and the dependent variable (e.g., mimicry by the participant), they are exploring a concept called *moderation*. In other words, the researchers are investigating whether participants' personality characteristics *interact* with the confederate's behavior in predicting the outcome (participant mimicry). If such an interaction exists, participants' personality characteristics are said to *moderate* the extent to which participants demonstrate the chameleon effect.

If your team is interested in looking for potential moderators, it is crucial to go back to a process of brainstorming. "Personality," for example, is a broad concept, and greater specificity is needed if you are to develop a meaningful hypothesis about how personality might moderate an effect. In their third (and final) experiment, Chartrand and Bargh hypothesized that a person's tendency to be empathetic (which is an individual difference characteristic) would predict that person's likelihood of mimicking the confederate. How did they measure empathy? A number of well-tested questionnaires have been developed to measure individual differences in empathy, and if your experiment includes a concept such as this, it is critical that you avoid reinventing the wheel. This is an instance in which a wise research team goes back to the literature, investigates how others in the field are studying the concept, and brings back the best current thinking and practices to inform the team's own investigation.

What Chartrand and Bargh discovered was that empathy is not necessarily a single concept. Instead, theorists tend to distinguish the emotional part of empathy (e.g., feeling another person's feelings) from the cognitive part of empathy (e.g., being able to take another person's point of view). Which component of empathy, the emotional or cognitive one, might moderate the chameleon effect? Chartrand and Bargh decided to set up a horse race between the two competing moderators. That is, they measured both components of empathy in order to see the relative impact of each one. And, of course, they went into their third experiment with a hypothesis: They predicted that the cognitive component of empathy would be a more important moderator of the chameleon effect than the emotional component. They made this prediction because their earlier studies suggested that the chameleon effect can occur even in the absence of an emotional response or connection to another person. (If you recall, Experiments 1 and 2 involved a picture-rating task that did not elicit much if any emotional connection between the participant and the confederate.) As a consequence, the researchers predicted that participants who pay more attention to others and are skilled at taking another person's perspective (that is, those who possess the cognitive component of empathy) would be more likely to display the chameleon effect than those who do not have such a tendency. Furthermore, they predicted that this cognitive component of empathy alone, *not* the emotional component, would moderate the effect of the confederate's behavior on the participant.

The procedure for Experiment 3 was similar to that used in the first two studies. The participant and confederate completed a task in which they judged pictures, and this time the confederate engaged in face rubbing *and* foot shaking throughout the entire interaction. The confederate's facial expression remained neutral. As in Experiment 1, the participants were videotaped, and their mannerisms were coded for the amount of time they engaged in each type of movement. After the interaction with the confederate, participants completed the empathy questionnaire, which measured both the cognitive and the emotional aspects of empathy.

But why did the empathy questionnaire come *after* rather than *before* the interaction with the confederate? Does the order of manipulation and empathy measure matter? The concern here is that one aspect of the study (interacting with the confederate) might influence another aspect of the study (self-reported empathy) or vice versa. Recall that the prediction is *not* that confederate behavior should influence participant empathy. Instead, the prediction is that participant empathy will strengthen or weaken the extent to which mimicry occurs. This means that the researchers do not want responses on the survey to be affecting *or* affected by the interaction with the confederate. One way of handling this concern is to separate measurement of the moderator from the experimental paradigm. In this case, the researchers could have administered the empathy questionnaire days or weeks in advance of the experiment. As you might imagine, however, this can be difficult to achieve. The reality of experimental work is that resources (e.g., participants) are limited, and it might be difficult to count on having access to the same participants over time.

If practical limitations require you to measure a potential moderator within the experimental paradigm, as was the case in Chartrand and Bargh's study, you ultimately must ask which concern is greater: the measure's impact on the experimental manipulation or the impact of the experimental manipulation on the way participants respond to the measure. The answer to this dilemma is not an easy one, but in this case there was something very important to preserve: the believability of the cover story. If the participant first fills out a questionnaire that asks about his or her ability to take another person's perspective and the extent to which he or she feels an emotional connection to another person's experiences, the participant might be *primed* to think about these aspects of empathy during the experimental interaction. Moreover, the participant might become suspicious of the study's real intent and begin to question the behavior of the confederate. This would present great problems for the integrity of the research design. In contrast, empathy is considered to be an individual difference characteristic that is stable over time. So although a participant's responses to the empathy questionnaire conceivably might be influenced by the interaction he or she just had with the confederate, the influence is likely to be very small. It is through weighing these pros and cons that researchers determine the order of manipulations and measures in an experimental design.

So what did Chartrand and Bargh find? As predicted, they found that participants who scored higher on the cognitive component of empathy (perspective taking) rubbed their faces and shook their feet significantly more times per minute than did those who scored lower on this measure. However, the emotional component of empathy (empathic concern) did *not* moderate the chameleon effect. In other words, only the participant's perspective-taking ability (and not his or her empathic concern) influenced the extent to which the participant imitated the confederate. Again, the researchers' hypotheses were supported, and their findings added to the overall understanding of the chameleon effect.

Conclusion

As you have likely observed in reading this chapter, there are numerous considerations to juggle during the experimental design process, and we have covered only a subset of them. The overarching challenge your team must meet in designing your study is to be highly organized, systematic, and meticulous. You will find that the beginning of the design process is characterized by chaos; your team is likely to consider manipulating and measuring everything and anything. Once you target a few key variables, the chaos will subside and a sense of order will begin to take over. From this point on, feasibility should be a key component of all your design decisions; there are clear restrictions on what can be done in a single study (ethical constraints, time limitations, and limited finances being just a few).

When you consider concepts such as validity (i.e., is your experiment measuring what you think it is?), we encourage you to focus on *internal validity* rather than *external validity*. That is, it is critical to strive for an elegant, tightly controlled, clearly orchestrated study, regardless of whether the study takes place in the lab, online, or on paper. It is less important to be able to conclude, at the end of just one study, that your findings have broad implications for the "real world." With any line of research, the experimenters must aim to understand the effects as completely as possible, but this understanding does not come after one or two or even three studies. Over time, a team of researchers will work to understand multiple facets of a phenomenon. Scientists use the phrase *line of research* deliberately. Each individual experiment continues along this "line," moving the question forward in a systematic fashion. We challenge your team to let go of the *ideal* design in order to pursue the best *possible* design, one small step at a time.

References

Cella, D. F., Jacobson, P. B., Orav, E. J., Holland, J. C., Silberfarb, P. M., & Rafia, S. (1987). A brief POMS measure of distress for cancer patients. *Journal of Chronic Diseases, 40,* 393–342.

Chartrand, T. L., & Bargh, J. A. (1999). The chameleon effect: The perception-behavior link and social interaction. *Journal of Personality and Social Psychology, 76,* 893–910.

Cohen, J. (1990). Things I have learned (so far). *American Psychologist, 45,* 1304–1312.

Cronbach, L. J. (1951). Coefficient alpha and the internal structure of tests. *Psychometrika, 16,* 297–334.

Ekman, P., & Friesen, P. (1978). *Facial Action Coding System: A technique for the measurement of facial movement.* Palo Alto, CA: Consulting Psychologists Press.

Hurlburt, S. C., & Sher, K. J. (1992). Assessing alcohol problems in college students. *College Health, 41,* 49–58.

Mead, N. L., Baumeister, R. F., Gino, F., Schweitzer, M. E., & Ariely, D. (2009). Too tired to tell the truth: Self-control resource depletion and dishonesty. *Journal of Experimental Social Psychology, 45,* 594–597.

Spanier, G. B. (1976). Measuring dyadic adjustment: New scales for assessing the quality of marriage and similar dyads. *Journal of Marriage and the Family, 38,* 15–28.

CHAPTER 6

Statistics and Data

Seven Lessons (Plus or Minus Two)

1. Anticipate the data your team's research is likely to produce. This is an essential part of research design and must happen before you run any study.

2. Stay focused on the concepts of statistical reasoning. Symbols and math are useful tools, but more often than not they distract us from the concepts themselves.

3. Learning statistics is like learning a language: the more experience, the better. Fluency requires course work, repetition, and conversation.

4. Use statistics to make sound claims about meaningful ideas. Before you collect any data, you must be absolutely certain that your study is designed to illuminate important comparisons.

5. Build your thinking about statistics from a simple understanding of three sacred tools: the *mean* (a point of reference for making comparisons), the *standard deviation* (conceptually, the average distance between a typical observation and the mean), and the *standard error* (the standard deviation of a set of means).

6. The secret and real power of statistics rests in *correlation*. The vast majority of statistical techniques, reduced to their most basic components, operate on simple linear relationships between two variables at a time.

7. The pursuit of an explanatory variable that stands between the experimental manipulation and the study's primary outcome (and is responsible for this relationship) is the search for a *mediator*.

(Continued)

8. Redouble your efforts to simplify and strengthen your team's research design. Chance can wreak havoc with your data, especially if you have too many experimental conditions, employ a weak experimental manipulation, fail to recruit enough participants per condition, or use sloppy outcome measures.

9. Be meticulous (to the point of obsession) when you work with data. Develop routines that will minimize coding errors and detect anomalies.

Abelson's First Law of Statistics: Chance is lumpy.

—Robert Abelson (1995, p. xv)

If you are reading this book from cover to cover, you might wonder why we are discussing statistics *before* the chapter on conducting a study. A researcher needs to gather data before performing any statistical analyses, so it seems like we are getting ahead of ourselves. But this is one of many misconceptions about statistics. If you design and run a study without a clear sense of what your findings might look like and how you will tell a convincing story based on these findings, then you have not "designed" your study at all. Instead, you have thrown together some methods and are hoping blindly that things will turn out nice and neat. They generally won't. You must anticipate and reckon with the data your study is likely to produce *before* you finalize your study's design and run the study. That means you have to stop and think about statistics.

Our prescription to stop and think about statistics might sound like bitter medicine. *Statistics are boring. Statistics are terribly mathematical and beyond the mere mortals who study psychology.* Beliefs such as these abound. Fortunately, these misconceptions are dead wrong. Statistics are not at all what they seem. So over the next few pages, try to set aside everything you think you know about statistics. Because a plague of misconceptions and mathematical snobbery afflicts the field of statistics, we need to clear our minds. The best disinfectant, in our opinion, is irreverence. Math? Who needs it! Statistical models? Excuse me? Meeting certain assumptions before conducting a statistical test? Whatever! . . . That felt great!

Consider something that an otherwise praiseworthy statistician recently wrote: "Because statistical models of reality are mathematical ones, they can be fully understood only in terms of mathematical formulas and symbols." (It really does not matter who said this. Google it if you must.) We have warm fuzzy feelings about good data and the statistics that bring them to life. This is partly conditioning—we first kissed over a particularly good statistical analysis. But we would rather visit a dentist than listen to a lecture admonishing us that statistics "can be fully understood only in terms of mathematical formulas and symbols." There is no place in statistics for a rigid insistence that symbols and notation are all-important. Symbols are quirky tools useful only when they save time, and only as long as they do not distract from the *concepts* themselves. But you know what? Symbols and notation are a major distraction more often than not. So, for now, they are in a serious "time-out." They can be good kids, really, but we are not going to let them out until they can be on their best behavior.

BEGINNER'S MIND

Irreverence is refreshing. It can bring on a Zen-like state of beginner's mind, a powerful way of thinking that avoids preconceptions. This mind-set can help you understand and appreciate the powerful concepts that make statistics so very useful. This approach is not just for beginners. It grows more important as one's knowledge increases. What we think we know about statistics often interferes with our understanding because, as Jacob Cohen (1990) puts it, "some things you learn aren't so" (p. 1304). An irreverent return to beginner's mind keeps one honest and open to deeper understanding and new ideas.

It is no coincidence, then, that many of statistics' greatest teachers have been irreverent, surprisingly amusing characters. They include the following:

- An unassuming beer brewer who wrote as "Student" and rarely invoked anything more than a few basic statistical principles

- A Ping-Pong-loving college dropout with virtually no math beyond high school algebra who downplayed the importance of statistics and lampooned null-hypothesis testing by titling one of his articles "The Earth Is Round ($p < .05$)"

- An Ivy League professor who whimsically assigned the job of randomness to leprechauns and whose Zen-like "laws" of statistics (e.g., "Chance is lumpy"; "Never flout a convention just once"; "There is no free hunch"; "Don't talk Greek if you don't know the English translation") poke fun at statistics while inspiring us to use statistics more wisely

- A trailblazing woman famous for her love of cigars who ably brushed aside the egos of her legendary mentors, deriding them for being "vague" and envious of one another, and who protested getting a Ph.D. because it did not seem worth the fee of twenty British pounds

Yes, statisticians can be cool! Irreverence is not an excuse to be lazy, however, and knocking down conventions will not make you any smarter. So don't be smug. You should rely on beginner's mind to refresh your perspective, and you should engage the concepts of statistics playfully. But you must build your understanding of statistics in a disciplined manner. This is *serious* play, which can be a tough balance to strike. So let a trio of words—*irreverent, playful,* yet *disciplined*—serve as your mantra. With this, let the play begin.

FIRST OF ALL, DON'T PANIC!

Many psychology majors experience the following symptoms at some point when taking a course in statistics (e.g., just before stepping into the classroom for the first time or halfway through the first exam): trembling, dizziness, shortness of breath, racing heart, and an uncontrollable sense of vulnerability and panic. It is as if a course in statistics might sneak up and kill a person. It won't. But try telling this to a student in the throes of idiosyncratic panic disorder. This is an entirely made-up diagnosis; it cannot be found in a clinician's diagnostic manual. Still, many students experience moments of panic when their diffuse fear of math kicks up and makes the whole enterprise of statistics seem hopelessly overwhelming. For a student in the midst of a statistics panic attack, the world of numbers, formulas, and variability lurches and crashes down. Any previous sense of insight or mastery evaporates. This malady makes it all but impossible for the student to relax and learn statistics.

The notion of "statistics panic" may be tongue-in-cheek, but we have modeled the idea of it on panic disorder (PD), a very real and debilitating anxiety disorder. Individuals who suffer from PD experience severe anxiety attacks characterized by the physical symptoms and sense of impending doom described above. Fortunately, anxiety disorders such as PD are treatable. One empirically supported treatment is cognitive behavioral therapy (CBT), which trains individuals to confront the distorted cognitions that feed into panic attacks (e.g., "My heart is racing, I'm losing control, I'm having a heart attack and am going to die") and to remain mentally relaxed as they experience anxiety's intense physical symptoms. As a treatment for panic, CBT has been well validated. CBT works extremely well for most patients, and its effects are long lasting, despite the fact that it is a relatively brief form of therapy.

Although CBT works, scant evidence exists demonstrating that CBT works *because* it changes patients' distorted cognitions concerning panic attacks. This is a question of *mechanism*. Does CBT work for the reasons clinicians think? If not, clinical psychology does not understand CBT or panic all that well. Thankfully, a relatively recent study by Leanne Casey and her colleagues provides an answer to this question (Casey, Newcombe, & Oei, 2005). In this study, 36 patients were randomly assigned to receive 12 weekly sessions of CBT, while another 24 patients remained on a waiting list over the same period of time in order to serve as the experiment's control condition. Before and after the experiment, the researchers assessed *panic severity* (the study's primary dependent variable) as well as *panic self-efficacy* (a measure of the patient's perceived control over thoughts, sensations, and situations that might lead to a panic attack) and *catastrophic misinterpretation of bodily sensations* (a measure of the patient's tendency to misinterpret bodily sensations in a way that might lead to a panic attack). The researchers predicted that CBT's ability to increase panic self-efficacy and decrease catastrophic misinterpretations of bodily sensations would account for CBT's overall effectiveness in reducing panic severity. In other words, improvements in patients' distorted cognitions would account for CBT's effectiveness as theorized.

What a wonderful study! Here we have a real-world experiment concerning a disorder that afflicts millions of people, and it has been designed to test whether CBT works *because* it changes patients' distorted cognitions concerning panic attacks. This is the type of research that enables psychologists to pin down and advance the field's understanding of important phenomena. What could be more practical? If you know how a treatment works, you can refine and deliver the treatment as effectively as possible. This study's theoretical merits are complemented by its methodological elegance. The primary dependent variable (panic severity) is measured both before and after the treatment, as are two explanatory variables (panic self-efficacy and catastrophic misinterpretation). These explanatory variables are called potential *mediators* because they are believed to stand between the treatment and the outcome and literally transform the treatment into the outcome. That is the basic layout of the study, and it is refreshingly simple.

Now we can turn our attention to the statistical sophistication of this elegant study. The study's results were presented as a basic table of correlations (see Figure 6.1). All you need to recall about correlations for now is that they range from –1.0 to 1.0. Numbers closer to zero indicate little or no relation between two variables. Numbers approaching either extreme indicate a strong relationship. Related variables move either in the same direction as one another (*positive correlations*) or in opposite directions (*negative correlations*). For example, this study found a strong positive correlation between changes in panic severity and catastrophic misinterpretation of bodily sensations ($r = .71$). Panic severity tended to go down as misinterpretation of bodily sensations decreased. Conversely, there was a strong negative correlation between changes in panic severity and panic self-efficacy ($r = -.82$). Panic severity tended to go down as panic self-efficacy increased. Keep in mind that a correlation of .50 in either direction is considered to be a strong relationship in psychological research. That is, a negative correlation of –.50 is just as strong and meaningful as a positive correlation of .50. The only difference is the direction of the correlation.

Looking again at the table of correlations, we see that being in the "standard" CBT condition increased panic self-efficacy ($r = .81$), decreased catastrophic misinterpretations of bodily sensations ($r = -.77$), and decreased overall panic severity ($r = -.75$). You probably have learned that correlation does not equal causation, but remember that some things you learn aren't so. Correlation is just a statistical technique, and its meaning depends on the design of the study. This was a true experiment, with patients randomly assigned to either therapy or the waitlist condition. As a consequence, these correlations indicate that patients in the study did, in fact, benefit from CBT.

But did CBT reduce panic severity *because* it changed patients' distorted cognitions about panic attacks? Although this can be a rather sophisticated statistical question, the researchers provided a straightforward answer. If you simultaneously use panic self-efficacy (a mediator), catastrophic misinterpretation (another mediator), and CBT condition (the independent variable) to predict posttreatment panic severity, only the mediators

FIGURE 6.1 Table of correlations presented in Casey, Newcombe, and Oei (2005).

Variables	1	2	3
1. Panic severity			
2. Treatment condition	–.75***		
3. Panic self-efficacy	–.82***	.81***	
4. Catastrophic misinterpretation	.71***	–.77***	–.68***

Note: Treatment condition was coded "0" for Waitlist and "1" for Standard condition. Coefficients for panic self-efficacy and catastrophic misinterpretation refer to residualized change scores. Higher residual change score on panic self-efficacy reflected a shift toward greater self-efficacy at posttreatment being associated with a lower level of panic severity at posttreatment. In contrast, higher residual change scores in catastrophic misinterpretation reflected a shift towards greater catastrophizing (relative to the sample mean) at posttreatment being associated with higher level of panic severity.
***$p < .001$.

contribute to our statistical understanding of panic severity. In other words, CBT does not have an effect on panic severity *above and beyond* its effect on the mediators. CBT works, and it appears to work because it increases panic self-efficacy and decreases catastrophic misinterpretations of bodily sensations. Slam dunk!

Behind the scenes of this example are some rather complicated statistical techniques that can take years to master. And even then, researchers will quibble over the details of which particular technique is more accurate. Think of expert testimony at a legal trial—it is always possible to find opposing experts to contradict one another. But these quibbles are a bore, and they seriously undermine our ability to think clearly about what really matters: the *logic* of a study.

If you noticed, we used only a few numbers and no mathematical equations at all to explain Casey and colleagues' study. We emphasized concepts instead. Make no mistake, these are extremely powerful statistical concepts, and our goal in this chapter is to develop these concepts a bit further. Although we cannot teach you everything about statistics and data handling in such a short span of pages, we can equip you with a powerful, intuitive approach to statistics and data. Beyond this, there is no substitute for course work in statistics. Undergraduates interested in research should take an introductory statistics course as early as possible, and juniors (ideally) or seniors should seek out a second, more advanced course if they plan to complete a student-initiated research project or assume a leadership role in a mentor's lab. Learning statistics is like learning a language. The more experience, the better.

STATISTICS AS "PRINCIPLED ARGUMENT"

As the therapy study described above should make clear, the subject matter of statistics is not numbers or mathematical equations, but rather ideas. Statistical reasoning helps us make sound claims about meaningful ideas. This is an inherently human enterprise, not some stuffy mathematical affair. Yes, there is some math involved in statistics, but the most powerful statistical concepts emphasize logic rather than math, and they can be mastered by anyone with a decent high school background in algebra. These concepts enable researchers to tell intelligent stories about the world around us. As Robert Abelson (1995) argues, "Data analysis should not be pointlessly formal. It should make an interesting claim; it should tell a story that an informed audience will care about, and it should do so by intelligent interpretation of appropriate evidence" (p. 2).

Does the sun orbit the earth? Galileo, father of modern science, used data from eclipses to reason that the earth could not be the fixed center of celestial movement as his contemporaries believed. The earth must move around the sun instead. This idea, which shook the earth free of old ideas, was a product of statistical reasoning. This perspective on statistics treats statistical reasoning as a means of "principled argument" (Abelson, 1995). That is, we learn the logic of statistics in order to add a powerful tool to our scientific tool kit: Statistics enable us to make much better arguments, and arguments hashed out by a community of scholars are the basis of knowledge.

So what types of questions can statistics, in particular, help us answer? As Edward Tufte (1997), one of the many characters in the world of statistics, has said, "The deep, fundamental question in statistical analysis is *Compared with what?*" (p. 30). In other words, when we use statistics we are always comparing things. Newspapers, politicians, advertisers, and even scientific journal articles often present statistics without making clear what comparisons are being made. Take the statement that 15% of patients taking a new allergy medicine report experiencing headaches. Compared to what? Think about it. Does this sound like a possible side effect of the medicine? At first, perhaps. But the real answer is *not at all*. If roughly 20% of patients taking *any* allergy medicine, or for that matter a placebo (i.e., a sugar pill), would report experiencing headaches over the same time period, then the new allergy medicine is unlikely to be causing headaches. Perhaps it even *reduces* allergy-related headaches. Our interpretation of the statistic (15% incidence of headaches) depends critically on our answer to the question, *Compared with what?* What initially seemed like a potential downside of the new medicine might actually be an additional merit.

The role of a good study is to set up the most informative comparisons. Statistics then enables us to interpret these comparisons in a rigorous and principled way. Research that obscures important comparisons should make you suspicious of the source's methods, reasoning, or motives. The lesson here is straightforward: Before you collect any data, you should be absolutely certain that your study is designed to illuminate important comparisons.

THE BASICS: STATISTICS' THREE SACRED TOOLS

Virtually everything in statistics boils down to a few simple concepts that are embodied, for all practical purposes, in what we call statistics' three sacred tools: the mean, standard deviation, and standard error. These tools should be front and center in your mind whenever you work on a data set or pose a statistical question. When you discuss statistics with others, if you cannot connect what you are saying to these tools, then you really don't know what you are talking about. This holds true whether you are uttering an innocent phrase concerning statistics or attempting to explain a more challenging statistical concept to a member of your research team or another scientist interested in your research findings. Abelson (1995) puts it nicely: "Don't talk Greek if you don't know the English translation" (p. xv).

The goal, then, is to be able to explain even the most complicated statistics in the most basic terms, and to be able to translate these terms into plain English. If you cannot do this, or if you ever get into a jam and find yourself confused or stymied by a statistical procedure or discussion of statistics, then you need to step back and rework your thinking from a simple understanding of the mean, standard deviation, and standard error. Try to visualize statistics with respect to these tools whenever possible. Nothing is more important to the nuts and bolts of statistics than these tools. Nothing. The rest is commentary. So let's take up each of these tools in turn, beginning with the mean.

The Mean

This one is easy. It is just the plain-old average. Add together a column or list of observed values and then divide by the number of observations. A stickler would call this the *arithmetic mean* in order to distinguish it as much as possible from other measures of central tendency (such as the median and mode) and more exotic ways of calculating a mean (such as the geometric mean), but this is commentary. If your statistics instructor grumpily insists that you say "arithmetic mean," consider asking him or her to define *arithmetic*. The adjective itself really does not distinguish this simplest of means from anything else, so the terminology is a convention. Dismiss the jargon, and keep your mind on the concept itself.

The mean is simple to calculate, but as a concept it is rather profound. Remember, statistics is best thought of as a method of storytelling, and the foundation of any story is a point or frame of reference. As Archimedes said of physical objects, if you can identify and leverage a fixed, immovable point, you can move the world. A mean serves psychologically as a powerful point of reference, but in isolation it is of little value rhetorically. Consider per person consumption of electricity throughout the world (the following data are available online from the World Bank, 2011): On average, each person in Colombia uses the equivalent of about one 100-watt lightbulb 24 hours/day, 7 days/week. So what? Colombia has a mild tropical climate and is not the most prosperous country, so you probably had some sense that it consumes less electricity than other countries. Besides, saying "one lightbulb per person" is rather boring in isolation. Then again, if you use Colombia's mean as a point of reference, the story gets much more interesting. In comparison, each American uses the equivalent of about *16* 100-watt lightbulbs constantly. What a difference! Any hypotheses? And how about Iceland? Brrrrrrr. About *57* lightbulbs per person. Then there is Haiti, arguably one of the poorest countries in the world. In Haiti, 38 people must "share" the equivalent of only one 100-watt bulb. Using Haiti and Iceland as points of reference for each other, you can tell an even more dramatic story. The average family of four in Haiti uses an amount of electricity equivalent to just two tiny nightlights, while in Iceland the average family's ongoing electricity consumption is equivalent to well over 200 ultrabright 100-watt lightbulbs! Variability like this is extraordinary.

A single mean occasionally tells its own story, but only when an intuitive reference points already exists. For example, in Milgram's (1963) classic study of obedience to authority, participants were asked to deliver increasingly severe shocks to a fellow participant who was trying to memorize a set of word pairs. As you may recall, the "learner" was a confederate and did not, in fact, receive any shocks at all. But participants did not know this, and they delivered on average 24 to 25 shocks to the learner. This corresponds to shocks that were just under 370 volts, and at this level, the learner was no longer responsive and apparently gravely injured if not dead. Although the "compared with what" question was never answered, Milgram's results speak dramatically for themselves because the intuitive reference point for most of us is that participants should either refuse to deliver any shocks or stop after only a shock or two. They certainly would not kill someone. The mean number of shocks is never considered in isolation. Notice that Milgram's story would not be nearly as powerful if our intuitive reference point were that most people would deliver "a whole lot of shocks."

With your permission, at this point we will let symbols and notation out of their time-out, because they should play nicely by now. To calculate the mean, we sum up all of our observations and divide by the number of observations. Here is the straightforward, conceptual formula:

$$\overline{X} = \frac{\Sigma X}{N}$$

A quick note about notation. One of our professors at Yale had a habit of suggesting that the math behind statistical concepts was mathematically obvious. He would then scribble advanced calculus on the blackboard that hardly any of the Ph.D. students could follow. We prefer to take the opposite approach. If you think the formula for the mean is obvious, then move on. For those of you who don't think so, we offer a quick explanation of the notation even if it is relatively simple. Some of us, after all, are like deer in the headlights when we see a mathematical formula. So here is the way to approach the formula for the mean. Suppose we have measured the number of M&Ms consumed by participants while watching the movie *Nightmare on Elm Street* in our lab. (This is an interesting idea for a study, but the counting would be tedious.) We take this number for each participant (i.e., each X), and we add all of these observations together using a nifty little "adding machine" called summation (i.e., Σ). Divide the sum by the number of participants in the sample (i.e., N), and there we have it, the mean. The notation for the mean, $\overline{X}$, is cute. It is as if the bar on top of the X flattens or evens out all of the individual scores. That is a nice, visual way to think about the average.

As we have said, means serve as reference points, allowing us to make informative comparisons among different groups. For example, participants watching *The Wizard of Oz* might eat 45.3 M&Ms on average during the movie, whereas participants watching *Nightmare on Elm Street* might eat an average of 121.7 M&Ms. If a study like this were well designed and involved a sufficient number of participants, we would conclude that people snack more when they are scared, perhaps to comfort themselves or because their self-control is sapped by their efforts to stay calm.

Standard Deviation

The most common stories we tell with statistics involve comparisons between the means of different groups. But means serve as reference points in another, equally important way. That is, the mean is a reference point for each of the observations in the sample. This logic leads us to the second sacred tool of statistics, the standard deviation. This concept should be nearly as easy to understand as the mean, but the jargon gets in the way. Both *standard* and *deviation* give the impression of something sterile and detached, a concept you might expect to find in a brainy technical report.

So how can it be that the standard deviation is nearly as easy to understand as the mean? Here is the answer: *Conceptually, it is just an average.* After determining the mean of a sample of observations, you should then ask how far, on average, the typical observation is away from the mean. This is the variability that makes research exciting. If there is no variability in something, then each individual observation as well as the mean would be identical. That's no fun. The researcher who sets out to study the average number of wheels on a unicycle has a problem. But when observations are spread out around the mean, things get much more interesting. Conceptually, the standard deviation is just the average distance between the typical observation and the mean. That's it.

Even so, the mathematical path to the standard deviation involves a couple of tricks that are illuminating and really need to be explained. Suppose you play horseshoes, and you always throw the horseshoe in exactly the right direction. However, you sometimes throw too far; we will use a positive number of inches to identify these throws that go beyond the stake. Alternatively, you sometimes throw too short; we will use a negative number of inches to identify these throws that are short of the stake. The funny thing about the mean is that you might be a horrible horseshoes player, but the combined distances of the horseshoes you throw beyond the stake (positive numbers) might cancel out the combined distances of the horseshoes you throw short of the stake (negative numbers). So, *on average,* your throws might be perfect. But this is absurd, and statements like these give rise to groan-inducing statistics jokes such as, "You know, a person whose body is half in an oven and half in a freezer feels perfectly comfortable *on average.*"

The point of the standard deviation is to sidestep this absurdity. When we are trying to determine how far the typical observation is away from the mean, we do not want distances above the mean (positive numbers) canceling out distances below the mean (negative numbers). Instead, we want to get rid of the signs (+/–) of the distances. The mathematical trick used to solve this problem is to square each observation's distances away from the mean. These squared distances will always be positive (i.e., a negative number times itself is a positive number), so the *average squared distance* from the horseshoe stake will never be zero unless you are truly a perfect player. On the other hand, this number will grow larger (and larger and larger) to the extent that you are a less talented horseshoe thrower.

However, there are two problems with using the average squared distance from the mean as a measure of variability. First, it is a squared number, so it is not very intuitive. If you tell your friend that you typically miss the horseshoe stake by 144 square inches, this will only lead to confusion. This is an easy problem to address. Take the square root, and you are back to the original (unsquared) units of measurement. The square root of 144 is 12, so you can tell your friend that you typically miss the stake by about 12 inches, or 1 foot. This is much simpler and more meaningful. Technically, this might be called the "root mean squared deviation from the mean," but conceptually, it is just a tricked-out average.

The second problem with merely calculating the average squared distance from the mean and using this as a measure of variability stems from a distracting but somewhat important distinction. In psychological research, we almost always draw *samples* from larger *populations.* Try not to overthink this. We rarely if ever deal with entire populations. Even when we have the midterm grades of all the students in a class, we are not really interested in just those students. Instead, we want to generalize from any particular sample of students to all possible and potential students like these. This is science—we try to reach *general* conclusions from a *limited* set of observations. When we calculate the mean of a sample, this is our best guess of the mean of the entire population. That's a very nice thing about the mean. But when we try to use the average squared distance between each observation and the *sample mean* to guess the variability between the scores and the true *population mean* (and never forget that this is our goal), we run into a problem. Our sample mean is just a *guess* of the population mean, and to the extent that it is wrong, each sample score will be artificially closer to the sample mean than to the true population mean.

Think about this for a moment. Drawing a sample of observations from a population is a chance process, and, as Abelson's first law of statistics states, chance is lumpy. One implication of this "law" is that samples tend to fall or lump slightly to one side or the other of the true population mean. And by definition, any "lump" of scores (i.e., the sample) will be closer to its own center (i.e., the sample mean) than to the true center of the population.

As a consequence, using the average squared distance between each observation and the sample mean to guess the true variability of the population results in an underestimate.

Fortunately, the lumpiness of chance is systematic, and we can correct upward from this underestimate. The extent to which samples tend to fall to one side or the other of the true population mean, what we call *sampling error,* is a direct function of *N,* the number of observations in the sample. Large samples are less lumpy. That is, large samples tend to be spread more evenly around the true population mean. On the other hand, small samples tend to fall substantially to one side or other of the true population mean. How far? We know the precise answer to this courtesy of statistics' *Central Limit Theorem.* On average, the squared distance between each observation and the sample mean "shaves off" 1/Nth of the squared distance between the observation and the true population mean. As a result, when you tally all of the squared distances between the observations and the sample mean (there are *N* of these, one for each observation), you end up *one* "average squared difference" short (i.e., *N* times 1/N). So rather than dividing by the number of observations (i.e., the number of squared differences going into the formula), the appropriate adjustment is to divide by one fewer, or *N − 1*. As a shorthand, we typically call this adjusted quantity, *N − 1,* the *degrees of freedom.* This is jargon, but it captures an important concept. We used up one unit of our sample's variability (i.e., that one "average squared distance" that seemed to go missing) when we calculated the sample mean and used it rather than the true population mean to estimate the standard deviation. In essence, we robbed the sample data of this one degree of freedom (i.e., one unit of variability) and now have only *N − 1* degrees of freedom remaining.

These considerations lead to the formula for standard deviation:

$$S_x = \sqrt{\frac{\Sigma(X - \overline{X})^2}{N - 1}}$$

This is not pretty, but don't let the notation blind you. Here is the way to approach this formula. Conceptually, the standard deviation is just an average. It is the average distance between each observation and the mean. Technically, however, we add up all of the *squared* distances between the observations and the sample mean so that the positive and negative distances do not cancel one another out. Then, instead of simply dividing by *N,* we divide by *N − 1* to adjust for the systematic underestimate associated with using the sample mean rather than the true population mean in estimating these distances. Finally, we take the square root of this to put the result back into the original units of our measure. So, yes, the standard deviation is a tricked-out average, but it is still just an average.

Standard Error

So far we have used the mean and the standard deviation to summarize a sample of *individual* scores. But in psychological research, we don't care very much about individual scores. We more often care about comparisons between *groups.* Suppose we conduct an experiment on how long people can hold their breath underwater. This is not a contest, and we are not going to recognize anyone for being Aquaman. We really don't care how long any particular person can hold his or her breath. Instead, we assign participants to one of three experimental conditions. Just before going under the water, each person sees one of three images displayed on a large poolside television: (a) a terrifying image of a shark, (b) a soothing image of an angelfish, or (c) a disgusting image of a rotting seal. At the end of the day, our only care for individual participants is that they do not drown. Otherwise, we rush home to calculate the group means and try to determine whether or not our experimental conditions differed from one another. We hypothesize that participants exposed to the shark image will have the most difficult time holding their breath because fear increases heart rate (and might consume oxygen more quickly), whereas participants exposed to the seal image will be able to hold their breath longer because disgust decreases heart rate (and might conserve oxygen somewhat). We hope that participants exposed to the angelfish image will fall somewhere between the other two groups because this is our neutral-mood control condition.

To understand the third sacred tool of statistics, the *standard error,* you need to focus on group means rather than on individual scores. Most of what we do in psychological research involves comparing the results (that is, the means) of two or more experimental groups. In our example, we are comparing the means of the shark, angelfish, and seal conditions. Our basic question is this: How much do these sample means vary from one another? This question is nearly identical to the question we asked in order to generate the standard deviation, but we are no longer interested in how far, on average, the typical *individual* score is away from the sample mean. Instead, *sample means are replacing individual scores,* and we want to know how far, on average, the typical sample mean is away from, well, let's just call it the *grand mean* (i.e., the mean of the sample means). In other words, the standard error is nothing but a standard deviation (which, again, is nothing but an average). That is, the standard error is the standard deviation of a set of sample means.

So what does the formula for standard error look like? You already know it because it is the *same* formula as that for the standard deviation. Really! However, we adjust the notation to remind ourselves that we are dealing with a set of sample means rather than a set of individual scores. Instead of having N individual scores, we now have k sample means, and we are squaring the distance between each sample mean ($\overline{X}$) and the mean of the sample means ($\overline{\overline{X}}$). You have to admit that the notation for the grand mean, $\overline{\overline{X}}$, is *doubly* cute. The double bar averages or flattens the sample means, each of which averages or flattens its underlying individual scores.

In any case, this gives us the following formula:

$$S_{means} = \sqrt{\frac{\Sigma(\overline{X}-\overline{\overline{X}})^2}{k-1}}$$

Again, this is not pretty, so here is the way to approach this formula. Conceptually, the standard error is just an average. It is the average distance between each sample mean and the mean of a collection of sample means. But we need to use the same tricks that we used to get the standard deviation. We add up all of the squared distances so that positive and negative distances do not cancel out one another, and we divide by $k-1$ in order to correct upward from the underestimate associated with using the sample means to estimate the true grand mean. We then take the square root to put the result back into the original units of our measure.

By now you might have noticed that statistics can be rather repetitive. But this is true in a way that is much like the incremental repetition of poetry. The incremental repetition of statistics first builds on the plain-old mean to get the standard deviation (i.e., the average distance of a set of individual scores from the mean). It then builds on these first two concepts to get the standard error (i.e., the average distance of a set of sample means from the grand mean). This scaffolding of ideas often throws students off when it goes unspoken. So let's be clear. Each of the three sacred tools of statistics is just an average: the average individual score ($\overline{X}$), the average distance between individual scores and the mean (s_x), and the average distance between sample means and the grand mean (s_{means}).

PUTTING THESE TOOLS TOGETHER

Although the logic behind the three sacred tools of statistics is somewhat repetitive, it leads to a place that is truly impressive. Revisiting our breath-holding experiment, suppose we have run 25 participants in each of the study's three conditions (i.e., exposure to the image of a shark, angelfish, or rotting seal). We want to compare the means of our three experimental groups, which is an instance of Tufte's fundamental question, *Compared with what?* The first thing we do is compute the sample mean for each condition, and we observe that the mean for the shark condition ($\overline{X}$ = 48 seconds) is somewhat lower than the means for the angelfish ($\overline{X}$ = 50 seconds) or the rotting seal ($\overline{X}$ = 52 seconds) conditions. To make things easy, assume that the standard deviation of individual scores within each sample (i.e., the average distance between the typical person's time and the mean of his or her experimental condition) is the same (s_x = 13 seconds). This is a rather large standard deviation—but as we all know, some people can hold their breath much longer than others.

At first glance, these data look great. The pattern of means clearly supports our prediction that the lowest mean would be in the shark/fear condition and the highest mean would be in the rotting seal/disgust condition, with the angelfish/calm condition falling somewhere in between. Time to celebrate? Not quite so fast. Remember, chance is lumpy. Even if the images that our participants viewed right before holding their breath had absolutely no effect on the length of time they stayed underwater, we would expect our samples to lump apart or away from one another just by chance. As it stands, our measure of how much the condition means vary from one another is the standard error of the means:

$$S_{means} = \sqrt{\frac{\Sigma(\overline{X}-\overline{\overline{X}})^2}{k-1}} = \sqrt{\frac{2^2 + 0^2 + 2^2}{3-1}} = \sqrt{\frac{8}{2}} = \sqrt{4} = 2$$

That is, based on our data, the typical distance between each of our sample means and the true grand mean is estimated to be 2 seconds, which is a pretty small effect. And remember, the typical individual within each of our samples fell plus or minus 13 seconds from his or her condition's respective mean. That is a lot of individual variability, or *noise*.

Given that individuals seem to differ so much in the length of time they can hold their breath underwater, how confident are we that the 2 seconds of variability between our sample means was caused by the study's experimental conditions and not just by chance fluctuations? This is the truly quintessential statistical question. If chance could easily account for the variability between our sample means, then our hypothesis seems doomed. How do we answer this question? Chance seems so mysterious. This question is sophisticated, and a full and complete answer to it would take a bit more time to develop.

But you will be able to answer this question definitively in just a moment even if your only understanding of statistics has come from reading this chapter. You need only one more insight.

Chance is mysterious, but we know its properties quite well. As we noted earlier, the lumpiness of chance is systematic, and what we call *sampling error* is a direct function of the number of observations in a sample. Larger samples lump less. How much less? Suppose that the images viewed had absolutely no effect on our participants. Then each sample was drawn at chance from the *very same* overall population of breath-holding times, just as if the participants saw no images at all. How far would the typical sample mean fall from the "no effect" or *null* mean just by chance? A wonderful thing known as the central limit theorem (developed in large part through the flipping of bazillions of coins and observation of countless other chance processes) tells us to expect that our samples of size $N = 25$, if drawn from a population with a standard deviation of 13 seconds, will have means that typically fall plus or minus 2.6 seconds from the null mean just by chance. Here is the formula for this:

$$S_{means} = \frac{s_x}{\sqrt{N}} = \frac{13}{\sqrt{25}} = \frac{13}{5} = 2.6$$

Wait, this looks like a calculation of standard error, and it is! Indeed, the central limit theorem gives us another way to approach standard error. The variability of sample means is expected, just by chance, to equal the variability of individual scores (in this case, $S_x = 13$ seconds) reduced through division by a function of the sample size (i.e., $\sqrt{N}$). That is, larger samples are *systematically* more accurate.

So now we have our answer. How confident are we that the 2 seconds of variability that we observed between our samples was caused by the study's experimental conditions and not by chance fluctuations? Not confident at all. The observed standard error in our study is 2.0 seconds, and this is *lower* than we might expect by chance according to the central limit theorem (i.e., 2.6 seconds). We actually observed a bit less variability between our sample means than we might expect to see just by chance. In other words, chance could easily account for the variability between our sample means. In the bizarre parlance of statistical hypothesis testing, we clearly "fail to reject the null hypothesis." We haven't proven anything. Note that we cannot prove the *null hypothesis* because the smallest of effects are almost impossible to distinguish from chance variability. But without a doubt, our predictions have been eviscerated.

This example would have turned out differently if the observed variability between the sample means had been a bit higher. If the observed standard error between these sample means had been 5 seconds instead of just 2 seconds, this would have been about *twice* the standard error expected just by chance. To make a clear decision, we then would determine the precise likelihood of chance fluctuations producing this much variability between our sample means. If this likelihood were very small (typically, less than 5%), we would conclude that our experimental manipulation caused a difference in participants' ability to hold their breath. In such a case, we would conduct appropriate follow-up calculations in order to describe the exact pattern of this effect.

Although there are many more details to learn about the type of statistical test described above as well as other statistical tests and techniques, it is worth noting that we just carried

TABLE 6.1 Statistics' Three Sacred Tools	
Always start by visualizing these three basic tools when you tackle any question in statistics:	
1. Mean	This is easy. The mean is just the common average. Add together the scores in a sample and divide by N (i.e., the number of scores) to get the *mean*.
2. Standard deviation	This is a bit tougher. Conceptually, the standard deviation is the average distance between a typical score and the sample mean. But the standard deviation is also just a fancy average. Subtract the mean from each score, square each of these *deviations*, and then add all of these *squared deviations* together. This quantity is known as the *sum of squares*, and dividing it by $N - 1$ results in the sample's *average squared deviation*, also known as the *variance*. Take the square root of the variance to get the *standard deviation*.
3. Standard error	This is the same equation as the standard deviation but in slight disguise. The standard error is the average distance between a typical sample mean and the *grand mean* (i.e., the mean of a set of sample means). In other words, it is the standard deviation of the sample means. Subtract the grand mean from each sample mean, square these *deviations*, and then add these *squared deviations* together. Divide by $k - 1$ (i.e., the number of sample means minus one), and then take the square root of this to get the *standard error*.

out a conceptual (and perfectly legitimate) *analysis of variance,* or *ANOVA.* (This term stems from the fact that we conducted an analysis in which we compared the observed variability between our sample means to the estimate of this variability derived from the central limit theorem.) Typically students need to take nearly a semester of statistics before they understand basic ANOVA. But if you have followed the logic of this section and understand the three sacred tools of statistics (summarized for your convenience in Table 6.1), then you already have a strong conceptual grasp of ANOVA. When you encounter ANOVA again, you will have a more intuitive understanding of this statistical test. Starting from these basic principles, you should be able to make sense of many if not most of the statistical arguments that you are likely to encounter as an undergraduate. As you learn more about statistics, always keep these sacred tools front and center in your mind. They are extremely powerful.

ADVANCED STATISTICS: A MATTER OF CORRELATION

The mean, standard deviation, and standard error are statistics' three most essential and sacred tools. But where there are sacred things, there are secret things as well. Ironically, these secrets often hide in plain sight. Conspiracy theorists will tell you that the mysterious Eye of Providence appears on the back of every U.S. dollar bill as a sign that the secretive Freemasons played a powerful role in founding the United States. Similarly, the secrets and real power of statistics rest in a ubiquitous, seemingly minor concept: correlation. As we noted earlier in this chapter, correlation is a relatively simple way to index the degree of association between two variables. Related variables move either in the same direction as one another (positive correlation) or in opposite directions (negative correlation), and correlation coefficients are computed such that they range from –1.0 (a perfect negative correlation) to 1.0 (a perfect positive correlation). Simple enough, and not that earthshaking.

When we discussed Casey and colleagues' (2005) compelling study of cognitive behavioral therapy, you might have been a bit disappointed that these researchers presented their findings as a simple table of six correlation coefficients. Undergraduates are taught to be wary of correlational studies (i.e., "Correlation is not causation"), and many instructors frown when students try to use a correlation to express the relationship between a categorical independent variable (e.g., therapy versus waitlist condition) and a continuous dependent variable (e.g., panic severity). Everyone knows that correlations should be computed only when both variables are continuous; and, besides, the honorable *t* test is the proper way to test the difference between the means of two experimental groups. (You probably know about the *t* test, but if not, you can think of it as a simplified version of ANOVA, which we just discussed.) But once again, some things you learn aren't so. Correlation is an extraordinarily versatile technique, and it can be used to do just about everything in statistics. That might seem like a stretch, especially if you have taken a first course in statistics. Introductory statistics textbooks typically set correlation off to the side as quite distinct from other statistical techniques. But it's not.

The General Linear Model

The key to understanding the power of correlation is to recognize that the vast majority of statistical techniques work with *two variables at a time* and assess *simple linear relationships*. However, one can generalize these techniques beyond two variables by carrying out a careful *series* of simple linear analyses. In addition, these techniques can be generalized beyond linear relationships through a sort of mathematical cheating—namely, transforming an original scale of numbers (e.g., by squaring each value) so that the resulting variable is more amenable to a linear analysis. The ins and outs of these two topics—transforming scales of measurement and building more complex analyses out of a series of simple linear analyses—give rise to a vast array of statistical tests and procedures. Reduced to their most basic components, however, these tests and procedures operate on simple linear relationships between two variables at a time. This is the basis of the *general linear model,* or *GLM,* the prevailing approach to statistics. The GLM is a powerful, *generalized* approach to statistical reasoning built on simple *linear* relationships, hence the name. And guess what? Those simple linear relationships are nothing but correlations.

Clearly, it is beyond the scope of this chapter to present the mathematics of correlation and then build the entire framework of more advanced statistics from this concept. Still, we can give you a feel for the power of correlation by showing you how a series of just two correlations can answer some of psychology's most important questions.

Statistical Mediation and Partial Correlation

Arguably, the greatest satisfaction in research comes from answering the questions of *why* and precisely *how* an effect occurs. It is one thing to observe that after ten days of drinking an opaque pink fluid, your child no longer has an ear infection. But *why* did drinking the fluid work? If you are told that the (not so) delicious elixir is an antibiotic, your child's cure makes complete sense. As we mentioned in the context of Casey and colleagues' (2005) study, what comes between an independent variable and a dependent variable is called the *mediator*. In this case we have a pink fluid that cures an ear infection. The mediator is the sustained, measurable concentration of antibiotic in the child's body. Although this is a medical example, psychologists are equally interested in why and precisely how the effects that they observe occur. Answering these questions is a matter of identifying, measuring, and evaluating the explanatory role of *mediating mechanisms*.

Consider a study by Kenneth Rice and Amy Van Arsdale (2010). These researchers were interested in studying the extent to which perceived stress leads to alcohol-related problems for college students. They assessed stress using the 14-item Perceived Stress Scale, and they measured alcohol-related problems using a 27-item questionnaire that includes questions about driving while intoxicated, doing poorly on school-related assignments, and experiencing headaches, nausea, and blackouts. The researchers found a modest positive association between these two variables ($r = .15$). The more stress reported by a student, the more likely he or she was to have problems with alcohol. The question, of course, is *why?* Said differently: What is the mediator of the relationship between stress and alcohol-related problems?

Rice and Van Arsdale proposed a cognitive mechanism to account for the link between stress and problems with alcohol. Namely, stress in students' lives will lead them to consider various potential coping strategies, and some stressed students will develop a belief that alcohol is an effective means of coping with their problems. To the extent that a student develops these "drinking to cope" motives, he or she will be more likely to experience problems with alcohol. Thus, the authors proposed that drinking to cope would be the explanatory link, or mediator, between stress and alcohol problems. In their study, they measured this potential mediator using a 5-item subscale of the Drinking Motives Questionnaire.

How do we test whether or not drinking to cope mediates the relationship between stress and alcohol problems? The pivotal test we use to answer this question is quite elegant. We need to calculate a *partial correlation*. Conceptually, a partial correlation is a sequence of two correlations. In this case, we first calculate the correlation between the explanatory variable (drinking to cope) and the outcome (alcohol-related problems). The relationship between these two variables is rather strong ($r = .45$). Next, we leverage the power of correlation to do something clever. Because drinking to cope is associated with alcohol problems, we can use each student's drinking to cope score to predict his or her experience of such problems. This prediction technique is called *regression,* and if you are willing to think in terms of standard deviations, it is quite easy to explain. If a student's drinking to cope score is one standard deviation above the mean, then we would *predict* that his or her alcohol problems score would be .45 standard deviations above the mean. In other words, for every standard deviation change in the predictor variable, we *predict* a change in the outcome variable equivalent to *r* standard deviations. Our predictions will not be perfect, but they will get us a bit closer to students' actual experience of alcohol-related problems.

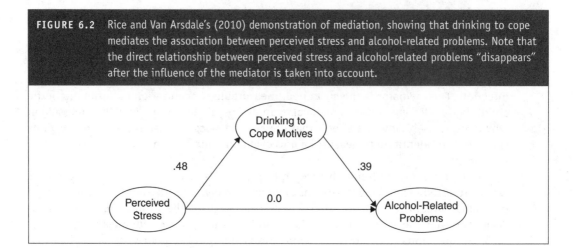

FIGURE 6.2 Rice and Van Arsdale's (2010) demonstration of mediation, showing that drinking to cope mediates the association between perceived stress and alcohol-related problems. Note that the direct relationship between perceived stress and alcohol-related problems "disappears" after the influence of the mediator is taken into account.

For each student, the difference between our prediction and the student's actual experience of alcohol-related problems has a concrete value, and this set of "residual" values is something we will now try to explain. Specifically, we will calculate a second correlation to see if the original variable of interest (i.e., stress) statistically explains any of the residual variability in alcohol-related problems. This correlation between stress and "alcohol problems not otherwise accounted for by drinking to cope" is a partial correlation (technically, it would be more accurate to say that this is one aspect of a partial correlation, but the distinction is minor), and it will help us answer our question about mediation. In Rice and Van Arsdale's study, this relationship was essentially zero (see Figure 6.2). In other words, stress did *not* account for students' problems with alcohol above and beyond the role played by the mediator, drinking to cope. This is solid evidence that drinking to cope mediates (that is, explains) the effect of stress on problems with alcohol.

The implications of this study provide a strong rationale for why testing for mediation (and, by extension, understanding partial correlation) is so important. College support staff such as resident advisers, counselors, and health advocates might assume that they should teach stress reduction as a way of reducing alcohol-related problems among students, when in reality the link between stress and alcohol problems is quite modest. What really seems to matter is the mechanism identified in Rice and Van Arsdale's study: college students' use of alcohol as a coping strategy. This might be a much more effective locus of intervention. College support staff should consider interventions that directly target students' beliefs that using alcohol is an effective way to cope with their problems.

STATISTICS AND EXPERIMENTAL DESIGN

A firm grasp of the core principles of statistics will help you and your team develop a compelling research project that is likely to produce meaningful results. Before finalizing the design of your research project, you and your teammates should dedicate one meeting to envisioning the likely results of the project. Start by diagramming the key comparisons you will make when your study's data are analyzed. How many experimental conditions are there? Which of these conditions should differ from one another, and why? Is it realistic to think your data will live up to these expectations? What other pattern of findings might be just as likely to occur, and why? Will the study be meaningful if one of these alternative results is obtained? You might be surprised that a project can make it to this stage without the researchers being able to answer these questions. This exercise is an extension of Tufte's (1997) cautionary reminder that the fundamental goal of a research project is to make clear and cogent comparisons. And as Abelson (1995) argues, you must be able to make a principled argument that the results of your research are meaningful. Your team can achieve these goals if you think carefully about how statistics' core principles will influence your study's results.

As an overarching approach, your team should take Abelson's first law of statistics to heart: *Chance is lumpy.* The most important implication of this law is that your study's findings are unlikely to be neat and tidy, especially if you have too many experimental conditions or fail to recruit enough participants per condition. In such cases, chance can and will wreak havoc with the comparisons you hope to make. To combat this, your team should do several things:

1. *Redouble your efforts to simplify the research design.* If you limit the number of experimental conditions in any single study, your statistical comparisons will be more focused. The chance of muddled findings increases dramatically even when you move from two to three experimental conditions.

2. *Recruit at least 30 participants per experimental condition.* Although something called a *power analysis* can help your team determine the number of participants needed in order for your study to produce meaningful results, these analyses are more of an art than a science. In general, 30 participants per condition is a respectable goal. If you have the opportunity to learn about power analysis from your instructor or research mentor, you should do so. However, utilizing this list of recommendations is just as important as a formal power analysis.

3. *Make sure your experimental manipulations are consistent, distinct from one another, and as strong as possible.* Subtle manipulations occasionally have profound effects, but more often than not a subtle manipulation will translate directly into a small, undetectable effect. The lumpiness of chance will interfere much less with the larger effect produced by a stronger manipulation.

4. *Keep your outcome measures clean and simple.* Chance thrives on the statistical noise of everyday life. Poorly worded questions and ambiguous behaviors are rife with such noise and lead to standard deviations that are hopelessly large. Because the reliability of your sample means (i.e., standard error) is a function of this noise (i.e., the standard deviation of individual scores), noisy dependent variables will blur any comparisons you hope to make. Simple questions and clear, concrete outcome behaviors make the best dependent variables.

5. *Use a few (rather than too many or just one) interrelated outcome measures.* If you measure too many things, your statistical analyses will be unfocused, and the chance of muddled findings will increase. On the other hand, using a single question or behavior as

a study's sole dependent variable is too risky, because no single question or behavior is perfect. If you triangulate on an outcome using a few interrelated measures, the statistical noise in any single measure will be less of an issue. (This parallels the idea that sample means are more reliable than individual observations.)

Following these recommendations will improve your team's research project. Of course, conducting a single focused study will answer only, at best, one or two focused research questions. So it is likely that you and your teammates will want to extend your research in follow-up studies if there is time to do so. One of the most promising ways to extend a line of research is to hone research findings and then propose and measure a potential mediating mechanism, such as those discussed in Casey and colleagues' (2005) and Rice and Van Arsdale's (2010) research. You can measure a mediator just as you would any other dependent variable (e.g., by asking participants a few questions that tap into the proposed explanatory variable). Again, you should include a modest number of interrelated questions and focus on keeping the measures clean and simple.

WORKING WITH DATA

Once you have a good conceptual understanding of statistics, it is time to think about the realities of working with data. Data can be messy. If you have ever transferred survey responses or coding sheets manually into a computer spreadsheet, you know that data entry can be extraordinarily tedious and prone to mistakes. The ambiguity of participants' handwritten responses can be unnerving: "Did this person circle a 3 or a 4 for this question, or both?"; "What do I do if the participant circled both a 2 and a 6 and then explained in the margin that the answer depends on the circumstances?"; "I can't make out this handwritten number—is it even a number?"

Fortunately, data are more often collected using computers these days, so responses are more uniform and unambiguous than in the past. Still, computers have their own glitches (e.g., "How can the response be 11 when the scale goes from 1 to 7?"), and they make it possible for researchers to collect massive amounts of information that can be difficult to manage (e.g., thousands of reaction times or millisecond-by-millisecond psychophysiological measurements). Moreover, storing data on computers can be a nightmare: "Why do I have 10 different data files for this study?"; "Which computer has the most up-to-date file?"; "Oh no, my hard drive just crashed!" For all these reasons and more, your team needs to develop and follow a systematic procedure for entering, checking, and archiving research data.

The overarching goal in working with data is to minimize errors. Errors and ambiguities can introduce potentially catastrophic noise into your statistical analyses. Think back to our discussion of standard error and standard deviation within the breath-holding example. In order for you to be confident that an observed experimental effect is real and not a product of chance, the size of the effect must exceed the level of noise within your data. To the extent that errors in data entry occur, this noise will be artificially inflated. For instance, a coding error that assigns someone a 52 for a question scored from 1 to 7 will "explode" that variable's standard deviation. Any means that you compute using this variable will be dramatically skewed, and any statistical tests that you carry out will be potentially meaningless.

How can you eliminate errors during data entry? The single best method of ensuring that data from paper-and-pencil surveys are nearly error-free is to enter the data twice, each time independently. This is where working as a team is extremely helpful. One person should set up a data spreadsheet with short descriptive variable names in the first row. Then your team should create two copies of the spreadsheet, one each for two separate teammates to use in entering the data as carefully as possible on their own. After both spreadsheets are completed, you can use the spreadsheet program to compare the two files for differences. (If the program you are using does not have this option, save the data files as text files and compare them using Microsoft Word's simple-to-use "Compare Documents" feature). Your team should scrutinize the results of the comparison and make corrections wherever differences are identified between the independent data files. You can follow a similar procedure with computer-generated data as well. Whenever you transfer a computer-generated file into a data spreadsheet or make any changes to data files, you should have two teammates do this independently and compare results to identify and correct any inconsistencies.

Of course, some paper-and-pencil data are ambiguous; data collected on a computer might suffer from technological glitches; and, inevitably, some errors manage to find their way into any data file. These realities require your team to do two things. First, you must develop decision rules (before conducting any analyses) for clarifying any ambiguous data. If a person circles two responses on a survey item, do you use one of these responses, average the responses, or record no response at all? The answer to this will depend on the type of item under consideration and whether you can decipher the participant's intent. You need to work together as a team to make objective rules that will allow you to handle such cases systematically and to explain your data-handling procedures to others.

Second, you must produce comprehensive printouts, reports, and visual depictions of all your data in order to check files for errors. Print out the entire data spreadsheet and scrutinize the columns of data for anomalies. Create reports for each variable, including basic descriptive statistics (e.g., the mean, standard deviation, range, and number of observations), as well as response frequencies. Be on the lookout for skewed means, inflated standard deviations, dropped cases (i.e., unexpected dips in the number of observations), and scores that are outside the valid range of responses. In particular, scrutinize the frequencies of items that you expected to be skewed in one direction. If the report reveals the exact opposite skew, you might have coded the variable in the wrong direction! Finally, graph your data using histograms or scatter plots. All too often researchers fail to appreciate how much information visual depictions of their data can convey; when you generate such depictions, the first thing you will often notice is a potential problem with the data that needs to be addressed.

If our description so far of data handling sounds a bit paranoid and excessive, trust us. We are speaking from experience. Small data errors in our own research (and in countless student projects that we have supervised) have led to huge blunders. Coding errors have gone undetected until they were pointed out during a lab presentation. Interesting findings have vanished upon the identification of an erroneous score. Studies that seemed to have failed were saved at the last moment because someone recognized that a massive problem was caused when the data were sorted incorrectly. You probably cannot avoid such disasters entirely, and that should make you feel deeply unsettled. You should channel this feeling into constant vigilance. Being meticulous at all times and in all ways when you work with data should be a personal goal, and you should make this a norm within your team. Trust no one in this respect, least of all yourself. Watch out for errors made by your teammates, and encourage your teammates to double-check your own efforts.

Conclusion

Many undergraduates in psychology believe they are not "numbers people," so they avoid statistics. This is a terrible mistake. Ultimately, the vision guiding any research project and the story told by any particular study will be contained in the data and expressed through statistics. Yes, some of the details of statistics can be complicated, but the most powerful concepts driving statistical reasoning can be mastered by anyone. You and your teammates can help one another achieve this mastery and take ownership of the results of your research. There is nothing like sitting down together to analyze the results of a study and learning that your hypotheses were correct. Equally emotional are those times when a study seems to fail right in front of your eyes as you analyze the data with your teammates. Our students liken the process of analyzing data to participating in a high-pressure, but exciting, athletic competition (which our lab fondly refers to as "the data show"). Together, you and your teammates will experience the thrill of victory, the agony of defeat, or perhaps a bit of both. And maybe, just maybe, these emotions will be accompanied by a nagging desire to do more research.

Learning statistics is very much like learning a language. In order to be fluent, you must engage in conversation, and you must seek out more opportunities to learn the grammar, syntax, and nuances of statistical reasoning. We encourage you to review the logic developed in this chapter with your teammates. To cement in your mind a basic understanding of statistics, there is nothing like playing with statistical concepts, helping others understand them, and learning from your peers' perspectives about ways of approaching these ideas. We also encourage you to pursue more course work in and readings about statistics. Indeed, a vast array of statistics resources is available online and in print; to get started, see the up-to-date list of these resources we maintain at http://go.lclark.edu/detweiler-bedell /teams. Armed with a more intuitive understanding of statistics' core principles, you might be surprised to discover that learning and doing statistics can be great fun.

References

Abelson, R. P. (1995). *Statistics as principled argument*. Hillsdale, NJ: Lawrence Erlbaum.
Casey, L., Newcombe, P., & Oei, T. (2005). Cognitive mediation of panic severity: The role of catastrophic misinterpretation of bodily sensations and panic self-efficacy. *Cognitive Therapy and Research, 29,* 187–200.

Cohen, J. (1990). Things I have learned (so far). *American Psychologist, 45,* 1304–1312.

Milgram, S. (1963). Behavioral study of obedience. *Journal of Abnormal and Social Psychology, 63,* 371–378.

Rice, K. G., & Van Arsdale, A. C. (2010). Perfectionism, perceived stress, drinking to cope, and alcohol-related problems among college students. *Journal of Counseling Psychology, 4,* 439–450.

Tufte, E. R. (1997). *Visual explanations: Images and quantities, evidence and narrative.* Cheshire, CT: Graphics Press.

World Bank. (2011). *World development indicators.* Retrieved from http://data.worldbank.org/data-catalog/world-development-indicators

CHAPTER 7

Piloting a Study

Seven Lessons (Plus or Minus Two)

1. The pilot study serves as a dress rehearsal for the "real" experiment. It will illuminate invaluable information about the participants' experiences, the flow of the methods, and your team's level of preparedness.

2. Three central aims of piloting include testing the adequacy of the research materials, identifying logistical problems, and training the experimenters.

3. In piloting, test components of your team's experiment individually and together so you can be sure the manipulations and measures work as intended.

4. Maximize the efficiency of piloting by assigning team members the roles of coordinator, evaluator, and storyteller.

5. Prepare for the pilot study by creating a standardized script and practicing the script as a team.

6. Construct an extended debriefing that includes broad questions about the study's purpose and specific questions about areas of confusion, followed by a focused explanation of the study and a conversation about potential areas for improvement.

7. Use piloting feedback judiciously. Make significant changes to the experiment only if you observe a worrisome pattern of responses across a number of pilot participants.

We may never be able to predict how particular people will respond to novel situations . . . . We also may never be able to predict how people in general or particular groups will respond to novelty. Situations are highly complex, and so are people's interpretations of them.

—Lee Ross and Richard E. Nisbett (1991, pp. 17–18)

Many situations, from those we encounter in our daily lives to those we create when we design an experiment, are extraordinarily complicated. For this reason, it can be quite difficult to know ahead of time which aspects of a situation will influence a person's behavior and which will matter little if at all. For instance, imagine that a construction worker wearing a light-blue shirt and a large tool belt approaches you as you walk across campus to your midday class. He stops you to ask for directions to a building on the other side of the campus. As you describe how to get to the building, two individuals carrying a large door pass between you and the construction worker, temporarily obstructing your view of each other. After the door is out of the way, you continue to give directions to the construction worker. But something has changed. He is no longer wearing a tool belt, and he is now sporting a *black* shirt rather than a blue one. Nevertheless, if you are like most people who have experienced this sequence of events, you keep giving directions without missing a beat (Simons & Levin, 1998). Believe it or not, you fail to notice that you are now giving directions to an entirely different person!

As it turns out, people are very poor at identifying seemingly obvious changes in their visual world if their attention is even briefly interrupted or misdirected, a phenomenon called *change blindness* or *inattentional blindness* (Simons & Rensink, 2005). In a classic study of this phenomenon, participants watch a minute-long video of two teams of three people (one team wearing white shirts, the other team wearing black shirts) bouncing a basketball back and forth. Participants are asked to count the number of passes the white team makes during the video. At a point 35 seconds into the clip, a gorilla (that is, a person wearing a full-body gorilla suit) walks through the scene, stops right in the middle of the players to face the camera, thumps its chest, and then walks out of the scene. The gorilla spends almost 10 seconds on the screen, yet only 50% of participants notice it (Simons & Chabris, 1999). If you were to show this video to a group of your peers, about half would slightly chuckle when the gorilla appears, and afterward they would ask, "What was that gorilla all about?" Upon hearing this, the other half of the group would be dumbfounded. "What gorilla?" Students who are shown this video often insist, somewhat emotionally, that there was *no* gorilla, and they demand to see the video again (to watch this and other videos from Daniel Simons's lab, visit http://www.simonslab.com/videos.html). Change blindness is fascinating because it is so counterintuitive. It also is a frightening illustration of how easily humans fail to notice and appreciate important aspects of the world around them.

In designing and carrying out a research investigation, noticing what matters is crucial. Unfortunately, researchers typically focus their attention on what they *expect* to happen in a study. This leads to something very much like inattentional blindness. Even the best researchers can be distracted and fail to notice the most important details of a study. As a result, they miss glaring errors that creep into their methods as study materials and procedures are revised, and they fail to appreciate the extent to which participants will construe the experimental situation and study questions differently than intended. In this chapter, we discuss an essential tool that helps overcome this challenge. This tool is the *pilot study*. After you have narrowed down your ideas, completed the initial design for a study, and anticipated your plans for analyzing the study's findings, it is time to test your team's study on a small scale and systematically assess whether participants are experiencing the study in the manner you intend.

This is the meaning of the quotation we selected to open this chapter. Experimental situations are complex, and they unfold within specific contexts. Context matters a great deal in determining how people will interpret and react to an experiment. Unfortunately, our intuitions (even when they are based on past research findings) often lead us astray in predicting how participants will construe and respond to our procedures and study materials. A good bit of "tinkering" and careful pretesting are essential to the finalization of a study's design.

WHAT IS A PILOT STUDY?

A pilot study is a trial version of an experiment. Your team's pilot study is an opportunity for you to pretest individual components of your study design (such as the manipulations and measures) and to evaluate how participants experience the study as a whole (Teijlingen & Hundley, 2001). Pilot studies typically involve only a small number of participants, but a substantial amount of time is dedicated to debriefing. During the debriefing, the experimenter's objective is to learn as much as possible about the participants' experience of, responses to, and impressions of the research paradigm. The pilot study enables you to test out your team's procedures while the stakes are still low, so piloting is the place to identify and correct mistakes. Measures and materials are often fine-tuned as a result of piloting. This careful refinement of a study maximizes the chance of getting meaningful results when the full study is conducted. Most institutions require institutional review board approval before pilot studies can be conducted, so it is important that you check with your research adviser or professor about what is required before initiating your team's pilot study.

There are a number of specific reasons for conducting pilot studies, many of which are summarized in Table 7.1 (Teijlingen & Hundley, 2001). For the purpose of our discussion, we will emphasize three of these aims: testing the adequacy of a study's research materials (i.e., manipulations and measures), identifying logistical problems with procedures, and training the experimenters.

Testing Research Materials

Great experiments in the behavioral sciences are focused and elegant. They manipulate a theoretically compelling independent variable in a clear and convincing way. They then assess the effects of this manipulation on a few carefully selected outcome measures. The best experiments are, as a result, surprisingly simple. But it takes a great deal of effort to hone one's experimental manipulations and outcome measures to such precision. Before launching their studies in their entirety, many researchers wisely pilot test individual components of their projects.

The Experimental Manipulation

Let's start with the piloting of a study's experimental manipulations (i.e., the independent variable or variables). For example, a research project might aim to manipulate

TABLE 7.1 Reasons for Conducting Pilot Studies
• Developing and testing the adequacy of research instruments
• Assessing the feasibility of a full-scale study or survey
• Designing a research protocol
• Assessing whether the research protocol is realistic and workable
• Establishing whether the sampling techniques are effective
• Assessing the likely success of proposed recruitment approaches
• Identifying logistical problems that might occur using proposed methods
• Estimating variability in outcomes to help determine sample size
• Collecting preliminary data
• Determining what resources (finance, staff) are needed for a planned study
• Assessing the proposed data analysis techniques to uncover potential problems
• Developing a research question and research plan
• Training a researcher in as many elements of the research process as possible
• Convincing funding bodies that the research team is competent and knowledgeable
• Convincing funding bodies that the main study is feasible and worth funding
• Convincing other stakeholders that the main study is worth supporting

Source: Teijlingen and Hundley (2001; http://sru.soc.surrey.ac.uk/SRU35.html).

participants' mood states by randomly assigning each participant to view one of three images: a well-dressed woman encountering a snarling attack dog, a man removing a dead and decaying mouse from the floor of a room, and a smiling child eating birthday cake. The researchers hope that these images will elicit fear, disgust, and joy, respectively. But how do they know if the manipulation actually works? Sure, the procedure has a certain degree of *face validity*. If participants empathize with the person in the picture or otherwise "feel" the emotional tone of the picture, the manipulation should be effective. But we cannot know for certain whether this is a *good* mood induction procedure unless the images are systematically selected and piloted.

Ideally, the process of selecting stimuli would start out with a much larger pool of images, and a small number of participants (perhaps 10–15) would be asked to view and rate each image on its emotional qualities. This would help ensure adequate *stimulus sampling,* which is just a sophisticated way of saying that you should pretest a wide range of possible stimuli so you are relatively certain that you ultimately select strong, reliable stimuli for your experiment. In this example, you would probably narrow the stimuli down to the images that rate highly and "cleanly" on the target emotions (i.e., fear, disgust, joy). In other words, the best candidates for effective images are those that rate highly on the target emotion and *only* on the target emotion. It might be difficult to find a fear image that does not rate highly on anxiety as well, but you should nonetheless strive to make your experimental manipulations as distinct as possible.

Once you have selected the best "candidate" images for your study, you might want to run a ministudy to see if these images actually *elicit* the targeted emotional responses. Although you can do this within the full-blown study itself using a *manipulation check* (i.e., directly assessing participants' emotional reactions right after the images are displayed), you might want to know ahead of launching the larger study that participants will actually feel the targeted emotions after viewing the images. Moreover, you might not want to include a manipulation check within the study itself because doing so might call participants' attention to their emotional states. This can cause participant *reactivity* (i.e., a change in how participants respond to the experimental situation because they identify the purpose of the study or intended effect of the manipulation). If during a pretest of your stimuli you are unable to produce the intended effects (e.g., the desired emotional states), you will want to consider using alternative stimuli or perhaps a different procedure altogether.

What if your team is relying on an experimental manipulation that has been tested and used previously by other experimenters? A tried-and-true manipulation might need less piloting than a procedure your team has created from scratch (e.g., you might not need to pretest the independent variable in isolation), but you might need to make minor adjustments in the manipulation in order for it to be maximally relevant to your participant pool. For example, consider Leon Festinger and James Carlsmith's (1959) classic cognitive dissonance experiment. In this study, participants were brought to the research lab and asked to complete a torturously boring set of tasks. They were asked to place 12 spools in a tray, then empty the tray, and then fill it again. After thirty minutes of this, they were asked to do another task: to turn 48 square pegs in a clockwise direction, over and over again. After their work was complete, the experimenter thanked them for their participation and described a dilemma he was facing: the second experimenter (who was supposed to describe the task to the next participant) hadn't shown up. Would the participant be willing to describe the tasks to the next person as "fun" and "exciting"?

This is when the experimental manipulation occurred: Half of the participants were told they would be given $1 for helping out, whereas the other half were told they would be given $20. All of the participants agreed to help the experimenter, regardless of condition. You probably know the results, which were counterintuitive at the time: Those who were paid $1 to describe the tasks as fun and exciting later reported liking the boring tasks much more than those who were paid $20, supporting Festinger and Carlsmith's theory of dissonance-reducing attitude change in the face of insufficient justification.

Imagine that you would like to replicate this dissonance manipulation today, more than 50 years after Festinger and Carlsmith completed their classic study. Should you use the same monetary values? Maybe, maybe not. In today's dollars, the $1 condition is now equivalent to approximately $7. However, if you can get all of your present-day participants to agree to describe the task as fun and exciting for only $1, this would be ideal; $1 is even less justification for such a "fib" as compared to 50 years ago. But to make the dissonance manipulation a success, you need to identify the smallest *effective* incentive in order to replicate the $1 condition. So realistically you might need to raise the stakes to $2 or $5 to ensure compliance. As for the $20 condition, this amount is equivalent to about $150 today. It is hard to imagine that offering only $20 would have the same effect as it did 50 years ago, but $150 seems excessive. What is a clear price point at which participants will say, "I just did it for the money"? Perhaps $50 or $80. Perhaps more. Careful trial and error through piloting would be needed to set the amount.

The Outcome Measures

Another critical use of piloting is to refine the study's outcome measures. Has your team designed a questionnaire from scratch? Have you modified an existing measure? Are you certain your pool of participants will respond to a widely utilized questionnaire in the manner you predict? In all of these cases, it would be helpful to have a small group of individuals run through the materials to test out how effective they are in isolation. The items on a questionnaire may make perfect sense to the members of your research team, but a naive participant might find the questions confusing. A common difficulty researchers encounter when creating questionnaires is the use of jargon. Terms that are familiar to psychologists (e.g., *self-efficacy, experimental trial, stimulus*) might be totally foreign to or interpreted differently by the average participant. Piloting a questionnaire by having a small number of participants read and attempt to respond to the items will allow you to catch issues such as these.

Sometimes your team may wish to use a subset of items from a questionnaire that is widely utilized by other researchers. After selecting the particular items you wish to include, you will want to pretest the instrument to confirm that participants still respond in a manner that is consistent with expected responses to the original, full version of the questionnaire. In some cases, pretesting might lead your team to conclude that an otherwise well-validated questionnaire is not appropriate after all. Perhaps the questionnaire is limited in its utility because of the characteristics of the sample you plan to use, or perhaps the questionnaire takes much longer for participants to complete than you had anticipated. Finding out this information early on will allow your team to make the necessary revisions before launching the study.

Identifying Logistical Problems

A pilot study also serves as a dress rehearsal for the official, full-scale "performance" of your team's experiment. Whether or not you pilot individual components of the research, it is always a good idea to do a full run-through of your study with a small number of participants before beginning data collection in earnest. The full run-through allows you and your teammates to practice the logistics of the study (see the discussion of training experimenters, below), determine how long the study takes, and get detailed feedback about the participants' experiences with the paradigm. It is not uncommon for a pilot of the full-scale study to reveal that the experiment takes much longer than the experimenters anticipated. It is also likely that participants will need more "hand-holding" during the experiment, in the form of additional instructions or guidance from the experimenter, than expected. Or you might find that participants respond to your team's study in a very different way than you anticipated, leading you to reconsider your choice of experimental manipulations or outcome measures.

What is the appropriate number of participants to include in a pilot of the full study? There is no definitive answer to this question, and the number often depends on practical concerns. How many volunteers are you and your teammates able to enlist for the pilot? How much time do you have before official data collection must begin? We would recommend, as a simple rule, that you pilot using a number of participants equal to about

10% of your planned total sample size, especially for smaller studies. Moreover, we recommend having at least two or three pilot participants per experimental condition. For example, if your team's experiment has two conditions, and you are planning to run 60 participants, it would make sense to have about three pilot participants in each of the two conditions. Ideally, pilot participants should be similar to participants who will be completing the full-scale study, so, generally, you should avoid using friends and family members as pilot participants unless you and your research adviser consciously decide that a *convenience sample* such as this is acceptable.

What might piloting tell you? At the extreme, identifying too many logistical problems might suggest that it is not feasible to conduct the full-scale study "as is." Your team might need to make substantial changes in your experimental situation or measures in order to increase the chances that the study is a success. For instance, you might find that the initial design is so tedious or time-consuming that participants fail to complete the study in its entirety or simply "zone out" and complete measures toward the end of the study unreliably. Similarly, if you are hoping to recruit a special population of participants (e.g., people from a particular demographic group), you might learn during piloting that the recruitment process is far too slow to allow you to complete your project in a timely matter. In this case, you might need to tailor your team's research to a wider range of participants to ensure the feasibility of the study. These are but a few of the logistical problems that can be identified through piloting.

Training Experimenters

Even the strongest set of manipulations and measures can be undermined by experimenter error. Here is a snapshot from the laboratory of Linda Bartoshuk, a professor in the Department of Community Dentistry and Behavioral Sciences at the University of Florida. Data collection in a study of taste perception had just begun:

> After just a glance at her graduate student's notes, Linda Bartoshuk knows that the results of today's experiment will have to be thrown out. The concentration of quinine, a bitter chemical used in this study of taste perception, is one-tenth of what it should be. The student, Adilia Blandon, suddenly realizes her mistake. Blandon had given the quinine to a team of undergraduate assistants to gauge volunteers' sensitivity to different flavors, but with the wrong standard for bitterness, she can't compare these data with previous results. Blandon turns to Bartoshuk with a cringe and groan. Behind her, the doomed experiment continues. Moments like these test a busy scientist's patience. But without missing a beat, Bartoshuk nods and says, "Don't worry. This is why we call it a pilot study. Now is the time to catch mistakes." (Bohannon, 2010)

It never feels good to mess up, but making mistakes in the context of a pilot study feels a great deal better than making mistakes in the context of your full-scale experiment. As much as we would like to believe that our performance as experimenters will be perfect, perfection is an exception rather than the rule. Moreover, as Bartoshuk notes, mistakes go hand in hand with good science because good science requires researchers to take risks, try something new, and occasionally employ methods that are somewhat complex or otherwise challenging to pull off (Bohannon, 2010).

Although the novelty and complexity of an experimental procedure increase the likelihood of mistakes, even a simple experiment can be doomed if not piloted appropriately. With some chagrin, we would like to share an example from our own research laboratory. The study was the final of three experiments designed to test methods for enhancing the likelihood that participants would carry out a health behavior. It was by far the simplest of the three studies, and it was carried out entirely online. In addition, it was almost identical to the first experiment, making the design of the study quite straightforward. Both studies involved contacting participants twice, one week apart. The only element that varied from Experiment 1 to Experiment 3 was a minor change in the content of the intervention given in the first week (that is, the independent variable).

Perhaps because of overconfidence, knowing we had used the same basic procedure with success in the past, or perhaps because of time pressure, we did not pilot Experiment 3. We launched the study, collected data from more than a hundred participants, and analyzed the data. We found significant results. We rejoiced! A number of months later, as we were writing up the paper, we discovered something shocking: All of the participants in Experiment 3 had been assigned to the exact same experimental condition. The independent variable had not varied at all! Although the chance of a type I error, or "false positive," such as this is small, statistical significance at the $p < .05$ level means that 5% of the time you will discover a spurious significant effect when there truly is no difference. This certainly happened in our case because, after all, every single participant had been exposed to the exact same experimental manipulation.

Fortunately, we discovered our error before we had submitted our paper for publication. But wouldn't it have been better to discover this error during pilot testing? If we had done a full run-through of the experiment, we would have scrutinized the study's manipulation check, and during debriefing we would have learned directly from our pilot participants that they all experienced the same experimental manipulation. This would have been a simple error to catch during piloting. The computer algorithm used to assign participants to the study's two conditions wasn't set up properly. But we were overconfident and wanted to launch the study as quickly as possible. There's nothing like wasting the time of more than a hundred participants and more than $500 in compensation fees to teach you an important lesson: Never underestimate the value of piloting.

The value of piloting stems from the pitfalls inherent in transitioning from the "big idea" and initial design of the study to the realities of conducting the study itself. The work of theorizing, hypothesizing, and proposing an experimental design is rooted in the overarching, abstract purpose of the study. By contrast, implementing the study and tweaking the experimental design are hands-on activities. Piloting plays a pivotal role in reconnecting researchers to the concrete methods of their studies. Without this crucial step, it is all too easy to overlook problems with a study. This is, as we have said, a problem of inattentional blindness. By training all team members in as many elements of the experimental process as possible, your team becomes refocused on the details of the study. These details are crucial, and they are where errors often occur. Of course, the process of piloting contributes to making you and your teammates more experienced researchers, but most important, it ensures that the "ideal" of the study is supported by careful attention to the realities of the study.

CONDUCTING A CAREFUL PILOT STUDY

We have described the rationale for piloting an experiment, and now we focus on the practicalities of piloting. Working with a research team is invaluable when it comes to piloting a study. We strongly suggest that before you officially recruit pilot participants, you and your teammates pilot the study with one another. Take turns being the participant and the experimenter. Try to approach the study from a new perspective; imagine what it would be like if you were experiencing the manipulation and measures for the very first time. Be on the lookout for errors, both large and small, and try to set up safeguards that will help you avoid such errors in the future.

Another way to capitalize on the strengths of the team is to create various "subspecialties" for each team member to focus on. First, there are the logistics of data collection. Recruiting pilot participants, setting up the laboratory or survey, and practicing the paradigm are elements of piloting in which all team members can and should be involved. We have found, however, that it is extraordinarily helpful for *one* person to be given explicit responsibility for organizing and overseeing these logistics. This minimizes the likelihood that something will be forgotten or overlooked. This *piloting coordinator* also should keep track of when participants are scheduled (as well as what types of individuals are recruited for piloting) to minimize any conflicts or other problems.

As we discussed earlier, piloting is crucial for helping you gain a better understanding of the effectiveness of your manipulations and measures. A second team member should be in charge of this evaluative component of piloting. Again, all team members will want to be involved in *doing* the piloting and assessing how well the experiment is working, but consolidating this information in one place is essential. This *piloting evaluator* should create a system for gathering and summarizing all of the specific feedback collected from participants (as well as the experimenters) during the piloting process. In addition, this person should be the one to halt the piloting process if something serious is going awry.

Whereas the coordination and evaluation roles require attention to specific details of the study, a third role requires a much broader focus. The *piloting storyteller* should be in charge of the overarching flow of the procedure, stepping back and asking general questions, such as, "Are the timing and progression of the study's components right?" and "Overall, is the paradigm testing what we think it is?" It is often helpful for this person to play devil's advocate. This is the last time to make significant changes in the design, so it is important to ask not only "What are we doing well?" but also "What else can we be doing, and should anything significant be changed?" Once your team formally launches the study, which we will discuss in the next chapter, it is crucial for all team members to work in lockstep with one another. But the piloting phase affords just enough flexibility to the team for one individual to ask tough questions.

Location

Whether you decide to have your final study take place in the lab, online, or over the phone, pilot studies are ideally conducted face-to-face. (You can do smaller, additional piloting online or over the phone to ensure that the particular venue of data collection is problem-free.) The idea here is to have a quiet place where you can give participants part (or all) of your materials and then carry out a structured discussion with them about their experiences. The location of the pilot study will depend on what resources are available to you. Some students will have access to a mentor's research laboratory for piloting. Others will use empty classrooms, study rooms, the library, or a (quiet) common area or campus lounge. Having minimal distractions is important, because you would like to maximize the amount of attention your pilot participants pay to the materials. The greater their attention, the more valuable their feedback is likely to be.

Compensation

Compensation for pilot participants also depends on available resources. Often individuals will volunteer to help out a friend of a friend by participating in a pilot study, in which case you may not have to pay them anything. However, the downside of recruiting people you know to pilot your study is that they may not respond in exactly the same ways as individuals who don't know you at all. A method that works well on college campuses is to offer an inexpensive candy bar in exchange for participation. In our experience, college students agree to participate at a much higher rate when offered a 50-cent candy bar than when offered $1 or $2 in cash, probably because the candy bar is an immediately useful "social" thank-you (much better than the meager economic payment of a dollar or two). However, some pilot studies are time-intensive for participants because of the additional debriefing, and you might be recruiting from a non–college student population. In these cases, your team will need to offer an effective incentive, perhaps paying pilot participants even more than you plan to offer participants in the full-scale study.

The Script and the Extended Debriefing

Creating a detailed script for the pilot session is essential. Your team wants to be sure that each participant is asked the same questions, and that each experimenter knows what to ask. The key features of the piloting process include obtaining informed consent (yes, this should be done in the context of piloting as well as in the context of running a full experiment), delivering a brief but clear set of instructions, and describing what needs to be done once the participant finishes the questionnaires or other tasks. After delivering the initial instructions, you wait patiently and unobtrusively while the participant completes these tasks. Then, when he or she is done, you carry out the single most important part of the pilot study, the extended debriefing.

The extended debriefing is your team's opportunity to learn what it was like to take part in the experiment from the participant's point of view. Whether you are pretesting a subset of the final study or running the whole shebang, your team will want to develop a number of questions to assess how well the manipulations, measures, and procedure are working. The extended debriefing can be thought of as an hourglass shape, where you start with open questions, narrow your focus, and then broaden again. We conceptualize the extended debriefing as a process of bringing the participants from a place of naïveté to a place of information and then to collaboration. The process should treat participants as informants who have unique insights into how well your study is functioning.

The first line of questioning should allow the participant to speculate about what the study was investigating, describe any times during the experiment when he or she felt confused, pinpoint particular items on the questionnaires that could be worded differently or better, and share general comments about the experience. You should avoid leading the participant to any conclusions during this process. Instead, you need to allow the participant to try to put things together for him- or herself. For instance, when you first ask the participant to speculate about the purpose of the study, keep the question as open as possible and avoid using language that might hint at your study's hypotheses. Be patient as the participant considers these open-ended questions. Then, as you narrow your questioning, focus on specific aspects of the participant's experience. In many cases it is helpful to hand the participant a fresh set of study materials or a list of the dependent measures and ask, "Was there anything in today's survey that you found puzzling or difficult? If so, how could this be improved? Were any of the instructions confusing or unclear? If so, how could these be changed?"

After you have touched on a number of specific issues, it is time to provide the participant with a vision of what the study is about. Initially, this part of the extended debriefing should feel most similar to a standard debriefing. That is, you will carefully explain the background, theory, and hypotheses of the experiment. However, as you describe the purpose and predictions of the research, you should treat the participant as a collaborator. This is critical in setting the stage for what comes next. The final part of the extended debriefing is designed to convey a shared sense of ownership of the experiment with the pilot participant. Get the participant's opinions about problems with the study and potential improvements now that he or she knows exactly what you are hypothesizing. For example, you can ask, "When we conduct this study with a larger number of people, do you think we'll find what we're predicting? Why or why not?" and "Can you think of any problems with or changes you would make to this study that would make it a better test of our predictions?"

Finally, thank the participant for his or her time and for making a contribution to the research project, and give the participant the opportunity to leave contact information with you so you can later inform him or her of the results of the experiment. A sample script for a pilot study, which includes an extended debriefing, is provided in Table 7.2.

USING PILOTING FEEDBACK

Once you get feedback from your participants, it's time to regroup as a team and decide what (if anything) to change. Let us stop and emphasize the "if anything" in the preceding sentence even though it appears in parentheses. Remember, two of the three goals

TABLE 7.2   *Sample Piloting Script With Extended Debriefing*

Hi, _____. Thanks for coming in to help us with our research. Please have a seat. You'll notice that I'm reading off of a script today; this is so that all participants' experiences are the same. Today you'll be completing a survey and then answering a few more questions. Do you have any questions before we begin? (*Wait for questions.*) Okay, great! Please begin by filling out the survey on this computer. When you have finished, the computer will prompt you to come out and get me so we can start the next part of the study.

Stand up and check the computer for the welcome screen. Exit the room and close the door behind you. Sit in the main room of the lab and quietly wait for the participant to come get you. Get the debriefing questions ready.

Extended Debriefing Questions:

- Thank you for filling out the survey. I now have a couple of questions for us to go over together. Do you have any questions for me before we start?
- First, we would like to get an overall sense of what you thought of the study. Do you have any general comments for us?
- What was your initial reaction when you were given instructions to bring samples of dental floss home with you after the study? How did you feel?
- Was there anything confusing or misleading about the computer survey? (*Hand the participant the printout version.*) Please take a moment to go through the survey and point out any typos or confusing sections.
- What do you think the study is about?

Extended Debriefing Study Description:

Thank you again for participating! Please do not discuss any information about this study with others who have not yet participated in the study. Doing so could influence their responses and cause their data to be unreliable.

In this study, we are looking at how to best persuade people to improve their flossing behavior. We are examining two different frames: one that emphasizes the potential harm that could come from not flossing (loss frame), and another that emphasizes the potential benefits that could come from flossing (gain frame). This study examines how message framing influences attitudes, intentions, and behaviors regarding flossing.

Previous research has identified a difference in the effectiveness of these frames in promoting oral health behaviors (Sherman, Updegraff, & Mann, 2008), but there is not a clear understanding about what might influence a particular frame's effectiveness. We believe the reason has to do with underlying thought processes. The underlying thought process (or mind-set) of an individual has been studied by Fujita and colleagues (2006), who found that individuals interpret events in one of two ways: (1) abstractly, in which the individual focuses on the global and far-reaching implications of an event (i.e., the big picture), or (2) concretely, in which the individual focuses on the local and specific details of an event (i.e., the specific steps involved).

To investigate this claim, we asked you to think either about HOW you floss or WHY you floss. This task is meant to encourage either a concrete or an abstract mind-set, respectively. We hypothesize that participants in an abstract mind-set will be more receptive to gain frames, whereas participants in a concrete mind-set will be more receptive to loss frames.

(Continued)

TABLE 7.2 (Continued)

Final Questions:

- When we conduct this study with a larger number of people, do you think we will find what we're predicting? Why or why not?
- Can you think of any issues or changes we could make to the study that would make it a better test of our predictions?

Please remember that your individual data will never be released or reported. All data are anonymous and analyzed in groups. We hope that you feel your participation in this study has been worthwhile. If you have any further questions, please feel free to direct them to our research adviser, Dr. Jerusha Detweiler-Bedell. Thank you!

of piloting that we have highlighted concern practicing the flow of the whole study and having an opportunity for the researchers to be trained in the procedure. These important goals do not entail making any changes to the study. Indeed, you should make changes in your dependent or independent variables with great caution and only if similar concerns are repeated across participants. In addition, not all concerns should necessarily lead you to make changes. For example, a pilot participant may complain that the mood induction video she watched was too short. (She wanted to see more!) If your piloting demonstrates that this short video induced a strong mood across your pilot participants, there is no reason to extend the viewing time.

Although your team should make significant changes to the study only if you see a worrisome pattern of reactions across a significant number of pilot participants, there are exceptions to the multiple-participant rule. Take, for example, the experience Dan Ariely describes in his book *The Upside of Irrationality* (2010, pp. 21–33). The study he designed with his collaborators aimed to test the impact of financial incentives on performance. This experiment was conducted in India, and (because of the favorable exchange rate between rupees and dollars) the "bonus" given to participants who performed well on the experimental task was—depending on experimental condition—the equivalent of one day's pay, two weeks' pay, or five months' pay. The initial design called for giving the participants the money to "hold" while they completed the experimental tasks. The first pilot participant who was assigned to the five months' pay condition was unable to carry out any of the tasks with success because he was practically paralyzed by the stack of cash sitting before him. As for the second pilot participant in this condition, "the poor fellow was so nervous that he shook the whole time and couldn't concentrate" (p. 33). At the end of the experiment, this participant grabbed the money (despite having earned none of it) and fled. Two pilot participants were enough. At this point the researchers changed their design and instead gave the participants the money at the end of the procedure and only if they "earned" the bonus. (What, by the way, did this study find? Contrary to the notion that bonuses serve as effective motivators of performance, those who had a bonus equal to five months' pay weighing on their minds performed the worst, *not* the best.)

LEARNING FROM EXPERIENCE

To a certain extent, it is difficult to imagine what it feels like to carry out a pilot study until you are in the midst of doing it. However, most researchers feel a mix of excitement, nervousness, and anticipation. Getting the pilot ready to go is tremendously time-intensive, and the team will feel invested in having it go well. In our first year as professors, one of the research teams in our lab had worked for a number of months designing a study to test the effect of mood on cognitive dissonance. This study was to take place in our research laboratory, which at the time meant the participants would be tested in a very small room in the middle of a long hallway. The research team of three was excited. Finally it was time to see what the participant's experience would be like. The team prepared the lab room and waited for the participant to arrive. Shortly thereafter, we (the research advisers) walked down the hall to check on how the piloting was going. What we saw stopped us in our tracks: All three researchers were crammed into the tiny testing room, hovering over the participant and eagerly watching her as she filled out the questionnaire. We intervened at once, recognizing with some amusement that although we taught our students many things about piloting, we had failed to emphasize that you should give pilot participants the same sort of privacy while they are completing the study that other participants will have when the actual study is conducted. This was an example of togetherness taken too far!

Indeed, the piloting period is a time when the development of togetherness is emphasized. Most researchers feel that the piloting process elicits feelings of nervousness and vulnerability. (See Table 7.3 for some of our own students' accounts of their first experiences with piloting.) You will not be alone if you are experiencing these feelings, but rather than being paralyzed by negative emotions, you and your teammates should capitalize on them and use them to create a constructive atmosphere. Channel your team's energy back to the vision for the project. It is easy to lose sight of the vision during the transition from the idea phase to piloting, so one member of the team may need to be tasked with reminding the team continually of the bigger picture. Pilot studies help ensure that your team is doing what you think it should be doing, and the final synthesis of the study's design (that is, when piloting is over and adjustments or improvements have been made) will renew the team's sense of ownership. With this progress comes a deeper commitment to the project.

Conclusion

In a chapter titled "Research in Social Psychology as a Leap of Faith," Elliot Aronson (2004) describes two ways to do science. Some individuals take months or even years to design their studies; they aim for perfection the first time around, and, as a result, they start and stop their research, fine-tuning the details until—at last—they are satisfied that they have an ideal final product. Other researchers (and Aronson puts himself in this camp) quickly take a plunge, designing and conducting daring investigations that are far from perfect,

TABLE 7.3   First-Person Accounts of Piloting

It was both an exciting and nerve-wracking experience. I knew what I was supposed to say, but I was worried that I would forget it when the time came. I showed up in the lab about an hour early, even though it took less than 20 minutes to prepare. I double- and triple-checked to make sure each of the materials was in place, ran through the process over and over in my head, and finally sat down and waited. My participant was five minutes late, and it felt like an eternity. When she finally arrived, and I started off by saying, "Hi, thanks for coming in today. I'm Rachel," everything got easier. Although it was never actually a question in my mind, it became clear that the participant wasn't going to judge me—she had no idea if I was saying the right lines or not, and she was probably nervous too! Once I realized that I was in control and the participants were just listening to me, I calmed down and everything went smoothly.

—Rachel Ludovise, Class of 2011

I had very little practice with the script and realized quickly the difference between reading it over a few times in my head and actually running a person through it. The first time was very awkward, and I felt hopelessly unprepared. During any interaction with a participant you want to radiate professionalism while also cultivating a comfortable environment through body language, tone, and demeanor. Without practice, confidence in yourself, and familiarity with the material, this is a ridiculous proposition. One important part of practicing is identifying areas you need to memorize as well as places you want to look up or pause. Working on your own and then again with your lab group is an effective method, and the more you can standardize the process with the other experimenters the better. Posture is also something I struggle with; it not only conveys professionalism, but also acts as a reminder of your role. Again I cannot emphasize practice enough—ideally you can work with a group who is willing to make little nitpicky comments and adjustments. It can be easy not to take piloting seriously, but the purpose of the task is to test your experiment. You want to see if what you have designed will be effective at measuring what you want it to.

—Richie LeDonne, Class of 2011

I was terrified! I felt a lot of pressure not to mess up because I didn't want to ruin everything for our study and let down my faculty advisers. As a result of this I was super nervous and acted more awkward than I should have . . . . I probably stumbled over a few words, but I didn't make any real errors. The fact that I didn't trust myself was really the biggest issue, and if I had just mellowed out and not gotten so worked up about it, I wouldn't have had any problems. This experience taught me to breathe while reading my script and to trust myself!

—Kelsey Domann, Class of 2011

For me the biggest part of piloting, at least for in-lab studies, is getting to the point where you are in the role of the experimenter. Early on, I was a little afraid of the participant: Were they going to be a good participant? Would they ask a lot of questions? Would they analyze any tiny mistake I made? After the pilot I thought to myself that much like humans who are terrified of spiders, the case is that spiders are usually much more frightened of us than we are of them.

—Dmitri Ian Alvarado, Class of 2012

but are fun and stimulating. Scientists in this latter camp rely on the reactions and feedback provided by colleagues in the field who see the results of this research presented at conferences or written up in manuscripts submitted for publication. These colleagues help the daring investigator identify and correct imperfections in the work. "Since I believe that science is a self-correcting enterprise," argues Aronson, "I prefer to be provocative than right" (p. 6).

But wait a minute! Doesn't Aronson's statement fly in the face of what this chapter has been all about, namely, the careful testing, in advance, of the measures and procedures of your study? Not at all. The daring researcher may design a study relatively quickly, but he or she relies on careful pilot testing to avoid being sloppy. As Aronson says, piloting a study is the process of "seeing where you went wrong, recasting it, and then running it as best as you can at the moment" (p. 5). So whether you fall into the camp of the slow and cautious (most common if you are working with a professor on a line of research that has been under way for years) or the quick and daring (most common if you are working on a project for class), please remember: Piloting is essential.

References

Ariely, D. (2010). *The upside of irrationality*. New York: HarperCollins.

Aronson, E. (2004). Research in social psychology as a leap of faith. In E. Aronson (Ed.), *Readings about the social animal* (9th ed., pp. 3–9). New York: Worth.

Bohannon, J. (2010). A taste for controversy. *Science Magazine, 328,* 1471–1473. doi:10.1126/science.328.5985.1471

Festinger, L., & Carlsmith, J. M. (1959). Cognitive consequences of forced compliance. *Journal of Abnormal and Social Psychology, 58,* 203–210.

Fujita, K., Trope, Y., Liberman, N., & Levin-Sagi, M. (2006). Construal levels and self-control. *Journal of Personality and Social Psychology, 90,* 351–367.

Ross, L., & Nisbett, R. E. (1991). *The person and the situation: Perspectives of social psychology*. New York: McGraw-Hill.

Sherman, D. K., Updegraff, J. A., & Mann, T. (2008). Improving oral health behavior: A social psychological approach. *Journal of the American Dental Association, 139,* 1382–1387.

Simons, D. J., & Chabris, C. F. (1999). Gorillas in our midst: Sustained inattentional blindness for dynamic events. *Perception, 28,* 1059–1074.

Simons, D. J., & Levin, D. T. (1998). Failure to detect changes to people during real-world interaction. *Psychonomic Bulletin and Review, 5,* 644–649.

Simons, D. J., & Rensink, R. A. (2005). Change blindness: Past, present, and future. *Trends in Cognitive Science, 9,* 16–20.

Teijlingen, E. R., & Hundley, V. (2001, Winter). The importance of piloting. *University of Surrey Social Research Update, 35.* Retrieved from http://sru.soc.surrey.ac.uk/SRU35.html

CHAPTER 8

Conducting a Study

> **Seven Lessons (Plus or Minus Two)**
>
> 1. Successfully conducting an experiment requires constant vigilance. Even subtle cues can have dramatic (and unexpected) effects on participant behavior.
>
> 2. Your team's goal during data collection is to ensure that the only systematic difference between your experimental conditions is the experimental manipulation.
>
> 3. Organization is the first line of defense against threats to the integrity of your team's experiment. Arrange all materials in advance, stick closely to a script, and keep the methodology consistent throughout data collection.
>
> 4. Even when your team is fully prepared, the unexpected will occur: Delays, no-shows, errors, and other snafus are realities of experimentation.
>
> 5. Don't hesitate to admit moments of confusion, distraction, or error. It is crucial to catch, document, and remedy issues (large and small) as soon as possible.
>
> 6. All forms of data collection have their strengths and weaknesses. Be aware of and attempt to remedy any challenges associated with your team's design choices.
>
> 7. Maintain a regular meeting time with your team during data collection in order to share experiences and reflect on the larger meaning of what you are accomplishing.

Human behavior is incredibly pliable, plastic.

—Philip Zimbardo (2003)

The time has come. Data collection has begun. Your study is in full swing. But a day or two into the study, one of your teammates reports that his participants have been rushing through the questionnaire. Another teammate reports that her participants keep interrupting her before she is done explaining what to do next. Interestingly, you haven't noticed either of these problems with your own participants. Assuming that your teammates are accurate in their self-reflections, should you be worried about their participants' behaviors? If you were a student of New York University professor of psychology John Bargh, you would most certainly answer *yes* to this question. Something in the experimental situation, perhaps something that differs between you and your teammates as you run the study, might be causing participants to behave in these ways.

Research conducted by Bargh, Chen, and Burrows (1996) suggests that even the most subtle cues, called primes, can trigger meaningful changes in people's behavior. In a now-famous series of studies, these researchers demonstrated that a simple task of unscrambling words to form sentences had a noticeable impact on participants' actions. In one study, participants were given a 30-item survey. Each item included five words in no particular order, and the participants were asked to write a sentence using four out of the five words. The control condition included words such as *thirsty* and *private*. In comparison, the experimental condition included words such as *ancient, Florida, lonely,* and *bingo.* In case you haven't guessed already, the experimental condition was designed to prime a stereotype of the elderly. The control condition contained relatively neutral words not associated with any particular stereotypes.

After completing the survey, each participant was told that the experiment was over. But it wasn't over just yet. Hidden from view, a confederate started a stopwatch the moment the participant exited the laboratory. The confederate stopped the watch when the participant reached the end of the long hall leading away from the lab. This was the study's primary dependent measure, and it was at this point that the experimenter caught up with the participant and fully debriefed him or her. What, exactly, was being studied? Bargh and his colleagues hypothesized that exposure to words associated with stereotypes of being old would have a direct impact on participants' stroll down the hall. And that is exactly what they found. Participants in the experimental condition took longer to walk the length of the hall compared to participants in the control condition.

What range of behaviors can be influenced by such subtle primes? In another study, participants were exposed to a similar sentence-generation task, but this time the first experimental condition included words such as *rude, bother, obnoxious,* and *intrude.* A second experimental condition included words such as *polite, respect, courteous,* and *behaved.* The control condition included neutral words. After completing the sentence-generation task, the participant needed to walk down a short hallway to another lab room, where the experimenter was waiting. But when the participant arrived at the other room, he or she found that the experimenter was engaged in a conversation, apparently describing the procedure of a different study to a very confused participant (who was actually a confederate of the experimenter).

How long would the true participant patiently wait for the experimenter to finish this conversation? A surprisingly large percentage of participants (regardless of experimental condition) never interrupted the conversation, which was scripted to last 10 minutes. Yet the priming of rude versus polite behaviors significantly influenced participants' willingness to interrupt. Less than 20% of participants in the polite condition interrupted, about 40% of those in the neutral control condition interrupted, and more than 60% of those in the rude condition interrupted (Bargh et al., 1996). If a simple sentence-generation task can influence everything from walking speed to social grace, we have to assume that every small detail in the experimental environment matters and might be a potential source of influence.

Let's return to the scenario that opened this chapter. Is it possible that subtle aspects of the experimental situation could *unintentionally* prime participants to hurry through the study or interrupt the experimenter's instructions? Absolutely! Perhaps the teammate whose participants have been rushing through the study has been administering the questionnaire in the library, near a large clock that ticks loudly as the second hand moves. This could easily prime a sense of time pressure. And your other teammate? To her chagrin, she might recall that a book she is reading for her sociology class, *Incivility: The Rude Stranger in Everyday Life,* has been sitting in plain sight of each of her participants.

AVOIDING THREATS TO INTERNAL VALIDITY

The subtle cues we just described were imagined, but details like ticking clocks and misplaced sociology texts are ubiquitous in any experimental situation. They are a real problem for two reasons. First, they can add considerable variability or *noise* to how participants experience and respond to your team's experiment. Extraneous factors such as these will make it much more difficult for you to detect any systematic effect of your study's experimental conditions. Second, and even more problematic, is the difficulty that arises when the small cues themselves differ between your experimental conditions. This introduces an unwanted *confounding variable* in how participants experience and respond to the experiment. That is, any difference between the experimental conditions might be a result of this confounding influence rather than the experimental manipulation. This represents a significant threat to the study's *internal validity*. Indeed, when your team is conducting the experiment, your overarching goal is to avoid threats to internal validity by decreasing the influence of extraneous variables on your participants. To the extent possible, the *only* systematic difference between your experimental conditions should be the experimental manipulation. If an extraneous variable such as a subtle environmental cue differs between experimental conditions, the results of your entire study are in jeopardy. In order to avoid such threats, you must collaborate closely with your teammates and rely on the guidance of your research mentor or instructor.

Be Organized

We have found that a researcher's first line of defense against threats to internal validity is to be meticulously organized. Having materials ready for the entire study well before running the first participant, sticking closely to a script, and keeping your methodology consistent throughout the data collection process all help to ensure a high level of consistency in how the experiment is conducted. Much of your initial organizational work will have taken place during pilot testing, but making sure that your team stays focused on the details throughout the course of data collection is essential. Remember, seemingly inconsequential details can have profound effects. By tightly organizing the experimental procedure, you can minimize the likelihood of something unexpected sneaking in.

Minimize Differences Among Experimenters

A common source of threats to internal validity in a lab-based experiment is the experimenter. The experimenter's expectations, clothing, tone of voice, and body language are just a few of the many factors that can influence participant responses. Carefully practicing the experimental procedure in advance of launching your team's study is one of the best protections against these concerns. Again, this is something that should be done during piloting; ideally, you and your teammates already will have given each other extensive feedback on how best to interact with participants. But, of course, human beings are not robots. Despite rigorous training, there will be some differences from one experimenter to the next. So long as these differences are modest, they should not present much of a problem. Some variability, or noise, is unavoidable.

Minimize Demand Characteristics

What you *can* avoid, and would like to avoid at all costs, is systematic variability that masquerades as or masks the effect of your team's experimental manipulation. How do you avoid this? First, a well-designed study either keeps experimenters from knowing each participant's assigned condition or, at minimum, puts safeguards in place to limit the influence that such knowledge has on the participant's response to the experimental manipulation. The most straightforward way of achieving this is to keep experimenters *blind* to the participants' assigned conditions. For example, in Bargh and colleagues' priming studies, the experimenter did not know which of the sentence-generation tasks the participant had just completed. The task was in a sealed envelope, presorted by other members of the research team, and not seen by the experimenter. The concern here is that if the experimenter is aware of the participant's assigned condition *and* knows the hypotheses of the study, subtle aspects of the experimenter's behavior might change. These changes tend to bias participants' responses to the experimental situation in a manner that favors the hypotheses of the study.

This type of influence is one source of *expectation effects* or *demand characteristics,* which are described by Orne (1962) as cues that arise in the experiment that suggest to the participant how he or she should act. In some cases, participants might deduce or even be told the hypothesis of the experiment during the consent procedure. This information can bias participants' responses, which is why many researchers avoid describing (or use cover stories to conceal) the predicted relationship between different parts of a study. Even so, experimenters might convey their expectations inadvertently (e.g., by making eye contact or spending more time with participants who are responding in a manner that supports the study's hypothesis). These subtle cues are problematic, as are all demand characteristics, because they can bias participants' responses in a number of ways. Weber and Cook (1972) identified four potential "roles" that a participant might take on: the good subject, the negativistic subject, the faithful subject, and the apprehensive subject (p. 274). The good subject aims to confirm your hypotheses (how helpful!), whereas the negativistic subject aims to rebel against you (how annoying!). The faithful subject is someone who wishes to "help science" by following the rules, either by taking on a passive role ("just tell me what to do") or by taking on an active role ("no matter how suspicious I am, I will *not* allow my responses to be biased"). Of course, either of these approaches leads to artificial responses by the participant. Finally, there is the apprehensive subject: a participant who is concerned that his or her behavior could be evaluated negatively. This role, too, can influence the participant's responses. Weber and Cook found that only the faithful subject role and, in particular, the apprehensive subject role are common. Indeed, many participants are anxious about how they will be evaluated by the experimenter, and you and your team should keep this mind as you design your study and interact with participants.

Of course, it can be difficult or impossible to keep experimenters blind to condition in some experimental situations. For instance, the experimenter might read aloud instructions that contain the manipulation, or a confederate's actions might serve as the manipulation. In these cases, following a precise script is an important safeguard that limits the unintentional influence the experimenter might have on participants. Likewise, it is generally a good idea to minimize contact between the experimenter and the participant.

Distribute Participants Across Experimenters

Beyond expectation effects, each experimenter's unique style or actions (e.g., running the experiment in a particular testing room, as in the example that opened this chapter) might have a distinct effect on participants. For this reason, it is important to distribute participants in a balanced manner across different experimenters. It is a good idea for each teammate to run about the same number of participants overall. Moreover, it is absolutely essential that each experimenter runs roughly an equal number of participants from each experimental condition. Otherwise, your experimental manipulation will be confounded with the person acting as the experimenter. Taking these precautions will distribute any "experimenter effects" roughly equally across conditions, and your statistical analyses might be able to identify and correct for these effects.

Control the Experimental Environment

More generally, another potential source of threat to internal validity is the experimental environment. In what is now a classic study in psychology, researchers Berkowitz and LePage (1967) investigated the impact of objects in the testing room on participant behavior. Imagine being invited to participate in their study, which was described as an investigation of the effects of stress on problem solving. When you arrive in the lab, you are introduced to another participant (actually a confederate) and told that each of you is responsible for generating a solution to a problem. You will be evaluating each other's solutions by assigning ratings from 1 (*best*) to 10 (*worst*). To raise the stakes, these ratings have a tangible meaning: They refer to the number of electric shocks you will have to endure! In other words, if your partner thinks highly of your solution, you will get only one shock, but if your partner thinks your solution is lousy, you could get as many as ten shocks. So with this threat hanging over your head, you complete your task and receive your partner's evaluation. You learn that your partner has decided that you should endure seven shocks for your (not so great) solution. (What you don't know is that this number of shocks was predetermined.) You now must determine how many shocks your partner deserves for his or her solution. One? Ten? Seven?

Here is where environmental demand comes into play. In one condition of the experiment, two badminton rackets are lying next to the shock generator. In another condition of the experiment, a rifle and a revolver are next to the generator. In both cases, you are told to disregard these objects because they were left in the room for another experiment. (Yes, this was much easier to pull off before "zero tolerance" for weapons became commonplace in educational settings.) So how many shocks will you give? Perhaps not surprisingly, participants gave significantly more shocks in the weapons condition than in the innocuous stimulus condition. More recent research on this topic has replicated this effect, demonstrating that simply looking at images of weapons elicits aggressive thoughts (Anderson, Benjamin, & Bartholow, 1998). In these examples, the researchers predicted that the presence of weapons would elicit aggressive responses, and it did. The point for our purposes, however, is that biases can enter an experimental paradigm unintentionally, easily interfering with the effect you are trying to investigate.

Some *random noise* will enter your study no matter what you do. Participants differ from one another in countless ways. The time of day or day of the week can influence participant behavior. Even the weather can add noise to your data. Then there's the effect of pure chance. Moment-to-moment differences in how participants attend to, interpret, and respond to the experimental situation are a fact of life. Human behavior emerges from an incredibly complex, dynamic system. As complexity theory suggests (Gleick, 1987), the smallest of factors can have a disproportionately large effect in any given situation. Unfortunately, the more noise in your data, the harder it is to see an effect of your experimental manipulation. Systematic noise or bias poses an especially large problem. For instance, if you accidentally run only men (or people falling within any other particular demographic) in one of your experimental conditions, you will not be able to tell if any effect you observe is caused by the experimental manipulation or by the *confounding variable*. So your team should make every effort to minimize random and systematic noise by carefully standardizing the way in which your experiment is conducted.

PRIMER ON RUNNING PARTICIPANTS

With all the concerns discussed above looming, launching a study can be anxiety producing. To reduce the stress you feel, we offer the following primer on running participants (the items addressed below are summarized in Table 8.1).

Prepare and Stick to a Script

When a study takes place in the lab, we like to think of the research team as embodying the roles of playwright, director, and actor. The first and most important task the team faces is to prepare a script for what should happen during the experiment. A script, complete with a list of "props" and detailed "stage directions," greatly minimizes the unintentional addition of noise to your study. The top of the script should include a checklist of the items that need to be set up prior to each participant's arrival and tasks that need to be completed after his or her departure (see Table 8.2 for an example). Explicit directions covering where the experimenter should stand, where the participant should sit,

TABLE 8.1 A Primer on Running Participants

- Prepare and stick to a script.
- Memorize your opening and closing.
- Be polite and professional.
- Appear confident and competent.
- Arrive early.
- Wear a "lab coat."
- Expect delays and no-shows.
- Expect the occasional snafu.
- Document, document, document.
- Reveal any deception with compassion.

TABLE 8.2 Sample Checklists for a Study on Dental Flossing Behavior

Checklist of materials needed:

- ☐ Clipboard
- ☐ Working pen
- ☐ Folder with cover letter form
- ☐ Informed consent form
- ☐ Correct experimental pamphlet
- ☐ Envelope of seven dental floss packets, correctly labeled
- ☐ Example dental floss packet, unlabeled
- ☐ Survey with participant ID number (loaded on computer)

Checklist for lab preparation:

- ☐ Before the participant arrives, gather the necessary materials, as listed above.
- ☐ Tidy up the lab. Place one chair at each computer.
- ☐ Set up surveys by going to www.surveymonkey.com.
- ☐ Make sure table is clear, and put away any loose items.
- ☐ Wait for the participant outside the main door to the laboratory.

Checklist of things to do after the participant leaves:

- ☐ Write down date of experiment and date of e-mail contact on folder and master list.
- ☐ Note anything unusual or possible mistakes on cover of folder.
- ☐ File folder in appropriate cubby.
- ☐ Close all Web browsers and turn off computer monitors.
- ☐ Leave lab coat on hanger for next experimenter to wear.
- ☐ Clean anything you left behind.

when movement should occur, and so forth, are what we consider to be "stage directions." Although it may seem absurd to map out the progression of the study at this level of detail, remember that the smallest of deviations can lead to striking inconsistencies in participant behavior.

Once piloting is complete and a final script has been prepared, it is time to practice the protocol yet again with your team members before launching the full-scale study. A team member who takes on the role of director should pay particular attention to the implementation of the script and ask questions aimed at refining the details. For example, does each experimenter carry out the procedure similarly? Do the experimenter's words sound natural? This second question is important because instructions created for a written survey often sound stilted when read aloud by an experimenter. For this reason, you and your teammates will want to practice reading the script to one another in order to make sure the instructions flow well. It is ideal to memorize most, if not all, of the script, but still keep the script in front of you throughout the experiment and let the participant know that the script is being used to keep the information identical for all participants. When in doubt, stick to the script. It is much better to err on the side of reading your lines than to "improvise."

Memorize Your Opening and Closing

It is especially important at the beginning of each experimental session to welcome the participant and maintain eye contact as you smoothly deliver a two- or three-sentence scripted summary of what's to come. This should be memorized. After that you can eyeball your script to keep the study's instructions as consistent as possible. Because obtaining informed consent is likely to come first, you may want to say something like: "The consent form tells you more about the experiment. Please read it carefully and sign it if you agree to participate. If you have any questions, please feel free to ask."

Likewise, although it is common to read the debriefing to participants, having a closing sentence or two committed to memory is ideal. Maintaining eye contact as you close the study will help the participant feel at ease, increasing the likelihood that he or she will leave the study feeling as if the time spent was worthwhile.

Be Polite and Professional

The experimenter should always be polite and professional. We carefully coach our researchers to adopt a calm, measured tone of voice, and we work to make simple things such as posture, positioning in the room, eye contact, and even use of hand gestures consistent across experimenters. Beyond this, you should try to treat participants in the same way you would want to be treated if the tables were turned and you were the participant instead. The role of a welcoming receptionist at a doctor's office provides a good model to follow. This kind of professional goes about his or her routine in a relatively neutral manner, but with a touch of warmth that promotes a sense of comfort. This is the same balance you want to strike. However, you want to avoid any small talk because unscripted, friendly conversations will naturally differ from participant to participant. This would add yet another source of noise to your data. For instance, do not talk about the weather, the day's news, or the upcoming weekend. If a participant tries to initiate any small talk, you should respond briefly but then move on.

As we discussed earlier, the experimenter should ideally be blind to the participant's experimental condition, but sometimes this is not feasible. Especially in these cases, but as a general rule, tone of voice, how quickly or slowly instructions are read, placing emphasis on certain words, and reinforcing participants with facial expressions can have real and significant impacts on your participants and your data. Be aware of your tone and pace throughout the experiment, not just at the beginning.

Appear Confident and Competent

This advice is easier said than done. It is perfectly natural for you and your team members to feel uneasy at the start of data collection. As a result, you may feel unsure of yourself. Nevertheless, you should try to emanate an air of confidence and competence. Otherwise, participants will pick up on your insecurity or confusion. Participants who begin to second-guess the experimenter are likely to take the study less seriously, and the data you collect will be negatively affected. To increase your sense of confidence, practice the protocol as much as possible. If you are well prepared and well rehearsed, and if you remind yourself that you know a great deal more than the participants do about the purpose and details of the study, you will be fine.

Arrive Early

Experimenters always should arrive at their sessions early enough to set up the necessary materials without feeling rushed (for a typical study, 10 minutes before the participant arrives works well). If you are a person who tends to run late, pretend that the study starts earlier than it actually does. Rushing to set up an experiment is likely to induce some degree of anxiety in you, and this emotion is readily conveyed to your participant. As we discussed earlier, the participant is likely to be apprehensive, so it is your goal to be as calm, prepared, and organized as possible. You can further convey a sense of calm by greeting the participant at the door, and this avoids the awkward conversation that comes from having a participant walk in while you are still in the midst of preparations. When you greet each participant, be sure to ask if he or she has come to take part in *your* experiment, because participants sometimes get confused, especially in settings where multiple experimenters are conducting studies at the same time.

Wear a "Lab Coat"

To minimize variability across experimenters, it is helpful if all members of your team wear something similar while conducting the study. The traditional white lab coat is one option, but in our own research lab, we have experimenters wear a simple, solid-blue T-shirt and a nice, clean pair of dark-colored pants or jeans. When we were graduate students, one of the professors required all of his experimenters to dress more formally—men in suits and ties, women in slacks and blouses. Although this may have worked at a large, East Coast Ivy League school, we simply cannot pull this off at our small, Pacific Northwest liberal arts college—overly formal dress would be an experimental manipulation in and of itself! The idea is to adopt a standard, innocuous dress code that fits in and goes relatively unnoticed in your particular environment. If you are conducting research over an extended period and as part of a professor's research lab, it is a great idea to keep "uniforms" in the lab.

Expect Delays and No-Shows

Participants are fallible, and many of them will forget about the experiment or arrive late. To minimize the likelihood of this happening, establish a three-part reminder process: (a) e-mail each participant a few days before his or her appointment to confirm the date and provide directions to the location of the study; (b) the night before the appointment, leave a voice mail reminder for the participant; and (c) the morning of the appointment, send another e-mail reminder, again providing directions to the location of the study. Each of these steps is absolutely critical. Whenever experimenters in our lab skip a step, the rate of no-shows spikes.

Still, it is impossible to avoid no-shows and late arrivals entirely. If your protocol allows it, give participants fifteen minutes beyond the scheduled start time to arrive. Document the names and contact information of participants who do not show up, so that you can make an attempt to reschedule them.

Expect the Occasional Snafu

No study is pulled off without a hitch, so you undoubtedly will encounter a problem at some point. Today, errors are often technical: A Web page fails to load properly, software crashes, or a video clip freezes partway through. In cases such as these, do the best you can in the time you have. Try not to convey your distress to the participant; keep a calm external demeanor in place as you try to remedy the problem. If this proves unsuccessful, let your participant know that the session will have to end prematurely and then jump right to the debriefing. Tell the participant what he or she would have experienced if all had gone well, explain your hypotheses, and compensate the participant (if applicable) as you would normally. In short, treat the participant as you would any other.

In some cases, however, the error is human. As Sternberg and Sternberg (2010) note, "Experimenters, like subjects, sometimes get distracted" (p. 97). Human error takes every shape and form, and if you are anything like us, you will never forget the mistakes you make. The very first laboratory study that one of us conducted as an undergraduate, which we discussed in our opening chapter, was designed to investigate the impact of cognitive load on eating behavior among restrained eaters (Ward & Mann, 2000). As you may recall, this study compared the eating behaviors of dieters (i.e., restrained eaters) and nondieters who were asked to do simple versus complex tasks. The hypothesis was that dieters in the simple task condition would eat very little of the tasty snack food made available to them during the experiment because they would have plenty of cognitive resources available to restrain their eating. In comparison, nondieters would eat more when they were doing the simple task because they weren't especially busy and the snacks looked delicious! The reverse would be true among participants who had to do a complex task. Dieters who had to juggle complex tasks would eat *more* food because their cognitive resources would be taxed, and they would rebound and violate the strict "rules" they typically followed. Nondieters would eat *less* in this condition because they were keeping too busy to eat. This was an interesting prediction that ultimately was supported by the data.

The job of the experimenter was to set up food for the participant and, in the complex task condition, to run a slide show in conjunction with a computer-generated program that made random beeping noises. Each participant in the complex condition was asked to memorize the slides and to push a button on the floor as fast as he or she could whenever the computer beeped. In other words, the participant was asked to multitask. One day, after setting everything in motion for a participant in the complex task condition, I (JDB) left the laboratory to take my assigned post outside the room. It was only after the experiment was over and I was conducting the debriefing that the participant asked, "So how did telling me the computer would beep when it actually didn't fit into what you guys were looking for?" I was momentarily confused, but then what she was saying registered. The computer never beeped for her because I had forgotten to activate that part of the computer program. In hindsight this may not seem so bad, but at the time I was mortified. After explaining my inadvertent error to the participant, I then trekked downstairs to my research mentor's office and told him about my mistake. He was very understanding. After all, these things happen. But as a consequence, we had to throw out the participant's data.

Document, Document, Document

Experimenter errors, technological glitches, unforeseen deviations from a study's protocol, and odd participant behavior during the experiment are to be expected from time to time. It is human nature to overlook or minimize such problems. But as scientists, you and your team must keep track of these events in a systematic way. We suggest that you write down any abnormalities, including your own embarrassing errors, on a participant "control sheet" or "participation log." Many researchers make use of control sheets or logs in which they record participant numbers along with experimenters' observations about unusual events, including questions asked by participants (if any), the answers provided, and any overarching concerns or difficulties they experience.

Any time you encounter a serious problem, your team and research adviser should discuss the situation and make a decision about what to do with that session's data *before* you look at the data or conduct any analyses. In such cases, it is unethical to preview a participant's responses before deciding whether or not to exclude him or her from the study. Why? Because you are more likely to retain data from participants whose responses confirm your predictions and remove participants whose data seems "wrong," which is the definition of bias. Of course, there may be times when a participant's responses themselves are problematic (e.g., a participant answers only half the study's questions). It is best to have decision rules in place for dealing with such instances before you look at your data. For example, it may be reasonable to set a rule that you will exclude participants who fail to answer at least two-thirds of the study's questions.

Reveal Any Deception With Compassion

When you begin the debriefing, you are in the home stretch. You no longer have to worry that something you say or do could bias the participant. However, you want to leave a good impression on the participant, so that he or she feels appreciated and leaves believing that psychological research in general and your project in particular are important. If the experiment includes deception, you need to take care not to embarrass the participant or make him or her feel duped. Instead, normalize the participant's responses to the study and explain that the study was deliberately designed to make all participants believe the cover story. Take your time in providing the debriefing, and allow the participant to ask questions after the fact. An essential part of debriefing is giving something back to the participant so that he or she leaves having had a worthwhile educational experience.

PARTICIPANT RECRUITMENT

Once you are organized, well practiced, and as ready as possible to handle the unexpected glitches that almost certainly will arise while you are conducting the study, it is time to bring participants into the lab. If only this were the easy part! The success of any study depends on the efficient recruitment of participants, and this should never be taken for granted. How do you track down the elusive participant and ensure that each shows up as scheduled? The answer to this question depends on the type of participants you plan to include in your study, your location, and the resources you have at your disposal.

Challenges Associated With Participant Recruitment

As much as your team might want to recruit participants from a particular population (e.g., Alzheimer's patients, fourth-grade children, elderly persons, couples who have just started dating), our first bit of advice about this would be to *think twice*. Unless your research absolutely requires you to recruit from a restricted population (which may be the case if you are working in a research adviser's lab), your first priority is to make sure your project is *doable*. We have seen too many research projects flounder or fail because recruiting from a special population proved to be too challenging or too slow. And everyone winces (students and faculty alike) when a study planned for 60 or 100 participants is cut off with only a handful of participants per condition because of a deadline or the ending of the academic year. Don't allow your team to get into this situation. If at all possible, design a study that allows you to recruit from the broadest, most readily available population suitable for your research question. In many cases, it is better to adapt your research question to a more convenient population of participants—especially for course projects, senior theses, and initial studies in a line of research—than to struggle to recruit participants of a certain type. If, however, your mentor's line of research requires a particular type of participant or you are otherwise determined to use a more restrictive subpopulation, be realistic in planning how long it will take to complete the study. You will need to get an early start in running participants and remain focused and persistent in your efforts throughout the study.

Your location and access to participant recruitment resources will have considerable influence on your success in recruiting and running participants efficiently. If you are a student at a small college in the tiny town of Nearnothington, you might discover that finding participants is among the most challenging tasks you will face. If, in contrast, you are a student at a research university in a major metropolitan area, you are likely to have access not only to a large number of potential participants but also to a "subject pool" composed of university students enrolled in classes such as Introduction to Psychology, who are required to participate in a certain number of experiments during the term.

Convenience Sampling

It is important to keep in mind that the criteria for participant selection for research studies that are part of a research mentor's line of research or have gone through the IRB process are likely to be much stricter than the criteria for participant selection for research conducted solely within the bounds of a class project. Class projects typically allow greater use of *convenience sampling,* which is the use of participants who are maximally accessible and maximally likely to volunteer their time.

Because random assignment should help to correct for any systematic differences among participants across experimental condition, recruiting fellow students to be study participants is not necessarily a problem. More problematic are the demand characteristics and other threats to internal validity associated with casual recruitment strategies (e.g., e-mails to friends, Facebook posts). When your participants know one or more members of the research team, they may be more inclined to try to "please" the researchers (recall the "good subject" discussed earlier). They also may have heard something about your team's study or your hypotheses. And if they complete the study in the research lab, you may have more difficulty interacting with them professionally during the experimental procedure than you would with participants you don't know. So although there is a time and place for gathering participants through word of mouth (or the technological equivalent), your team should be cautious in doing so. If you know a participant, have a team member who doesn't know him or her run that session in the laboratory. If you've talked about your study with certain friends, don't later ask those friends to complete the survey. If you feel there are clear demand characteristics associated with your experiment, try to limit your convenience sample to first-year students, who may be more naive to psychological research than older students. If your team keeps such safeguards in place, you can feel more comfortable taking advantage of these easy recruitment strategies.

Participant Compensation and Scheduling

Recruitment resources also include the types of enticements (i.e., compensation) you have access to. If your research is being conducted in collaboration with a mentor who has grant funding, paying each participant is likely to be an option. If, in contrast, you are working with your research team on a class project, you have to rely on money from your own pockets or on the kindness of strangers who are willing to volunteer without pay. Entering participants in a lottery is sometimes an excellent incentive. You and your teammates can decide how much money you are each willing to pitch in for the study. Even a single prize of $20 (in the form of cash or a gift card from a local bookstore, for example) can be a potent motivator, especially to a college student sample. On the other hand, compensating each participant with at least a token item or payment often works best. As we discussed in Chapter 7, we find that offering a small or full-size candy bar to college students (at a cost of 10–50 cents per person in bulk) is much more effective than small cash payments. Similarly, a $1 lottery scratch-off ticket tends to be more effective than the same amount in cash. There are many ways to be creative in coming up with incentives, but do not be afraid to ask for volunteers. Plenty of people are still willing to help out simply for the "sake of science."

Finally, your team will need to develop a system of scheduling and actually running participants once they are recruited. The reality of experimentation is that sometimes you'll be doing nothing, and sometimes you'll be doing nothing but running participants! Working with a team, you have the advantage of splitting up the process of data collection. Scheduling lab-based research is a tricky process. Many teams attempt to spread the commitment relatively evenly across experimenters, but we have found that a truly even distribution of participants across team members is rarely achieved. Why? We attribute it to that fickle creature *chance*. During the first few days that you are scheduled to collect data, you might find that four of the five participant slots are empty and the one person who has signed up doesn't show. Your teammate, on the other hand, might experience a flood of back-to-back participants. The next week your roles might reverse. Simply knowing this is possible and being flexible enough to balance the workload as you go along is the best course of action. Just as important, and because recruiting takes work, you want to get started early and never let up. It bears repeating that far too many studies stall or drag on because participants were not recruited consistently or scheduled efficiently. Be tenacious!

STUDIES CONDUCTED "IN THE FIELD" OR ONLINE

Much of our discussion so far has focused on advice for conducting studies in the lab. But what if you conduct a study entirely online or in a more naturalistic environment? Whenever you complete a study with participants outside the lab, you will need to take into consideration the challenges associated with *field research*. Researchers conduct field studies to observe behaviors in more real-life, *ecologically valid* settings, such as medical clinics, elementary schools, retirement homes, and supermarkets. Although investigations of most psychological phenomena can be adapted to lab research, some types of research require or lend themselves to field studies. We once conducted a field experiment comparing the effectiveness of two different persuasive messages in promoting sunscreen use (Detweiler, Bedell, Salovey, Pronin, & Rothman, 1999). Naturally, we ran the study in midsummer at the beach! A beachgoer's decision to use sunscreen is a highly relevant, immediate health issue, and this setting contributed to the study's credibility.

Likewise, in a classic study of the impact of physiological arousal on romantic feelings, Dutton and Aron (1974) utilized an attractive female experimenter who surveyed men as they walked across a "five-foot-wide, 450-foot-long, bridge constructed of wooden boards attached to wire cables . . . [that had] a tendency to tilt, sway, and wobble, creating the impression that one is about to fall over the side [of the] very low handrails of wire cable . . . and [experience] a 230-foot drop to rocks and shallow rapids below the bridge" (p. 511). Did the men feel a heightened sense of attraction to the experimenter after crossing this bridge compared to a much less dramatic bridge? Yes, they did! What a compelling way to test this idea. Of course, not all field environments are as exotic as the beach or a harrowing suspension bridge. If you are looking to include a sample consisting of young children or the elderly, you might arrange to conduct a study at a local preschool or retirement home, respectively.

Challenges Associated With Field Studies

Although field studies, in comparison with lab studies, take place in more realistic settings, this typically comes at a cost. The world outside the lab is filled with countless extraneous influences. For instance, participants in our sunscreen study came to the beach with their family or friends, stayed at the beach different lengths of time, might or might not have gone swimming, and potentially observed or interacted with participants in the other experimental condition. In other words, our participants completed the study in a relatively uncontrolled environment. In the study of physiological arousal and emotional attraction, it was possible that men who were willing to walk across the scary bridge in the first place (i.e., risk takers) were more likely than men walking across the "boring" bridge to call the female experimenter later on. (This was Dutton and Aron's key dependent variable, by the way.) In both of these examples, participants' responses to the experimental situations were subject to countless extraneous influences, resulting in noisier data and the potential for alternative explanations for any observed effects between experimental conditions. This reflects the frequent trade-off between *external* validity and *internal* validity: A rich, real-life environment often gives the impression that a phenomenon is robust and likely to extend to other important settings (i.e., increased external validity), but it also tends to expose a study to significant concerns about potential confounds (i.e., decreased internal validity).

If you plan to conduct a field study, how can you guard against potential confounds and minimize the introduction of noise into your data? One answer is that you cannot guard against these problems completely. Field studies are inherently messy. Instead, your best bet is to include field studies alongside well-controlled lab studies in any line of research. If you are able to replicate a finding in both an artificial, well-controlled lab setting and a more realistic, albeit noisier field setting, the persuasiveness of both types of studies is increased. The likely external validity of the lab study is extended by the field replication, and the internal validity of the field study is shored up by the lab replication. This strategy reflects the ever-increasing need to replicate a finding across a number of varied studies in order to convince critics that your results are valid and robust.

On the other hand, the advice to replicate field studies in lab settings is not an excuse to conduct sloppy field studies. Being sensitive to the challenges associated with most field studies should lead your team to develop additional procedures to increase experimental control. In our sunscreen study, for instance, we embedded the experimental manipulation (i.e., two types of persuasive messages) entirely within brochures. This kept the experimenters blind to each participant's condition, eliminating any experimenter bias and making it less likely that participants would overhear the persuasive appeal of the alternative experimental condition. Moreover, only one person per beachgoer group was allowed to participate in the study, and participants were asked to refrain from discussing the study with their friends until they left the beach that day. This also reduced the likelihood of participants being "contaminated" by the other experimental condition, and it cut down somewhat on extraneous influences. In other words, if you conduct field research, remember that real-life settings can and should be standardized as much as possible.

Online Studies

Today, more and more studies are conducted entirely online, and a number of companies are devoted to the creation of Web-based surveys (e.g., SurveyMonkey, Qualtrics). Of course, Web-based studies are not "in the field" if participants fill out questionnaires online while sitting in the laboratory; these are best characterized as lab studies. Instead, we are referring to studies completed online by participants outside the lab and at their convenience. Although online studies often look just like simple laboratory-based experiments (e.g., when the experimental manipulation is embedded in a packet of questionnaires), these studies suffer from the same drawbacks as field studies because each participant is completing the study in an uncontrolled environment. A participant might be working on a desktop computer in a library, classroom, or office, but he or she is just as likely to be using a laptop while hanging out at a coffeehouse, riding a train, or lying in bed. It is impossible to control whether the participant is alone or surrounded by bickering roommates, in a quiet setting or listening to death metal. Maybe the participant is focused entirely on the survey; then again, he or she might complete the survey while talking on the phone, using FaceTime, or watching YouTube. This is a serious downside of online studies, and, unfortunately, such real-life influences are not what make field studies more convincing. Most experimenters would rather conduct computer-based studies entirely in the controlled setting of a research lab, but the convenience of running an online study often outweighs this ideal.

Because the environments in which participants complete online studies are outside the direct control of the experimenters, we recommend that you include additional instructions whenever you conduct an online study. At the outset of the survey, encourage the participant to find a quiet environment in which to complete the study without interruption. Then, at the end of the study, the survey should follow up on this instruction by asking the participant to report on the environment in which he or she completed the questionnaire (e.g., by asking whether there were any disturbances or technical difficulties). Your team can come up with decision rules, *prior to data analysis,* about what types of situations pose enough concern that a participant's data should be omitted from the sample.

It should be noted that there are some advantages to online studies. Chief among these is the ability to recruit greater numbers of participants than can be recruited for lab studies. This can help compensate for the increased noise associated with data gathered online. In addition, online studies can reach a wide array of participants beyond the typical college student, and such studies are especially attractive to potential participants because of their flexibility.

Despite these advantages, there are unique challenges associated with getting participants to complete online studies. Below we present some concrete tips for how to overcome these challenges. The challenges fit into three broad categories: lack of awareness, inadequate incentive, and technological difficulties.

First, some potential participants may not learn of the opportunity to participate in your team's study because the e-mailed invitation was shuttled automatically into their spam folders. Or perhaps it appeared in their in-boxes, but the subject line on the e-mail ("Win Cash!") looked so much like spam that they deleted it immediately. Perhaps the e-mail was received midweek, when they were swamped at work or school, and by the time things slowed down (and their desire to procrastinate resurfaced) they had forgotten about your invitation. Molasso (2005) offers some concrete solutions to the problem of getting your online study noticed. First, you should tailor the e-mail subject line, making it as clear as possible who is conducting the study. It also is ideal to send individual invitations (rather than a mass mailing), with the participant's name included in the invitation. Cook, Heath, and Thompson (2000) recommend using multiple invitations, but they note that sending more than three separate e-mails to a potential participant does not increase the response rate significantly and could be interpreted as harassing the individual. Finally, sending invitations on different days of the week (e.g., midweek, weekend) may increase the likelihood of getting a response.

Another reason those invited might not agree to participate (or might not finish the entire survey) is that they have little incentive to do so. This is a problem particularly when they perceive the survey to be too long, either because it has a large number of pages to complete or it has multiple open-ended questions to answer. Truth in advertising is essential—giving an accurate estimate of how many minutes it will take a participant to complete your survey will increase the likelihood that those you invite will agree to take part and complete the entire study. You also can increase incentive to participate by providing some form of compensation. Your team could choose to compensate all participants by sending them cash, but this means you would have to mail compensation to each person individually, greatly increasing the cost to your research team in terms of both money and time. If this is feasible, it can be very effective. Alternatively, we and others (e.g., Molasso, 2005) have found that one of the best methods of offering compensation to online survey participants is to enter them into a lottery for one or more prizes. Of course, you will need to take into account the characteristics of your participants in determining what types of prizes will be most attractive to them.

Finally, individuals may not complete your study if they experience technological problems. Some of these problems are under your team's control. You need to be sure that the link to the survey works and that the layout of the survey makes sense no matter what type of browser a participant is using. (Alternatively, if the layout works in only one type of browser, let your participants know this in advance.) If your survey is overly complex, it also is possible that it will be slow to load on the Web page. Such minor frustrations are usually powerful enough to cause participants to discontinue the study prematurely. To detect these problems, Molasso (2005) suggests testing online surveys on different computers and doing shorter projects first (i.e., running subsets of the larger planned survey). It is also essential to pilot the survey, first among members of the research team and then with pilot participants. You should always double-check that random assignment to conditions (if applicable) works as you would expect. You certainly don't want to replicate our lab's error of inadvertently assigning all participants to the same condition on a Web-based survey!

COORDINATING YOUR TEAM'S EFFORTS

Whether you are conducting a study in the lab, in the field, or online, close coordination among your teammates is essential throughout the entire process of data collection. Although careful piloting will help you catch and avoid most potential problems in the first place, new problems and occasional errors will inevitably occur once you launch the study. You should communicate regularly with your teammates, and your team should have contingency plans in place for these instances. Likewise, retaining a running list of questions participants have asked (along with your responses to these questions) helps to maintain consistency among experimenters throughout the data collection process. In any case, do not be afraid to admit moments of confusion, distraction, or error. It is critical to catch problems quickly, even when they are small, before they grow more serious and threaten to undermine the entire experiment.

Although your team will need to identify and handle problems throughout the study, there is an important distinction between the launch of the full-scale study and the piloting process. During piloting, and up until the full study is launched, your team can make changes to the procedure and materials. Indeed, identifying problems during piloting is useful to the extent that the nature of these problems helps you to refine your study. Once you have formally launched your study, however, deviations from the norm are documented for a very different reason. Your team should not make any systematic changes at this point; it's simply too late for that. Now, your documentation of problems will be the basis for excluding a participant's data if absolutely necessary. It is much better to exclude a participant from the sample than it is to allow faulty data to enter your final set of analyses. In Table 8.3, we present a list of real-life concerns that your team should document during data collection, as these might be grounds for excluding participants.

Experimenter error and puzzling participant behavior are not the only reasons an experimenter might decide to exclude a participant from the data set. We recommend that your research team develop a standard set of questions to ask each participant at the very end of the study, after your dependent measures but before the debriefing. The questions we often ask include the following: What do you think we are studying? What is the highest-level psychology class you have taken? Have you recently taken any courses in social psychology? (We've found that social psychology students tend to be very suspicious of all experiments!) Have you heard anything about this study before participating (e.g., from friends or family who have already participated)? Were you able to finish the

TABLE 8.3 Potential Reasons for Excluding Participants
• Failed to follow directions • Answered questions incompletely or carelessly • Appeared to be intoxicated or extremely fatigued • Talked on cell phone or sent text messages during the experiment • Navigated to unrelated websites while completing online questionnaires • Rushed through the procedure • Needed to leave before the study was complete • Described preexisting knowledge of the design and hypotheses (e.g., because a roommate had participated in and shared details of the study)

study as instructed, with minimal distractions? Were there any technological difficulties that interfered with your participation?

Although we frequently ask this series of questions, we only occasionally exclude data based on answers to a particular item. Some studies are more sensitive than others to demand characteristics; some studies may require undivided attention more so than others. These determinations need to be made on a case-by-case basis. However, we remind you that there are a number of cardinal rules underlying the decision to exclude data from your sample: (a) Ideally, this should be done only according to preestablished decision rules for the particular study; (b) in the case of unexpected problems, the research team must reach a decision *before* the data are analyzed; (c) the decision criteria must be applied equally to all participants; and (d) these criteria and any exclusions must be reported when the study's methods and findings are presented. If you are ever on the fence about whether or not to include a participant, never give in to the urge to analyze the data to see what it looks like with versus without the participant. This is unethical. Instead, consult with your research mentor or instructor and your team, and establish a clear-cut and consistent approach to inclusion criteria. Stick to this predetermined approach no matter what the data end up looking like.

Pilot testing is specifically designed to identify problems with a study before it begins, but after your official "launch" you can still check for problems by running a first wave of the study with relatively few participants. (If, for example, you plan to have 80 participants in the study, include just 10 in the first wave.) The assumption you are making is that everything will go smoothly. However, because there is always a chance that significant problems might be identified, running a small initial wave of participants allows your team to come together, discuss any problems, check on the participants' experiences (including their random assignment to condition), and decide to complete the second (and often final) wave of data collection. If there are no problems, you can continue the study and include this initial wave of participants as your first data points. If you find a systematic problem, you can treat the first wave as a second pilot study. This requires throwing out all of the data collected in the first wave, correcting any problems, and starting fresh. This is never an easy choice to make, but it is much easier to discard a small batch of initial participants than it is to find a fatal flaw in your study after all of the data collection has been completed.

Conclusion

Just before you launch your study, you and your teammates are likely to experience a heightened sense of anticipation and exhilaration. All of your collaborative work is paying off. Together you have transformed an initial, vague idea into a well-conceived, concrete study. Your individual contributions to this effort should have you feeling a strong sense of ownership of the project, and the shared vision your team has developed will be evident in your hopes that the study's findings will confirm your predictions or otherwise lead to a compelling and convincing story. Because you have generated this project and these hopes as a team, your feeling of togetherness with your teammates is likely to be at its peak.

However, the realities of data collection rarely sustain these positive feelings. You will expend a tremendous amount of effort attending to your study's critical yet mundane details. As your team moves the project from the planning stage to its implementation, practical issues and logistics will overshadow the broader analytical approach that characterized the earlier idea and design phases. This may lead your team to neglect the principles of togetherness, ownership, and vision, or to believe that these principles have become less important. But paradoxically, to conduct a successful study, you must keep these principles foremost in your mind. Collecting data can be isolating to the extent that team members are likely to have duties that do not overlap. Maintaining a schedule of regular meetings of the whole team helps to keep alive a sense of togetherness. In these meetings, team members can report back on successes, share uncertainties, and admit mistakes. You and your teammates also need to rely on the relationships you have built with one another in order to maintain the stamina necessary to make it through data collection to the analysis phase.

Ownership begins as you take an idea, play with it, shape it into a research question, and design a study to test it out. But something changes once you begin conducting the study. Ownership takes on a whole new meaning when you watch your team's idea come to life in the minds of your participants. As this happens, your role in the process takes on new meaning as well. As one of our students describes:

> My experience with running a study was a real growth and transition period for me. The first study I ever ran was an in-lab experiment that required much preparation, scheduling, and planning in order for things to go smoothly. By the time everything was ready, our initial tenacity had expired, and we were waiting for our second wind. What I remember very clearly was that I started the experience thinking, "Who am I to be running a participant?" But after the first participant, even with errors here and there, I felt like a genuine researcher. (Dmitri Ian Alvarado, Lewis & Clark College, Class of 2012)

A deepening sense of ownership develops as you become a "genuine researcher" while in the trenches of running the study. But being in the trenches also means that you are immersed in nitty-gritty details, and sometimes it is all too easy to get lost in these details. This can cause the big picture of your research to fade into the background. The members of a well-functioning team will remind one another, actively and explicitly, *why* they are doing the hard work of running a study. By regularly stepping back, reflecting on the importance of what you are doing, and remembering that you are moving ever closer to your end goal, your team can maintain a strong shared sense of vision throughout this busy time.

References

Anderson, C. A., Benjamin, A. J., & Bartholow, B. D. (1998). Does the gun pull the trigger? Automatic priming effects of weapon pictures and weapon names. *Psychological Science, 9,* 308–314.

Berkowitz, L., & LePage, A. (1967). Weapons as aggression-eliciting stimuli. *Journal of Personality and Social Psychology, 7,* 202–207.

Bargh, J. A., Chen., M., & Burrows, L. (1996). Automaticity of social behavior: Direct effects of trait construct and stereotype activation on action. *Journal of Personality and Social Psychology, 71,* 230–244.

Cook, C., Heath, F., & Thompson, R. L. (2000). A meta-analysis of response rates in Web or Internet-based surveys. *Educational and Psychological Measurement, 60,* 821–836.

Detweiler, J. B., Bedell, B. T., Salovey, P., Pronin, E., & Rothman, A. J. (1999). Message framing and sunscreen use: Gain-framed messages motivate beach-goers. *Health Psychology, 18,* 189–196.

Dutton, D. G., & Aron, A. P. (1974). Some evidence for heightened sexual attraction under conditions of high anxiety. *Journal of Personality and Social Psychology, 30,* 510–517.

Gleick, J. (1987). *Chaos: Making a new science.* New York: Viking.

Molasso, W. R. (2005). Ten tangible and practical tips to improve student participation in Web surveys. *Student Affairs Online, 6*(4). Retrieved from http://studentaffairs.com/ejournal/Fall_2005/StudentParticipationinWebSurveys.html

Orne, M. T. (1962). On the social psychology of the psychological experiment: With particular reference to demand characteristics and their implications. *American Psychologist, 17,* 776–783.

Sternberg, R. J., & Sternberg, K. (2010). *The psychologist's companion: A guide to writing scientific papers for students and researchers* (5th ed.). New York: Cambridge University Press.

Ward, A., & Mann, T. (2000). Don't mind if I do: Disinhibited eating under cognitive load. *Journal of Personality and Social Psychology, 78,* 753–763.

Weber, S. J., & Cook., T. D. (1972). Subject effects in laboratory research: An examination of subject roles, demand characteristics, and valid inference. *Psychological Bulletin, 77,* 273–295. doi:10.1037/h0032351

Zimbardo, P. (2003, August 27). Professor Philip Zimbardo: The interview, by Hans Sherrer. Retrieved from http://forejustice.org/zimbardo/p_zimbardo_interview.htm

CHAPTER 9

Presentations

Seven Lessons (Plus or Minus Two)

1. After data collection and analysis are complete, your goal is to share your team's findings with others.

2. Presentations take many forms, but the two most common in psychology are research talks and poster presentations.

3. Craft a compelling story when describing your team's idea, predictions, methods, and data. Treat the members of your audience as blank slates, but quick studies.

4. Use PowerPoint wisely by including minimal text and maximally informative graphics.

5. A successful presentation hinges on your devoting adequate time to practice. Although it is natural to feel nervous, convey professionalism through your pace, tone, body language, and eye contact.

6. Even null results can be compelling. Regardless of the study's outcome, conclude your presentation with a discussion of what your team has learned and what questions remain unanswered.

7. Creating an effective poster requires setting aside time for drafting, editing, and printing.

(Continued)

8. Poster presentations are more casual than research talks, but practice (especially of a 2-minute "elevator talk") remains essential.

9. The success of any presentation can be measured by the extent to which the audience becomes invested in the researchers' vision, develops a sense of shared ownership, and feels connected with the research team.

Our responsibility is less to assume the role of experts . . . than to give [psychology] away to the people who really need it—and that includes everyone.

—George Miller (1969, p. 1071)

If you had been in the audience for the American Psychological Association's presidential address in 1969, you may have fallen off your chair in a state of shock. When APA president George Miller took the podium, he "committed the heresy of exhorting [the psychological establishment] to go public, get real, get down, give it up, and be relevant" (Zimbardo, 2004, p. 340). Miller was not a radical activist living on the fringe of the discipline; he was a famed research psychologist and author of—among many other scientific papers—"The Magical Number Seven, Plus or Minus Two" (1955), which, as you may recall, inspired the title for the "lessons" that jump-start each chapter of this text. Today's psychology students might take for granted the importance of using and sharing psychological research to increase the understanding and welfare of society as a whole. But in 1969 there was a long-held prejudice against goals such as these, and Miller tackled it head-on in his presidential address. How do you make the world a better place? You conduct research that matters. And what do you do after you analyze and interpret your data? You give it away to others.

Even if your team's project is limited in scope or applicability, every well-conducted research project should be shared with an audience, ranging from your roommate or grandmother to your classmates, a local community group, or a gathering of professional psychologists. No single presentation is likely to affect the general welfare of society, but over time, presentations of progressively more substantial research get psychologists closer to lessons that will help humanity. You need not identify yourself as an expert in order to give your team's research findings away through presentations. Instead, think of yourself as a person who is helping friends learn something new, or think of yourself as a scholar who is helping other psychologists consider a direction for future research that they might not have imagined otherwise. Psychology can be given away in a number of different venues, ranging from dorm rooms and dining halls to research laboratories and classrooms, to college-wide or community gatherings, to national or international conferences (see Figure 9.1).

By the time you are reading this chapter, it is likely that your team has ushered your project from hypothesis to design to data collection and analysis. You may be

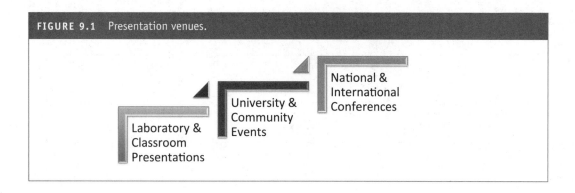

FIGURE 9.1 Presentation venues.

planning to write a paper based on your research (a topic we discuss in the next chapter). But at this point, you should consider presenting your team's work. What does a typical presentation look like? In psychology, two types of presentations are most frequently encountered at professional conferences, and students and faculty often give these same types of presentations on their own college campuses. One is a lecture, or "research talk," typically using PowerPoint. The length of the talk can range from 5 minutes to more than an hour. Some talks are given collaboratively (with members of the research team trading off), whereas others are given by an individual speaker who represents the team. Using tools such as PowerPoint to help structure and guide the talk is typical in most settings. When we were students in the 1990s, PowerPoint was so new that it was considered to be too glitzy for serious academics. Most presenters created transparencies of their handwritten or laser-printed bullet points and graphs, which they flipped between (often clumsily) and displayed using overhead projectors. Thankfully, pretty much everyone in the field now has come around to supporting the use of more sophisticated technologies.

The second type of presentation is a poster. A poster is a summary of your team's findings displayed on a large (typically 4 feet by 6 feet) upright bulletin board. The body of a poster looks much like an abbreviated version of an APA-style paper, including sections labeled "Introduction," "Method," "Results," and "Discussion." Going back again to the time of our graduate training, creating a poster meant printing out a series of 8.5-by-11-inch pages that were then pasted onto sturdy poster board or, alternatively, pinned up one by one onto a bulletin board. Again, thanks to modern technology (this time the advent of the large-format printer), you can now design your entire poster on a computer, enlarge it, and simply unroll a beautifully printed single piece of paper to display your poster presentation.

In the second half of this chapter, we give concrete advice on exactly how to create a research talk and a poster presentation, keeping in mind that these presentations are likely to be done in collaboration with your teammates. We begin, however, with a more in-depth discussion of the rationale for giving presentations and of the general characteristics of strong presentations. To help you to adopt the appropriate psychological mind-set for

FIGURE 9.2   Thought exercise: Why?

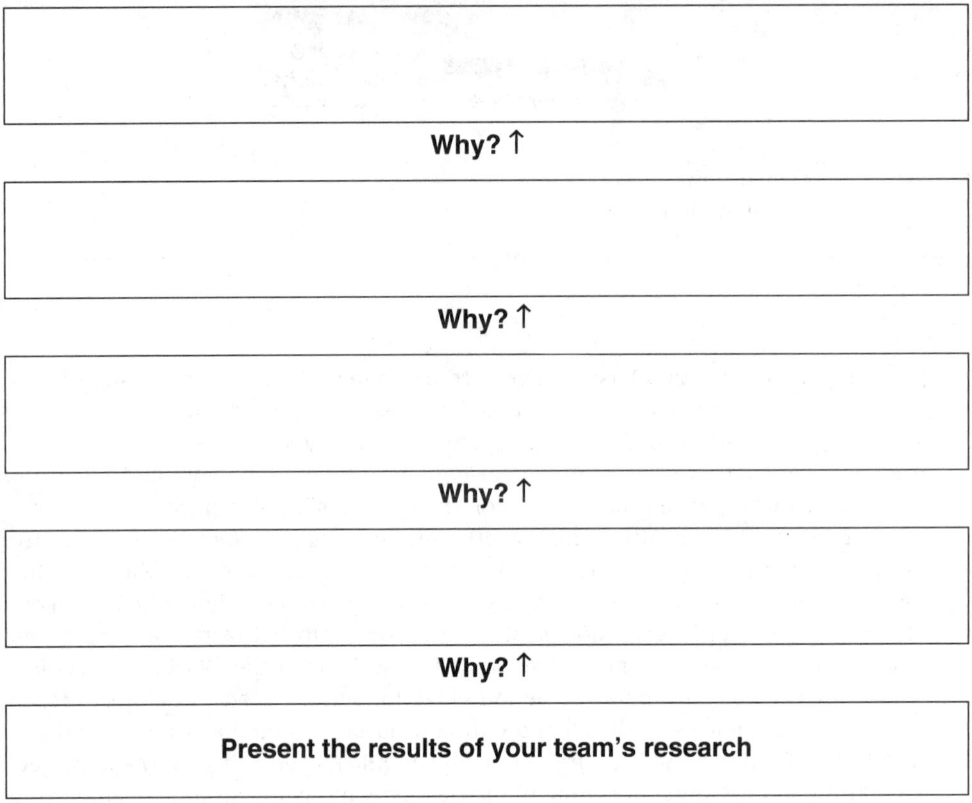

[empty box]

Why? ↑

[empty box]

Why? ↑

[empty box]

Why? ↑

[empty box]

Why? ↑

Present the results of your team's research

considering these issues, take a moment and complete the exercise in Figure 9.2. Think first about the goal in the lowermost box: *Why* would you present the results of your team's research? Write the answer to this question in the box immediately above the prompt. Perhaps your answer is, "Because it's a class requirement." Take this answer and again ask the question "*Why?*" Write a response in each box, working your way upward by indicating why you would pursue each successive goal.

The exercise you just completed was designed to put you in an abstract mind-set (Freitas, Gollwitzer, & Trope, 2004). According to the research findings of Yaacov Trope and colleagues, objects and events are mentally represented at two distinct levels: *Abstract, high-level* construals capture the overarching meaning and central, superordinate features of an object or event, whereas *concrete, low-level* construals consist of the immediate experience and specific, incidental features of an object or event (Fujita, Trope, Liberman, & Levin-Sagi, 2006). For example, studying for an exam can be construed as a means of being a good student and as a step toward accomplishing one's long-term goals (abstract), or it can be thought of as an urgent task involving hundreds of pages of reading and attendance at tonight's study session (concrete). One of these mind-sets will tend to dominate a person's thinking at any given time, and a person's responses to a situation will differ depending on whether he or she is in an abstract or concrete mind-set.

In a series of studies, researchers investigating mind-set found that individuals in an abstract mind-set displayed greater self-control and physical endurance and were better able to recognize temptations that undermine self-control than were individuals in a concrete mind-set (Fujita et al., 2006). Said differently, the mind-set in which you experience a situation or event can influence your ability to overcome barriers and, returning to the topic of this chapter, may play an important role in how you tackle the next piece of the collaborative research process: presenting the results of your project. So with the aid of an abstract mind-set, let's begin.

THE PITFALLS IN PRESENTING

It is important for leaders to know their stories, to get them straight, to communicate them effectively, particularly to those who are partial to rival stories, and, above all, to embody in their lives the stories they tell.

—Howard Gardner (1996, p. xi)

To be a successful presenter, you must craft a compelling story out of your team's idea, predictions, methods, and data. You then must convey this story to others. What constitutes a compelling story? At the heart of telling a good research story is remembering what it was like knowing little or nothing about the topic. All too often, presenters are stuck in their own heads and wind up telling stories that only they understand. This is because researchers often take the big picture for granted, especially after they have been immersed in the concrete details of running a study and analyzing the data. They are stuck in a concrete mind-set and tell a story that emphasizes incidental details, numbers, and jargon at the expense of the overarching meaning of their work. Although the details of your experiment and your team's findings are important, you must put these details in context for your listeners. This means you should lead with the broader vision motivating the research and then guide the audience from your team's original idea through the rationale for your specific predictions. In other words, you should begin your presentation in the abstract and then gradually and systematically focus on concrete details.

If you follow this advice, you will be well on your way to telling a coherent and compelling story. But you are likely to face a related problem that plagues most presenters. It is challenging to remember what it was like to know little or nothing about your research topic, and this makes it difficult to calibrate the pacing, amount of information, and level of detail you convey in a presentation. Some presenters act as though their ideas are far too complex for the audience to understand in the course of a brief talk. As a result, they stretch out the background and logic of their story so much that the presentation drags on and often runs out the clock before they can describe the study itself or the findings. Other presenters err on the side of brevity and skip key steps in their story because they take for granted many of the important ideas that gave rise to their team's research. Unfortunately, these two failures are not mutually exclusive. Quite the opposite: The same presenter who bores an audience with incidental details (i.e., information the presenter no longer thinks much about but nevertheless seems relevant) may gloss over important aspects of the logic motivating the study's design (i.e., information the presenter thinks about all the time and therefore seems too obvious). This is another sign that the presenter is stuck in his or her own head and, in a sense, is presenting to him- or herself rather than to the audience.

How do you calibrate the pacing, amount of information, and level of detail of your presentation? Our mantra is that audience members should be treated as "blank slates, but quick studies." That is, you should assume they know little, but you must challenge them because they are capable of rapid learning. A presentation must be crafted so that it (a) inspires others with the key question underscoring the line of research and (b) quickly and convincingly develops the research story based on the presenter's own "detached" appreciation for the most important, compelling elements of the story. Developing this detached perspective is a real skill that cannot be taught directly. It takes work to distill your team's complex ideas and efforts into compelling stories, and the only way to do this is through practice and through seeking (and carefully listening to) feedback from your audiences. Conceptually, however, your goal is clear: You should adopt the perspective of your listeners and forget everything you know, then build your story quickly and efficiently from the most basic and relevant principles.

A good presentation engages and inspires, and it gives listeners the conceptual tools they need to generate the predictions of the study presented. This leaves the listeners satisfied with how the research topic was handled, and yet intrigued. They then should be able and inspired to generate their own questions and directions for future research. In other words, it is your team's goal to give the project away to your audiences by bringing them to the point where they can elaborate on your team's story and incorporate the take-home message into their own way of thinking.

PRINCIPLES OF GOOD PRESENTATIONS

There are many reasons for presenting your team's research project. As a student, you may want to gain some experience in public speaking. Or perhaps your professor or mentor wants to view a presentation in order to evaluate your team's work. Although being "evaluated" might feel threatening and unidirectional, keep in mind that this allows others to make suggestions about your research. A presentation can serve as a catalyst for next steps, ranging from conducting additional analyses to launching a follow-up study. At the same time, creating a presentation can help to give your research team a sense of closure. Finally, there is the most common goal of presenting, stemming from the scientific method itself: sharing your findings with others. Giving a presentation allows for others to grapple with the questions you asked and the results you found.

No matter which purpose of presenting you embrace, we believe that the success of your presentation will depend on your fostering vision, ownership, and togetherness among members of your audience. Vision is the hook that draws your audience in. By sharing your team's vision early on in the presentation, you can encourage the audience to feel included in the goal or larger story of your research investigation. Ownership develops, first, as you put the audience in the place of the investigator (that is, make the audience part of your team) in describing how the research question was developed. Remember how your team winnowed many ideas for the project down to *the idea*? Make sure your audience shares an appreciation for why you and your teammates decided to pursue the hypotheses that you did. Next, put your audience in the place of the participant. Describe your team's methods in vivid detail so that each listener can feel as if he or she participated in your study. Finally, solidify a sense of ownership by putting your audience in the place of the storyteller; that is, immerse your listeners in the immediacy of the presentation, so they find themselves asking with great anticipation, "What is going to happen next?" When you share your team's findings, be sure to help audience members make sense of them by linking the findings to something they know or care about.

Togetherness builds from this vision and ownership. The first step is to feel united as a team during the presentation. Not every team works perfectly together, and sometimes your team's "united front" is not as truly united as you would like it to be. However, this is the time to put aside differences and difficulties and to focus outward, on your audience. A good marker of whether you have created a sense of togetherness with your audience is how you and your listeners feel about asking questions. If you have conveyed the vision of your team's project effectively and imbued your audience with a sense of ownership, then you won't feel defensive when audience members ask your team tough questions. After all, listeners who share your vision and are given a sense of ownership become your newest collaborators, and their ideas might help you out. This togetherness makes it more, not less, likely that they will ask tough questions, and you will be more likely to ask them questions in return (prodding them to "say more" or "elaborate on that"). If you don't know the answer to an audience member's question, you should feel excited, not ashamed. A reasonable course of action on your part is to remark that the question is intriguing and that you haven't had the opportunity to consider it. In other words, it is worth looking into. Then brainstorm a possible answer *with* the audience. If you do this, a difficult question may end up making a significant contribution to your work.

ORGANIZING YOUR PRESENTATION

How do you go about creating a compelling presentation? To answer this question, let's start with a description of research investigating the impact of a disorderly environment on norm violations. In a series of experiments, researchers Kees Keizer, Siegwart Lindenberg, and Linda Steg, all affiliated with the University of Groningen in the Netherlands, investigated whether disorder is contagious. That is, if you find yourself in an environment that has been damaged (e.g., broken glass is strewn on the sidewalk), are you more likely to add to the disorder in a new way by littering, trespassing, or even stealing? As Keizer and colleagues reported in a 2008 article in the journal *Science,* "disorder" was operationalized slightly differently across a series of six studies. In the first study, the disorderly environment was one where graffiti had been spray-painted on the wall of an alley. In the second study, bicycles were chained to a fence despite a sign proclaiming, "Geen fietsen aan het hek vastmaken." (Although we do not speak Dutch, the sound of the words alone seems to convey a strong message that bikes should not be attached to the fence!) The third study took place in a parking garage where shopping carts had been abandoned in violation of a sign requesting that customers please return their carts to the store. The fourth study cleverly incorporated acoustic disorder in the form of fireworks being set off at a time and place in which this was prohibited. The fifth study again utilized graffiti, and the sixth conveyed disorder through a collection of littered paper, orange peels, cigarette butts, and empty cans.

All six of these studies were done in the field, with participants who never knew they were being observed. For example, the first study took place in an alley where people typically parked their bicycles. There was one independent variable in this study: whether the wall of the alley was tagged with graffiti (disorder condition) or was clean (order condition). In both conditions a large sign in the alley stated that graffiti was prohibited. Before data collection began, the experimenters systematically placed a white flyer on the handlebars of each bicycle in the alley. The flyer was securely attached with a rubber band and the note on the flyer wished the recipient "happy holidays" on behalf of a (fictitious) business. The dependent variable was straightforward: What did the bicycle owners do with the frivolous flyers, given that there were no garbage cans in the alley? Did they carry the flyers out? Did they surreptitiously move the flyers from their own handlebars to other bicycles? Or did they drop the flyers on the pavement? For the purposes of this study, hanging a flyer on another bike or dropping it on the ground was considered to be "littering" (i.e., adding disorder to the environment).

What were this study's results? As the authors predicted, the bicyclists who were in the graffiti-covered alley were significantly more likely to drop the flyers on the ground (or move them to other bikes) than were those in the (same) graffiti-free alley. Specifically, 69% of individuals in the disorder condition littered, whereas 33% of those in the order condition littered. What a compelling demonstration of the authors' hypothesis! This is certainly a study that has results worth sharing, so let's take Keizer and colleagues' line of research and try to shape it into an effective presentation. To guide our recommendations, we draw on the researchers' own presentation of their findings in their published paper and in supplemental online materials associated with their project (Keizer et al., 2008a, 2008b).

Provide a Compelling Context

As you begin to think about your team's presentation, step back from the details of the study and ask yourself, "Why should my audience care?" Your goal is to get the audience to share in your team's vision. To do this successfully, you and your teammates need to remind yourselves of the purpose of the research project in the first place. This is not a trivial exercise. The purpose of most studies is multifaceted, so you will have to make a conscious choice of which aspect of the purpose to highlight when you introduce your study.

Keizer and colleagues had to make this choice. Should they begin the presentation by talking about the environmental problem of littering in public spaces? Or should they begin by talking about the research on social norms and rule violations? In their published scientific paper, they chose the latter. Why? Because the initial argument they wanted to make was *not* about how to reduce littering; rather, it was about how one type of norm violation (e.g., graffiti) can lead to another type of norm violation (e.g., littering). But don't be fooled. The opening sentences of the authors' presentation do not focus on the social psychological distinction between injunctive and descriptive social norms. This "tantalizing" theoretical argument may be important to the research, but it doesn't appear until later. Instead, the beginning of their presentation is devoted to real-world issues. The authors begin their discussion of the research with a vivid description of then New York City mayor Rudy Giuliani's aim to improve the quality of life in New York in the mid-1990s. As portrayed in the *New York Times Magazine,* "The key to Giuliani's quality-of-life campaign was the idea that there was a collective right to safe and orderly public space that trumped the individual rights of the squeegee operators and aggressive panhandlers and street vendors and graffiti artists who were abusing that space" (Traub, 2001, p. 65). In order to tell the best story, Keizer's research team uses Mayor Giuliani's quality-of-life campaign to persuade the scientific audience that their topic of research matters, is engaging, and has potential real-world applications.

After grounding their research in the actions of Mayor Giuliani, the research team describes the broken windows theory (BWT), which argues that disorder is contagious (Kelling & Wilson, 1982). So far, so good. Then they introduce a controversy: Despite the intuitive appeal and widespread application of the BWT (even in cities as big as New York), scientific research findings provide very little evidence to support this theory. It is only at this point that the authors begin to talk about injunctive norms (that is, behaviors that people approve or disapprove of) and descriptive norms (that is, behaviors that are common in particular situations; Reno, Cialdini, & Kallgren, 1993). Audience members, with broken windows and the streets of New York City looming large in their collective imagination, are now ready to hear how these social scientists went about tackling their research question. In other words, the very first ideas you present to your audience make a difference in how well the audience is hooked and then drawn into a shared vision of your research.

Shape the Context Into a Hypothesis

Once you've provided a context, it is your job to lead the audience toward the primary hypothesis (or hypotheses) of the research. A skillful presentation draws the listeners in, leading them to envisage what you will be predicting. As a result, they will feel satisfied when your hypothesis matches what they had imagined. To accomplish this, you should use past research and findings as key stepping-stones in working toward your hypothesis.

Keizer and colleagues draw on past work by Cialdini and colleagues suggesting that other people's behaviors are particularly influential in shaping our own expectations about what is the correct or wise thing to do. They then extend this work by suggesting that when there is a conflict between an injunctive norm (e.g., a sign reminding us that graffiti is prohibited) and a descriptive norm (e.g., a graffiti-covered wall), we are likely to let go of our own internal goals to act in an approved manner. We may begin to think, "Other people aren't following the rules, so why should I?" As a result, we will be more likely to pursue hedonic goals (i.e., anything that improves our mood or increases our resources). This has the potential to produce a "cross-norm inhibition effect," whereby one norm violation spreads to another type of norm violation. If this prediction is supported, then perhaps there is some truth to the BWT after all. Seeing graffiti where it is prohibited may not only make you more likely to spray-paint your own initials on the wall, but it may also "free" you up to litter or to trespass.

Could this possibly be true of the average person? If so, what does this mean about *you*? At this point in the presentation, the audience should feel the satisfaction of putting together a jigsaw puzzle. Many pieces remain, but the border and general theme of the puzzle have clicked into place. The audience is now ready and excited to complete the picture.

Describe Your Methods Vividly

When it comes to describing studies, the best presentations put the audience in the place of the participants. One way to accomplish this is through a demonstration based on one or more of the experimental conditions. Having the audience experience some aspect of the experimental procedure can be extremely effective. If this is not feasible, you can share concrete details of the study's procedure and ask audience members to imagine being a participant. Or you might describe the study vividly from the perspective of the experimenter. In their written work, Keizer and colleagues include a number of photographs. This is somewhat unusual for a published scientific paper, but in this case it is especially important for the reader to understand the settings in which the experiments took place. In a research talk, Keizer and colleagues might include a photo of each setting (e.g., alley, parking lot) to make the participants' experiences tangible *and* to usher the audience along from one study to the next. But in a poster, space is limited. In this context they might include only one or two images. Take a moment to view the photos in Figures 9.3 and 9.4. Which set of two would you include in a poster presentation if you had to choose?

Both oral presentations and posters benefit tremendously from the judicious use of visual stimuli, but there is a clear trade-off when space is limited. On one hand, these researchers could provide images that allow the audience to visualize more than one of the settings in which the research took place (as in Figure 9.3). On the other hand, the researchers could provide images associated with two experimental conditions in the same setting (as in Figure 9.4). Ultimately, the best story has to be grounded in the predictions, and, by extension, the best visuals depict the experimental manipulations in action; thus, in this case, the set of photos in Figure 9.4 would be the better choice.

Vivid descriptions matter because they facilitate the audience's understanding of a study, but they do so by *constraining* the audience's thinking to the essential features of the procedures. This suggests a need for caution. Illustrations of a study's procedures can be misleading if they fail to stay true to the participant's experience or if they focus the audience's attention too narrowly. For instance, you might notice a potential problem with presenting the photos in Figure 9.4 to a predominantly American audience. In the United States, the typical sign prohibiting a behavior has a diagonal red line *across* an image symbolizing the behavior. To an American, the sign from this study, which says "graffiti," might be perceived more as an endorsement of defacing the alley walls than a warning

FIGURE 9.3 Photographs of two experimental settings.

Source: Keizer, Lindenberg, and Steg (2008a, p. 1683). Reprinted with permission from AAAS.

against doing so. Audience members who focus too much on the sign in the picture might conclude that there was graffiti on the wall simply because the behavior was encouraged by the sign. Without a clear description of what this sign means in the Netherlands (where the research was conducted), the whole idea that graffiti was prohibited by an injunctive norm might be lost on an American audience. Of course, careful listeners will keep in mind

FIGURE 9.4 Photographs of two experimental conditions. Bicycle riders were more likely to litter (by dropping the white flyer from their handlebars onto the ground) in the graffiti condition. In both cases, the sign indicates that graffiti is prohibited.

Source: Keizer, Lindenberg, and Steg (2008a, p. 1682). Reprinted with permission from AAAS.

the theories that underlie the research question and will give the benefit of the doubt to the presenter. Still, it is best to avoid confusion of this kind. Although you should accentuate key details of your team's study with vivid descriptions and illustrations, you must take care to present these details clearly so they do not undermine the audience's understanding of your methods and logic.

Tell a Clear and Concise Story With Your Data

When you go about analyzing your data, you are likely to spend hours poring over descriptive statistics and subjecting your findings to countless statistical tests. You will try to identify outliers and other irregularities in your data. You will look to see if there was an effect of gender on your primary hypotheses. You might explore whether mood interacted with your variables of interest. And so on. After torturing your data by testing everything you can think of, you are likely to start to lose sight of the big picture. This is why, as you might recall from our chapter on experimental design, Jacob Cohen admonished his students to streamline the number of variables included in any given study. The number of possible analyses grows rapidly and becomes exponentially more unwieldy as a study becomes more complex. Even the most straightforward research project typically results in an overwhelming amount of statistical output.

In shaping the presentation of your data, should you share all of this output in order to demonstrate your team's statistical prowess? Should you walk your listeners through every analysis you conducted so they feel as if they sat with you as you crunched the numbers? No, and no. When you describe your team's predictions and research methods, your goal is to bring the audience along on a journey. But as you transition to your presentation of the data, it is time to complete the journey and tell the best story you can. To do this, you need to simplify as much as possible. Highlight only the most targeted analyses. Be sure to depict your data visually. Streamline your presentation by stripping out unnecessary statistics. The best oral presentations generally include little if any discussion of statistics. Instead, one or two key slides per study should provide visual depictions of the main findings and embedded indications of the *size* and *reliability* of these effects. For example, standard deviation bars within a graph and a *p* value just under the graph are enough information for most listeners. If someone in the audience asks you to describe your analyses in greater detail, you can go ahead and provide a lengthier description. Otherwise, stick to these essential details.

Although Keizer and colleagues' findings are presented in a somewhat detailed journal article, the authors nevertheless streamlined their findings in order to tell a good story. For instance, they coded for participant sex at first, but as they found no association between sex and the dependent variables, they do not discuss this variable at all in presenting their results (and in fact they dropped coding for participant sex from the design of their later studies). In addition, they held constant two variables that would have otherwise been treated as covariates (that is, variables that could explain systematic noise in the data): the time of day and the weather. The experimenters collected data only in the afternoon and on days when there were cloudy skies. As past research suggests, sunshine can have an impact on self-reported mood, helping behavior, and interpersonal judgments (Cunningham, 1979; Redelmeier & Baxter, 2009). Rather than worrying about the potential impacts of extraneous influences such as the weather, the researchers were able to hold the environment relatively constant in order to eliminate the need for additional statistical tests.

Choose Visual Depictions of Data That Enhance Understanding

What type of graphs, charts, or summary tables should you use to tell the story of your team's data? Visual depictions of data should enable the audience to understand an effect quickly and precisely, and well-designed graphics are one of the most powerful means of communicating statistical information (Tufte, 2001). This doesn't mean that a graph should be simplistic. Instead, the best graphs are *efficient* in how they depict critical comparisons. Achieving this efficiency entails highlighting meaningful information while eliminating less useful clutter.

Consider Keizer and colleagues' journal article. Does it include a graph of the averages we described earlier? No. An audience readily comprehends a comparison between two simple means or percentages. Creating a graph out of these data would be redundant, and this redundancy might undermine the presentation of the study's findings. Instead, the authors present this effect in the text alone. Visual depictions of data are more important when a study has more than one independent variable. Take, for example, some of the original work by Reno and colleagues (1993) that influenced the line of research we have been describing. Imagine that you are walking back to your car after picking up a book at the local public library. As you approach the parking lot, you see a college-age person drop a bag from a fast-food restaurant on the ground and continue walking. When you get to your car, you find a large flyer under the driver's-side windshield wiper, reminding you to "drive carefully." What do you do with the flyer? Take it into the car? Or throw it to the ground? And how might your behavior be different if you hadn't just passed by a person who littered? Better yet, how would you behave if you instead had just passed by a person who *picked up* a fast-food restaurant bag from the ground? You might predict that the behavior of the person who either littered or picked up litter (in this case, a confederate of the experiment) would influence your own behavior, and you would be right. But this wasn't the only independent variable in the study. The researchers also were interested in the descriptive norm, or what was *generally done* in the particular setting. In half of the conditions, "the parking lot had been heavily littered by the experimenters with an assortment of handbills, candy wrappers, cigarette butts, and paper cups" (p. 105). In the other half of the conditions, the parking lot had been cleaned of all litter.

The primary dependent variable (whether or not the participant takes the flyer from the windshield and drops it on the ground) depends on the confederate's behavior *and* on the cleanliness of the parking lot. When the confederate litters, the descriptive norm (the cleanliness of the environment) is made salient. When the confederate picks up the bag, the injunctive norm (the societal expectation that one should not litter) is made salient. That is, we have two independent variables (norm salience and environmental condition).

This design is not particularly complex, but the pattern and meaning of the findings resulting from it can be more challenging to grasp. This is where a graphic can be tremendously helpful. See Figure 9.5, which depicts the pattern of results for the behavioral measure of littering. A simple display such as this tells the complete story. In the control condition (where the confederate simply walks past the participant), more than one-third of participants littered with the flyer, regardless of the cleanliness of the environment. When the confederate dropped trash in a litter-strewn environment, participants' likelihood of littering was the same as it was in the control condition (30% is not significantly different from 37% or 38% in this case). However, when the confederate littered in a clean environment, participants' likelihood of doing the same went down dramatically (to 11%), and when the confederate modeled an antilittering norm (by picking up the bag), participant littering went down significantly in *both* the the clean and the littered environments. This graphical display presents a series of profoundly important comparisons that we needed four sentences to summarize. In other words, the information presented in the graph is not simple, but the graph itself is *efficient*.

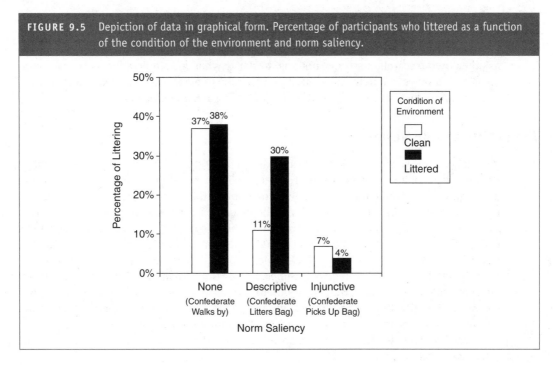

FIGURE 9.5 Depiction of data in graphical form. Percentage of participants who littered as a function of the condition of the environment and norm saliency.

Source: Reno, Cialdini, and Kallgren (1993, p. 106).

Leave the Listener Satisfied, but Craving More

As you approach the conclusion of your presentation, your goal is to tie up loose ends, allowing the audience to feel satisfied with what your team has shared. Ideally, your data will enable you to reach a compelling conclusion. Reno and colleagues (1993) argue that the tools of social change are easy to apply. For example, no matter what the environmental conditions may be, having someone pick up a single piece of garbage (thus activating an injunctive norm) can have beneficial ripple effects on naive observers. They even suggest that similar patterns of behavior could be observed in other settings, such as roads where the speed limit is regularly violated or neighborhoods where people are unlikely to turn out to vote (p. 106). Similarly, Keizer and colleagues (2008a) go all out in the discussion of their data by saying, "There is a clear message for policymakers and police officers: Early disorder diagnosis and intervention are of vital importance when fighting the spread of disorder" (p. 1685).

Even if your study does not lend itself to a strong "take-home" message, you should still describe what you and your teammates (and your newest collaborators—the audience) have come to understand, along with the questions that remain unanswered. Indeed, it is usually better to stick rather closely to the data and not stretch the implications of your findings too far; otherwise, you might damage the credibility of your story. Even so, you can conclude by discussing unanswered questions, directions for follow-up studies, and how your findings fit into the big picture. Here is where the audience can be left craving more. Audience members should want your team to continue pursuing research. And they should be inspired to ask their own research questions, not only to clarify what you studied but also to take your ideas and findings in a new direction. If you are able to elicit this feeling of *wanting more,* you will know that you have succeeded in presenting a compelling story.

The Reality of Null Results

Throughout this section, we have used a highly successful study as an example to shape our discussion of how to present your results. Of course, not all projects are successful, and although we are rooting for you, it is likely that your study did not turn out exactly as you expected. Null results are common in psychological research, and very often a study that finds "no difference" is never spoken of again. This is something psychological scientists call the *file drawer problem* (Rosenthal, 1979): The data are stuffed away in a file drawer, never to see the light of day again. There's even a journal aimed at combating this problem, fittingly titled the *Journal of Articles in Support of the Null Hypothesis.* The journal's website welcome statement notes: "In the past other journals and reviewers have exhibited a bias against articles that did not reject the null hypothesis. We seek to change that by offering an outlet for experiments that do not reach the traditional significance levels ($p < .05$). Thus, reducing the file drawer problem, and reducing the bias in psychological literature" (http://www.jasnh.com).

So if you and your teammates find yourselves needing to present null results, remember that you are in good company. Remember, too, that the absence of results is something worth presenting and talking about. When you get to the concluding segment of your presentation, your team can share hypotheses for why the experiment did not turn out as planned. Perhaps there were problems with the measures. Perhaps the independent variable was too subtle. Perhaps the difference that you predicted really doesn't exist. The only way to know for sure is to continue your program of research. If you become hooked on research, you will find that another study is always just around the corner. In our own lab, we hardly give ourselves time to take a breath after analyzing data before we begin to sketch out "what's next."

THE NUTS AND BOLTS OF PRESENTING YOUR RESEARCH

Now that we have described some of the abstract principles underlying successful research presentations, it is time to get more concrete. First, let's revisit the mind-set exercise that you completed at the start of this chapter. This time, however, we take the goal of presenting the results of your team's research and then ask *how* we can accomplish this and each successive goal. We have completed the exercise based on our discussion so far (see Figure 9.6). Rather than asking *why*, we are now focused on *how,* which should elicit a concrete mind-set. Concrete, here-and-now thinking provides a good starting place for focusing on the work of creating a presentation.

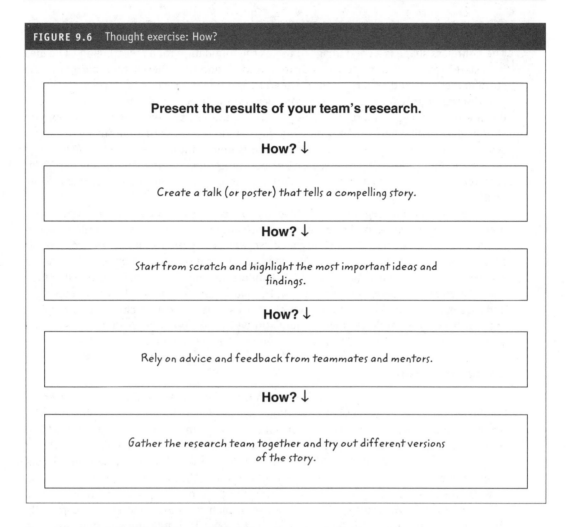

FIGURE 9.6 Thought exercise: How?

> **Present the results of your team's research.**

How? ↓

> Create a talk (or poster) that tells a compelling story.

How? ↓

> Start from scratch and highlight the most important ideas and findings.

How? ↓

> Rely on advice and feedback from teammates and mentors.

How? ↓

> Gather the research team together and try out different versions of the story.

Creating and Delivering an Effective Research Talk

First, we focus on advice associated with an oral presentation, a format you will encounter both in classes and at conferences as a vehicle for psychologists to share the highlights of their research. As we mentioned at the start of the chapter, the lengths of oral presentations vary tremendously, so determining how long your presentation must be is an important first step in the process. Your team also will need to confirm that you will have access to the projection equipment necessary for the use of PowerPoint (this tends to be ubiquitous in classrooms and conference halls these days, but you shouldn't take access for granted). Although the timing and format of research talks vary, the basic advice we share here can be applied to how you go about structuring your presentation regardless of whether your talk is 5 minutes, 15 minutes, or 45 minutes; just bulk up or slim down the talk accordingly.

Structuring Your Presentation

The hourglass shape is a good image to use as the foundation for a research talk. The idea is to start broad as you introduce your team's ideas and hypotheses, then narrow to the specific methods and results of your research, and finally broaden your presentation as you discuss your team's results and consider the implications of the findings. You will begin with the background research, but be sure to emphasize ideas, not authors. Yes, you should give credit where credit is due, but you can do this on your slides using just a *few* select citations within parentheses. Although it is important to stress the big picture and the logical implications of past research, the best presenters rarely focus on any particular researchers' past work in depth, and it is not necessary to give full citations during the talk itself.

The most important segment of the research talk conveys your team's own hypotheses, methods, and results. An oral presentation is constrained by time, so you should be selective (though always truthful) in what you share. Presenting the results of your research is an exercise in framing and focusing. Remember, the goal is to tell a compelling story. Do not neglect what audience members *need* to understand, but be sure to focus on what they will be *excited* to understand. End the talk by sharing three or four take-home messages and suggested directions for future research. It is also customary to include a slide displaying your references and acknowledgments (in which you thank individuals who helped your team with the project). For a sample outline of a research talk, see Table 9.1.

Using PowerPoint

As we noted earlier, it is typical to use PowerPoint as a presentational tool. Research conducted on the effectiveness of PowerPoint suggests that students rate professors who use PowerPoint higher in terms of organization, clarity, and even likability compared to professors who do not use it (Apperson, Laws, & Scepansky, 2006). But not all PowerPoint presentations are equal in their effectiveness. Can you recall a time when an instructor held you captive and tortured you with PowerPoint slides? If so, you are not alone. PowerPoint used poorly has been called everything from "a big waste of time" (Tufte, 2003a, p. 25) to "evil" (Tufte, 2003b). The use of pictures and sound effects, especially those that are irrelevant to the text, has been shown to undermine student learning outcomes and liking of the presentation (Bartsch & Cobern, 2003). Apperson, Laws, and Scepansky (2008) surveyed 275 students (from a state university and a private liberal arts college) and found that they disliked when presenters read word-for-word from slides or included too much text. Instead, the students expressed a strong preference for presenters to use key-phrase outlines along with visuals (such as relevant pictures, graphs, or movie clips). They also expressed a preference for presenters to elaborate on slides by adding concrete examples, thus encouraging active engagement of the audience. As Tufte (2003b) observes: "PowerPoint is a competent slide manager and projector. But rather than supplementing a presentation, it has become a substitute for it. Such misuse ignores the most important rule of speaking: Respect your audience." Respecting your audience includes encouraging involvement in your presentation, and your use of PowerPoint should facilitate rather than hinder this process.

TABLE 9.1 Sample Outline of a Research Talk

Promoting Dental Floss Use in a College Student Population

I. Source of ideas
   a. Health message framing
   b. How can we encourage healthy dental behaviors?
   c. Previous research
      i. Sherman and colleagues
      ii. Health message framing research

II. Hypotheses

III. Concrete predictions

IV. Methodology
   a. Phase I: In lab
      i. Pretest
      ii. How/why manipulation
      iii. Pamphlets
      iv. Post measures
      v. Floss packets
   b. Phase II: At home and follow-up survey 1 week later
      i. How/why follow-up
      ii. Floss behavior questions
      iii. Problem checks and debriefing

V. Results

VI. Real-world implications and conclusions
   a. How can we better motivate people to floss?
   b. Possible pitfalls and limitations
   c. Future research

VII. References and acknowledgments

When it comes to PowerPoint slides, we again tout the idea that *less is more*. Use short phrases or words on your slides, not complete sentences. Be judicious in your use of levels of bulleting on any given slide. It is all too common to see the most important points on a slide placed on the lowest level, hidden in small font (Tufte, 2003a). The goal is to employ PowerPoint to outline the structure of the talk; it is the speaker's job to elaborate verbally. Make sure that all fonts on your slides are big enough and clear enough for the audience to read easily, and use open or white space well (i.e., slides should be visually elegant and balanced rather than "crammed" or "vacant"). And by all means avoid distracting templates and glaring colors, and never have the program produce a quacking, chirping, or ringing noise as you advance from one slide to the next. Excessive bells and whistles and funky transitions undermine the professionalism of your talk.

Using Presenter Notes

It is natural to feel apprehensive as you envision giving a talk. One of the ways some people cope with this feeling is to prepare highly detailed written scripts of their presentations. If you fall into this camp of presenters, please (oh, please!) avoid the temptation to read your script aloud to your audience or to memorize the script verbatim. This undermines the content of a talk because audiences tend to be distracted by the overly controlled, often stilted style that comes with reading or memorizing. It isn't wrong to write down what you want to say, but after you do the writing, you should streamline these notes by identifying your key points and then putting these key points on note cards or summarizing them in outline form. (In addition to key points, knowing what you want to say next is particularly important when you are transitioning between slides or ideas.) If you are presenting just one segment of your team's talk, a broad outline that fits on your hand might be enough (see Figure 9.7). Another approach is to print out your PowerPoint slides and write a few key phrases under each slide (see Figure 9.8) or to use a series of note cards (see Figure 9.9). With experience and practice, you will develop a style of presenter notes that works best for you.

FIGURE 9.7   Presentation notes on hand.

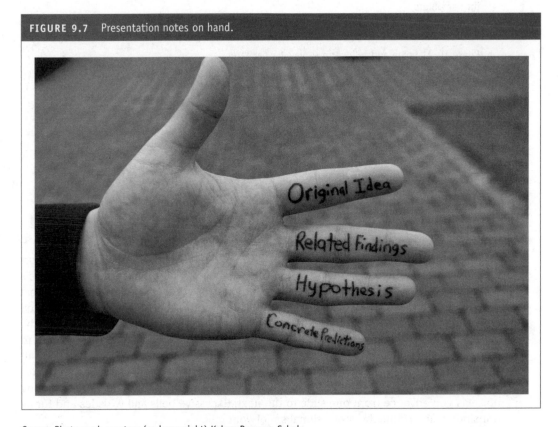

Source: Photograph courtesy (and copyright) Kelsey Domann-Scholz.

FIGURE 9.8 Sample PowerPoint slides with notes.

Motivational illusions: "Framing"

A typical study…

- You start with $10. If you solve enough puzzles, you will earn a $20 bonus. *Approach*

  OR

- You start with $30. If you fail to solve enough puzzles, you will lose $20 of this.

  Avoid

- From an economic standpoint, there is <u>no</u> difference.
- But which do <u>you</u> prefer?

Gains or losses…

- Negative information captures our attention and losses loom large.

- But many circumstances are ambiguous.
  - Which stand out, the positives or the negatives?

- Interpreting something in terms of <u>gains</u> or, alternatively, <u>losses</u> adds meaningful "depth."

- We prefer gains and are motivated to avoid the negative
- ≠ Freudian repression Instead mindlessly discarding junk mail

---

Revisiting control

Recall Idea: Negative consequences of aging due in part to loss of control, so give more control

Study: Retirement home residents visited by college students over a two-month period:

- Some participants were able to control or at least predict the frequency and duration of these visits.
- Compared to visits at random or no visits.

- What's important is our subjective perception
- Gaining / losing a few $ in the lab may not seem meaningful
- BUT… remember the nursing home study?

As a reminder…

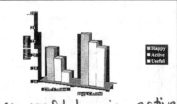

- Happy
- Active
- Useful

Schulz (1976)

More useful, happier, active

- Control is great, yes?
- Yes. But only if control ISN'T LOST
- What happened after the study ended?

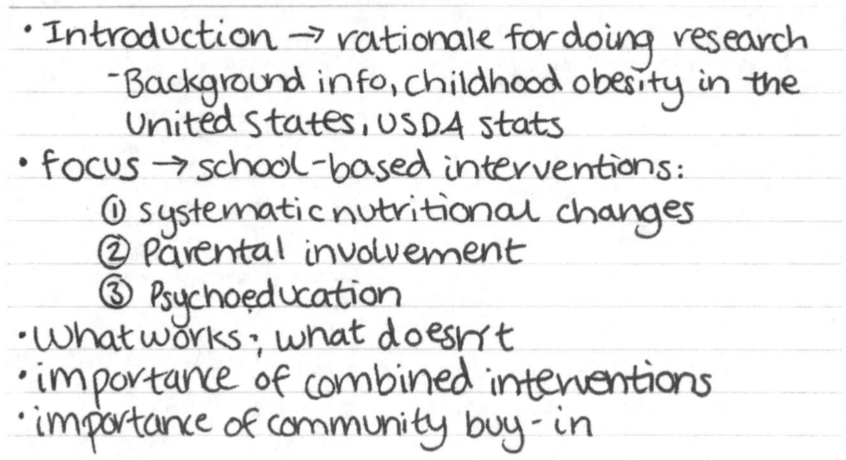

FIGURE 9.9 Sample presentation note card.

- Introduction → rationale for doing research
    - Background info, childhood obesity in the United States, USDA stats
- focus → school-based interventions:
    1. systematic nutritional changes
    2. Parental involvement
    3. Psychoeducation
- What works; what doesn't
- importance of combined interventions
- importance of community buy-in

Presentational Style

In developing a presentational style, your goal should be to harness and control the natural anxiety you feel rather than giving in to it. Even the most seasoned speakers often feel anxious immediately before they begin a talk. We recall the advice given to us early on in our careers: When you no longer feel nervous prior to giving a lecture, it's time to retire. Some speakers feel more comfortable if they acknowledge to the audience that they are nervous. You may be able to pull this off if you do it judiciously, but if each member of your team stands up and starts by saying, "I'm anxious!" it won't go over well with the audience. Some speakers make a point of scripting something to elicit audience involvement at the beginning of their talks (e.g., asking for a show of hands in response to a question relevant to the talk's topic); others make a habit of starting off with a joke. Remember that the hardest part of the talk is the beginning, and once you get through the first few minutes the rest will feel easier.

The best speakers come across as expert but approachable, as well as poised but conversational. How can you achieve this? You can convey professionalism and poise through your tone, body language, and eye contact. Allow your eyes to move around the room, and if actual eye contact makes you nervous, look at the tops of people's heads instead. The pace of the presentation is crucial. Most speakers who are nervous tend to talk too fast, but occasionally the opposite is true, so you will have to adjust your pacing depending on your own predisposition. In addition, many speakers use habitual filler words and sounds (e.g., "um," "ah"), and it is important that you identify such habits in your own speech and try to minimize them. Train yourself to replace your filler words with small pauses. Pauses are not just acceptable; they are often quite useful. Pausing intentionally can help you make a point or add suspense. The overarching goal in pacing your presentation is to speak clearly, succinctly, and deliberately.

In order to come across as approachable and conversational, speakers must be able to react to their audiences, read what the audience is thinking and feeling, and respond in kind. This is why it is important to be able to speak from notes rather than a complete script. Your audience will view you as less accessible if they hear you reciting a memorized spiel. It also is important to sidestep jargon whenever possible; when jargon is unavoidable, tuck it behind the concepts and make sure that everyone is following you. Face the audience (avoid looking too much at your notes, the computer screen, or—worst of all—the screen behind you). Finally, allow yourself to be responsive to questions rather than defensive. Remind yourself that the audience is rooting for you, and rather than thinking of audience members as your adversaries, think of them as your newest collaborators.

Refining Talks Through Practice

Editing as a Team

Successful presentations result from careful editing and repeated practice. Your team will need to work together to edit if you are giving a joint presentation. This typically requires some time, so ideally the pieces of your talk will be pulled together at least a few days before the presentation itself. A common approach to take when giving a talk in collaboration with members of a research team is to divide the sections of the talk among the different individuals. Each person then drafts the PowerPoint and text associated with his or her part of the talk. After this is done, it is crucial for team members to come together to review and edit the slides. During this process, the team should focus on at least three aspects of the presentation, the first of which is the formatting and style of the PowerPoint slides. It probably goes without saying that the same template should be used by all presenters, but far more subtle details also matter. You and your teammates should examine the slides for consistent uses and styles of titles, bullets, font sizes, and overall organization of the visual aspects of the slides. If you fail to coordinate the appearance of the slides, your audience will be distracted from the content of your talk.

Second, your team should look for consistency in use of terms. Something as simple as using the word *Study* versus *Experiment* is important to keep constant. Even more important is the language used to describe the ideas driving your project. If one member of the team is presenting the background research and hypotheses and another is presenting the methods and results, the language used to link the two is going to make or break your audience's understanding of what you found. For example, look at the flowcharts in Figures 9.2 and 9.6, which we utilized earlier in this chapter; these flowcharts are designed to change your psychological mind-set to be more abstract or concrete. In the research literature, abstract versus concrete thinking is referred to not only as *mind-set* but also as *construal level*. In our own lab, we have watched presentations in which the first speaker has referred to mind-set and the second to construal level. The audience, however, cannot be expected to know that these terms refer to the same construct. Agreeing on and sticking to a common set of terms is essential.

Third, your team needs to edit the content of the talk to make sure that each speaker's segment flows naturally into the next. This requires careful attention to areas of overlap as well as potential gaps between ideas. Sometimes two speakers inadvertently provide descriptions of the same concept (e.g., a dependent variable of importance is described in detail during the background research segment and again during the segment on research methods). Equally often, one speaker assumes that another speaker will have given background information that, in reality, has been omitted. The problem of overlap may lead to boredom among members of your audience, and the problem of omission may lead to an even bigger problem: confusion. It is only through careful editing that your team can avoid these mistakes.

This is another good time to assign one team member to the devil's advocate role. This person should ask questions such as, "Is this the best way to introduce our background research?" and "Are the numbers right?" Eventually, your team will feel confident that the gaps have been filled and the overlaps have been omitted. This, combined with attention to the consistency of terms and coordination of visuals, prepares you for the next stage of the presentation process.

Practice, Practice, Practice

Once your team's presentation has been carefully edited, it is time to practice. Studious practice will allow you to be familiar enough with the key points that they come naturally and easily. And, of course, you should be aware that practicing sometimes highlights additional aspects of the talk that will need editing. The best way to think about practice is in terms of layers: alone, informally with your team, and formally with your team (ideally) in front of a practice audience. When you practice alone, you might begin by going over the words silently in your mind. But the next step is to speak aloud, perhaps using the "talk to the mirror" method. The most important thing to keep in mind when you are practicing your talk aloud is that you should act as if the audience is in the room with you. Imagine the pace of the presentation and the way it will sound to your eventual audience.

When you practice informally with your research team, you might pause midstream to ask your teammates a question, discuss a particular slide, or make the case for what you are saying. The idea at this stage of practice is to catch errors and polish the content. This leads naturally into the "real" run-through of your talk, for which it is ideal to gather a friendly audience who will give you helpful feedback. If you are presenting research for class, perhaps one of the other teams would be willing to give feedback to your group in exchange for the same. Or perhaps you could gather a group of team members' housemates to listen to what your team has to say. It is important that you encourage this audience to take notes during the talk and to be unabashed in giving feedback. It is much better to have your nervous habits and confusing word choices pointed out by a friend than by a professor. It is our belief that anyone can become a confident, competent speaker with practice.

Creating an Effective Poster Presentation

Up until now, we have focused on creating and delivering an effective research talk. However, the most common type of presentation in psychology (at least in terms of sheer numbers represented at regional, national, and international conferences) is the research poster. A poster presentation resembles an APA-style paper in terms of its organization but differs in terms of its length (see Figure 9.10 for an example).

FIGURE 9.10 Poster presentation example.

The space limitations of a poster are such that you will have only a paragraph or two for your introduction and a paragraph or two for your discussion. You are likely to have five or fewer references in your poster. What comes in between (the methods and results) can be more or less detailed depending on whether you are describing a single study or many. But no matter what, you will rely heavily on carefully placed visuals, allowing the procedure and data to come across clearly to the audience.

Who, you might ask, is the audience of a poster presentation? It certainly isn't a captive group of individuals sitting in a lecture hall. Instead, the audience of a poster presentation is a group that walks and mingles, loiters or hurries. In a conference setting, you never know until you get there whether 50 people will spend 10 seconds each looking at your poster or if 5 people will spend 10 minutes each. Sometimes a poster session is modestly attended, but other times you will be engulfed by a crowd (see Figure 9.11). Being prepared for either of these scenarios (and anything in between) is essential.

FIGURE 9.11   Poster session at a meeting of the Society for Neuroscience.

Source: Photograph courtesy (and copyright) Dominique Naegele-Clifford.

An overarching piece of advice about creating a poster is to leave plenty of time for drafting, editing, and printing. Various snafus can interfere with the poster creation process, so the more time you can set aside to carefully construct and check your team's poster, the better. In general, a poster's creation can be broken down into the six steps detailed below.

Step 1: Writing Up the Text

A poster includes the same sections as an APA-style paper: Introduction, Method, Results, Discussion, and References. We discuss these in great detail in the next chapter on writing. Abstracts are typically excluded from poster presentations, but on this point you should check with your professor (if the presentation is for a class) or with the conference website (if you are presenting your poster at a professional meeting). If you will be presenting your poster at a conference, you will need to write and submit an abstract during the application process (conferences typically use a peer-review process to decide which posters are accepted), so by the time you're creating the poster, this part of the process will be done.

The most important and time-consuming part of creating a poster is writing the main body of the text, so you will want to do this part first. Although the content of the poster will ultimately be placed into a layout program such as PowerPoint, we encourage you to draft the text using a typical word-processing program (e.g., Microsoft Word). This will allow you to focus on the content and quality of the writing without being distracted by the formatting. There will be plenty of time for making formatting decisions later. The best way to go about writing the text is to act as if you were writing up a short version of a paper. Throughout the writing process, ask yourself: "What is the most important part of the story?" and "What information is essential for my audience?" The goal is to be both comprehensive and concise in your writing.

As Swarthmore College professor Colin Purrington (2011) notes on his website devoted to poster creation: "The number one mistake is to make your poster too long. Densely packed, high word-count posters are basically manuscripts pasted onto a wall, and attract only those viewers who are for some reason excited by manuscripts pasted onto walls." No matter how concise your writing is, more likely than not you will need to do some significant editing. Editing is an extremely important part of any writing process, and in creating a poster, your research teammates can be especially helpful to one another in completing this task. Different members of the team initially can be responsible for drafting particular subsections. After the first drafts are completed, team members can exchange work and begin editing. Once you feel satisfied with the quality and content of your writing, you are ready for the next step.

Step 2: Selecting the Graphs and Visuals

If you already have given an oral presentation, it is likely you have graphs prepared, and all your team has to do is decide which one or two graphs best represent the findings. Because a concise presentation of your data is extremely important in a poster, you may want to include a table of correlations (rather than describing the correlations in the text). Usually, this information can be copied directly from the data analysis program you have been using (e.g., SPSS). A word of caution: Any visual depiction of data that you include in poster presentations must be carefully labeled. Of course this is also good advice for oral presentations, but the reality is that you will walk the audience through your tables and graphs when you are giving a talk. In contrast, poster presentations have to speak for themselves, allowing the transitory audience to understand the information without additional descriptions from you. In addition to a visual depiction of the data, your team may want to include a sample of the experimental manipulation (e.g., vignettes from different conditions) or critical visual stimuli (e.g., video capture or images used in the study). As a general rule, the total number of visual components on your poster should range from two to four.

Step 3: Formatting the Poster

This step in the process fluctuates between fun and frustrating, but if you follow the basic template illustrated in Figure 9.12, your team will produce a very nice-looking poster. At the top of the poster you will include the title of the presentation (font size of 50 point or above), your team members' names (font size of 30 or above; typically arranged in alphabetical order if all members contributed equally or, if contributions varied, in order

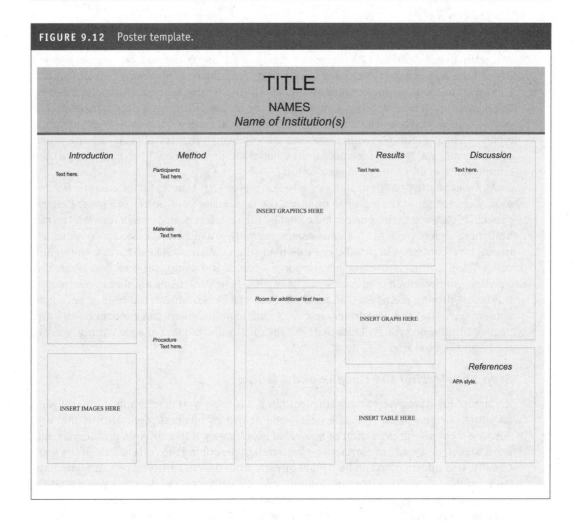

FIGURE 9.12   Poster template.

of the amount of involvement from greatest to least), and your affiliation (your college or university's name). If your research lab has a logo (or if you want to use your university's logo), leave room in the lower right-hand corner to display this along with relevant contact information (e.g., team members' e-mail addresses).

The best poster layouts include from four to six columns of text, with the visuals interspersed throughout. This helps to ensure that the text is easy to read when the poster is printed in large format. If at all possible, you should try to avoid breaking up smaller sections into different columns (e.g., the Introduction should be contained in a single column). The font size of your subheading titles (e.g., Introduction, Results) should be 30 point or larger. The text of the body of your poster should be no smaller than 18-point font. At this stage, you and your teammates will need to become diligent copy editors. It is likely that you will find you have too much or too little text for the poster, so you will need to add or remove content. This opens up the door for error, so be sure to triple-check your resulting text scrupulously. There is nothing more frustrating than catching an error when you are standing in front of your poster and your audience.

Step 4: Printing the Poster

The way that you save and print your poster depends on the software you used to create it and the printer you will be using. Although this process is becoming more and more straightforward, serious technological glitches can and still do occur. You should plan to print your poster at least a few days before you need it to be done in case you need to troubleshoot problems. If you use PowerPoint to create your poster, we suggest saving the file in three or four formats: (a) the default PowerPoint format, (b) an earlier PowerPoint presentation format (optional, but useful if you are using a recently updated version of the software), (c) a PDF file, and (d) a high-resolution PNG image file. If you use another program to create the poster, saving it as a PDF and a PNG file will work best because these are rather universal formats that most computers and printers can handle without any problem. Your team will want to have enough time to reprint the poster in case you run into a copier malfunction or the printing software transforms the Greek in your chi-square symbol into the shape of a mailbox (yes, this has actually happened). Once your poster is printed, you will need to take care of it. A good way to store and protect it is to place it in a cylindrical poster tube that is labeled with your team members' or research lab's contact information.

Step 5: Preparing Handouts

Especially at conferences, it is customary to hand out copies of your poster on regular (8.5-by-11-inch) paper. This allows busy conference attendees to get information about your study without stopping to read the whole poster. If you are using PowerPoint, the most efficient way to create a handout is to print the final version of your poster using the "scale to fit paper" option. This produces a small but legible copy. If you choose this option, make sure that the contact information is also clear and legible (you may want to enlarge its font). The number of handouts you need will vary depending on how many individuals are expected at the poster presentation, but usually the number ranges from 25 to 75. If you are attending the conference where your poster will be presented, be sure to make your handouts prior to your team's departure for the conference location. Although printing and photocopying may be available on-site, it is usually expensive and stressful to print conference materials on the day of your presentation.

Step 6: Practice!

A common mistake is to assume that one need not practice for a poster presentation. Although a poster presentation is far more spontaneous and casual than a PowerPoint talk, practice is invaluable nonetheless. We recommend that you and your teammates take turns being "visitors" to the poster, asking questions about your predictions, methods, and findings. Here is where a 2-minute-long "elevator talk" comes in handy. The premise of an elevator talk is that you should be prepared to summarize your entire study succinctly in the time it would take for you to ride an elevator from the top to bottom floor of a midsize building. And if you attend psychology conferences, you may find that your companion on this elevator is the author of your Introduction to Psychology textbook or—better yet—the person who inspired your team's line of research!

When you are presenting a poster, you will often get requests to "give me a quick summary of what you found." In translation, this means "I'm too busy or tired to read your poster, so give it to me in a nutshell, please." The nutshell version of your poster is infinitely more effective when it is rehearsed. You and your teammates might try out different versions of the summary to determine which is most compelling. You can then practice the selected version alone, informally with friends, on the phone with your grandma, and finally in front of someone who knows nothing about your project. Getting and incorporating feedback from each of these individuals will greatly enhance the quality of your spiel. When the poster presentation day arrives, you may naturally feel quite nervous and give rather rough summaries the first few times, but you will quickly adjust and polish your pitch. If a visitor to your poster does not engage you directly, feel free to initiate a conversation by offering to give a brief overview of your team's project. When done well, the 2-minute elevator talk can transform your team's findings from a semester-long research project into an appetizing morsel to be shared with acquaintances, the press, or even that famous psychologist or U.S. Senate committee chairperson who crosses your path.

Conclusion

Whether you are giving a research talk or presenting a poster, remember to resist the urge to discuss every step of your thinking, methods, and analyses in exhaustive detail. Instead, step back and imagine knowing very little about your topic. Recognize the key logical building blocks of your team's research that, put together, will tell the story efficiently. Even if the members of your audience have some expertise in this area of research, treat them as blank slates. Start with basic concepts and build quickly and efficiently to the idea, predictions, and methods. Then wow them with the findings and conclusions.

As you prepare and give any research presentation, always keep in mind that your goal is to hook your audience with the team's vision. You are crafting and telling a compelling story. This means that you need to develop your story in a way that enables the audience to elaborate on and envisage how the research and specific studies unfolded. If you accomplish this, the audience will feel a sense of ownership of the research and a sense of togetherness with your team. When people talk about psychological science as comprising a *community* of scholars, this is precisely what they mean.

References

Apperson, J. M., Laws, E. L., & Scepansky, J. A. (2006). The impact of presentation graphics on students' experience in the classroom. *Computers and Education, 47,* 116–126.

Apperson, J. M., Laws, E. L., & Scepansky, J. A. (2008). An assessment of student preference for PowerPoint presentation structure in undergraduate courses. *Computers and Education, 50,* 148–153.

Bartsch, R. A., & Cobern, K. M. (2003). Effectiveness of PowerPoint presentations in lectures. *Computers and Education, 41,* 77–86.

Cunningham, M. R. (1979). Weather, mood, and helping behavior: Quasi experiments with the sunshine Samaritan. *Journal of Personality and Social Psychology, 37,* 1947–1956.

Freitas, A. L., Gollwitzer, P., & Trope, Y. (2004). The influence of abstract and concrete mindsets on anticipating and guiding others' self-regulatory efforts. *Journal of Experimental and Social Psychology, 40,* 739–752.

Fujita, K., Trope, Y., Liberman, N., & Levin-Sagi, M. (2006). Construal levels and self-control. *Journal of Personality and Social Psychology, 90,* 351–367.

Gardner, H., with Laskin, E. (1996). *Leading minds: An anatomy of leadership.* New York: Basic Books.

Keizer, K., Lindenberg, S., & Steg, L. (2008a). The spreading of disorder. *Science, 322,* 1681–1685. doi:10.1126/science.1161405

Keizer, K., Lindenberg, S., & Steg, L. (2008b). The spreading of disorder: Supporting online material. *Science.* Retrieved from http://www.sciencemag.org/content/early/2008/11/20/science.1161405/suppl/DC1

Kelling, G. L., & Wilson, J. Q. (1982, March). Broken windows. *Atlantic Monthly.* Retrieved from http://www.theatlantic.com/magazine/archive/1982/03/broken-windows/4465/

Miller, G. A. (1955). The magical number seven, plus or minus two: Some limits on our capacity for processing information. *Psychological Review, 101,* 343–352.

Miller, G. A. (1969). Psychology as a means of promoting human welfare. *American Psychologist, 24,* 1063–1075.

Purrington, C. B. (2011). Designing conference posters. Retrieved from http://colinpurrington.com/tips/academic/posterdesign

Redelmeier, D. A., & Baxter, S. D. (2009). Rainy weather and medical school admission interviews. *Canadian Medical Association Journal, 181,* 933. doi:10.1503/cmaj.091546

Reno, R. R., Cialdini, R. B., & Kallgren, C. A. (1993). The transsituational influence of social norms. *Journal of Personality and Social Psychology, 64,* 104–112.

Rosenthal, R. (1979). The "file drawer problem" and tolerance for null results. *Psychological Bulletin, 86,* 638–641.

Traub, J. (2001, February 11). Giuliani internalized. *New York Times Magazine,* SM62–67, 91, 100–101.

Tufte, E. (2001). *The visual display of quantitative information.* Cheshire, CT: Graphics Press.

Tufte, E. (2003a). *The cognitive style of PowerPoint.* Cheshire, CT: Graphics Press.

Tufte, E. (2003b, November). PowerPoint is evil. *Wired, 11*(9). Retrieved from http://www.wired.com/wired/archive/11.09/ppt2.html

Zimbardo, P. G. (2004). Does psychology make a significant difference in our lives? *American Psychologist, 59,* 339–351.

Research Write-Ups

Seven Lessons (Plus or Minus Two)

1. Whether or not writing comes easily to you, mastering the subtleties of APA style is part of becoming a research psychologist.

2. The key to successful writing is to break the process up into small, manageable steps.

3. Collaborative writing is an iterative process, characterized by periods of solitary writing, peer editing, exchanging ideas, and team-based discussion.

4. Set deadlines, gather references, and outline your paper before you begin to write.

5. Every APA-style research paper has the same sections: Abstract, Introduction, Method, Results, Discussion, References.

6. When writing a collaborative paper, avoid giving ownership of sections to particular individuals. Instead, conduct round-robin editing, where team members trade sections and take turns adding to and editing content.

7. Seek formal feedback from a peer editor who is knowledgeable about psychology but not directly involved in your team's research project.

8. The best psychology papers are written with clarity and concision, mimic the style and structure (but not the content) of published papers, hold the attention of the reader by being rigorous yet conversational, use technical terminology and direct quotations infrequently, and always avoid plagiarism and biased language.

9. The process of writing consolidates your team's vision, feeling of ownership, and sense of togetherness. A finished paper gives meaning and longevity to your team's research project.

Everything comes out wrong with me at first; but when once objectified in a crude shape, I can torture and poke and scrape and pat it till it offends me no more.

—William James (1890/1920, p. 297)

To William James, arguably the best writer in the history of psychology, writing did not come easily. His first drafts came out so *wrong* and *crude* that they *offended* him, and he only succeeded after struggling to *torture*, *poke*, and *scrape* these initial efforts into better shape. James's vivid description of his own "ceaseless toil in rewriting" underscores what any honest author will admit: *Writing is an emotionally draining process!* This process ranges from mundane to anguishing to gratifying. The goal, of course, is to tip the scale toward a more positive and productive writing experience. To do this, you must be comfortable and proficient with the rather dull requirements of "APA style," and you must be confident in your ability to organize your exciting ideas and research into the structure and language of a standard research paper.

In Chapter 9, we discussed research talks and posters. These abbreviated presentations require a "stage presence." Their purpose is to excite the audience, outline the basics of your work, and encourage follow-up questions and discussion. By design, talks and posters allow you to leave out many details of your work in anticipation of the audience's opportunity to ask questions. In contrast, papers must be more comprehensive and yet still concise, coherent, and compelling. If you think of a talk or poster as the chorus from your favorite tune, a paper is the entire song. Just like the chorus of a song, a talk or poster should be accessible to people with different interests and levels of expertise. A paper is more detailed, technical, and formulaic. Some readers will "listen" to your paper casually, glossing over certain sections until they get to the chorus. Other readers will closely scrutinize your paper just as a music professor would analyze a composition. And regardless of the audience, readers are free to choose how much time they spend "listening" to you. They can and will tune out, especially if your paper is sloppy, loses focus, or drags on. Your goal, then, is to capture and keep the reader's attention from the introduction of your team's idea through the sections on method, results, and discussion.

In this chapter, we focus on how to write an APA-style research paper—that is, a paper that conforms to the format and style laid out in the *Publication Manual of the American Psychological Association* (2010). If you are writing a different type of paper such as a literature review or research proposal, be sure to consult additional resources. But read this chapter first. APA-style research papers contain virtually all of the elements of psychology writing. A research proposal, for example, is a special type of research paper aimed at a particular audience, such as your research adviser or the institutional review board, and written with an eye toward both expected and alternative possible results. Similarly, a literature review can be thought of as an extended introduction to a research paper.

Students are often quizzed on APA style in their research methods courses, but very few people memorize every small detail of the APA's *Publication Manual*. To complicate matters, new editions of the APA manual periodically introduce changes in style requirements that result in a good bit of confusion. Even your instructor or research mentor is likely to get tripped up on occasion by proper APA style. For these reasons, you should keep the latest edition of the *Publication Manual* by your side throughout the writing process and consult it when in doubt. It is authoritative, and it contains a wealth of examples that you can (and should) emulate. Our advice builds from the *Publication Manual*, but it cannot act as a substitute for the comprehensive information contained in this hallowed guide.

COLLABORATIVE WRITING

Our approach in this chapter reflects the overall approach of this book—that is, we emphasize collaborative writing. As a student, you probably are more familiar with writing papers individually. Most college writing is solitary work, involving just you, a keyboard, and the ideas that flow from your mind to the screen. However, research psychologists and others in the sciences almost always cowrite their papers, and there are many approaches to cowriting. The writing process usually occurs after a research team has run a number of individual studies. This allows for a natural division of responsibility, where (for example) a graduate student will write up her experiment as Study 1, and the research adviser will write up the lab's follow-up work as Studies 2 and 3. One person will take on the role of "first author," which (in the field of psychology) refers to the person who does the bulk of the work and whose name is listed first on the finished paper. It is possible that some of the individuals listed as authors on a paper (e.g., other graduate students who played central roles in helping with experimental design and data collection) have not done any original writing for that paper, but instead have edited semifinal drafts. For the purposes of this book, however, we focus on a more engaged and egalitarian method of collaboration, where the assumption is that you and your teammates have completed data collection together and are ready to synthesize the results into written form.

Cowriting a paper does not mean sitting side by side with your research team, taking turns typing away at the computer. After all, as Scott Adams (1996) has observed, "few things in life are less efficient than a group of people trying to write a sentence. The advantage of this method is that you end up with something for which you will not be personally blamed" (p. 45). More seriously, groups who literally write "together" often find that one person ends up doing the majority of the work; typically this is the person sitting in front of the computer or the person who is most vocal or best able to articulate his or her thoughts aloud. Writing en masse also disrupts the flow of the writing process. The writing proceeds too slowly, and collaborators with different writing styles and habits can become frustrated with one another.

Instead of clustering around the computer to write, you and your teammates should take individual responsibility for writing sections of the paper and then pass your drafts back and forth among one another. In other words, coauthoring a successful paper requires your team to divide and conquer tasks systematically. Collaborative writing should be an *iterative* process characterized by alternating periods of solitary writing, peer editing, and team-based discussion and feedback sessions. This can be a challenging process to organize, but keep in mind that the best writing comes not from a muse but from a *routine*. Scheduling weekly time devoted solely to writing, setting realistic goals, and being accountable to your writing routine is crucial (see Silvia, 2007). This chapter will help your team establish an efficient writing routine.

For the reader who is writing a paper individually, the advice we offer here about the general process (e.g., deadlines, outlining) and the nuts and bolts of writing (e.g., tone and style, citation and quotation) will be equally relevant to you. Moreover, the iterative nature of collaborative writing and the division of labor among coauthors mirrors many practices that the individual writer should adopt. No matter your situation, the key to successful writing is to break the process up into small, manageable steps.

Fortunately, the structure of an APA-style research paper lends itself to breaking up a project into smaller tasks. Every paper includes the same basic sections: Abstract, Introduction, Method (further divided into subsections on participants, materials, and procedure), Results, and Discussion. This organization of the manuscript will help your team divide the labor of writing across people and across time. However, before you and your teammates divide up the writing tasks, you should all come together to crystallize the paper's overarching argument and to sketch a rough outline. (Individual team members can outline each section of the paper in more detail, as we discuss later in this chapter.) Each team member should then take on the actual writing of a particular section, working alone to flesh it out. After this initial round of writing, the team should alternate between group meetings (to discuss the paper's progress) and individual writing tasks (aimed at improving each section of the paper and, later, the paper as a whole).

USING DEADLINES

Starting a writing task is often the hardest part of all, and most of us will put off the work until there is an urgent need to get something done. Working as a team is an excellent way to combat this tendency to procrastinate. After you have broken up the writing process into smaller tasks, you and your teammates should set and stick to regular deadlines for completion of these tasks and to move the paper forward. If your paper needs to be completed within a tight time frame, you might need multiple deadlines each week, perhaps daily, until the paper is done. Otherwise, weekly deadlines that coincide with regular team meetings are a great way to make steady progress on a paper that might otherwise slip in priority. Either way, the prospect of letting down one's collaborators can be truly motivating.

Importance of Regular, Well-Spaced Deadlines

Whether you are working individually or as a team, the benefits of well-spaced, self-imposed deadlines are immense. Don't just take our word for it. Ariely and Wertenbroch (2002) carried out a compelling series of studies reported in a journal article titled "Procrastination, Deadlines, and Performance: Self-Control by Precommitment." First, the researchers observed that students understand the importance of spreading work out rather than cramming it all in at the last moment. They set up classroom-based situations that allowed students to set their own assignment deadlines (i.e., due dates for three papers), but within these constraints: The self-imposed deadlines had to be on or before a certain date (e.g., the last day of class), the deadlines could not be changed, and late papers would incur a penalty (e.g., one point deducted for each day late). What should students do? To avoid incurring *any* penalties, a perfectly rational student would tell the professor that all of her papers would be turned in on the last possible date, but she wouldn't wait until the last day to complete them. She would set personal deadlines throughout the semester and systematically complete and turn in the papers one by one. After all, there was no penalty associated with turning in papers early!

But the students in Ariely and Wertenbroch's studies did not set their assignment deadlines rationally, at least not according to the strict economic definition of rationality. Instead of imposing a single end-of-term deadline for all three papers in order to avoid any otherwise "needless" penalties, they committed to deadlines spread out over the semester because they were aware of the human tendency to procrastinate. In other words, people are quite willing to give up some degree of their own flexibility and choice because they recognize that their day-to-day decisions often fail to serve their long-term interests.

The next question is whether spreading out deadlines results in a better product. The answer, according to Ariely and Wertenbroch's research, is yes, but only if the deadlines are spaced rather evenly throughout the time period available to complete the work. One of their studies illustrates this point beautifully. In this study, participants were asked to proofread three 10-page papers, each of which contained 100 spelling and grammatical errors. The number of errors correctly identified provided an objective measure of each participant's performance. Participants were randomly assigned to one of three experimental conditions. Those in one group were told to turn in all of the papers three weeks later. Those in another group were told to set a self-imposed deadline for each of the three papers; these participants tended to space the deadlines over the allotted three-week period, but not always evenly. Participants in the third group were required to turn in one paper every seven days. Regardless of condition, participants were paid for each error they correctly identified minus a $1 per day penalty for missing a deadline.

In this study, Ariely and Wertenbroch found that evenly spaced deadlines dramatically improved participants' performance, resulting in more errors detected, fewer missed deadlines, and higher earnings for completing the proofreading tasks (see Figure 10.1). Moreover, self-imposed deadlines that were more evenly spaced were nearly as effective as the experimenter-imposed evenly spaced deadlines. This means that the limitation of

FIGURE 10.1 Benefits of evenly spaced deadlines.

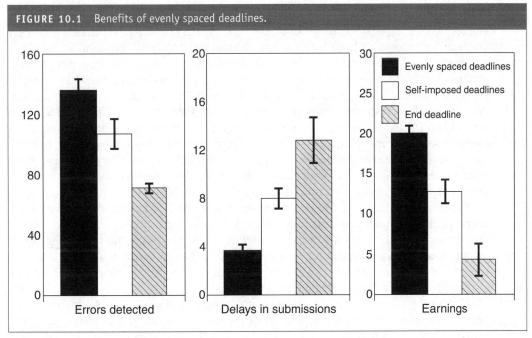

Source: Ariely and Wertenbroch (2002).

self-imposed deadlines is not that they lack the authority of the professor or experimenter. It is, instead, the nature of the deadlines themselves. We simply need to be aware that self-imposed deadlines are often spaced suboptimally.

Setting Deadlines as a Team

How can you apply this lesson to your own writing project? First, you cannot be lax about setting and sticking to deadlines. Have your group's most organized "taskmaster" clarify and write down each person's next goal and then send the group a follow-up e-mail listing everyone's tasks. If you are writing a paper on your own, recruit a friend or family member to receive regular e-mails from you that state your next goal moving forward and indicate whether or not you accomplished your previous goal. Your recipient does not have to respond to your messages; you just need a way to externalize your deadlines.

In addition, you have to think carefully about how you "portion" and space the various writing tasks. As we have already noted, the typical structure and sections of an APA-style research paper lend themselves well to breaking up the project into smaller tasks, and the nature of research means that there is a natural progression to the writing process. You can get an early start on writing your paper by drafting the introduction and methodology sections while data collection is under way. The results and discussion come next, and the abstract (although it appears first in the final paper) comes last in the writing process. Just make sure that your goals and deadlines are reasonable. Depending on the complexity of your research, drafting an entire introduction or discussion section in a single round might be too much to expect of one person. If so, break each section up even further between people or over time.

Throughout the writing process, editing and reworking of the content are crucial. This is where coauthoring a paper really contributes to the final product's overall strength. After one team member initially writes a section, another person should substantively edit (not just proofread) that material. The assumption here is that your first draft is not a great draft. If you struggle with perfectionism, as many writers do, your initial goal should be simply to get some words down on paper, no matter how rough. The team as a whole then can discuss and resolve questions about content, structure, and style. Likewise, if the introduction was drafted while the research was still under way, someone other than the original writer should revisit and rework that section in light of the actual results of the research. In other words, you should break tasks up not only by section but by iteration as well. Thoroughly editing and reworking parts of your paper from the different perspectives of your research team members will make for a much stronger final product.

If you find yourself procrastinating, try some strategies for combating writer's block, such as talking through the paper out loud to yourself or to a friend, breaking down the task into even smaller steps, starting in the middle of a section rather than at the beginning, or setting up a reward system for small accomplishments. For additional advice on this topic, see Conrey and Brizee's (2011) discussion of the symptoms and cures for writer's block on the Purdue Online Writing Lab's website.

Of course, you may not have the luxury of imposing your own schedule on the writing process. You may be taking a class in which the professor has already broken up the project into smaller components. (If so, and if the components are evenly spaced over time, be sure to thank him or her!) You may be working with a research team, with each person's schedule influencing the progression of deadlines. Or you may be working with collaborators (e.g., graduate students or faculty at other institutions) who move to the rhythm of their own internal clocks. Nevertheless, you are likely to have at least some control over the timing of the many tasks involved in the writing process. Our advice is that you assert yourself as much as possible up front, doing your best to organize and tackle the project in a step-by-step manner. And whenever you can, explicitly commit yourself and your cowriters to deadlines throughout the process.

CREATING OUTLINES

The entire process of writing will be much more manageable if, before you sit down to write, you take the time to make a careful outline. Many of you will have a rough draft in the form of an institutional review board proposal or research proposal previously assigned by your professor. Then again, your paper might exist only as a rough idea in your mind's eye, so the real work of writing begins now. Either way, the paper will need thorough organizing, writing, editing, and rewriting. Even the highest-quality draft produced before the research began will need substantial revision based on the actual progression of your work and the story you end up being able to tell with your data.

Gather References

No matter what the shape of your paper, a few key steps will help you write an effective outline. First, you should consolidate your references, many of which you may have gathered at an earlier stage of the project. It is likely that you will have a rather extensive set of sources in hand before you begin to write. As you bring together and add to this collection, it may be helpful to take advantage of one of the digital resources available for managing references. RefWorks is an extensive online research management tool that many colleges and universities make available (http://www.refworks.com), EndNote is a software program that helps you organize and cite your sources (http://www.endnote.com), and Zotero is open-source software (available online free of charge) that allows you to collect, organize, cite, and share your sources (https://www.zotero.org).

Whatever process you use to organize your references, it is essential that you have a digital or physical copy of every paper you plan to cite. As you write, you are likely to need to go back to the literature to fill in gaps in your logic. Just be sure to obtain and add copies of any additional papers to your collection. You will use the bulk of your references in your introduction, but some (e.g., those related to a questionnaire your team used) may be included in the method section and others (e.g., those related to ideas for future research) may be included in the discussion.

One strategy that many writers find useful is to create a note card (or the digital equivalent) for each source. On each card, you summarize the reference's content and relevance. This resembles the process of creating an annotated bibliography, where the reference is listed alongside a paragraph-long description of the source's content. Such annotation goes beyond copying and pasting the paper's abstract. Instead, you should think carefully about how you will integrate the source into your paper and then highlight these connections in your summary. (For detailed guidance on annotated bibliographies, see http://library.ucsc .edu/help/howto/write-an-annotated-bibliography.) As you move into the outlining phase, you can draw from your note cards or annotated bibliography to shape the structure of your paper.

Organize Writing Tasks

Once you have studied and organized your references, it is time to make a rough outline of what you want to cover in your paper. The organization of an APA-style research paper is always the same: It begins with an introduction of the topic, followed by a description of the research methods, a report of the results, and a discussion of the findings. Given this structure, your group should start by organizing writing tasks around a very basic outline. It should look something like this:

I.   Abstract

II. Introduction

III. Method

    A. Participants

    B. Materials

    C. Procedure

IV. Results

V.   Discussion

VI. References

In order to begin the outlining process and help shape the initial draft of your paper, your team should talk through the main argument you plan to make. This will become the paper's thesis statement. A good thesis statement is a concise summary of your team's idea and predictions, and it should leave very little to the imagination. Many students mistakenly think that a thesis statement merely identifies the topic of the paper, but this is inadequate. When you write a scientific report of your research, you are *not* writing a mystery. Your thesis should appear early in the introduction, take up the better part of a paragraph, and foreshadow the paper's complete story. This is true even if you found something unexpected. By the time you settle on the story you plan to tell, you will have developed a clear idea of what you found and, more important, *why* you found it. This theoretical insight should be reflected in the thesis statement. The only exception is when your story pits two, or maybe three, clear alternative outcomes against one another. In such a case, you have a horse race between these competing ideas, and your thesis should make a succinct case for each alternative.

Once you and your teammates have agreed on your paper's main argument, it's time to divide up writing tasks, which will roughly correspond to the typical sections of an APA-style paper. Individual team members will need to outline their own sections of the paper in detail before they begin to write. However, it is worthwhile for the team as a whole to have a separate conversation about each section of the paper just before this. If your team has the time, you should assign someone other than the initial writer of each section to keep detailed notes of the discussion. These notes will provide a "bird's-eye view" of the section for the writer that he or she can then use as the basis of a more detailed outline. These conversations can be extremely rewarding. They will remind your team of the reasoning behind each aspect of the project, all the way from the idea to the methods. After this, the team members will be in a perfect position to complete their writing tasks separately but with a strong feeling of togetherness.

Outline Each Section of the Paper

Below, we offer some section-by-section advice for you and your teammates as you sit down individually to outline different parts of the paper:

Introduction

Begin by listing the points you want to make throughout the introduction. Each point of your argument should be a *complete sentence,* not just a term or phrase. This is crucial because sentences will begin to reveal the logic and flow of your argument, and you will be able to match your references to the specific assertion each citation supports. As you do this, you should put the references that you plan to use in parentheses immediately after each sentence. This is a good point to assess whether you need to collect more references and to determine the relevance of those you already have. As you add details to the outline of the introductory section, examine both your list of topics and the related references to make sure they are in the best order possible. As you outline, you may find that the flow of ideas needs to change or that pieces of your argument are missing. Now is the time to reorganize the structure of your introduction and to fill in the weak spots of your argument.

Once you have organized the overall structure, you may find it helpful to write transitional sentences between main topic ideas as a further check that everything flows well together. In addition to checking the flow of ideas, you should evaluate the relevance of your content. The content you include in the paper's introduction should be directly applicable to the experiment you conducted. It is possible that your team initially read and reflected on ideas from sources that no longer tie in with the study you carried out. Exclude these reflections and focus instead on information the reader needs in order to understand your team's project. The introduction should end with a clear statement of your team's hypotheses and how the research was designed to test these predictions.

Method

The guiding principle in presenting your methods is that the information you provide should allow another investigator to replicate your research. The method section is quite formulaic, so there is very little room for creativity. And although you need to be comprehensive in describing your methodology, you should also strive to be concise. Toward this end, you must include a brief description of the participants in your experiment, including the methods of recruitment and any relevant demographic characteristics (e.g., sex, age, ethnicity). For animal research, you need to report the genus, species, and sex of your subjects as well as any other relevant details about them. The materials section is the place to describe the instruments used in the study, ranging from key equipment (e.g., the type of eye-tracking equipment utilized) to the explanation and basis of any behavioral measures (and, if relevant, the rating or scoring procedure) to the specific items included in any written questionnaires. After your data have been collected, you need to compute and incorporate the appropriate reliability estimates for any multi-item scale (typically Cronbach's alpha) or multiple-rater scoring procedure (typically the interrater reliability). Under the "procedure" subheading, you will carefully outline the design of your study. A good way to approach this important subsection is to outline the procedure step by step from the participant's point of view and then incorporate into this outline the methodological considerations behind each of the steps (e.g., the experimental design and conditions, rationale for any important instructions or deception, and so on).

Results

Brevity and clarity are the guiding principles of a well-written results section. When you begin to outline this section, you should assume that your reader has a sophisticated understanding of statistics, so there is no need to describe *how* a basic statistical test works. Instead, simply describe your prediction, identify the statistical test used to test the prediction, and report the test statistic and the few associated details that are critical to understanding your findings (e.g., any means, standard deviations or standard errors, and perhaps a measure of effect size). Immediately after you report any statistical test, briefly describe the pattern of findings and whether this pattern supports your prediction.

Here is an example of how to report data, first in outline form, then as complete sentences:

IV. Results

    A. Primary prediction = odor influences cooperation

    B. Primary finding = significant effect of condition on cooperation: $t(34) = 3.10, p < .01$

    C. Report means and standard errors by condition

    D. Note that the hypothesis was supported

We predicted and found that the manipulation of ambient odor (pleasant versus noxious) significantly influenced participants' willingness to cooperate, $t(34) = 3.10$, $p < .01$. Participants in the pleasant odor condition were significantly more likely to cooperate with the confederate ($M = 3.47$, $SE = .30$) than were participants in the noxious odor condition ($M = 2.37$, $SE = .21$). These results are consistent with our hypothesis that odor, even when it is clearly attributable to something other than one's partner, can have an effect on prosocial behavior.

Discussion

Your outline of the discussion should begin with a clear restatement of your findings. You may feel that APA-style papers are repetitive at times, and the reality is that they are. If a reader has enough time only to read your discussion, he or she should find adequate information there to understand what you were predicting, what you found, and why you think you found what you did. After you restate your findings, your objectives are to interpret them, discuss their limitations, and explore their implications and applications. Although the discussion section is the place to elaborate and explore, you must be careful never to lose sight of the data. You should discuss only the *direct* implications of your findings, and when you bring up possible applications, be sure to base these applications on the direct implications. The reader of your paper should find your ideas to be plausible and compelling. If you reach too far (e.g., by describing how your team's investigation of odor's effects on cooperation has the potential to improve relations between Democrats and Republicans in the U.S. Congress), the reader will begin to come up with counterarguments, which in turn will undermine your otherwise interesting findings.

Don't be surprised if you find that your discussion changes shape as you develop the remainder of the paper. It is likely that you will be making changes and adding ideas to the outline of the discussion as your paper's deadline approaches. But once your paper's outline is complete, writing the paper itself becomes a matter of fleshing out the details. The time you invest up front in outlining pays off tremendously when you sit down to write.

OVERCOMING THE CHALLENGES OF GROUP WRITING

> *The main goal of group writing is to ensure that every sentence satisfies all the objectives of every person in the room. This can be problematic if all the participants have different objectives. You can minimize the impact of different objectives by focusing on the goal that all parties can agree on: 1. Don't convey any information whatsoever. 2. See number one.*
>
> —Scott Adams (1996, p. 46)

When you envision the process of writing in collaboration with a group, what is your initial reaction? Relief? Dread? Confusion? When we asked some of our own students this question, most said that they see group writing as difficult and sometimes annoying, but often necessary. Group work, as we all know, presents a number of challenges. This is certainly true of collaborative writing. But contrary to what Scott Adams suggests in the quotation above from his satirical book *The Dilbert Principle*, we believe it *is* possible to succeed at conveying important information through writing in collaboration with a team.

Some scholarly and professional disciplines pride themselves on individual thinking and analysis (e.g., philosophy, art history), which often lead to single-author papers. Among psychologists, however, cowritten papers are the rule rather than the exception. As we have already suggested, your team can make the process of cowriting much more manageable by being willing to organize the project and your time carefully. This means taking our advice about setting evenly spaced deadlines. It is essential that you and your teammates establish clear expectations of what each person is committed to accomplishing. This also means following our advice about writing an outline. Once the placement and flow of ideas have been determined, team members can split up the sections, take their first cracks at writing alone, and then come back together for the editing process.

Even with this level of organization, your team cannot avoid all of the challenges associated with collaborative writing. What are the most typical problems associated with group writing, and how can your team strive to avoid them? Many students are troubled by the potential for disparities in workload across team members. Before we offer a solution, let's do a reality check. Teamwork does not entail a perfectly "even" distribution of work. Some sections of the paper are going to be longer than others. Some sections of the paper are going to feel more difficult to write than others. And some sections of the paper are going to need more revision than others. That said, you can strive to spread out the work of writing the paper by using a round-robin method of drafting and editing. After you have drafted the main outline, have each person select which section they plan to tackle first. Then set a deadline for all team members to come back together with their best possible work completed. When you come back together, trade sections and create a shared expectation that these sections will be edited and *added to* by the next person. Continue to trade sections until each person has had the opportunity to read and edit each section. Of course, competing assignments and obligations might make this process of trading sections difficult to pull off, but if you work backward from your final deadline to determine a schedule, it is likely you'll find that you can still fit this in, even if each person has only a day or two to do work on a given section before passing it along.

A number of the problems associated with group writing can be addressed through this style of round-robin drafting and editing. First is the problem of particular individuals not following through on their commitments, either by checking out all together or missing their deadlines. Holding one another accountable is much easier if you have a series of small deadlines rather than one or two large ones. You will be able to identify early on if a team member is having trouble making deadlines, and you can intervene right away to get him or her back on track. If this doesn't work, you can always enlist the aid of your mentor or instructor. We know from experience that mentors have an easier time helping students address challenges within a team if they are alerted early on. When groups fail to seek assistance until their papers' final deadlines loom large, mentors are much less likely to be able to help. Successful collaboration takes time and sustained effort, and no one can make a faltering group "whole" at the very last minute.

Another problem that can be addressed if you use this style of editing is the lack of cohesion in the "voice" of the paper that is often apparent after the various sections written by team members are combined. All coauthors, including the most seasoned researchers, have to cope with the unique and at times quirky individual writing styles of their collaborators, and coauthors' styles of writing may clash with one another regularly. However, inconsistencies among styles can be smoothed out substantially if each person has an opportunity to work with every section of the paper, and if *substantive* reworking and expanding are the norm of the group's editing process rather than the exception. If the paper remains disjointed even after this process, a good approach is to nominate one team member to take on the role of editing the final paper for flow and style. This person is likely to allow his or her own style to dominate in the editing, so it makes sense to assign this role to a person the team considers to be a strong writer. However, team members should be aware that this task is often a much bigger one than it seems to be at first glance. To protect the person who takes on this role from an undue individual burden, you and your teammates should be sure to assign other tasks (such as putting the references in APA style, writing the abstract, and formatting the tables and figures) to others.

Sometimes the challenges faced by a team are rooted in individual differences and the nature of each writing task. Some team members are going to be better or more efficient writers overall, some are going to be more familiar with APA style, and still others will be more skilled statisticians. Your goal is to identify your own strengths and weaknesses, to be as straightforward as possible with the team about these, and then to make a personal commitment to working on your weaknesses while capitalizing on your strengths. This model of building on your strengths while at the same time making a commitment to broaden your skill set will serve you well long after your collaborative research paper is a distant memory.

A healthy and somewhat easier problem to deal with is disagreement between team members about specific aspects of the paper. These disagreements can range from small issues, such as verb tense and word usage, to bigger questions concerning the level of detail that should appear in any given section. There also may be more subjective disagreements about the content of sections, such as the flow of ideas in the introduction or the choice of which points to cover in the discussion. When disagreements like these surface, it helps to get outsider feedback and advice. Ideally, your team will be able to turn to your professor, mentor, or teaching assistant for guidance on these issues. These are times to listen to your mentors and learn about the mechanics, style, and substance of scientific writing. When it is not possible to consult a mentor, your group should keep in mind that the goal of scientific writing is clarity. Which choice of language or ordering of ideas is most clear? If the group as a whole is having a difficult time resolving an issue, make it into an empirical question and ask a few peers, preferably other psychology students who are informed but have enough distance from your project to consider things from a fresh perspective.

PEER EDITING

Trading drafts with your research teammates is critical to generating and improving a cowritten manuscript, and peer feedback is just as important when you are writing a paper independently. Even professional journals rely on the peer-review process to improve each paper's reliability and lucidity. Whereas professional peer reviewers give feedback not only on the quality of the writing but also on the importance of the topic, student peer reviewers simply need to make sure that the paper is clear, coherent, and informative. Peer editors can help you to identify what you've left out, catch citation errors, point out unexplained jargon, and give suggestions for sections that need to be restructured or explained differently. Peer editing, when done well, can transform your paper from satisfactory to excellent. But receiving good peer feedback depends, in large part, on the way you set up the peer-review process. Here are some concrete tips about the peer-editing process.

Who Should Edit Your Paper?

If you are writing an individual paper about your team's research project, a natural choice of peer editor would be someone from your team. It is always a good idea to check in with your professor about this to ensure that reading and giving advice to team members about their write-ups is allowed. Assuming that it is, your ideal choice for a peer editor would be a team member who has strengths that will complement your areas of weakness. For example, if you are concerned about how you have written up the results of the study, you may find it helpful to ask the most statistics-savvy member of your team to edit your paper.

Whether or not you are able to solicit feedback from your teammates about your manuscript, you also should seek out a knowledgeable peer editor who was not involved directly in the research. A person who has some distance from the project, and who is unaware of the details of your predictions and procedures, can offer an important additional perspective to your work. It is crucial, however, that this person have a base of knowledge that will be helpful to you. This means that your peer editor could be another psychology major, ideally someone who already has taken a research methods class. Alternatively, your peer editor could be someone who is a skilled writer and can give you straightforward feedback about how and where your writing can be improved. If this person is not familiar with APA style, you will have to rely on someone else's feedback to help you double-check the organization of your paper as well as your use of citations and references. If you are worried about imposing on someone, keep in mind that the barter system works well with editing: offer to return the favor by editing something your peer editor has written, or provide pizza while he or she edits your draft.

When Should You Solicit Peer Feedback?

In an ideal world, the answer to this question is "early and often." Realistically, however, you need to be wise and balance the following considerations. On one hand, it is ideal to give your peer editor a very solid and mostly complete draft. On the other hand, you should give your peer editor plenty of time to devote to your paper the careful scrutiny it deserves, and you, in turn, will need time to incorporate changes based on your editor's feedback. These considerations are often at odds, so it is essential that you plan ahead. If you take our advice and set up and stick to small deadlines throughout the writing process, you will be able to let your peer editor know when to anticipate a knock on the door with a request for feedback. Of course, the constraints of real life will sometimes result in your needing to pass along an incomplete draft to your peer or to ask for a faster turnaround time than you would like, but some peer editing is certainly better than none.

What Instructions Should You Give Your Peer Editor?

Open-ended requests to "take a look at and edit this paper" generally lead to low-quality feedback. Your peer editor might not know what type of feedback will be most useful, and it is understandable if he or she is reluctant to be critical of a friend's or acquaintance's writing. The solution is to be systematic. Specific guidance is essential to the peer-editing process, and it is up to you, the paper's author, to provide it. If you are writing the research paper for a class, begin with the professor's instruction sheet. Create a checklist of the requirements your professor lists, and give this checklist to your peer editor. Leave space under each item for comments by your peer editor. Whether or not you have received an instruction sheet from your professor, it is also helpful to create a peer-editing worksheet similar to the one depicted in Table 10.1. One of the most useful tasks for a peer editor to

---

TABLE 10.1 *Peer Editing Instruction Sheet*

  A. **Basic Proofreading.** Please read for basic syntax and grammar. There is no need to correct errors. Instead, just CIRCLE questionable words, phrases, punctuation, and APA-style errors.

  B. **Organization.** Please outline the paper *on the second page of this sheet*. Begin by identifying the thesis and hypotheses/predictions of the paper, and then paraphrase the topic sentence of each supporting paragraph. In the space to the RIGHT of the outline, make comments related to the following questions:

  - What revisions would make the hypothesis or point of the paragraph more clear?
  - Reviewing the outline, are there places where the organization could be strengthened?
  - Are transitions between paragraphs logical and smooth?

  C. **Sections of the Paper.** In the spaces below, offer brief evaluations of the following sections of the paper:

  - Abstract:

  - Introduction:

  - Method:

  - Results:

  - Discussion:

  - APA-Style References:

  D. **Clarity.** Now focus on the clarity of the draft:
     1. Pick one good example of clear, informative, professional writing. (BOX this section of the paper and label it with a CIRCLED STAR.)
     2. Now select a section you find dissatisfying and explain in the space below why you find it problematic. (BOX this section and label it with a CIRCLED MINUS SIGN.) For instance, is the writing too casual or jargony? Does it assume something is obvious when it is not? Would you like more (or less) information and detail?

  _____

  _____

  _____

  _____

  E. **Concluding Remarks.** Make some final remarks, offering helpful advice to the author for the next step.

  _____

  _____

  _____

  _____

(Continued)

TABLE 10.1 (Continued)

F. Thesis and Hypotheses:	Comments:
_____	_____
_____	_____
_____	_____

G. Supporting Paragraphs:

1. _____	_____
2. _____	_____
3. _____	_____
4. _____	_____
5. _____	_____
6. _____	_____
7. _____	_____
8. _____	_____
9. _____	_____
10. _____	_____
11. _____	_____
12. _____	_____

do, as indicated on this worksheet, is to complete a topic sentence outline based on your paper. It is often through *reverse outlining* (i.e., outlining after the draft has been written) that illogical transitions, missing concepts, and repetition of ideas are identified.

How Should You Incorporate Feedback?

Once you have received your peer's feedback, it is time to incorporate any needed changes. As we mentioned earlier, having adequate time to review and respond to the feedback carefully is highly desirable. Keep in mind that even the best editor will provide some good and some not-so-good advice about your paper. Your job is to evaluate the feedback you receive before incorporating any particular suggestions. Sometimes you will need to check with someone else before incorporating certain changes (e.g., if you are uncertain whether the peer editor's advice about how to reference a source is correct). At other times, you may not be convinced that a suggested change is appropriate, perhaps because you feel that it would dilute or confuse the argument you are trying to make. Most of the time, however, you should trust the impressions of your peer reviewer and attempt to make the prose associated with his or her suggestions more clear. This is especially true if your editor had trouble following the logical progression of your ideas or had difficulty outlining your paper. It can be painful to admit that certain aspects of your paper need to be changed, but it is much less painful to do so during the editing phase than when you get a so-so grade from your professor or a rejection letter from a journal editor.

THE MECHANICS OF GOOD WRITING

In the remainder of this chapter, we focus on the mechanics of writing an APA-style paper. Much of our advice highlights information available in the most recent (sixth) edition of the *Publication Manual of the American Psychological Association* (2010). For additional advice and detailed descriptions, we suggest that you consult your own or a library's copy of this manual.

Tone and Style

Contrary to popular belief, a scientific paper can be pleasurable and interesting to read. One of the best ways to become familiar with the typical tone and style of psychological research papers is to read published empirical papers. What you will see as you read others' papers is that the tone is *rigorous yet conversational*. Although you might be tempted to immerse your readers in technical details in order to make your paper sound "more professional," fight this temptation and keep your writing accessible. The best-written psychology papers use technical terminology sparingly. When they do employ technical terms, they tend to introduce the terms' meanings concretely before switching to use of the terms as convenient shorthand.

Whenever possible, you should try to write in a style you would be comfortable speaking out loud. Many students find that the strategy of "talking" the text of a paper helps them avoid getting stuck. Spoken words are likely to be more focused than written text, and as you listen to yourself speak, you can incorporate your natural choice of words into your paper. As you strive to adopt an engaging tone, it helps to imagine the person who will be reading your paper. If it feels too intimidating to imagine a professor or journal editor reading your work, instead imagine a person who inspires confidence in you: perhaps a peer, a teaching assistant, a parent, or a friend.

As discussed in the APA *Publication Manual*, the use of transitional words (e.g., *next, therefore, however*) can help to create a clear flow of ideas and a "smoothness of expression" (p. 65). A related goal of this style of writing is to be concise. Avoid the temptation to meet a target number of pages by filling the paper with tangential or redundant ideas. "Economy of expression" (p. 67) is the guiding principle of APA-style writing, and a beneficial side effect of eliminating extra words and elaborating on ideas only when necessary is that your paper will be more enjoyable to read.

Verb Tense

Choosing the appropriate verb tense is often a tremendous challenge for novice writers. Keep in mind that changing the verb tense in the middle of a paragraph or section is likely to undermine the flow of ideas in your paper, so consistency is key. As a general rule, you should use past tense or past perfect tense to describe something concrete that already happened, such as your own or others' experimental procedures and results (e.g., "Kaufman tested the hypothesis that . . ."; "Grossman and colleagues have explored . . ."). When describing a theory, however, you should use present tense (e.g., "Dissonance theory suggests that . . ."). These guidelines mean that the introduction to your paper will include both present and past tense. In contrast, the method and results sections will be dominated by the use of past tense (e.g., "Heart rate was significantly higher in the experimental condition than in the control condition"). In the discussion section, you will continue to use past tense when you are referring to the results, but you will use present tense to discuss the implications of the results (e.g., "These findings lend support to the idea that . . ."). As a final consideration, keep in mind that the active voice (e.g., "The experimenters administered the questionnaire") is generally better than the passive voice (e.g., "The questionnaire was administered by the experimenters"). These and other tips about the use of verbs can be found in the *Publication Manual* (see pp. 65–66, 77–78).

Table 10.2 presents excerpts of text from the introduction, method, results, and discussion sections of a coauthored paper (Detweiler-Bedell, Detweiler-Bedell, Hazlett, & Friedman, 2008). These excerpts help demonstrate the way in which verb tense varies within the body of a paper.

Headings

Although scientific papers can be pleasurable and interesting to read, they afford very little room for creativity when it comes to section headings. In APA style, headings are typically quite formulaic; the required method of formatting headings is specified in the

TABLE 10.2 Examples of Verb Tense		
Section	**Text**	**Rationale**
Introduction	Even individuals with objectively equivalent symptoms often **perceive and cope** with their symptoms in different ways (Mechanic, 1986; Meyer, Leventhal, & Gutmann, 1985) . . . . Illness cognition models **predict** important factors related to illness outcome, such as treatment seeking behavior and adherence to treatment regimens, for a variety of physical as well as mental illnesses. However, the application of illness cognition models to the study of mental illnesses (i.e., psychological disorders) **is** still relatively new (see Lobban, Barrowclough, & Jones, 2003, for a review).	*Present tense:* The introduction describes theories and the state of current research, so it is written primarily in the present tense (except when stating what researchers previously did or found, in which case the past tense is used).
Method	Participants **were** 139 undergraduate students who **completed** the study online. As compensation, participants **were given** a chance to win one of twelve cash prizes ranging from $10 to $40. The sample **was** predominantly female (70% women, 30% men) and **had** an average age of 19.5 years . . . . After reading the vignette, participants **wrote** about what it would be like to experience these symptoms and then **filled out** a series of measures **designed** to assess their perceptions of the causes of and potential cures for the symptoms. Participants also **answered** general demographic questions and **reported** on their previous level of knowledge of depression and heart conditions.	*Past tense:* The method section describes the procedure followed in the conduct of the study, so it is written in the past tense.
Results	There **was** a significant main effect of experimental condition on participants' perceptions of the extent to which physical factors generally not subject to internal control **caused** their symptoms, $F(3, 134) = 4.36$, $p < .01$, and the extent to which psychological factors generally subject to internal control **caused** their symptoms, $F(3, 134) = 14.69$, $p < .001$. Specifically, participants who **were told** that their symptoms of depression **were** due to a heart condition **felt** the causes were more physical ($M = 2.64$, $SE = .12$) than participants in the depression ($M = 2.07$, $SE = .12$) condition.	*Past tense:* Research findings are described in the results section in the past tense.
		(Continued)

TABLE 10.2 (Continued)		
Discussion	In sum, the results of our first study **suggest** that the diagnostic label **influenced** participants' interpretation of the (otherwise identical) symptoms of depression. Participants **asked** to imagine they had depressive symptoms reflecting a heart condition **perceived** their symptoms as having more physical (less controllable) causes and as improving due to luck or medical care . . . . Another potential direction for future research **is** to manipulate perceptions of reward among individuals likely to have an opportunity to provide social support to someone with depression. The first step in this direction **is** to identify the specific short- and long-term rewards associated with creating or maintaining a relationship with a depressed individual.	*Present and past tenses:* The discussion section is where the research implications are described in the present tense and the findings are described in the past tense.

Source: Excerpted from Detweiler-Bedell, Detweiler-Bedell, Hazlett, and Friedman (2008).

Publication Manual (pp. 62–63). The one section of the paper that does *not* include a heading is the introduction. This first section simply comes immediately after the centered title of the paper on the paper's opening page. All other sections include headings bearing their names: Method, Results, Discussion. Within the body of the paper, subsection headings may be used when needed. Any headings that you choose to include should be concise and clear, conveying to the reader the key point of the subsection. As in outlining, subsection headings should appear at any given level only if more than one subsection is needed; a single subheading under a main heading is regarded as superfluous. APA style allows for five levels of headings, but the typical paper has no more than three or four levels. Table 10.3 presents a fictitious example of the levels of headings in each section of a paper, formatted according to APA style.

Statistics

Reporting statistics with clarity and precision is essential, and successfully doing so takes a good deal of practice. We urge you to model and mimic one or more published articles reporting on studies that have used research methods similar to yours. You will find that all research papers refer to the primary results in sentence form within the body of the paper, and many papers include tables and/or figures to summarize more complex statistical information (such as depicting an interaction between two independent variables in a graph or including a series of correlations in a table). The APA *Publication Manual* includes detailed advice on presenting statistical information (pp. 116–124) and on displaying results (Chapter 5). The approach to reporting data follows a predictable sequence. You note your prediction, the pattern of data (e.g., means, standard errors), and the statistical

TABLE 10.3 Example Headings Formatted According to APA Style

Farming's Positive Influence on Physical and Emotional Well-Being

Personality Characteristics of Farmers
Open Spaces and Well-Being
Caring for Plants and Livestock

Method

Participants
Procedure
Measures
        Demographics.
        Personality characteristics.
        Physical activity and health status.
        The Green-Thumb and Cow-Liking Scales.
        Measures of emotional well-being.

Results

Impact of Farm Life on Well-Being
        Physical health.
        Emotional health.
Moderating Role of Caring for Plants and Livestock

Discussion

The Costs and Benefits of Farming
The Importance of Intrinsic Motivation
        Caring for plants.
        Caring for animals.
Conclusions and Future Directions

test (e.g., ANOVA, *t* test, chi-square). This is then followed by a very brief statement of how the results relate to the hypotheses of the research.

Citations and Quotations

We encourage you to read published articles in order to model the style and tone of writing by well-established authors. Modeling and mimicking can be especially helpful when it comes to the frequency and style of in-line citation, quotation, and referencing. *In-line citation* refers to naming the sources of any ideas, theories, or findings that you mention within the body of the paper. Whenever you refer to a source directly or otherwise rely on a source to make an assertion, you should cite the source in parentheses, typically at the end of the relevant sentence.

In APA style, the most common method of citation is to insert in parentheses the last name of the author(s) of the source being cited, followed by a comma and the year of the publication. When more than one source is being cited in a given sentence, the sources are listed in alphabetical order by the first author's last name, separated by semicolons. An example citation of multiple sources is as follows: (Banaji & Mitchell, 1999; Salovey & Pizarro, 2000; Whisman & Friedman, 1996). However, when the names of the authors being cited are part of the sentence referring to their work, you should cite the publication date in parentheses following the names; for example, "As Lemm and colleagues (2009) found . . . ." Online sources, sources without authors, and sources without dates are cited somewhat differently; you should refer to the *Publication Manual* for advice on these kinds of citations. Whenever you are quoting, paraphrasing, or extending the ideas of another author, you need to cite that author. If you are uncertain about whether or not to cite an author, err on the side of caution and do so.

Incorporating the exact words of another author into your paper is known as direct quotation. Before we discuss the mechanics of using quoted material, let us first make a rather blunt point: *You should use direct quotations only rarely.* The purpose of your paper is to report your own work, not to quote other authors, and most of psychology writing should be in your own words. You must have an excellent reason for using any direct quotation. If you need to be precise or you find it impossible to paraphrase another author's assertion accurately, a direct quote might be appropriate. But be careful. It is all too easy to turn these good reasons into an excuse: "I just couldn't find a way to say it as well as the original author did!" If you find yourself using direct quotations more than a few times in your paper, revisit the quotations during the editing process and do your best to paraphrase (and, of course, cite) the ideas instead.

When you do quote a source directly, the original words should appear in quotation marks, and the citation must include the name of the author(s), publication year, and page number in the original source where the quotation is found. If the quotation is 40 or more words long, it should appear as an extract or block quotation, broken off from the rest of the text and indented, with no quotation marks. This description from the *Publication Manual* illustrates this formatting:

> Start such a *block quotation* on a new line and indent the block about a half inch from the left margin (in the same position as a new paragraph). If there are additional paragraphs within the quotation, indent the first line of each an additional half inch. (American Psychological Association, 2010, p. 171)

References

The reference section comes at the end of your paper, immediately following the discussion section, but beginning on a new page with the heading "References". This is where you list all of your cited sources in alphabetical order by author name, using APA style. Creating a reference list in APA style initially will seem cumbersome and foreign, and you will find yourself referring frequently to the *Publication Manual* for detailed advice on how to format certain kinds of references. We also recommend that you visit the Purdue Online Writing Lab (http://owl.english.purdue.edu/owl/), which is an excellent source of information about APA style (Angeli et al., 2011).

One mistake that some students make is including in their reference sections sources that are not cited in the body of the paper. The reference section is intended to be a list of works cited, not a list of works consulted. If a given article or other source influenced your thinking, cite it within the paper and include it in the references. Omit from your references any materials you may have read in an earlier stage of your work that did not end up being related to the content of your paper. After you have a complete draft of your paper, you will need to double-check that everything you cite does, indeed, appear in the reference section, and that nothing appears in the reference section that you do not cite. Before you turn in your final paper, you should double-check your citations and references yet again, because it is possible that ideas were added to or taken away from the body of the text during the editing process, leading to changes to the citations that must be reflected in the reference section.

Another common question we hear from students is how they should cite a study that is cited in someone else's paper. The short answer is that you should always track down the original paper yourself, read it, and then cite it directly. For example, imagine that you have read the following sentence in a paper by Brownell (1991): "Our beliefs about control influence how we feel about our bodies and our health (Campbell, 1981; Rodin, 1986; Taylor & Brown, 1988)." You would like to refer to this line of research in your own paper, and the Brownell article provides a concise summary of it. You are tempted to echo Brownell and write: "The control we have over our daily lives, even perceptions of having control, can be beneficial to our psychological and physical well-being (Rodin, 1986; Taylor & Brown, 1988; as cited in Brownell, 1991)." Is this appropriate? The answer is no. Although it is extraordinarily convenient to rely on other scholars to distill complex information for you, it is your job as an author to track down and read all sources that you cite in your paper. The *Publication Manual* urges psychology writers to use secondary sources (e.g., the Brownell paper in our example) *only* when a primary source is unavailable, out of print, or not written in English (p. 178). If you fail to follow this advice, you risk playing a game of "telephone" or "whisper down the lane," in which information that is cited secondhand invariably gets distorted over time. This inaccuracy runs counter to science's core values. By reading each original source, you can be assured that what you are reporting is as accurate as possible.

Though we urge you to track down and read everything you cite in your paper, there is a practical exception to this blanket rule in the case of collaborative writing. Of course, it is ideal for every contributor to read every reference. But when you coauthor a paper, the reality is that not every author will have read every source that is referenced in the paper. Different coauthors have different areas of expertise; one author may focus on the literature review as his or her contribution to the paper, while another author focuses on the statistical analyses and write-up of the results. It is the job of all coauthors to talk to one another and to describe the various references they have read that contribute to the paper. In team-based psychology writing, although it is unlikely that every author has read every source, every source should have been read by someone on the team. In addition, we would argue that the first author of any paper is ultimately responsible for the paper as a whole. It would be prudent, then, for the first author to consult every source and ensure that it is being cited accurately. Moreover, if you are cowriting a paper for a class, be sure to check with your professor about course expectations regarding this issue. In all likelihood, a course paper will require only a limited number of references, but every person on the research team might be expected to read every one of these.

Avoiding Plagiarism

The process of writing a psychology research paper is different from the process of writing a creative arts paper. Psychology writing calls for a somewhat detached, professional tone, a lack of embellishment, and the incorporation of multiple sources. You are expected to know past research well and to link your ideas to others' arguments and theories. As Stolley and Brizee (2011) note, professors often place students in a difficult position by presenting somewhat contradictory sets of instructions:

> There are some intellectual challenges that all students are faced with when writing. Sometimes these challenges can almost seem like contradictions, particularly when addressing them within a single paper. For example, American teachers often instruct students to:

Develop a topic based on what has already been said and written	**BUT**	Write something new and original
Rely on experts' and authorities' opinions	**BUT**	Improve upon and/or disagree with those same opinions
Give credit to previous researchers	**BUT**	Make your own significant contribution
Improve your English to fit into a discourse community by building upon what you hear and read	**BUT**	Use your own words and your own voice

Instructions such as these plant seeds of insecurity in many of us, and a common response is to cling too closely to the work of others. The risk is that clinging too closely to others' work can lead to plagiarism.

The Council of Writing Program Administrators (2003) provides this definition of plagiarism: "In an instructional setting plagiarism occurs when a writer deliberately uses someone else's language, ideas, or other original (not common-knowledge) material without acknowledging its source" (p. 1). Consider the etymology of the word *plagiarize.* According to the *Oxford English Dictionary,* the classical Latin word *plagiārius* is defined as a "person who abducts the child or slave of another; kidnapper; seducer." Our advice to you is to avoid, at all costs, kidnapping the words of others. Some forms of plagiarism are blatant, such as when a student takes part or all of another person's paper and turns it in as his or her own. Some forms of plagiarism are more subtle, but also problematic, such as when a student steals specific sentences or ideas from another source without using quotation marks and proper citation. In this digital age, it is all too common for students to be tempted to copy and paste helpful descriptions or phrases from materials written by other people. In the spirit of efficiency, students may tell themselves that they are using the lifted words as "placeholders," and that they will come back and put those sentences in their own words later. But "later" may never arrive, or by the time it does, the students have become so familiar with and attached to particular phrases that they have difficulty remembering that the words are not their own.

Contrary to popular belief, professors are not encyclopedias. But we, too, live in the digital age, and a Google search can quickly identify the true origins of sentences that seem out of place in a student's paper. Simply stated, you must avoid the temptation to copy and paste material. If you cannot part with a particular sentence or phrase, use quotation marks and proper citation when you put it into your text. Whenever your thinking has been shaped or influenced by another person's research or theories, cite that person's work. Referencing the sources of your ideas is essential, and your default position should always be to cite your sources. The penalty for citing too much or too often is negligible: Typically it takes the form of constructive feedback from your professor. The penalty for citing too little or not at all is severe: Typically it ranges from failure of an assignment to expulsion from one's school or workplace. Thus, it is crucial that you understand exactly what plagiarism is and learn how to avoid committing it. The Purdue Online Writing Lab offers additional descriptions of and exercises related to plagiarism that are well worth exploring before you begin the writing process (see Stolley & Brizee, 2011).

How can you, as a student, grapple with the challenging task of learning to be a skilled writer of psychology research papers without crossing into the territory of plagiarism? The answer is simple, but the work takes time: You should become an avid reader of publications that appear in the best psychology research journals. Your research mentor can suggest the top journals in fields related to your research project, but a good starting place for most students is the journal *Psychological Science,* which publishes short and longer research reports on a broad array of topics (see http://www.psychologicalscience.org/index.php/publications/journals/psychological_science). Published by the Association for Psychological Science, *Psychological Science* is the top-ranked empirical journal in the field of psychology, and the articles found in the journal tend to be fascinating and relatively accessible. Reading as many of these articles as you can will help you begin to appreciate the way in which psychologists write about their research.

Because APA-style papers are quite formulaic, the key is to become familiar enough with the approach of other writers so that you can mimic the style and structure—but *not* the content or ideas—of previously published papers. This is especially useful when it comes to learning how to use subheadings or to cite and reference sources properly, but it is equally beneficial when it comes to grappling with appropriate tone and style of writing. When we talk about mimicking, we are referring to a process of using a well-written, peer-reviewed paper as a *model* of APA-style and the typical structure, form, and flow of psychology writing. This is very different from plagiarism.

Avoiding Biased Language

Every writer needs to be conscientious about avoiding the bias that can creep into the language of any research paper. Bias often stems from faulty assumptions that have been incorporated over time into careless language. These include the assumption that the reader or study participants are male, or that the race, age, ethnicity, or sexual orientation of a group is homogeneous. To correct some of these biases, the proper action is to be inclusive (e.g., by using plural pronouns such as *they* rather than singular pronouns such as *he*). To correct other such biases, the proper action is to be precise (e.g., by identifying your sample's ethnic identity in specific terms).

The American Psychological Association's commitment to avoiding bias in writing is summarized by three general guidelines in the *Publication Manual*: (a) describe at the appropriate level of specificity, (b) be sensitive to labels, and (c) acknowledge participation (pp. 71–73). The first guideline urges us to err on the side of specificity by referring, for example, to the age ranges of our participants and to avoid using the words *sex* and *gender* interchangeably. At the same time, this guideline suggests it is important to mention differences only when they are related to what you are reporting (e.g., is it relevant to mention the sexual orientation of your participants if it is not linked with your predictions or findings?). The second guideline reflects the fact that bias can arise from the use of loaded or judgmental language, such as "the borderlines" or "the old people." Instead, in these cases, you might refer to "individuals diagnosed with borderline personality disorder" or "older adults" (pp. 71–72). The third guideline reminds us to be cautious in our use of depersonalized descriptions of the individuals who participate in our research studies. Psychology writers refer to specific characteristics of their samples in the method sections of their papers (e.g., college students, patients, retirement home residents), but throughout the remainder of their papers, the people who took part in their studies are referred to as *participants* or *subjects* or *the sample*. Most writers today use the word *participant,* but it is still appropriate to use the other terms, especially when these are grounded in statistical terms such as *sample size* or *within-subjects design* (p. 73). For additional details on reducing bias based on gender, sexual orientation, racial and ethnic identity, disabilities, and age, please refer to the *Publication Manual* (pp. 73–77).

Conclusion

Scientific writing is storytelling, and by telling the story of your research in its entirety, you are sharing the vision of your team's project. A sense of closure comes from a completed write-up, and there is no deeper sense of ownership than what you feel when you see your semester-long, year-long, or seemingly never-ending project captured in page after page of carefully crafted text. When you engage in collaborative writing, you are putting your team's togetherness to a final, challenging test. Difficult tasks help to unite a team, and there is no doubt that writing is difficult. Completing a write-up of psychological research can be deeply satisfying, because doing so solidifies the authors' vision, ownership, and sense of togetherness. Whether your research teammates are your peer editors or your coauthors, you will find that providing feedback and asking for help along the way will link you with one another in a deep and significant manner.

Stated simply, writing the results of a research study is the best way scientists have of communicating their findings with precision. Writing is also ideal for disseminating information to individuals you may never meet face-to-face. By writing up your research, your

TABLE 10.4 Specialized Venues for Publication of Undergraduate Research Papers

- *Canadian Undergraduate Journal of Cognitive Science (CUJCS)*
- *Journal of Psychological Inquiry (JPI)*
- *Journal of Psychology and the Behavioral Sciences (JPBS)*
- *Journal of Student Research (JofSR)*
- *Modern Psychological Studies (MPS)*
- *Psi Chi Journal of Undergraduate Research (PCJ)*
- *Stanford Undergraduate Research Journal (SURJ)*
- *Undergraduate Journal of Psychology (UJOP)*
- *Undergraduate Research Journal for the Human Sciences (URJHS)*
- *Yale Review of Undergraduate Research in Psychology (YRURP)*

team gives other people the opportunity to be inspired by, to build on, or to extend your team's work. If you are collaborating with a faculty mentor, your research article might be submitted to and published in one of psychology's many research journals. Moreover, some journals, such as those listed in Table 10.4, focus specifically on publishing papers written by students.

So, yes, with some hard work, you can publish your research. But even if your audience is limited to a single professor and the members of your research team, putting the results of your research in writing gives your project longevity. Although presentations are efficient methods of engaging a broad audience in your topic, they are ephemeral. Papers, especially in this digital age, have an infinite shelf life.

References

Adams, S. (1996). *The Dilbert principle: A cubicle's-eye view of bosses, meetings, management fads and other workplace afflictions*. New York: HarperCollins.

American Psychological Association. (2010). *Publication manual of the American Psychological Association* (6th ed.). Washington, DC: Author.

Angeli, E., Wagner, J., Lawrick, E., Moore, K., Anderson, M., Soderland, L., . . . Keck, R. (2011, May 28). APA style. Purdue Online Writing Lab. Retrieved from http://owl.english.purdue.edu/owl/section/2/10/

Ariely, D., & Wertenbroch, K. (2002). Procrastination, deadlines, and performance: Self-control by precommitment. *Psychological Science, 13*, 219–224.

Brownell, K. D. (1991). Personal responsibility and control over our bodies: When expectation exceeds reality. *Health Psychology, 10*, 303–310.

Conrey, S. M., & Brizee, A. (2011). Symptoms and cures for writer's block. Purdue Online Writing Lab. Retrieved from http://owl.english.purdue.edu/owl/resource/567/1

Council of Writing Program Administrators. (2003, January). *Defining and avoiding plagiarism: The WPA statement on best practices*. Retrieved from http://www.wpacouncil.org/positions/WPAplagiarism.pdf

Detweiler-Bedell, J. B., Detweiler-Bedell, B., Hazlett, A., & Friedman, M. A. (2008). The effect of diagnosis and perceived reward on perceptions of depressive symptoms and social support. *Journal of Social and Clinical Psychology, 27*, 1–35.

James, W. (1920). Letter to Mrs. Henry Whitman, July 14, 1890. In H. James (Ed.), *The letters of William James* (Vol. 1, p. 297). London: Longman, Green.

Plagiary. (2006). In *Oxford English dictionary* (3rd ed., September 2011 version). Retrieved from http://oed.com/view/Entry/144942

Silvia, P. J. (2007). *How to write a lot: A practical guide to productive academic writing*. Washington, DC: American Psychological Association.

Stolley, K., & Brizee, A. (2011). Avoiding plagiarism. Purdue Online Writing Lab. Retrieved from http://owl.english.purdue.edu/owl/resource/589/01

Student-Initiated Research

Seven Lessons (Plus or Minus Two)

1. The best psychological research is always collaborative, even when you take on the role of *principal investigator*.

2. Identify professors who have the potential to be strong mentors. Assess the extent to which their interpersonal styles and areas of research interest are compatible with your own.

3. Meet early on with potential mentors. Explore and engage in conversation with them about their research and teaching.

4. Once a mentoring relationship has been established, have an explicit discussion with your mentor about general expectations, frequency of meetings, project timeline, and resource issues.

5. Confirm that your project is doable with the time and resources you have available.

6. Seek out students who are engaged in similar research experiences and create a peer-mentoring network. The ability to share successes, hopes, and concerns among peers is invaluable.

7. Consider recruiting younger students to assist you with your project. You will gain the experience of being a mentor and benefit from their perspectives.

8. Student-initiated research projects provide unique opportunities for you to be deeply involved in every step of the research process.

You know my methods. Apply them, and it will be instructive to compare results.

—Sir Arthur Conan Doyle (1890, p. 96)

Team-based psychological research often occurs as part of a methodology class or within a laboratory run by a professor, postdoctoral student, or graduate student. There is no substitute for these organized research projects. As an undergraduate, you should be introduced to the research process in a structured and supportive collaborative environment, and research labs in particular serve as the quintessential model of what it is like to be a research psychologist. But what if you are encouraged (or even required) to complete an "original" senior thesis? What if you have a deep desire to go beyond instructor- and mentor-initiated research? These situations call for you to take the next step in your education, but you should not feel like you are stepping off a cliff. The goal is for you to take primary responsibility for a project's vision and execution. All too often, such a project is described as *independent research,* but this term is misleading and potentially harmful. We believe quite strongly that the best way to do a student-initiated project is to allow it to grow naturally out of your other research experiences and to seek the guidance of a research mentor. As we will make clear in this chapter, the best psychological research is always collaborative, even when you assume the role of *principal investigator.*

Before you decide to pursue a self-initiated research project, you should step back and identify your personal reasons for doing so. Here are a few stereotypes of students who propose their own research projects:

- *The competitive student:* "It'll look good on my resume."

- *The idealistic student:* "I want to make the world a better place!"

- *The curious student:* "I need to solve this question!"

- *The trapped student:* "I'm required to do this thesis."

These caricatures undoubtedly oversimplify things. Most students resonate to some extent with all of these motives because, underlying the stereotypes, there are some very good reasons to do a student-initiated project. You might want to apply theory and research to a "real-world" problem. You might want to learn more about the field of psychology or understand better how researchers go about their work. Perhaps taking the lead role in a research project will help you gain insight into or prepare for future career paths. In any case, the experience will enable you to hone and demonstrate a number of skills that will be attractive to graduate schools and employers. All of these are valid reasons for pursuing a more independent, if not truly autonomous, research project.

Whatever you do, don't be fooled into thinking that student-initiated research entails a better, more impressive research experience. This is a mistaken impression and the wrong reason for pursuing an independent project. In most cases, you should pursue the best possible research, and faculty-initiated projects tend to be better grounded and more likely to succeed. But such projects are not necessarily available to every student who wants the experience, and even if the opportunity is there, you may find that your own interests take you in a different direction. Our advice is that you learn as much as possible from more directed research experiences and take on a self-initiated project only to augment those experiences.

Before we discuss how to go about initiating a research project, it is important to acknowledge that there are a number of different types of independent work, and the exact requirements will vary from one institution to the next. Many colleges and universities require a "capstone" class in the psychology major that acts as the culmination of all that the student has learned. This course often requires a significant APA-style paper, but it typically takes the form of a literature review rather than a write-up of novel empirical research. Writing a literature review requires a great deal of reading and synthesizing of information (much like writing an extended introduction to a research paper), and it can be done within the time span of a semester.

In contrast to a literature review (and as you already know if you have read the other chapters in this book), conducting an original research study is much more time-consuming once you take into account the need for institutional review board approval, survey design, piloting, data collection, data analysis, and write-up. For this reason, institutions that *require* original research of all students may offer a class in the junior year that helps guide the development of the students' projects. But perhaps more common than a required thesis is the *option* of doing one's own research project, which is encouraged at some institutions and merely "allowed" at others. Typically, this kind of project takes the form of an honors thesis or independent study research. Sometimes research methods class projects help pave the way for these independent projects. In other instances, students search out inspiring ideas or draw connections between theories they have been exposed to in their course work.

In all of these cases, the student is in the driver's seat and takes primary responsibility for the generation of an idea, creation of the hypotheses, and design of one or more studies. Once again, however, it is a mistake to view these projects as truly independent. Conducting a successful research project necessitates reliance on the expertise and contributions of a skilled mentor, and recruiting and mentoring younger research assistants can be an effective and rewarding way to complete a research project. In other words, you should seek out or create a team environment even when you initiate your own project.

SUCCESSFUL SELF-INITIATED PROJECTS

The key to the success of a self-initiated project is to develop an idea that engages you and your research mentor. You are looking for a happy collision of imagination, daily life, past research experiences, and course work. Of course, all of the advice about idea generation from Chapter 2 still applies, but as the principal investigator you will need to sustain the project. This means that you must identify a topic and a particular question that will capture and keep your attention over an extended span of time. In other words, the question really needs to grip you. Likewise, your mentor will be more involved in your efforts and will provide better, more extensive mentoring if your idea relates to his or her research. This is a simple fact of academic life. Mentors are specialists by training, and they can be extraordinarily busy, so the best way to capture their attention and time is to propose a relevant, irresistible idea. Besides, there is nothing better than pursuing an idea that exhilarates both you and your mentor whenever you meet.

Let's say, for example, that you have always wanted to have a better understanding of the behavior of young children. Previously, you wrote a paper on young children's play styles for your developmental psychology class, and you studied infant brain development in human physiology. Engaged by this course work, you began serving as a research assistant late in your sophomore year in a child development laboratory. Now, for winter break of your junior year, you head home and have the opportunity to play with your two nieces, Nola (13 months old) and Cori (21 months old). You remember a game that you played with them when you last saw the girls four months earlier in August. As you pretended to drink tea using a doll's cup, you "accidentally" knocked the cup over and exclaimed, "We have to clean up!" The two little girls (then 9 and 17 months old) laughed and laughed as they held paper towels in their tiny fists and mimicked you cleaning the imagined mess. Home for winter break, you decide to see if they still remember the game. You go through the same motions, knock over the teacup, and exclaim, "We have to clean up!" Cori begins to laugh and immediately grabs a paper towel to scrub the table, but Nola looks perplexed. After watching her cousin play, however, Nola again joins in the fun. What explains the memory differences in the older versus younger child? You recall from your class on brain development that the frontal cortex develops rapidly for one-year-olds (Herschkowitz, Kagan, & Zilles, 1997). Does this period of brain development help explain the differences in memory that you observed? Although Nola didn't remember the game this time around, will she remember it when you return home again during spring break? With these questions, the seeds of a self-initiated research project have been planted.

The scenario we just described is imagined, but it was inspired by the work of Conor Liston, who, as an undergraduate at Harvard University, carried out a senior thesis that asked these same questions. In his study, he brought 9-, 17-, and 24-month-old children into the research lab and presented playful actions to them like the "cleanup" example described above. Four months later, these same children returned to the research lab, were exposed to the props used previously, and were given a verbal prompt (e.g., "cleanup time!"). The experimenter observed whether or not the children were able to recall and reenact the actions they had imitated months before. As predicted, the 21- and 28-month-old children were able to recall the playful actions they had performed four months earlier, but the 13-month-old children were not. This supported the idea that long-term memory is associated with development of the brain's frontal lobe during the transition into the second year of life (Liston & Kagan, 2002). Liston's thesis, titled *Self-Recognition, Language, and the Origins of Long-Term Event Memory: Implications for Infantile Amnesia,* won Harvard's Psychology Faculty Prize in 2002, but even more impressive, Liston published his experimental work in the journal *Nature,* which is an extraordinary accomplishment for an established professor, let alone for a senior biology-psychology major!

What contributes to successes such as Liston's? Are there common factors underlying the most successful student-driven research projects? Even though an individual student's experience is likely to be as unique as the project he or she pursues, we believe the answer is yes. Typically, students like Liston have served as research assistants, and in the course of doing so they have found that their colleges or universities offer opportunities for independent study or honors work. In addition, some programs require each undergraduate psychology major to conduct an independent research project to meet a graduation requirement. But as we have already noted, the idea of truly "independent" research departs from the team-based model we advocate. Researchers in psychology rarely work in isolation, and collaboration is critical to almost all psychological research. By extension, successful student-initiated projects are almost always built on the groundwork of previous experiences, and the best "independent" projects are those, ironically, that are meaningfully *dependent*. Conor Liston's research was done under the supervision of Jerome Kagan, one of the "fathers" of developmental psychology (Haggbloom et al., 2002), and Kagan coauthored Liston's *Nature* article. Even doctoral dissertations involve close collaborations with faculty advisers and peers.

This last point brings up the issue of "ownership." Does the student have perpetual ownership of the self-initiated project, leading to first authorship of writings and presentations related to the project? The answer depends on the context. A student is typically the sole author of the write-up of his or her thesis and of any on-campus presentations of the research (with acknowledgments and thanks given to the mentor and other individuals who helped with the project). Formal presentations at regional or national professional meetings are far more likely to be coauthored. If the presentation is closely tied to the student's work, then he or she may be the first author. Otherwise, the adviser may take on the first author role. And if the student is fortunate enough to have his or her project lead to additional studies and eventual submission to a professional journal, the issue of authorship must be visited yet again. It is rare to have an undergraduate project lead to a first-authored publication because additional follow-up studies are typically carried out after the student has graduated. Liston's case is the exception rather than the rule. More often, a successful student-initiated project leads the student to be a coauthor on a peer-reviewed manuscript. In cases where a student's original study sparks a line of research but does not warrant inclusion in the submitted manuscript, the student may have no authorship status at all. These choices depend on the nature of the project, the findings, the timing, the mentor, and, of course, the student him- or herself.

THE MENTORING RELATIONSHIP

Ideally, student-led research should complement work that has been done already and should be related to the work of an experienced research mentor. Thus, your first goal is to develop a strong mentoring relationship with a research adviser. One of the ways of identifying a mentor is to build on past collaborations. Perhaps you carried out a project for your research methods class, and your professor approached you with explicit encouragement for you to continue this line of research. Or perhaps you have been engaged in summer or academic-year research with a particular faculty member, and you feel prepared to propose a study that is related to the work you have been doing. If either of these scenarios applies to you, consider yourself lucky. You have a ready-made (and well-earned) mentoring relationship.

But what if you are inspired to pursue self-initiated research but don't know whom to approach for guidance? Seeking out a good research mentor is a process, and the more deliberately you go about matching your interests to those of a potential mentor, the more successful your project will be. Below, we describe the process of seeking out the best possible mentor.

Identify a Pool of Potential Mentors

The first step in looking for a mentor is to take stock of the people in your academic circle who might be willing to work with you. The most obvious choices of mentors include full-time faculty in the psychology department. But depending on the setting in which you are a student, there may be other choices. In some academic settings, adjunct or visiting professors might be willing to take on research students. At larger universities, master's and doctoral students might be eager to serve as research mentors. Quite often, a doctoral student will supervise an undergraduate's research project on a day-to-day basis, but the undergraduate might have the opportunity to sit in on larger weekly lab meetings or meet occasionally with one of the graduate student's faculty advisers. And if your research interests are interdisciplinary, you might want to look to a professor outside of psychology as a potential mentor or, at least, coadviser. Whatever the case, you ideally should come up with a pool of two or three potential mentors. There are many reasons your initial choice of a mentor could fall through, and besides, it is useful to speak to as many potential mentors as possible in order to learn more about various researchers' interests and work styles.

The criteria you should use to identify potential mentors at this early phase are three-fold: the person's (a) area of expertise and (b) interpersonal style, as well as (c) your past interactions with him or her. First and foremost, you need to know something about the area of expertise of each of your potential mentors. Broadly speaking, what is the potential mentor's subdiscipline (e.g., social, clinical, cognitive, developmental) and what areas of study interest you the most? If you are a student at a small institution, there may be only one faculty member for each area. Even so, you might be surprised to learn that a faculty member in a seemingly unrelated area has interests that overlap with yours (e.g., a cognitive psychologist might study the influence of video games on cooperation and aggression). On the other hand, larger research universities can have dozens of faculty members, postdoctoral students, and graduate students per area. If you are in such a setting, you will need to peruse potential mentors' research interests by tracking down their publications, paying close attention when your course instructors mention their own research, and even wandering the halls of the psychology department striking up conversations with faculty and graduate students alike.

The second criterion for you to keep in mind is the interpersonal style of each of your potential mentors. Is he or she easygoing or strict, hands-on or hands-off, accessible or intimidating, popular or relatively unknown? Although it may be counterintuitive, your goal is not necessarily to choose the easygoing, hands-on, accessible, and popular professor as your research mentor. You may thrive under the guidance of a strict mentor, or you may be the type of person who needs a great deal of independence and would feel stifled by a hands-on, more directive approach to mentoring. It is *not* important that a mentor's style duplicates your own; instead, you are looking for a mentor whose style works best for you. You need to get along with your mentor, of course, but perhaps it is best if his or her style complements (or should we say compensates for?) your own weaknesses. If you tend to be a bit disorganized, you might need a taskmaster as an adviser. If you tend to be overly anxious about academic work, perhaps you need a more easygoing adviser.

Keep in mind, too, that the most intimidating of mentors might be a brilliant scientist who nevertheless is a softy at heart. You might have difficulty approaching such a person initially, but you might find that he or she has been waiting for the energies of an undergraduate to bring life to an otherwise formulaic line of grant-driven research. Alternatively, the most popular professors might be surprisingly hard to work with or, in all likelihood, extremely busy. They may be admired for good reasons, but they may not be the best mentors if they are stretched too thin.

Finally, you should think about your past interactions with potential mentors. Have you taken classes with these individuals? Visited them in office hours? Asked them for guidance? How did they respond to you? Could you imagine seeking them out for advice in the future? A word to the wise: It's never too early to meet with potential mentors. Even as a first-year or second-year student, you should make use of your professors' office hours for more than just help with your courses. Go and talk with them about their research or how they ended up becoming professors. The more often you visit your professors, ask questions, and show curiosity, the more likely they are to remember you and treat your ideas for self-initiated research favorably.

Read Potential Mentors' Syllabi and Publications

In order to narrow your pool of potential mentors, you will want to look for a match between your own interests and the expertise of the mentor. General area of expertise should have been the first criterion you considered, but once you have a pool of two or three potential mentors it is time to learn more about each person's current interests. The best way to understand your potential mentors' interests is to look at their recent teaching and research experiences. Familiarize yourself with the classes they teach and read their syllabi online. If they have their own websites, navigate to their "research" and "publications" pages. Alternatively, search for their names using PsycINFO and Google Scholar. What kind of research have they published recently? At this point, carefully read a few of their most recent research publications. If you are a student at a college where the faculty have numerous teaching responsibilities, it's possible that potential mentors might not have large numbers of publications. If this is the case, go online and try to track down their résumés (or curricula vitae, or CVs, as they are known in academic circles) to see if they have been doing presentations of their research at conferences. If you can't find your potential mentors' CVs independently, e-mail them to ask if they have presented any recent talks or posters at national or regional conferences. They might be able to send you copies of these presentations.

The purpose of this phase of selecting a mentor is not only to assess fit but also to begin to develop your research ideas. If you find yourself being interested in or (better yet) inspired by a potential mentor's research or teaching, then the likelihood that you will come up with a well-grounded, mutually rewarding research idea is significantly greater. The time and effort you spend now trying to learn about your potential mentors will pay off later. Also, when the time comes to approach your potential mentors, they will appreciate (and might be impressed or even flattered) that you did background work about their interests in advance of meeting with them.

Approach a Potential Mentor With Your Ideas

When you have exhausted your background search, it is time to step back and consider your pool of ideas. Earlier, we described how imagination, real life, and your education up until this point must come together as you develop an idea for a self-initiated project. The key here is to identify ideas that are both interesting to you and related to work done by your potential mentor. Draw connections based on these ideas, and brainstorm a list of potential hypotheses to pursue. There is no need to flesh out the project completely. Instead, focus on hypothesis generation and bring a number of these ideas to a potential mentor with the hope of getting his or her guidance. E-mail the potential mentor to set up an appointment. If he or she has open office hours, you can just stop by, but it is always a good idea to send an e-mail to (re)introduce yourself and to say that you plan to come by during office hours to discuss some possible research ideas.

When the day of the meeting arrives, go prepared with paper and pencil (or a fully charged laptop). Before you share your favorite ideas with your potential mentor, briefly describe the process you went through in getting there. For example, first tell him or her about a general topic that interests you (e.g., child development), then tie that into your potential mentor's past work (e.g., frontal lobe development in infancy), and finally share the background for your hypotheses (e.g., a research paper you wrote in developmental psychology and observations you made over winter break while playing with your nieces). Ask your potential mentor if he or she knows of anyone who has studied this particular topic or hypothesis (in this example, the nature of the relationship between memory and frontal lobe development around 12 months of age). Finally, ask him or her for input about your idea.

Refine, Respond, and Revisit

In some cases, a potential mentor will respond with enthusiasm to your ideas, but then will break the news that he or she is not able to take on new students at this time. In other cases, a potential mentor will listen to your idea and either suggest that you are not yet prepared to pursue a project or refer you to someone else in the department with more closely related interests and expertise. If you receive some variation of these responses, don't be discouraged. Keep in mind the fundamental attribution error (Ross, 1977): You should attribute reactions like these to the situation (e.g., this person must be swamped with other obligations), not to you or this potential mentor (e.g., my ideas are awful; this person's a jerk). This is why we encourage you to create a pool of two or three potential mentors. Although one of the mentors may have risen to the top, it is likely that you will need to revisit your list, further refine your ideas, and go on to ask someone else to work with you.

With some luck, you'll soon find a mentor who will be interested not only in your idea but also in the opportunity to work with you. Even so, your potential mentor is likely to send you away with feedback that leads you to make changes to your hypotheses or to pursue additional background reading. It is your obligation to respond to that feedback, make the necessary revisions, and then visit him or her again to talk more concretely about the project.

Commit to a Mentoring Relationship

The commitment to a mentoring relationship may be more or less formal, depending on the norms of your institution. Regardless of the degree of formality demanded by your college or university, we encourage you to have an explicit discussion with your mentor about his or her expectations, including the frequency of one-on-one meetings, the timeline associated with the progression of the project, and resource issues (e.g., access to laboratory space, funds for compensation of participants, ability to recruit younger students as research assistants). Clarifying these expectations up front will help you avoid future misunderstandings and will contribute to a more successful and rewarding project.

DEVELOPING THE PROJECT

As you work with your research adviser in designing your research project, keep in mind the following tips. First, be realistic about the amount of time you have to complete the project. Depending on your circumstances and your institution, the time you have can range from more than a year to a mere three months (i.e., the length of a term in the quarter system). Work backward from the final due date of your project and give your best estimate of when you will need to be finished with each stage of the process. In some cases the incremental and final due dates will be fixed (e.g., when a senior thesis class is required of all majors). In other cases there will be no concrete deadlines, and if this is true for you, ask your mentor for advice about how best to structure your time.

Although all projects and each institution's requirements are unique, in an ideal world you would have at least eight months (i.e., a full academic year) to usher your research study from the development of an idea to the presentation of the final product. The most successful student-driven projects are typically under way more than a full calendar year before the expected deadline. We present the timeline in Table 11.1 as an ideal, keeping in mind that you may not have the "luxury" of spending this much time on a single study. Regardless, the specific steps (e.g., idea development, data collection, write-up) are likely to apply, and coming up with a detailed timeline for your project will serve you well.

After sketching a schedule for yourself, you should think carefully about your participant pool. Will you have ready access to the people you hope to recruit as participants? If you are interested in carrying out research with special populations (e.g., infants, older adults), make sure that your research adviser already has established connections with those populations. It takes a great deal of time to cultivate these connections, and access to special populations is predicated on trust between the potential participants and the

---

TABLE 11.1 An Ideal Timeline for a Student-Initiated Research Project

- **Formalize the idea:** 4 weeks
- **Write the Institutional Review Board (IRB) application:** 4 weeks
- **Refine materials and procedure while waiting for IRB approval:** 8 weeks
  (but this could be significantly longer or shorter, depending on the institution)
- **Collect data:** 8 weeks
- **Analyze data:** 3 weeks
- **Write paper:** 4 weeks
- **Prepare presentation:** 2 weeks

researcher. Yes, your summer internship may have put you in regular contact with health care workers, but if you want to study the impact of fatigue on health-related decision making, you may find that your contacts in the health field fade into the woodwork when you try to recruit them to take part in your study.

Aside from the IRB review process (much of which is outside your control, yet can take a good deal of time to complete), the data collection phase has the greatest potential to slow you down. We have seen the projects of some of our most talented students grind to a halt because they were unable to recruit enough participants. Even under the very best circumstances, participant recruitment can be a challenge. For this reason, we believe that undergraduates should seriously consider designing projects that can be completed using *convenience samples* of other college students unless you truly have ready access to other populations (e.g., by piggybacking your study onto a line of research in your mentor's lab). Although college students are not appropriate participants for every study, it is still the case that most psychology studies draw their samples from this convenient population, so if you do the same you will be joining a long line of psychologists who have followed this tradition.

Finally, we urge you to keep in mind a sobering truth: The ideal project you dream of may end up looking somewhat different from the realistic project you actually do. Because a research project is time-consuming even under the best of circumstances, it is critical that you confirm that your proposed project is *doable*. It must be doable with the resources and participants that you have at your disposal, and in the time you have to complete the project. If at all possible, you should design a project that is related to past research that you have conducted in collaboration with your research adviser or that you have already explored in the context of one of your classes.

Experience has taught us that the appeal of more complex projects is far outweighed by the practical limitations of what is doable. Let us give you a concrete example of this potential pitfall by describing an actual student-initiated project that was conducted by beginning graduate students (the two of us) but failed as a result of its complexity. As graduate students, we were interested in determining how individuals perceive and respond to emotional conflict within a group. All groups are likely to experience some level of conflict at some point in time, but this conflict is often subtle and perhaps even unspoken. This type of subtle, unspoken negativity can lead to "bad vibes" among group members. We hypothesized that the potential negative outcomes of group conflict would be moderated by group members' abilities to accurately perceive and effectively repair their own emotions and the emotions of others. Specifically, we proposed that there may be individual differences in the ability to manage bad vibes, and these individual differences might be related to a person's "emotional intelligence" or ability to understand and manage emotions.

The method we came up with to test this hypothesis was to invite groups of three participants into the lab and to ask them to take part in a role-play in which their group's goal was to resolve a hypothetical labor negotiation. Upon arrival, participants filled out a packet of questionnaires, including measures of their emotional competencies. For each role-play, two of the participants were randomly assigned to represent a coalition of doctors and nurses from a private hospital. One participant was asked to represent the doctors, and the other was asked to represent the nurses. These participants were asked to work together as a team, even though some of their specific concerns differed. The third participant was assigned to play the part of a representative of the hospital's board of trustees, who was meeting with the doctors and nursing staff to negotiate issues such as the quality of the workplace environment, the delivery of medical services, and compensation.

Midway through the negotiation session, participants were asked to fill out an additional series of questionnaires. For those playing the roles of doctor and nurse, one of these measures assessed their impressions of their partners. Unknown to the participants, the research team later modified these impressions to be more negative and then shared the questionnaire with the partner. Knowledge of these lukewarm impressions created a subtle interpersonal conflict within the doctor-nurse coalition (i.e., participants were clearly offended that their partners didn't think more highly of them), but the conflict went unspoken because the impressions were shared individually with the participants and the participants had no time to discuss them before the negotiation resumed. The key dependent measure for this study was the extent to which the doctor and nurse could nevertheless work together and help reach a final, mutually beneficial resolution in the face of the bad vibes that we had created.

Admittedly, this study was filled with theatrics. That was part of the appeal! But the cover story was too complex, there was deception involved, and (worst of all) the study could be done only when all three participants showed up as planned and on time. Looking back almost 20 years later, we are stunned that we took on such a convoluted experiment. Somehow we managed to run 22 groups of participants over the course of an entire academic year, but this really was not enough to perform the complicated data analyses required when groups of participants interact and influence one another's behavior. Alas, the results we obtained after spending an exceptional amount of time planning and conducting this study were hardly decipherable.

The lesson we learned from our experience is that there are clear advantages to keeping a study simple, straightforward, and uncomplicated. In order to feel better about a decision to keep your study simple, think of your self-initiated project as the first in a series of studies. After all, it is rare to see fewer than two or three studies in a published paper. If a relatively basic first study leads to strong results, it is likely that you, your mentor, or another researcher will spend time refining, replicating, and extending your work. Of course, hindsight is always 20/20, but we recognize now that our "bad vibes" study should have been preceded by a simpler questionnaire-based study. For example, we could have asked participants to read hypothetical scenarios of interpersonal conflict and make judgments about how they would handle the situations. After this, we could have created a more realistic but well-controlled role-play involving just one true participant and two confederates. Today, we could implement such a study entirely online, so the participant could do the negotiations with virtual partners whose responses were scripted by the researchers. As you can imagine, there are many ways to test any question of interest. The wise choice is to keep your study as manageable as possible and as closely linked to past work as you can.

PEER MENTORING

Although you should design any self-initiated project under the guidance of a faculty or graduate student adviser, the mentoring and collaborative process should not stop when you leave your adviser's office. Another shortcoming of the label *independent* is the assumption that it is up to you, and you alone, to move the project forward. Yes, you may be "in charge" of the vision and the development of the project, but the best academic work relies on the input of multiple people. In higher education, you are surrounded by one of the single greatest resources there is: other students. It is to your advantage to seek out peer mentors and collaborators to complement the guidance provided by your research mentor. In collaborating with other students, you will find solutions to many of the smaller problems that would otherwise require you to make an appointment and wait for your adviser's feedback. Peer mentoring is a form of *cooperative learning,* and research demonstrates that working with your peers will enhance your interpersonal relationships, self-esteem, and confidence as well as lead to greater academic success (Johnson, Johnson, & Smith, 1998).

Receiving Mentoring From Equally Experienced Peers

Where can you look for peer mentors, and what contributions should peers make to your project? Again, the answers depend somewhat on the practices of your institution or department. Your research experience may be formalized through enrollment in a class. One or more members of the psychology department may teach this class, and part of your participation is likely to include trading feedback with your peers. But what if you do not have a formal structure for this type of guidance? Is it possible to create something similar on your own? We believe that the answer is yes and that the effort you invest in creating a peer-mentoring network will pay off tremendously over time.

The first step in creating a network of peers is to find out if other psychology majors at your institution are conducting independent research. You may be able to locate these students through word of mouth, or you may need to seek the guidance of your professors to locate them. It is not necessarily important that all the students in your peer-mentoring network be engaged in similar research projects. Your goal is simply to identify other students who are carrying out empirical work and to assess whether they would be interested in working in collaboration with you.

The level of formality of the peer-mentoring process depends on your own and your peers' desires. Our own senior research students have found it helpful to meet on a weekly basis (about an hour each week) with a group of three to six peers. Typically, in the early stages, these meetings are spent sharing the details of one another's projects. As the students' familiarity with other group members' projects grows, the purposes of the meetings shift to providing updates, identifying problems, and brainstorming solutions. When you meet with your peer-mentoring group and provide a weekly project update, you should be sure to highlight something that is going particularly well; it is possible that your successes (however small) may inspire one of your peers. The updates you and your peers present should also be forward-looking, allowing each person to share goals for the upcoming week.

Perhaps the most useful part of peer-mentoring meetings is the problem-solving process. Do not be afraid to talk about concerns or shortcomings and to allow the group to help you find solutions. Sometimes solutions can be found within the group. For example, if one of you has been having difficulty recruiting participants, perhaps another member of the group has had greater success and can share the strategies he or she implemented to enhance participation rates. At other times, you may find the problem-solving process of your peer-mentoring group to be unproductive; this is an indication that you may need to meet with your research adviser to examine the problems you are having.

Providing Mentoring to Less Experienced Peers

The peer-mentoring process we have discussed so far involves forging relationships with other students who are in the same position you are. They, too, are carrying out self-initiated research and are interested in using peers as sounding boards throughout the span of their projects. In addition to developing a peer-to-peer mentoring network, you might consider acting as a mentor to younger students who are interested in assisting you with the research you are conducting. This means creating your own research team composed of one or two students who are willing to volunteer time to help you with tasks ranging from refining your materials and procedure to piloting and running participants. The students best suited to this task are likely to be fellow psychology majors in their sophomore or junior year. Ideally, these students will be bright and motivated at least in part by their desire to pursue their own projects in the future.

The benefits of this type of mentoring are bidirectional. You gain person-power and outside perspectives that will be invaluable in furthering your research project. You also have an opportunity to be a mentor, which can be a tremendous learning experience in itself. At the same time, these younger students gain the opportunity to conduct psychology research under the ongoing supervision of a more experienced peer.

Not surprisingly, we would encourage you to develop this type of arrangement if at all possible. This is the very essence of collaborative research that we have been promoting and describing throughout this book. Still, a cautionary note is in order. Before you move ahead and create your own research team, you should be sure to talk to your research mentor. It is possible that recruiting other students to help you conduct your research violates expectations of "independence" required by your mentor or your program of study. Although we advocate the creation of such teams because it can facilitate the success not only of your project, but also of the projects the younger students may do in the future, your mentor or institution might not consider a team-based structure acceptable in the context of an "independent" project. In our opinion, this is a serious potential shortcoming of requiring students to complete "independent" research projects—but, of course, you have to work within the requirements of your program.

FINDING FUNDING FOR STUDENT-INITIATED RESEARCH

Research that you conduct in the context of a classroom or a professor's laboratory requires resources, and these resources can be costly. Items ranging from equipment (including computers, printers, software) to research space to participant compensation all cost money, yet it is easy to take for granted the availability of these resources. When you decide to pursue your own project, it is likely that you will be responsible for getting some funding to support your efforts. Your need for funding will be minimal if your participants are going to be filling out a survey in the library or dining hall for no compensation. Your need for funding will be much greater if your participants are coming to the research lab to complete reaction-time tasks over the course of a three-day period. For such a study, your expenses will include (at a minimum) the costs of the reaction-time software and participant compensation. In any case, it is a good idea for you to become familiar with the sources of funding that are available for undergraduate students.

The first place to look for funding is close to home. Does your institution give small grants to students to support academic pursuits such as research? If so, apply! You also may want to ask your mentor if there are any local, off-campus funding opportunities that you would be eligible to apply for. Many institutions of higher education have personnel (sometimes on the faculty, other times on the staff) whose job it is to look for funding sources. Many of these opportunities will be directed toward faculty, but it is possible that there are sources of money for students as well. Ask your mentor if your institution has the equivalent of an office for sponsored research or a grants and awards coordinator.

Outside the bounds of your own institution, you can search for regional and national funding sources. One of the best resources for grants directed toward student work is Psi Chi, an international honor society in psychology. (Information about membership, and about starting a Psi Chi chapter at your institution, can be found online at http://www.psichi .org.) Psi Chi's list of potential sources of funding for undergraduates is extensive (see http:// www.psichi.org/awards/data_sheet.aspx), and not all funding sources require member- ship. Additional resources may be found through the American Psychological Association's Office of Precollege and Undergraduate Education (http://www.apa.org/ed/precollege/index .aspx) and the Social Psychology Network (http://www.socialpsychology.org).

The specific characteristics of individual grants vary. Some will fund equipment or materials, and others will fund participant compensation. Some will give a grantee a sti- pend to conduct research over the summer, and others will provide monies for travel to a conference to present the work. Sounds fantastic, right? The only downside of the grant submission process is the time it takes to get a grant application in order. It is important to keep in mind that the grant application process is a competitive one, and, like so much of research in psychology, it requires a good deal of planning and forethought. If you can plan ahead and make the time to apply for grants, it is certainly worth your while to attempt to get funding.

Conclusion

In this chapter, we have described how the best student-initiated projects are not as inde- pendent as the name *independent research* might suggest. By the time you are ready to take on your own project, the hope is that you have had the team-based experiences necessary to propel you toward a sophisticated, informed, and compelling research question. Relying on the contributions of mentors (both professors and peers) is critical, and some of the best student-initiated projects build on or complement earlier work that you have done in class or with your research adviser.

Despite the important role that collaboration can play, it does feel different when you are responsible for your own project. When you are conducting research as a member of a team, it is possible (and often expected) that you are involved only peripherally in some parts of the process (e.g., a teammate might take the lead on data analysis). With a self-initiated project, in contrast, you are personally and deeply involved every step of the way. The organization, design, and storytelling are ultimately placed in your hands. A spirit of togetherness is fostered not by the group, but by you, because it is your job to seek out experiences that nurture a positive atmosphere. Yes, you may delegate tasks and benefit from the input of others, but you will closely watch every detail. Others provide perspective when they act as sounding boards, check in on your progress, and help you to shape and stay true to your goals, but the vision for the project is yours.

References

Doyle, A. C. (1890). *The sign of four*. London: Spencer Blackett.

Haggbloom, S. J., Warnick, R., Warnick, J. E, Jones, V. K., Yarbrough, G. L., Russell, T. M., et al. (2002). The 100 most eminent psychologists of the 20th century. *Review of General Psychology, 6,* 139–152.

Herschkowitz, N., Kagan, J., & Zilles, K. (1997). Neurobiological bases of behavioral development in the first year. *Neuropediatrics, 28,* 296–306. doi:10.1055/s-2007–973720

Johnson, D. W., Johnson, R. T., & Smith, K. A. (1998). Cooperative learning returns to college: What evidence is there that it works? *Change, 30,* 26–35.

Liston, C., & Kagan, J. (2002, October 31) Brain development: Memory enhancement in early childhood. *Nature, 419,* 896. doi:10.1038/419896a

Ross, L. (1977). The intuitive psychologist and his shortcomings: Distortions in the attribution process. In L. Berkowitz (Ed.), *Advances in experimental social psychology* (Vol. 10). New York: Academic Press.

CHAPTER 12

The New You

Seven Lessons (Plus or Minus Two)

1. You have changed as a result of conducting team-based research. Engaging in accurate self-assessment is critical, but it is also notoriously difficult. Initiate candid discussions with your mentors and peers to identify your strengths and areas of weakness.

2. The top-rated skills sought by employers are ones you are likely to have gained through collaborative research: teamwork, critical thinking, analytical reasoning, and communication.

3. Information gathering and networking are important parts of the job search process. Set up *informational interviews* with people who work in careers that are of interest to you.

4. When you apply for a job, meticulously edit your résumé and your cover letter, paying close attention to detail.

5. When you apply to graduate school, the fit between you and the program is essential. Extensively research a variety of graduate degree programs to determine which program best suits you and your eventual career goals.

6. The graduate school application process is time-consuming, and you should typically begin preparing to apply at least a year before the program starts. Organization and planning ahead are crucial.

7. Keep in touch with potential recommendation writers after graduation. Contact professors early with your requests for letters and provide an organized set of materials to assist them in writing their recommendations.

(Continued)

8. Your personal statement should be compelling, professional, and very well written. It should highlight how your academic experiences and passions match up perfectly with the particular graduate program to which you are applying.

9. Completing a collaborative research experience in psychology should be viewed as a beginning rather than an end. Your participation in team-based research will have lasting impacts on your professional and personal development.

The content of most textbooks is perishable, but the tools of self-directedness serve one well over time.

—Albert Bandura (quoted in Stokes, 1986, p. 2)

When Kelsey was a toddler, her favorite toy was a stuffed unicorn. It slept in her crib, sat by her high chair, and accompanied her on every car ride. But over time her interest in the unicorn waned, and her mother put the toy away in a drawer. It wasn't until Kelsey was in second grade that she came across the toy again. With a mixture of awe and confusion she called out to her mom: "I don't understand . . . . How did you shrink my unicorn?"

This chapter is designed to help you reflect on a profound outcome you may otherwise fail to appreciate: You have grown and changed as a result of your involvement in collaborative research. Rather than seeing how far you have come, your natural assumption may be that you are merely keeping up with the pace of your education. It is all too easy to take for granted the unique skills you have acquired while ushering a project from an idea to a finished product.

The fallacy of mistaking a change in the self for a change in the world is more common than you might think. In a multipart study, Richard Eibach and his colleagues investigated how changes in one's knowledge, beliefs, or experiences can lead to a false belief that the world (not oneself) has changed. For example, in one study the researchers surveyed teachers and staff at a public elementary school to assess the extent to which "the risks and dangers kids face today" (Eibach, Libby, & Gilovich, 2003, p. 921) have increased or decreased over the past 30 years. Each participant compared the dangers of today to six specific times in the past: 5, 10, 15, 20, 25, and 30 years ago. All participants viewed the world as less safe today than it was in the past, and they felt as though they were assessing levels of danger based on objective indicators in the world around them. However, there was a strikingly large increase in perceived danger at a time that had nothing to do with changes in the world and everything to do with changes in the individual: the point in time when the participant first became a parent. Independent of age, sex, or length of parenthood, having one's first child coincided with a spike in perception that the world is a dangerous place for children.

This tendency to mistake a change in oneself for a change in the world is robust, but it can be modified with a relatively simple intervention. If you had been a participant in another of these researchers' studies, you would have been given the following instructions:

On the lines below please list 3 things about yourself (your personality, your attitudes, your perspective on things, etc.) that have changed since you were in high school. List one thing about you that has changed on each of the lines, for a total of 3 separate things about you that have changed. Be as specific as you can in describing each of the things about you that has changed since you've left high school and become a college student.

_____

_____

_____

(Eibach et al., 2003, p. 924)

Go ahead and try this out. After you've listed three things, ask yourself the following questions: How difficult was it to think of three ways you've changed since high school? How much have you actually changed? Over this same period, how much have your high school friends, parents, and hometown changed? Perhaps not surprisingly, Eibach and colleagues (2003, Study 4) found that having participants generate short lists of ways they have changed over time led them to believe that they had, in fact, changed and that the world around them (e.g., their parents and hometown) had remained relatively stable over time.

In this chapter, we will discuss how you can reflect on the ways you have changed through your experience conducting team-based psychological research. We also will help you to assess and understand how to market what you have learned through this process. The key is to take a step back and look at the bigger picture in terms of how this experience has shaped you and in terms of how you can put your new skills to use in the years after graduation.

REFLECTING ON YOUR EXPERIENCES

Having had experience conducting research prepares you to reflect on some of the broad questions about the research process. What, exactly, is the purpose of doing research? And what was the purpose of the particular research project you carried out? We would like you to imagine bumping into the kindly next-door neighbor who has been checking in on your well-being for years. "How are you doing, dear?" she asks. This is the type of person who is not satisfied with a "Fine, thanks." She wants a more detailed explanation, but she isn't an expert on anything you have been doing. What would you say to her about the purpose of doing research in psychology? And why should she care about your project? Being able to reflect on and articulate answers to these broad questions is essential. This will be the foundation of what you might say to future employers or mentors. So stop reading right now and try it out.

Another set of questions to consider relates to the amount and type of research that you have completed. What is the ideal amount of research that an undergraduate should do? In our experience, a psychology major ideally should pursue research beyond what is required as part of a research methodology class. This means pursuing a student-initiated research project, volunteering in a research lab, engaging in academic-year research, or conducting summer research with a faculty mentor. Out of all these options, a summer research experience can be the most transformative. Students often find a number of unique benefits to immersive summer research, among which are more undivided attention from research mentors and the luxury of not being distracted by the numerous demands of the academic year. The overarching benefit of pursuing additional research in psychology, regardless of the context, is that it gives you the opportunity to apply what you have learned and to pursue topics that interest you in greater depth. If you do have an opportunity to work in a faculty mentor's research lab, it is most advantageous for you to work there for an extended period (i.e., one or more years), as this will demonstrate to future employers or mentors that you have stamina and staying power. That said, this does not mean you should stick it out if the experience is unpleasant. Perhaps another research lab would be a better fit. And, of course, a life of research is not the best choice for everyone.

On a related note, what is the ideal balance between research and typical classroom-based learning? The reality is that your experience doing research is going to be enhanced by your progression in the classroom. If you have the opportunity to take advanced classes in statistics or classes that focus on empirical approaches to psychological questions, take them. When we asked our own students to reflect on this question of balance, they agreed that their appreciation for research grew as they advanced in the major. Still, they believed that *doing* research allows students to blaze a trail into something new and different and provides students significantly more learning per hour of involvement than a typical class does. In most cases, the amount of learning that happens in the lab surpasses what you might learn while passively absorbing material from a book or a lecture.

Many undergraduates wonder what is more important, the particular field of research or the general skills and techniques learned through the research process? At this stage of your career, the answer to this question is clear: Learning research methods and ways of thinking are far more important than learning about the specific field you are researching. Research experiences help to shape your likes and dislikes, and what you learn from lab-based work may guide you on a path toward a job or graduate school, but specialization can wait. When we were undergraduates, for example, one of us researched philosophical questions about death, and the other researched motivation in children. We went on to graduate school with these divergent experiences, but independently chose the same research adviser. Under the mentoring of our adviser, Dr. Peter Salovey, we immersed ourselves in the study of persuasion and health psychology. Would either of us have predicted this path when we were undergraduates? The answer is an unequivocal no.

Finally, what makes some research experiences better than others, and what is the ultimate goal of your research experiences? The best research experiences depend in large part on the nature of your collaborations, and learning to work as a team underlies the success of any given project. Likewise, being able to take an existing idea and then look at it or think about it in a new way is another characteristic of the very best research projects, and the ability to think creatively and scientifically is best developed in the context of teamwork. At the same time, the end goal of engaging in collaborative research is largely personal. Your experiences can and should help shape who you are and what you might do after graduation and beyond.

ASSESSING YOUR EXPERIENCES

Moving from reflection to assessment requires that you focus concretely on your own strengths and weaknesses. This process may feel intimidating, in part because it requires a great deal of objectivity and cognitive control. Therefore, we would like you to take a step back. In fact, we'd like you to take four steps back—literally. Yes, that's right, no matter where you are now (a library, coffeehouse, dorm room, kitchen) stand up and take four steps in a backward direction. After you have done that, read on. Trust us, there is a reason for this seemingly ridiculous request, and this reason will become apparent over the course of the next few pages.

Simply put, people are notoriously bad at self-assessment. In domains as diverse as education, the workplace, and personal health, our views of our skills, knowledge, and even well-being rarely match up with reality (Dunning, Heath, & Suls, 2004). In their comprehensive review of the literature on *flawed self-assessment,* David Dunning and colleagues describe how people tend to think of themselves as more erudite, accomplished, distinctive, healthful, skilled, and wise than those who surround them. These effects persist across the social and economic spectrum, with everyone from bungee jumpers and motorcycle riders to business leaders and college professors making flawed self-judgments. In short, almost everyone sees him- or herself as "above average" (Dunning et al., 2004, p. 72). However, these researchers discuss a number of promising solutions to the problems that people have with self-assessment, and, luckily, one of these tools is easily within your reach: feedback from peers and mentors.

Feedback From Peers

The team-based approach to psychological research provides you with a captive audience of experienced peers who will help you make more accurate assessments of your personal strengths and weaknesses. Peer assessment tends to be highly correlated with assessment by professors (Falchikov & Goldfinch, 2000), and Dunning and colleagues' review suggests that peer feedback can be particularly beneficial to students. Topping (1998) provides evidence that peer assessment of skills in a professional setting (e.g., practicum, internship) is reliable, and that open-ended, detailed feedback from peers enhances not only particular proficiencies (e.g., presentation skills, appraisal skills) but also the recipient's level of self-confidence. The overarching goal is to use peer feedback to encourage more accurate self-reflection, as well as to enhance learning (Falchikov & Goldfinch, 2000). One investigation found that some of the most successful research labs strongly emphasize group meetings in which peers with diverse yet overlapping areas of expertise ask challenging questions of one another (Dunbar, 1995). As described by Dunning et al. (2004), "Loved ones gently talk people out of crazy ideas, and peers give frank feedback when people overstep their abilities" (p. 96). Such frank feedback, in the context of a supportive and collaborative environment, can be a powerful catalyst for personal growth.

Feedback From Mentors

Of course, feedback from your mentor (e.g., classroom professor, teaching assistant, research supervisor) also is invaluable as you go about the process of self-assessment. If you have been getting college credit for your research experience, then it is likely you have received feedback in the form of letter grades on assignments, but the ideal assessment goes beyond grades. Your goal is to have a candid discussion with your mentor about your strengths and areas for improvement. Initiating such a discussion takes courage, but trust us, it is well worth it.

The first step is to alert your mentor that you would like to have a face-to-face meeting to talk about your strengths and areas for ongoing development as a researcher or psychology major. (You can be as general or as specific as you like.) It is essential to give your mentor some time in advance of your meeting to reflect on you and your performance. Your mentor is only human, and you don't want to catch him or her off guard by asking for an impromptu critique of your efforts and abilities. Your mentor will be able to provide more detailed, frank feedback if you give him or her an opportunity to formulate some thoughts. When the time comes for your meeting with your mentor, you can take the lead (at least initially) in shaping the discussion.

Table 12.1 depicts a broad general framework for a productive meeting with a mentor. First, let your mentor know that you would like his or her help identifying the skills you currently possess and the skills that you are still in the process of developing. In the example illustrated in the table, the student is a skilled writer but lacks confidence in the analysis and explanation of data. In addition to identifying your current and potential skills, it is critical to identify experiences that are going to propel you forward in your psychology major and in your postgraduate pursuits. What experiences have you had, and what additional experiences would you benefit from? Your mentor is a great resource for answering these questions. As you can see in the example, the student has already presented research at a conference, which is something to capitalize on. However, despite the student's success with a particular time-limited project (e.g., an assignment for a research methods class), she has not had the opportunity to pursue a longer-term collaboration.

Integrating Feedback

Allow the feedback you gather from peers and mentors to shape, not swamp, your own self-assessment. The value of the feedback you receive will depend, of course, on how well your peers and mentors really know you. It is possible that they have seen you function in one domain but that skills you possess in another domain are neglected, not because you lack these skills but because no one has had an opportunity to observe them. As you

TABLE 12.1	Framework for Soliciting Feedback From Mentors	
	I should capitalize on . . .	**I should develop further . . .**
Skills	Writing ability	Comfort with data
Experiences	Conference presentation	Longevity with a project

go about chronicling your areas of strength and areas that need further development, be sure to reflect on the various roles associated with the process of conducting psychological research. What skills have you developed in research design and analytics? To what extent have you been practicing and building on your abilities to tell a good story or write effectively? Did you play a role in the organization of the project, maintaining a bird's-eye view as you ushered your team's project from inception to completion? Use the framework of "capitalize on" and "develop further" as you reflect on these domains. Articulate your strengths and areas of weakness, and, most important, focus on progress. The process of learning and development continues far beyond any snapshot in time or any single project.

Once you have identified skills and experiences to develop further, think about how you will accomplish this. Many skills can be developed through course work. If data analysis is something you are interested in but do not yet feel confident about, find out whether there are other statistics classes you can take at your institution (or a nearby institution, perhaps during the summer). If writing is challenging for you, seek out (rather than avoid) writing-intensive classes in the major. You can work on developing additional skills outside the classroom through independently reading and writing about scholarly topics that interest you, and you can develop still other skills in the context of experiences you seek out, such as internships, practica, and faculty–student research. If you found enjoyment in carrying out your first team-based research project, seek out other opportunities to collaborate with mentors and your peers.

One concrete indicator of "success" in psychological research is to have your work reviewed by experts and deemed worthy of sharing with a larger audience. The larger audience can take the form of conference attendees or journal readers. Although the pinnacle of academic accomplishment is to publish your work in a peer-reviewed journal, the truth is that you are likely to reach a wider audience (that is, have more people actually hear about your work) if you attend a conference. If you have not had the opportunity to attend or present at a conference, now is a good time to pursue this option. The process of submitting to and registering for a conference begins many months before the conference itself. You can ask your mentor about upcoming regional and national meetings. Perhaps you will be able to find some local opportunities to present your work, or perhaps you will have a chance to apply for funding to attend a conference far across the country. Either way, conference attendance is an experience worth pursuing.

The Challenge of Self-Assessment

Now it is time to return to our request that you stand up and take four steps back. These instructions are inspired by the research of Severine Koch and colleagues, who were interested in studying approach versus avoidance motivations and their relationship to the motor system (Koch, Holland, Hengstler, & van Knippenberg, 2009). In a clever yet simple experiment, these researchers asked participants to complete the Stroop task (1935), which requires a great deal of *cognitive control*. In the Stroop task, one is asked to view a series of color words—such as *red, blue, green, black, yellow,* and *grey*—some of which are printed in colors different from those named by the words themselves; one's task is to name the colors of the ink while ignoring the meanings of the words (see Figure 12.1 for an example). Identifying the ink colors correctly when the words do not match them (i.e., on the incongruent trials) is challenging, and the natural tendency is to make mistakes and slow down when this happens.

Here is what Koch and colleagues hypothesized: Physically stepping backward should enhance participants' ability to complete the incongruent trials on the Stroop task accurately and quickly. Why? Because we tend to step back when we encounter something aversive, and when we encounter aversive stimuli, it is to our advantage to pay close attention and make more carefully controlled judgments. In other words, the fight-or-flight process of asserting cognitive control in order to protect or defend oneself is activated. Therefore, stepping backward in the laboratory should trigger this same system and enhance cognitive control. In contrast, stepping forward or sideways should not trigger this same level of control over thoughts and attention. Sure enough, this is what these researchers found. The specific number of steps (i.e., four) probably didn't matter as much as the sensation of movement itself. It is important to note that it was *not* the case that participants were faster on all of the backward-stepping Stroop trials as compared to the sideways- or forward-stepping trials. They were faster only when they stepped backward and were given an incongruent word-color combination.

Do we really think that backward movement will help you assess the skills that you have developed through collaborative research? Absolutely. For most students, taking stock of their skills, experiences, and weaknesses, especially as a precursor to marketing these skills to future employers or academic programs, is aversive. Your future might be bright, but you probably find thinking about it to be anxiety provoking if not downright frightening. The self-reflection process produces the same twist in the gut that comes from the dreaded questions often posed by family members: "Have the time and money spent

---

FIGURE 12.1   Example Stroop task. Name the font color as quickly as possible while ignoring the meaning of the word itself.

GREY	BLACK	WHITE	**GREY**
WHITE	WHITE	BLACK	GREY
GREY	BLACK	BLACK	WHITE
BLACK	**GREY**	GREY	BLACK

on college been worth it? Will you find a job after graduation?" You are likely to feel conflicted about your future, so why not capitalize on a simple movement that could activate additional cognitive resources for use during the process of self-assessment. As the study's authors conclude, "Whenever you encounter a difficult situation, stepping backward may boost your capability to deal with it effectively" (Koch et al., 2009, p. 550).

MARKETING YOURSELF TO EMPLOYERS

My job is one that requires involvement in the projects of a wide range of people who have varying interests and goals. Collaborative research provided me with highly applicable skills to take on and succeed in various roles in the course of working on these projects.

—Emily Umansky (Class of 2010, Lewis & Clark College)

Now that you have engaged in reflection and self-assessment, it is time to think about how these skills and experiences translate to the "real world." First, make a mental correction. You *have* been living in the real world all along. Yes, college offers certain luxuries and unique experiences that are not found as readily outside the halls of academia, but it is a myth that just because you have been a student (and, for some of you, just because you have been relying on someone else's income), the experiences you have had are not "real." You will find that identifying how these experiences have prepared you for the workplace is not as challenging as you might initially have feared. As the quotations in Table 12.2 demonstrate, former students describe how their research experiences matter in the world beyond college.

The experience of conducting high-quality team-based research leaves you with a number of decidedly desirable skills. A survey of more than 300 employers (including company owners, chief executive officers, presidents, executives, and vice presidents) found that employers most strongly value and emphasize the following skills, listed in order of importance: teamwork, critical thinking/analytical reasoning, and communication. When employers are making hiring decisions, they look for individuals who demonstrate evidence of being able to collaborate with others and work as part of a team. At the same time, however, 76% of the employers surveyed believed that colleges and universities do *not* put enough emphasis on collaboration and teamwork (Association of American Colleges and Universities, 2007). If you have had the opportunity (or, better yet, a series of opportunities) to engage in team-based research, you already have a competitive leg up in the workforce.

Bolstered by the knowledge that employers will find your experiences and skills valuable, you still must face the first challenge of deciding what type of jobs to pursue. This requires checking in with yourself about your areas of interest and general job characteristics that appeal to you. Do you want to work in a bustling environment or a quiet one? Do you want to work indoors or out? Do you want to be social or solitary? How much time do you want to spend talking versus listening, writing versus reading, computing versus communicating, applying versus creating? These are but a few of the many considerations to take into account as you begin to scope out a path toward a career. New York University's Wagner School of Public Service offers a number of excellent guidelines that

TABLE 12.2 Student Reflections on the Value of Team-Based Research and the Workplace

Team-based research made me a better employee at all of my jobs. I feel empowered to handle most any job's demands because I can organize and schedule people and tasks effectively. In addition, I honed many important presentational skills, ranging from the ability to project my voice when speaking to groups to the practice of carefully considering my audience when selecting what information to convey and how to frame it. Every time I prepare a presentation in my professional life I think, "I've presented complex statistical data to discriminating peers and leaders at countless research lab meetings. THIS is cake!"

—Kerry Balaam
(Writer and Program Administrator,
ʻIole land stewardship organization, Kapaʻau, Hawaiʻi)

What is evident now in my current office job is how much employers value effective collaboration. When my boss was interviewing me she was impressed with my research experience. I know that I work well in teams, but it was nice to have research on my résumé as further proof of that.

—Emilie Sanchez
(Office of Research and Assessment,
Lewis & Clark College, Graduate School of Education and Counseling)

One of the most helpful skills I gained was the ability to communicate with team members to accomplish complicated tasks together. College taught me to finish work on my own, but the reality of having a job is that everyone has to work together to get anything done, and if you can't communicate with mutual understanding and respect, nobody benefits.

—Kelsey Chapple
(Domestic Violence Program Legal Advocate, Anchorage, Alaska)

Being intimately involved in "making" statistics has changed the way I read and use other people's research in my professional life, looking for techniques and interventions that truly have been proven successful in helping kids learn. I read much more deeply into a paper; I don't just accept a significant result blindly; I look at methods more closely and critically. And having been involved in writing real papers for publication, I think I am much more comfortable using research and putting it into practice than I would have been without my experiences doing collaborative research.

—Zoey Cronin
(Special Education Teacher, Alakanuk School, Alakanuk, Alaska)

My experiences doing collaborative research absolutely contributed toward marketable skills postgraduation. My experiences with human subject research directly impacted my selection as an orthopedic surgeon's research coordinator. The many opportunities to practice communicating research— purpose, methodologies, results, etc.—were invaluable.

—Chelsea Heveran
(Master's student, Biomedical engineering, Boston University)

can help you identify the characteristics of a potential career that matter most to you; Table 12.3 lists the guiding questions suggested by NYU Wagner. Some of you may read these questions and feel prepared to answer them with certainty. Others of you may feel far less confident. Regardless of which camp you fall into, it is important that you find out additional information about yourself and about the actual experiences others have had in careers that interest you.

TABLE 12.3 Questions to Ask Yourself When Thinking About a Future Career
• What are my fields of interest? (e.g., children and youth, hospital administration, housing, international development) • What change do I want to make happen? (e.g., improve access to health care, reduce juvenile delinquency) • What roles might I want to play in an organization? (e.g., financial manager, policy analyst, urban planner, fund-raiser, program director, executive director) • When do I want to achieve these goals? (e.g., Do I want to be an executive director in 2 years or in 20 years?) • Is geographic location important? (e.g., New York City exclusively; Eastern Seaboard between Washington, D.C., and Boston; sub-Saharan Africa) • What skills do I have that I like to use? (e.g., analyzing, budgeting, writing, researching) • What work values are important to me? (e.g., advancement, creativity, independence, recognition, stability) • What leadership roles have I taken on? (e.g., task force at work, leader of student group, board member of a nonprofit organization) • What do employers look for when making hiring decisions?

Source: NYU Wagner (2005b).

Informational Interviews

In addition to conducting a careful self-assessment, you may find it valuable to seek out information from individuals who work in careers that interest you. These conversations can happen spontaneously (when, for example, you approach a guest lecturer after class and ask for more information about his or her career path) and informally (when, for example, you find out that a friend of a friend who is sitting next to you at a bar has an internship that seems exciting), or you can pursue them more formally, in what are known as *informational interviews*. Your goal in setting up an informational interview is to gather information by speaking (face-to-face or on the phone) with someone who works in a career that you are considering. The people you might seek out for informational interviews can range from family members to acquaintances to alumni of your institution to the colleagues of a friend of a friend. According to the guidelines provided by NYU Wagner (2005a), your goals in conducting an informational interview should be threefold:

1. To gather information (especially information that can't be found online or in a book)

2. To get advice (especially about what you should do in order to be successful in pursuing a similar career as your interviewee)

3. To be remembered positively (especially because your interviewee may be a source of connections to other people you should interview or to a future job) (pp. 27–28)

Although an informational interview is not a job interview, you should approach it with the same level of seriousness and commitment. It is up to you to guide the conversation, so you must come prepared with questions. Ideally, these interviews will provide you with a wealth of information and help you establish a strong network of connections in a field you think you might enjoy. You will find that most people are more than happy to spend some time talking about their own life paths and helping you think about how to achieve your career-related goals.

Cover Letters, Résumés, and Interviewing

Once you have narrowed down your areas of interest and have identified specific internships, jobs, or volunteer work to apply for, it is time to consider how to market your team-based research skills and experiences. To do this, you need to develop a compelling cover letter and résumé, to be followed by an impressive performance in a face-to-face interview. The cover letter is your first introduction to a potential employer, and the content you include is extremely important. Before you worry about how to discuss your skills and experiences, focus on two seemingly simple but crucial details: To whom should you address the letter? And what is the exact title of the position you are applying for? If either of these pieces of information is not clear to you, call the organization or company to find out. We have heard numerous tales of cover letters being tossed aside because they were addressed to "To Whom It May Concern" or because the job title the applicant mentioned was inaccurate. Two other details to attend to are the quality of your writing and your ability to find a good copy editor. Minor errors, wordiness, and confusing sentence structures turn employers off, so in addition to proofreading your own work carefully, you should seek out a peer or mentor to help you polish your final draft.

As you work to articulate the skills that you've gained through your research experiences in the body of your cover letter, back up your claims with specific examples. The ability to be a good team player and to collaborate with a diverse group of individuals is something you should emphasize, but be sure to illustrate the context in which you honed these skills. Being well organized and paying close attention to detail are attractive characteristics, but, again, you need to describe the experiences in which you developed these competencies. In addition to drawing on your research experiences, do not be afraid to mention course material, assuming that you can do so in a way that highlights the knowledge and skills the potential employer is looking for. Table 12.4 presents a sample of a well-thought-out cover letter.

Your résumé, also called a curriculum vitae, or CV, is the place where you provide details to support the ideas conveyed in your cover letter. Some employers specifically ask for single-page résumés; others accept résumés of any length. Be sure to find out about any length restrictions in advance of submitting your application. Like your cover letter, your résumé should include careful descriptions of your research experiences, even if they occurred in the context of classes. Remember that an ability to think analytically is very desirable to employers, so you will want to provide evidence of your role in developing your research and your understanding of scientific work. Give your role in the research project a name (e.g., "Research Team Member"), state the title of the project, and then give a one- or two-sentence description of the work you completed. For example, you might say

TABLE 12.4   Sample Cover Letter

Nicolia Eldred-Skemp   July 10, 2011
1 Main Street
Mytown, OR 10001

Dr. Letter Sample
Department of Neurology
University of Research
1 University Avenue
Worktown, OR 10011

Dear Dr. Sample:

I am writing this letter to express my strong interest in the Research Coordinator position in the Neurology Department. I feel I have both the experience and the enthusiasm that make me an ideal candidate for the job. I consulted with Dr. Detweiler-Bedell, Associate Professor and Chair of the Psychology Department at Lewis & Clark College, about the opportunity and was encouraged to apply.

I received my B.A. in Psychology in May from Lewis & Clark College, where I completed an upper-level Physiological Psychology course with an "A." I learned about a wide variety of topics in this course, including biological rhythms, psychopharmacology, and neuropsychological testing. This course sparked my interest and motivation to learn more about the field, and I gained valuable laboratory skills such as EEG recording, assessment of executive function, and brain dissection. For the past three years I have also worked as a Research Associate in the Behavioral Health and Social Psychology Lab, which gave me extensive experience in designing and conducting experiments with human subjects in a professional research environment, applying for and maintaining IRB compliance, and interpreting study data to present to lab members and faculty. I believe that my research and educational background have provided me with skills and experiences that I could successfully bring to the Research Coordinator position.

I am currently working as a Student Assistant for the National Health Measurement Initiative, and this internship has given me valuable experience in a research-based public health environment, while also allowing me to develop skills in reading grants, writing, interpreting statistical data, and preparing and editing presentations. In this position I am able to work independently and also to collaborate with supervisors on larger projects. This position and my recent completion of an upper-level Human Computer Interaction course both contribute to my computer proficiency, which would be useful in your research lab.

I am well organized, hardworking, and passionate about research, and I would love the opportunity to help coordinate and assist with physiological psychology experiments in the Research Coordinator position. Please refer to my attached résumé for a further summary of my qualifications, and let me know if you would like me to provide references from or contact information for any of my former employers. If you have any questions in the meantime, please do not hesitate to e-mail or call. Thank you for your time and consideration. I look forward to hearing from you.

Sincerely,
Nicolia Eldred-Skemp

Nicolia Eldred-Skemp

Source: Used by permission.

that you "worked in a team of three to develop a testable hypothesis, design experimental materials, administer the experiment to human participants, analyze data, write up the findings, and present the team's work."

In creating your résumé, keep the following tips in mind (adapted from tips offered by the Center for Career and Community Engagement at Lewis & Clark College):

- Consider your short-term and long-term goals.

- Highlight both your off-campus and on-campus experiences.

- Be specific when describing your skills and accomplishments.

- Use action verbs.

- Include both academic and professional references.

- Extensively research the organization you are applying to.

- Tailor your résumé to the specific job you are applying for.

- Create a visually appealing document.

- Proofread, proofread, proofread.

Table 12.5 lists the basic elements of a typical résumé, and Table 12.6 presents a useful activity to help you identify your skills.

If your cover letter and résumé allow you to rise to the top of the applicant pool, then you may be invited to interview. At the interview, you will have an opportunity to demonstrate that you are an effective communicator who can think critically about new ideas. Go to the interview prepared with an overview of the key experiences you have had that prepare you for this particular job, again backed up by concrete experiences. For example, if you plan to discuss how you are able to break up a large task into smaller component parts, a careful description of team-based goal setting would help to support your claims. If the content of the research you have done is related to the job, plan to give your 2-minute elevator talk to summarize the content of the research. Throughout the interview, do your best to convey a sense of self-confidence, collaboration, and willingness to face challenges head-on. These are the qualities that a solid research experience has instilled in you, so put them on display.

MARKETING YOURSELF TO GRADUATE PROGRAMS

After getting involved in collaborative research, my view of applying to graduate school changed. I never thought graduate school would be in the realm of possibility in my life. Now I know I can apply if I want to, and boy do I want to!

—Dmitri Ian Alvarado (undergraduate student, Lewis & Clark College)

One of the delightful side effects of a successful experience with collaborative research is the development of a passion for more: more ideas, more hypothesizing, more researching,

TABLE 12.5   Key Elements of a Résumé

Contact Information

- Name, address, telephone, e-mail
- Education
- Degree, school name, expected graduation date
- Major/minor or course emphasis, overall grade point average
- Relevant courses
- Overseas studies program name and location
- Special research projects or presentations (This is where you will highlight your research experience if you are going into a field that is research-intensive.)
- Special recognition (List any awards, honors, or other recognition you may have received.)

Related Experience

- Work experience (full-time, part-time, internship, etc.), including job title; company, agency, or institution; location; dates of employment
  - o Major responsibilities
  - o Major accomplishments, contributions, achievements
- Community service, campus activities, leadership
- Memberships (List job-related professional, civic, or campus organizations to which you belonged.)

Skills and Specialties

- Professional/specialized training (e.g., CPR, WFR)
- Special accomplishments (List publications, foreign language ability, special certificates, or talents such as music, art, drama.)
- Skills (demonstrated evidence of specific skills)

Source: Adapted from Center for Career and Community Engagement, Lewis & Clark College, "Resume Worksheet."

and, ultimately, more education. As students who have developed this passion attest (see Table 12.7), the pursuit of graduate school may be the perfect path forward in this case. But the path to graduate school is neither straight nor narrow—it is filled with twists and turns, challenges and opportunities. Still, when it comes to graduate school, the range of options is broad enough for anyone who feels a passion for ongoing learning in the field of psychology.

If you are someone who finds the prospect of attending graduate school to be attractive, the next step is to determine the type of graduate training you will pursue. The choices you have are extensive. Given that a review of the many graduate programs in psychology is beyond the scope of this chapter, we will discuss some of the considerations common to many graduate programs, with an emphasis on those that expect applicants to conduct research as part of their preparation for admission.

TABLE 12.6   Résumé Skills Identification Activity

Review the list and circle the four strongest skills that you want to demonstrate to an employer on your résumé:

Communication
Interpersonal
Listen
Present
Write
Instruct

Computer Skills
Databases
Internet/HTML
Spreadsheets
Word processing

Creativity
Design
Initiate new ideas &
evaluate likely success
Perform
Visionary; develop image of
how a system works in ideal
conditions

Flexibility/Adapt to Change
Change plans in midstream
Handle problems
Learn new roles
Take on new projects

Leadership
Delegate
Make decisions
Motivate others
Persuade
Social perceptiveness; aware
of others' reactions &
understanding why

Organization
Attention to details
Coordinate
Plan
Synthesize/Reorganize;
reorganize to get a better
approach to solve problem/tasks

Personal Management
Manage time
Manage finances
Work independently
Service oriented; actively looking
for ways to help people

Problem Solving/Critical Thinking
Evaluate options
Gather evidence through
research
Identify problems
Make conclusions

Teamwork
Complete assigned tasks
Cooperate
Negotiate
Contribute ideas within a team
Recognize and respect members'
strengths and weakness

Write down each skill you circled and identify experiences/positions, paid or unpaid, where you have used that skill.

Skill:
Experiences where you have used that skill:
_____

_____

_____

Skill:
Experiences where you have used that skill:
_____

_____

_____

Skill:
Experiences where you have used that skill:
_____

_____

_____

Skill:
Experiences where you have used that skill:
_____

_____

_____

Source: Adapted from Center for Career and Community Engagement, Lewis & Clark College, "Building a Resume."

TABLE 12.7 Student Reflections on the Value of Team-Based Research and Graduate School

As a result of my involvement in collaborative research, I experienced a significant boost in my professional confidence and public speaking skills. In applying to graduate programs, I believe this confidence helped me comfortably approach other scholars in the field to discuss shared research interests.

—Allison Sweeney, First-Year Doctoral Student
(Social Psychology, Stony Brook University)

Since beginning graduate school I have found that my experience with collaborative research has made me more confident in generating innovative ideas and seeking feedback from others to improve on these ideas. Overall, I find the collaborative model leads to research projects that are more creative and rigorous than studies students develop without a team-based approach.

—Miya Barnett, Second-Year Doctoral Student
(Clinical Psychology, Central Michigan University)

My experience doing team-based research gave me the skills to be an independent researcher, a collaborator, and a research consumer. These skills have helped me get research-related jobs, as well as aided me to get into and (more importantly!) through graduate school.

—Elena Welsh, Fifth-Year Doctoral Student
(Human Services Psychology, University of Maryland)

Collaborative research taught me the incredible value of being mentored and mentoring others. Whether in graduate school or in a career position, finding an experienced individual (or ideally several individuals) that can provide guidance and support is indispensable to your growth and success. When I began graduate school, advanced graduate students helped show me the ropes. Within a year or two, I was mentoring incoming graduate students and undergraduate research assistants. The relationships I cultivated then still play an important role in my life today (both professionally and personally).

—Julia Boehm, Postdoctoral Research Fellow
(Department of Society, Human Development and Health,
Harvard University School of Public Health)

I think the best part of doing collaborative research is that it allowed me to understand how research is more than simply reading a journal article or using SPSS; rather, research is about asking important questions about human behavior. This broader understanding of research prepared me for graduate school (and, ultimately, becoming a professor) because it helped shape me as an explorer and as a scientist.

—Anisa Goforth, Ph.D.
(Assistant Professor of School Psychology, Department of Psychology,
University of Montana–Missoula)

The collaborative aspect of research imparted a perspective on teamwork that I use both in my workplace (a university) and in everyday life. I now bring with me the appreciation that every individual in a group can make unique and valuable contributions and that a higher level of success can only be achieved by eliciting such contributions. Shared tasks are always easier (and more enjoyable) than those attempted alone!

—Lisa Williams, Ph.D.
(Lecturer, Faculty of Science, School of Psychology,
University of New South Wales)

Types of Graduate Degrees

Unlike some fields of study (e.g., law), the field of psychology includes a large number of different graduate degrees that you can choose to pursue. The broadest distinction is between master's-level degrees (i.e., M.A., M.S., MSW, MPH) and doctoral-level degrees (i.e., Ph.D., Psy.D.). The careers that you are qualified for after completing graduate school will vary depending of the type of degree you choose, so careful consideration of a match between the degree and your own interests is important.

Some students mistakenly assume that an individual must have a Ph.D. to do anything of substance in psychology. Although most of your professors have earned doctorates, the utility of a Ph.D. is relatively narrow; obtaining a Ph.D. is absolutely necessary only for those who hope to teach at a university or college, carry out high-level research, or perhaps direct a major program at a service agency. As we tell our own undergraduate students, you should pursue a Ph.D. only if you are 110% convinced that you enjoy research and if you have the experiences to prove this. The truth is that getting a Ph.D. is not for everyone. Although anyone *can* become prepared for and competitive in applying to doctoral programs, we have seen a number of extraordinarily talented, bright, and motivated individuals stop their programs without completing their degrees. The typical length of a doctoral program in psychology is five years, although it can take significantly longer. As you can imagine, this is a serious time commitment. Most doctoral programs in psychology expect that your number one priority is to conduct research. Teaching and other professional training activities (e.g., clinical work) come second.

Psychology Ph.D. programs can be found in each of the typical subfields in psychology, including cognitive, social, neuroscience, and developmental. However, the most popular Ph.D. programs by far are in clinical psychology. Gaining admission to doctoral programs is challenging because the number of qualified applicants is significantly greater than the number of open slots. Using the most recent data available from the American Psychological Association (2004), Norcross, Kohout, and Micherski (2005) calculated that the median acceptance rate to doctoral programs in psychology was about 21% across all subfields in the years 2003–2004, with the lowest acceptance rate of 11% for clinical Ph.D. programs.

The particular demand for admission into clinical psychology doctoral programs, along with a desire on the part of some applicants to focus their doctoral training on becoming practicing psychologists rather than researchers, is what led to the establishment of the Psy.D. degree. An individual with the Psy.D. (i.e., *doctor of psychology* rather than the more traditional *doctor of philosophy in psychology*) professional degree has been prepared for clinical practice in psychology much in the same spirit as a person with an M.D. degree has been prepared for medical practice.

The Psy.D. degree came into existence in the late 1960s in response to demand for doctoral-level training in psychology emphasizing practice rather than research. As with the Ph.D. degree, a Psy.D. program typically takes about five years to complete, and students are trained to be critical consumers of research. However, Psy.D. students do not engage in the same high level of intensive research training as do Ph.D. students. There has been a tremendous growth in the number of Psy.D. programs over the past 40 years, and although there are fewer Psy.D. programs than clinical Ph.D. programs, the number of Psy.D. graduates is significantly greater than the number of clinical Ph.D. graduates, because Psy.D. class sizes are quite large (Norcross et al., 2005). Data collected in 2007 suggest that the rate of admission at freestanding Psy.D. programs is much higher than the rate of admission at research-oriented clinical Ph.D. programs (50% versus 7%, respectively; Norcross, Ellis, & Sayette, 2010, p. 100). Figure 12.2 shows the typical employment settings of Psy.D. versus Ph.D. recipients.

If you find the idea of being in school for five more years daunting, or if the careers of doctoral-level psychologists are not for you, do not fear. Many students find that there are master's programs that offer just the right amount of training to prepare them for promising careers. As with the Ph.D., master's degrees can be found in just about every subfield of psychology. Overall, most master's programs take two or three years—significantly less time than is required by doctoral programs. In addition, some master's programs are geared toward enabling students to keep a work–school balance, holding classes in the evenings and on weekends, or even online. Another important factor to consider is that acceptance rates to master's programs are notably higher than acceptance rates to Ph.D. programs. The median acceptance rate across subfields was 57.9% in 2003–2004 (Norcross et al., 2005).

One of the reasons a student may pursue a master's degree is to use it as a stepping-stone to a doctorate. (For example, you may be interested in organizational

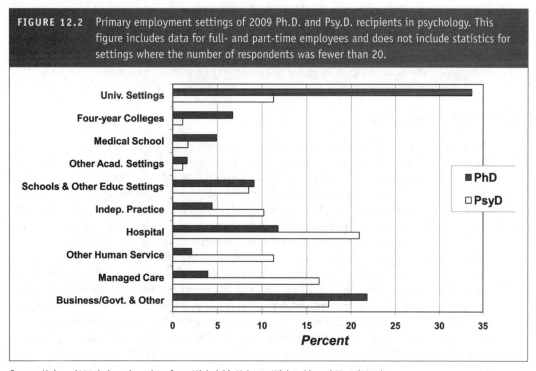

FIGURE 12.2 Primary employment settings of 2009 Ph.D. and Psy.D. recipients in psychology. This figure includes data for full- and part-time employees and does not include statistics for settings where the number of respondents was fewer than 20.

Source: Mulvey (2011), based on data from Michalski, Kohout, Wicherski, and Hart (2011).

behavior but not sure if the Ph.D. route is for you.) Be aware, however, that not all doctoral programs will transfer credits gained in master's programs, so this route might add a year or two to an eventual Ph.D. In addition, some programs actively discourage master's-level students from applying internally to their own doctoral programs. This is information you need to find out in advance of applying to any particular program.

More commonly, a master's degree leads right into a profession, and some professions (such as teaching) offer promotions to existing employees who obtain master's degrees that are relevant to their line of work. You should keep in mind, however, that some master's degrees are more attractive than others to employers. A master's in social work (MSW) or a master's in public health (MPH) is very marketable because the equivalent degree at the doctoral level is rare. In contrast, a master's degree in social psychology might be only somewhat helpful on the job market because the holder of such a degree must compete for jobs with individuals who have received Ph.D.s in the same field.

Another practical consideration to take into account is the cost of attending graduate school. Cost is undoubtedly an issue for many potential applicants, particularly those who are finishing up their undergraduate education with debt. Most graduate students continue to accumulate debt, and the longer the program, the greater the total cost. Ph.D. programs often help students with costs (in the form of tuition remission and stipends) in exchange for the students' working as research assistants in faculty members' labs or as teaching assistants. Similar arrangements can occasionally be found in Psy.D. and master's-level programs, but they are far less common. Because Psy.D. programs are considered to be professional schools, similar to medical or law schools, the total costs are likely to be higher than those for any other advanced degree in psychology. In a survey by Norcross and colleagues (2010), only 1% of students in freestanding Psy.D. programs were awarded full financial assistance, compared to 89% of students in research-oriented clinical Ph.D. programs.

The Process of Applying

Once you have identified the type of program you are applying to, it is time to begin the application process. Most individuals apply to a number of programs (e.g., between six and twelve). By being open to moving to a new location, you increase the odds that you will get the experience you are looking for. Choosing which graduate institutions to apply to is different from choosing which undergraduate institutions to apply to. Students describe choosing undergraduate institutions based on factors such as location, cost, reputation, and general characteristics of the student body. When you applied to colleges, your applications were likely similar no matter which institutions you were applying to, and the readers of your applications were members of the institutions' undergraduate admissions offices. In contrast, your choices of which graduate programs you will apply to are going to be based less on these factors and more on the *fit* you perceive between you and particular faculty members and the degree programs as a whole. Most likely, the readers of your applications are going to be professors, not admissions officers. Although institutional reputation as a whole might matter somewhat, the characteristics of particular degree programs and their faculty matter far more.

As a general rule, we suggest that you start the graduate program application process at least a full year in advance of when you hope to begin the program. This is especially important for doctoral and MPH programs, but beginning the application process a year in advance can be equally helpful for other types of programs. You will need this time to take entrance exams, prepare your materials, and, of course, wait to hear whether or not you have been accepted. Applying to graduate school is time-consuming, so you should build space for it into your schedule. If you are still a college student when you are applying, think of the application process as an additional intensive upper-division course. If you are working, be sure to set aside time in your off-hours to focus exclusively on the application process.

The following is a general overview of an application timeline, but you should keep in mind that exact time frames will vary based on the program and the degree:

- *July/August:* Finalize list of schools to apply to; take tests (e.g., Graduate Record Exam).

- *August/September:* Update CV; ask for recommendation letters.

- *September/October:* Send scores and transcripts; draft personal statements.

- *October/November:* Finalize all application materials (statement, CV, forms).

- *November/December/January:* Submit applications.

- *January/February/March:* Wait for notification of interviews (if applicable).

- *March/April/May:* Wait for notification of admission.

- *May/June/July:* Prepare for the start of the program!

It is very common to take time off after being an undergraduate before applying to graduate school. The advantages of doing this are numerous. First, you buy yourself time to figure out exactly what type of program you would like to apply to. Second, you give yourself the opportunity to gain additional experiences (e.g., research, internships) that will be attractive to the programs you plan to apply to. Third, you give employers and mentors who will be serving as your references additional time to get to know you, which will serve you well when it comes time to ask for recommendation letters. Finally, you give yourself time to study intensively for the Graduate Record Examination (GRE) or other entrance exams, depending on the type of program you are applying to.

Transcripts, Exams, and CVs

There are certain elements of the application process that you can and should check off your list early on. Well before it is time to send in your application, you should request a formal transcript from your institution so that you can review the grades you received and the classes that are listed to be sure that the information is accurate. After you have confirmed that your transcript is in good shape, you can request that your college or university send copies of the transcript to the programs that you are applying to.

In addition, many graduate programs require that you take the GRE. This is a standardized test that is reminiscent of the SAT; indeed, one good predictor of your performance on the GRE is your performance on the SAT. However, they are different tests, so it is important that you not allow your performance on a past standardized test to lead you to feel overly confident or pessimistic about the GRE. The single most important thing you can do is to prepare well for the GRE by consistently studying. The Educational Testing Service, which creates and administers the GRE, is one source of preparatory material for the exam. In addition, numerous self-guided books (many with testing software) are available in bookstores and online. Some students invest in preparatory classes (which can cost hundreds or even thousands of dollars) through companies such as Princeton Review or Kaplan. In our opinion, these courses are beneficial to the extent that they provide the structure necessary for regular, intensive studying. However, if you are able to structure your own time and take as many practice exams as possible in advance of the GRE, then you are likely to do as well as you would have had you taken a class. For better or for worse, your score on this test does matter. Often, as long as you score above a certain threshold (which varies depending on the program you are applying to), your application is likely to be considered. Scoring too low may increase the likelihood that your application gets overlooked.

Finally, many graduate programs require or at least allow you to submit a CV, and it is important to tailor it to the program you are applying to. Much of the advice we provided earlier in this chapter in the section on job applications is relevant here as well, but remember that in this context you are preparing an academic résumé, so certain experiences (e.g., being the receptionist at a local hotel) should be left off your CV.

Recommendation Letters

Most graduate programs require two or three letters of recommendation, and data from the 2004 edition of the APA's *Graduate Study in Psychology* handbook suggest that recommendation letters are among the most important criteria in admissions decisions for doctoral-level programs (alongside the applicant's personal statement) as well as for master's-level programs (alongside GPA; Norcross et al., 2005). It is typically a good idea to have at least two of your recommenders be college professors who know you well (i.e., you have had multiple classes with them and/or you have worked with them outside the classroom). The other recommender should be someone who has seen you work in a site that is relevant to the program you are applying to, such as a research laboratory or an internship.

The better your potential recommenders know you and are familiar with your ultimate career goals, the better your recommendation letters will be. It is important for you to stay in touch with your college professors after you graduate, especially if you have a sense that graduate school may be in your future. The last thing you want to do is contact someone who has a very hazy memory of who you are four years after graduation, because a detailed description of your accomplishments is a central feature of a strong recommendation letter.

The process of asking for a recommendation letter should happen well in advance of the application deadline. In fact, you should think of the entire time a professor, supervisor, or employer has known you as part of the recommendation process. Why? As Norcross and Cannon (2008) put it, you should think of your recommenders as "mirrors and recorders of your activity" (p. 25). In other words, the impression you have made on your recommenders throughout the time they have known you will have a direct impact on what they write about you. In addition, it is crucial that you waive your right to see your completed recommendation letters. Why? Put yourself in the position of the person who will be reading applications. Which recommendation letter will be perceived as the most complete and honest assessment of the applicant: the letter the applicant may have read and "approved" in advance or the letter the applicant agreed should be seen only by the recommendation writer and the graduate program? The answer is the latter. If you are concerned that your recommender may not compose a strong letter, then this is a clear indication that you should ask someone else to write for you.

The way you approach the person you ask for a recommendation also will have a direct impact on the quality and tone of the letter. Keeping this overarching perspective in mind, Norcross and Cannon (2008) share the following suggestions for ways to increase the likelihood that the letters you receive are strong:

- Start early.

- Ask the right people.

- Choose letter writers relevant to the graduate programs you are applying to.

- Ask the potential recommenders if they can write good letters.

- Waive your right to view the completed letters.

- Provide materials to your recommenders.

- Ask for the letters in person during formal meetings.

- Complete all of the (annoying) information on the recommendation letter forms. (p. 26)

Although we do not have scientific data to back us up, we believe the single most reliable predictor of receiving a strong recommendation letter (other than your own experiences and accomplishments) is asking for the letter in a professional and highly organized manner. Being professional means giving your recommendation writers plenty of forewarning—we recommend a *minimum* of six weeks in advance of the application submission deadline. In addition, being professional means giving your potential writers the opportunity to say yes or no depending on how well they feel they know you and how busy they are during the time that you ask. Psychology departments tend to be busy places to work, so professors are likely to be swamped with recommendation writing during the fall and winter months in particular. (This is yet another reason to get on their radar early.) Finally, being highly organized means that you provide your recommendation writers with all of the information they will need to write strong letters. This information should include, but is not limited to, the following:

- A chart that lists the names of the programs you are applying to and the degree(s) you are seeking, organized by the dates the letters are due, along with notations of the required form of submission (online, mailed, or given to you in a signed envelope)

- Your transcript

- Calculations of your psychology GPA and overall GPA

- Your scores on the GRE and any other relevant exams

- Your updated CV

- *If the recommender is a professor:* A list of the classes you took from the person and grades you earned, with a brief reflection on each class and any major assignments you completed; also, a list of any projects (e.g., independent study, faculty–student research) that you completed under the supervision of the professor

- *If the recommender is a supervisor or employer:* Your job title(s), with a brief description of the duties you performed and any major projects you completed while working for this person

- A bulleted list of the reasons you think you are a strong candidate for the program(s)

- A draft of your personal statement (if required by the program)

- Any required recommendation letter paperwork from the program, with all information (except for the evaluative material, of course) filled out by you (e.g., address and title of your recommendation writer)

- Stamped, addressed envelopes for any applications that are not to be returned online

- Any other information specifically requested by your recommender

This list is extensive, but the work that you put into creating it will serve both you and your recommender well.

The Personal Statement

Instructions on what should be included in your personal statement vary from one program to the next. Regardless of the requirements, the information you include needs to be compelling, well written, and *specific to the particular program*. A sloppy statement, with even a couple of glaring typos, might be cause enough for your application to be set aside. In addition, you need to convince each school that it is a great fit for you given your interests, experiences, and strengths. This means that you should tailor a significant part of your statement to each school, especially if the program emphasizes close faculty–student research collaborations. Doctoral programs, in particular, use personal statements as a central factor in making admissions decisions, because matching faculty members and students with one another is a priority at these schools.

If the program you are applying to is research based, it is critical that at least part of your statement identifies two or three professors with whom you believe you would work well, and you should discuss why this is the case. Remember, your application needs to catch the eye of a particular professor, not an admissions officer. To prepare to write this part of your statement, consider writing a *very brief* e-mail to a key faculty member at each school of interest. In this e-mail, your goal is twofold. First, ask if the professor is taking graduate students in the upcoming academic year. This question reflects the fact that even if you match perfectly with the interests of a given professor, if he or she has a full lab or is about to go on a year-long sabbatical, you have very little chance of being admitted. (This is also a great reason for listing two or three faculty by name in your personal statement, assuming, of course, that you actually have interest in working with each of them.) The first question also helps you to confirm that the person still works for that institution (even the best websites may not be completely up-to-date). We will never forget the early days of our first year at graduate school. We were discussing the graduate school admissions process with some of our peers, and one bemoaned the fact that she didn't understand why she wasn't admitted to a particular program that seemed to be a perfect fit on paper. When she said the name of the professor she had wanted to work with, a gasp went around the room. At the time she had applied, the professor had been dead for more than a year! To our friend's credit, she had done her research, but the department had not gotten around to updating its promotional brochure to reflect this fact.

The second question to ask your prospective professor is whether he or she has any research manuscripts that are under review or in press (accepted but not yet appearing in print) to share with you. This gives you early access to some of the professor's latest work and thinking. After all, fit is just as important to you as it is to the professor. If a prospective professor no longer works in an area that interests you, you might consider crossing him or her off your list. This question also shows that you understand the publication process and are serious about finding a good match with a mentor.

If you receive a response to your e-mail, wonderful. Be sure to send back a quick (i.e., one- or two-sentence) thank-you e-mail. If you do not hear back, don't worry. Professors can be quite busy, and some are inundated with e-mail requests. The key is to keep a relatively low profile as you put out these feelers, so whatever you do, avoid writing repeated e-mails asking for a response. You should be able to find answers to most of your questions through information available online, particularly if your prospective professors have Web pages listing their current work.

For more general guidance on writing a strong personal statement, look back at our advice about writing a cover letter for job applications (including the example cover letter in Table 12.4). You can work from much of this same information, regardless of the type of graduate program you are applying to. The key difference in writing a personal statement is that you should expand on your relevant academic experiences and passions and focus on the match between you and each program. Otherwise, you should maintain a "businesslike" style in selling yourself to graduate programs. We have seen too many personal statements become, well, far too personal. When we say that you should expand on your relevant passions, we mean that you should convey your intrinsic interest in the program of study. This is not the place to talk about your childhood or your experiences battling anxiety. In other words, this is not a college essay—it is much closer to a professional cover letter.

Waiting, Interviewing, Waiting, and Deciding

Although the feelings associated with sending in your final application by hitting "submit" or dropping the envelope in the mail may be euphoric, this euphoria will gradually transform into anxious anticipation—at least it does for most people. Uncertainty is never comfortable, and waiting for news from graduate school involves an extraordinary amount of uncertainty. Should you send an e-mail to professors at the school to see if they have received your application or to check in on how your application is faring so far? No. Not ever. Instead, your only contact person should be the administrative assistant or other person acting as a clearinghouse for all applications. Pestering potential research mentors will work against the likelihood of your admission, but double-checking with the right person that everything arrived on time is to your advantage. Technical glitches, human error, and the U.S. Postal Service can cause elements of your application package to go missing, and many graduate programs have a policy that applications will not be reviewed if they are incomplete. But after you have double-checked with the appropriate person that your materials have been received, you will have to keep on waiting.

Many graduate programs, especially Ph.D. programs, schedule interviews with a subset of applicants. If this is the case for you, it is important to say yes to the interview and, ideally, go to the school in person if invited. (Travel expenses associated with the interview are usually your responsibility. Phone interviews are always good backup plans, but if you can find a way to pay for the plane flight, do it.) As preparation for the interview, be sure to read up on the research interests of all the program's faculty, and do so in detail for those individuals you noted in your personal statement. Each school tends to handle the interview process in its own way, but you might be meeting with a large number and variety of professors. Try to come up with a couple of general questions to ask each person you meet, along with some specific questions for faculty members whose work interests you the most. You can ask everyone, for instance, what graduates of their program tend to do after they receive their degrees. You also can ask them to tell you more about their most recent research.

Of course, the interview is a time for the program to get a sense from you about your goals, motivation, postdegree plans, and so on. This is a chance for you to convey in person what you have described in your personal statement. You should strive to be professional yet down-to-earth and enthusiastic. The faculty will be evaluating how well you will fit into their program, how serious you are about your studies and research, and whether you are someone they would want to work with over the course of the program. After your interview, be sure to send a personalized thank-you message to each person who met with you. It does not have to be lengthy or detailed, but it should reflect your engagement in the conversation and your excitement about the program.

Interviewing leads to more waiting and still more waiting. But finally, the big envelope arrives—or, in the case of many graduate programs, the big phone call! With that in mind, make sure that your voice mail greeting is a professional one during this time period. Especially in a doctoral program, the admission decision is likely to be conveyed over the phone by the professor who plans to take you under his or her wing. You do not want to shatter this person's positive impression of you with a voice mail greeting that includes your personal rendition of Lady Gaga's "Telephone" ("*Hello, hello, baby, you called? I can't hear a thing. I have got no service in the club, you see, see*"). And when you answer a call from an unknown number with an unfamiliar area code, answer the phone professionally. First impressions are critical, and a professor might be calling to gather a last bit of information before making a final decision. Don't give him or her a reason to doubt you.

We won't tell you how to celebrate being admitted to a program. That is up to you. If you are fortunate, you might be admitted to multiple programs. If so, as you face the process of deciding which school to attend, the feeling of being fortunate is likely to wear off. Choice can be difficult, and choosing between two or more good options is more difficult still. Once you have been admitted to a program, you will find that the tables have turned. You are no longer trying to win them over—they are trying to win you! Doctoral programs are likely to pay your expenses for a campus visit. Other programs may not have the funds to pay your travel expenses, but if you have not visited already, now is the perfect time. In addition to meeting with professors, walking around campus, and finding out details regarding costs and funding, your top priority is to spend time with current graduate students. The graduate students are among your best resources if you want to learn the real scoop on a program. Explicitly ask what they are most happy with and what they find to be the program's biggest challenges. Ask them whether the atmosphere is competitive or collaborative. Ask them how much time they spend in class, on their own research, doing research with faculty, teaching, and so forth. Ask them if the program has met, fallen short of, or exceeded their expectations. To facilitate asking these questions, try to stay with a graduate student during your visit if at all possible. By the time you return home, you want to have as comprehensive an understanding of the program and its people as possible. Then, once you have visited each of the programs that has admitted you, it's time to make a list of pros and cons, talk with your current mentors and recommendation writers, and make a decision. Then you can really celebrate!

If you would like additional details about the various types of graduate programs in psychology and the processes of preparing and applying, you are in luck. A number of excellent resources are available, beginning with those published by the American Psychological Association: *Graduate Study in Psychology* (most recent edition, 2010) and *Getting In: A Step-by-Step Plan for Gaining Admission to Graduate School in Psychology* (2007). Other useful guides include Buskist and Burke's *Preparing for Graduate Study in Psychology: 101 Questions and Answers* (2006), Keith-Spiegel and Wiederman's *The Complete Guide to Graduate School Admission: Psychology, Counseling, and Related Professions* (2000), and, if clinical psychology is your field of interest, Sayette, Mayne, and Norcross's *Insider's Guide to Graduate Programs in Clinical and Counseling Psychology* (2010). If this list is not enough, you can find an extensive bibliography of student resources on the Social Psychology Network: http://www.socialpsychology.org/studentbib.htm.

HOW YOU HAVE CHANGED

Finally, it is time to be concrete in applying all of our advice to your own life. Whether you have completed team-based research in the context of a class or in the context of a mentor's research laboratory, you have changed substantially because of these experiences. What does your own list of self-changes look like? Before you answer this question, keep in mind an important caveat: Do not feel pressured to put together a lengthy list of changes you have experienced. You should focus on identifying just a handful of concrete changes, because forcing yourself to identify too many may backfire. How do we know this? Recall the study that we described at the start of this chapter, in which Eibach and colleagues

(2003) asked students to identify three ways they had changed since beginning college. What we neglected to tell you is that there was an important comparison condition in this experiment. Students in another group were given identical instructions, but they were asked to list not just three but *twelve* ways in which they'd changed. Most participants found the process of thinking of twelve changes to be challenging, and after this exercise they felt they had changed relatively little. Somewhat paradoxically, trying to think of twelve self-changes strengthened their belief that the world around them had changed and they had remained the same.

The moral, then, is that trying to generate a long list of self-changes may undermine your appreciation of the skills and knowledge you have gained over time. With this advice in mind, we'd like you to complete Eibach and colleagues' exercise, but this time with a slight modification to focus instead on your experiences with team-based research:

> On the lines below please list 3 things about yourself (your skill set, your ability to work with other people, your perspective on things, etc.) that have changed since you have been involved in collaborative research. List one thing about you that has changed on each of the lines, for a total of 3 separate things about you that have changed. Be as specific as you can in describing each of the things about you that has changed from the time you first began your collaboration up through now, when you are an experienced team-based researcher:

_____

_____

_____

When we asked some of our own students to reflect on how they had changed as a result of participating in collaborative research, they came up with a number of ideas. One is that they now view themselves to be more critical consumers of the media and pop psychology. Do you ever catch yourself thinking that the quality of the media is deteriorating and that depictions of psychological findings in the popular press are getting more and more distorted? Of course, these perceived changes have very little to do with the media and everything to do with your own understanding of research in psychology. Believe us, media coverage of research findings has been lousy for a long time! Another change commonly noted by our students is that they now approach questions about human nature in a very different way. Do you find yourself looking at everything through a psychological lens, much to the amusement (or annoyance) of your friends? Have you ever caught yourself saying, "Well, that's an empirical question"? Or when you hear that someone's data were "significant," does the word *statistically* immediately come to mind? Finally, our students reported that their abilities to understand scientific terms, to search the psychological literature, and to assess the quality of the articles they find have changed quite dramatically as well. They consider the nature and process of psychological research to be far less intimidating and time-consuming than they once did.

Not every change that you identify will be easy to explain to nonresearchers, and this can be frustrating. Many of our students find that their passion for building knowledge through well-designed research becomes so ingrained that they are surprised when others outside the field do not share their enthusiasm. One of us recalls being on a college-wide committee charged to address the following question: "How can we better encourage students to choose our college over others they have been admitted to?" A series of brainstorming sessions resulted in a proposal to mail admitted students a slick DVD about the college. Yes, this would be an expensive venture, but the cost just might pay off. The lone research psychologist in the room made what she thought was a very reasonable suggestion: "Let's take all the admitted students and randomly assign half of them to receive the DVD and the other half to get the usual mailings." The response from the room was swift and uncompromising: "But then half of the prospective students wouldn't be receiving something that might work well in getting them to enroll here!" Valiant attempts to explain the importance of experimental and control groups fell with a thud, and the plan went ahead without even a nod to experimentation. Yes, this was deeply disappointing. But years later, another committee tasked with the same admissions goals, yet made up of different individuals, fully embraced the idea of empirically evaluating student recruiting using random assignment. This time, admitted students were randomly assigned to receive a personal phone call from a faculty member or not. Did it work? The effect was very small, but the answer appeared to be yes. Thus, we urge you to persevere and hold true to the knowledge and values you have gained as a researcher.

Conclusion

As you complete your early journey with collaborative research, we hope you view this as a beginning rather than an end. The world truly needs more people skilled in evaluating and conducting research, and if you continue to build on the experiences you have had, you can become the newest expert in one of countless fields of study. Each of you has gained unique skills and perspectives, and you share an ability to see a research project all the way through from a mere idea to a well-articulated presentation of your findings. You have learned what it means to take responsibility for and share a commitment to a project. And you have developed an ability to work effectively and efficiently with other people. *Vision, ownership, togetherness*—learning how to foster these qualities in yourself and others is a skill that goes far beyond being attractive to future employers and graduate school mentors. These skills will help you move through the world with greater sensitivity, understanding, and confidence. Your experiences with a team-based approach to psychological research will have ripple effects throughout your professional and personal life. Embrace this continuing journey.

References

American Psychological Association. (2004). *Graduate study in psychology*. Washington, DC: Author.

American Psychological Association. (2007). *Getting in: A step-by-step plan for gaining admission to graduate school in psychology* (2nd ed.). Washington, DC: Author.

American Psychological Association. (2010). *Graduate study in psychology*. Washington, DC: Author.

Association of American Colleges and Universities. (2007). *How should colleges prepare students to succeed in today's global economy?* Retrieved from http://www.aacu.org/advocacy/leap/documents/re8097abcombined.pdf

Buskist, W., & Burke, C. (2006). *Preparing for graduate study in psychology: 101 questions and answers* (2nd ed.). Boston: Allyn & Bacon.

Dunbar, K. (1995). How scientists really reason: Scientific reasoning in real-world laboratories. In R. J. Sternberg & J. Davidson (Eds.), *The nature of insight* (pp. 365–395). Cambridge: MIT Press.

Dunning, D., Heath, C., & Suls, J. M. (2004). Flawed self-assessment: Implications for health, education, and the workplace. *Psychological Science in the Public Interest, 5,* 69–106.

Eibach, R. P., Libby, L. K., & Gilovich, T. D. (2003). When change in the self is mistaken for change in the world. *Journal of Personality and Social Psychology, 84,* 917–931.

Falchikov, N., & Goldfinch, J. (2000). Student peer assessment in higher education: A meta-analysis comparing peer and teacher marks. *Review of Educational Research, 70,* 287–322.

Keith-Spiegel, P., & Wiederman, M. W. (2000). *The complete guide to graduate school admission: Psychology, counseling, and related professions* (2nd ed.). Mahwah, NJ: Lawrence Erlbaum.

Koch, S., Holland, R. W., Hengstler, M., & van Knippenberg, A. (2009). Body locomotion as regulatory process. *Psychological Science, 20,* 549–550.

Michalski, D., Kohout, J., Wicherski, M., & Hart, B. (2011, June). *2009 doctorate employment survey*. Washington, DC: APA Center for Workforce Studies. Retrieved from http://www.apa.org/workforce/publications/09-doc-empl/index.aspx

Mulvey, T. A. (2011, April). *Debt, salaries, and careers in psychology: What you need to know*. Washington, DC: APA Center for Workforce Studies. Retrieved from http://www.apa.org/workforce/presentations/2011/rmpa-handout.pdf

New York University, Wagner School of Public Service (NYU Wagner). (2005a). *Career planning: Assessment and informational interviews*. Retrieved from http://wagner.nyu.edu/careers/resources/files/CareerPlanning.pdf

New York University, Wagner School of Public Service (NYU Wagner). (2005b). *Composing your career*. Retrieved from http://wagner.nyu.edu/careers/cyc/files/composing.pdf

Norcross, J. C., & Cannon, J. T. (2008, Fall). You're writing your own letter of recommendation. *Eye on Psi Chi,* 25–28.

Norcross, J. C., Ellis, J. L., & Sayette, M. A. (2010) Getting in and getting money: A comparative analysis of admission standards, acceptance rates, and financial assistance across the research-practice continuum in clinical psychology programs. *Training and Education in Professional Psychology, 4,* 99–104.

Norcross, J. C., Kohout, J. L., & Micherski, M. (2005). Graduate study in psychology: 1971–2004. *American Psychologist, 60,* 959–975.

Sayette, M. A., Mayne, T. J., & Norcross, J. C. (2010). *Insider's guide to graduate programs in clinical and counseling psychology*. New York: Guilford.

Stokes, D. (1986, June 4). Chance can play key role in life, psychologist says. *Stanford Campus Report,* 1–4.

Stroop, J. R. (1935). Studies of interference in serial verbal reactions. *Journal of Experimental Psychology, 18,* 643–662.

Topping, K. (1998). Peer assessment between students in colleges and universities. *Review of Educational Research, 68,* 249–276.

APPENDIX

Researcher's Toolbox

Chapter	Resource	Location
1	**Component Tasks of a Typical Research Project**	p. 10
1	**Examples of Undergraduate Research Experiences in Psychology** http://teachpsych.org/resources/e-books/ur2008/ur2008.php	References
1	**Research Skills Exercise**	Table 1.1
1	**Three Core Principles of Effective Collaboration**	Table 1.2
2	**49 Ways to Generate Creative Ideas** McGuire, W. J. (1997). Creative hypothesis generating in psychology: Some useful heuristics. *Annual Review of Psychology, 48,* 1–30.	p. 22 and References
2	**Four Approaches to Developing Research Ideas**	Table 2.2
3	**Tips for Using PsycINFO** http://helpdocs.apa.org/PsycNET-help.html http://www.apa.org/pubs/databases/training/search-guides.aspx http://www.apa.org/pubs/databases/training/psycnet-tips.aspx	References
3	**PsycINFO Search Strategies Summary**	Table 3.1
3	**Tips for Conducting Literature Searches**	Table 3.2
3	**List of High-Impact Journals in Psychology** See also: http://wokinfo.com/products_tools/analytical/jcr/	Table 3.3
4	**The Belmont Report** http://www.hhs.gov/ohrp/humansubjects/guidance/belmont.html	p. 51
4	**The Common Rule** http://www.hhs.gov/ohrp/humansubjects/commonrule/index.html	p. 52
4	**Animal Welfare Act** http://www.gpo.gov/fdsys/pkg/USCODE-2009-title7/html/USCODE-2009-title7-chap54.htm	p. 54

(Continued)

Chapter	Resource	Location
4	**Guide for the Care and Use of Laboratory Animals** http://www.nap.edu/catalog.php?record_id=12910	p. 54
4	**Association for the Assessment and Accreditation of Laboratory Animal Care** http://www.aaalac.org	p. 54
4	**Elements of Research Required by Institutional Review Boards** http://www.hhs.gov/ohrp/archive/irb/irb_introduction.htm	p. 55
4	**An Introduction to the Responsible Conduct of Research** Steneck (2006), http://ori.hhs.gov/images/ddblock/rcrintro.pdf	References
4	**Example Elements of Informed Consent Forms**	Table 4.3
4	**Sample Informed Consent Form**	Table 4.4
4	**Example of a First-Person Scenario**	Table 4.6
4	**Example of a Debriefing for a Study Involving Substantial Deception**	Table 4.7
5	**Research Methods Knowledge Base** http://www.socialresearchmethods.net/kb/index.php	p. 70
5	**20 Helpful Tips to Consider When Designing Measures**	Table 5.2
6	**Five Recommendations to Minimize the Likelihood of Chance Wreaking Havoc With Your Data**	pp. 107-108
6	**Representative List of Online and Print Statistics Resources** http://go.lclark.edu/detweiler-bedell/teams	p. 110
6	**Statistics' Three Sacred Tools**	Table 6.1
7	**The Role of Piloting** Teijlingen & Hundley (2001), http://sru.soc.surrey.ac.uk/SRU35.html	p. 115-116 and References
7	**Sample Piloting Script with Extended Debriefing**	Table 7.2
8	**Web-Based Survey Tools** http://www.surveymonkey.com http://www.qualtrics.com	p. 144
8	**10 Practical Tips to Improve Participation in Web Surveys** Molasso (2005), http://studentaffairs.com/ejournal/Fall_2005/ studentparticipationinwebsurveys.html	pp. 145-146
8	**A Primer on Running Participants**	Table 8.1
8	**Sample Checklists for a Study on Dental Flossing Behavior**	Table 8.2
9	**Website Devoted to Poster Creation Tips** http://colinpurrington.com/tips/academic/posterdesign	pp. 176-177

Chapter	Resource	Location
9	**Six Steps to Create a Poster**	pp. 176-180
9	**Sample Outline of a Research Talk**	Table 9.1
9	**Poster Template**	Figure 9.12
10	**The Official Guide to APA Style Writing** American Psychological Association. (2010). *Publication manual of the American Psychological Association* (6th ed.). Washington, DC: Author.	p. 184-208
10	**Tips for Productive Writing** Silvia, P. J. (2007). *How to write a lot: A practical guide to productive academic writing.* Washington, DC: American Psychological Association.	p. 185
10	**The Symptoms of and Cures for Writer's Block** http://owl.english.purdue.edu/owl/resource/567/1	p. 188
10	**Digital Resources for Managing References** *Refworks:* http://www.refworks.com *EndNote:* http://www.endnote.com *Zotero:* https://www.zotero.org	p. 189
10	**Guidance on Writing Annotated Bibliographies** http://library.ucsc.edu/help/howto/write-an-annotated-bibliography	p. 190
10	**Guidance on APA Style** http://owl.english.purdue.edu/owl/section/2/10	p. 190
10	**Guidance on Avoiding Plagiarism** http://owl.english.purdue.edu/owl/resource/589/01	pp. 206-207
10	**Peer Editing Instruction Sheet**	Table 10.1
10	**Venues for Publication of Undergraduate Research Papers**	Table 10.4
11	**The International Honor Society in Psychology: Psi Chi** http://www.psichi.org	p. 224
11	**An Online Resource Devoted to Research, Teaching, and Careers in Psychology: The Social Psychology Network** http://www.socialpsychology.org	p. 224
11	**Regional and National Funding Sources for Undergraduates** http://www.psichi.org/awards/data_sheet.aspx http://www.apa.org/ed/precollege/index.aspx	p. 224
11	**An Ideal Timeline for a Student-Initiated Research Project**	Table 11.1
12	**Résumé Creation Tips**	pp. 238-240
12	**An Overview of the Graduate School Application Timeline**	pp. 240-241

(Continued)

Chapter	Resource	Location
12	**Advice on Asking for Letters of Recommendation** Norcross, J. C., & Cannon, J. T. (2008, Fall). You're writing your own letter of recommendation. *Eye on Psi Chi,* 25–28.	pp. 248-250
12	**Information to Provide to Recommendation Letter Writers**	pp. 250-251
12	**Guides to Graduate Programs in Psychology** American Psychological Association. (2007). *Getting in: A step-by-step plan for gaining admission to graduate school in psychology* (2nd ed.). Washington, DC: Author. American Psychological Association. (2010). *Graduate study in psychology.* Washington, DC: Author. Buskist, W., & Burke, C. (2006). *Preparing for graduate study in psychology: 101 questions and answers* (2nd ed.). Boston: Allyn & Bacon. Keith-Spiegel, P., &Wiederman, M. W. (2000). *The complete guide to graduate school admission: Psychology, counseling, and related professions* (2nd ed.). Mahwah, NJ: Lawrence Erlbaum. Sayette, M. A., Mayne, T. J., & Norcross, J. C. (2010) *Insider's guide to graduate programs in clinical and counseling psychology.* New York: Guilford.	p. 253 and References
12	**Social Psychology Network's Bibliography of Student Resources** http://www.socialpsychology.org/studentbib.htm	p. 253
12	**Framework for Soliciting Feedback from Mentors**	Table 12.1
12	**Questions to Ask Yourself When Thinking About a Future Career**	Table 12.3
12	**Sample Cover Letter**	Table 12.4
12	**Key Elements of a Résumé**	Table 12.5
12	**Résumé Skills Identification Activity**	Table 12.6

Index